# SOPHIA, REGENT OF RUSSIA
## 1657–1704

Sophia: engraving by Abraham Bloteling of Amsterdam (c.1689)

# SOPHIA
# REGENT OF RUSSIA
# 1657–1704

Lindsey Hughes

YALE UNIVERSITY PRESS
NEW HAVEN AND LONDON 1990

Set in Linotron Goudy Old Style by
Excel Typesetters Company, Hong Kong

Printed and bound in Great Britain by
Biddles Ltd, Guildford and King's Lynn

**Library of Congress Cataloging-in-Publication Data**

Hughes, Lindsey, 1949–
    Sophia, Regent of Russia: ambitious and daring above her sex/
Lindsey Hughes.
        p.    cm.
    Includes bibliographical references (p.    ).
    ISBN 0-300-04790-8
    1. Sof'ia Alekseevna, Regent of Russia, 1657–1704.   2. Soviet
Union – History – Sophia, 1882–1889.   3. Regents – Soviet Union –
Biography.   I. Title.
DK125.H84   1990
947'.049'092—dc20
[B]                                                                              90-12288
                                                                                        CIP

# CONTENTS

# ILLUSTRATIONS

# ILLUSTRATIONS

# Note on Transliteration

For transliterating Russian proper names, terms and bibliographical items I have used a modified version of the Library of Congress system, including an apostrophe (') to indicate the soft sign (for example, strel'tsy). In the English text -y replaces -yi/-ii at the end of masculine proper names (Cherkassky, Vasily), which are, however, transcribed in full in Cyrillic bibliographical citations. Feminine Christian names with the alternative ending -'ia/iia have been standardised into -ia (e.g. Praskovia, Natalia). Most important, Sof'ia/Sofiia has been rendered Sophia throughout, with the stress on the first syllable. Peter is preferred to Petr/Pyotr, Aleksei to Alexis.

# Preface

The seeds of this book were sown back in the late 1960s and early 1970s when I was a student of Russian at the University of Sussex. A growing interest in Early Russian culture inspired by my tutors Sergei Hackel and Robin Milner-Gulland blossomed during a study visit to Moscow in 1969–70, when I wrote a rather naive undergraduate dissertation on seventeenth-century church architecture which transmogrified into my PhD thesis on Moscow Baroque architecture for the University of Cambridge, completed with the encouragement and guidance of the late Nikolai Efremevich Andreyev. By the time I took up my first academic post at Queen's University Belfast in 1974, my interest in the seventeenth century 'age of transition' had spread beyond architecture to encompass virtually every aspect of the era, including its leading personalities. My first book, on Prince Vasily Vasil'evich Golitsyn, himself a patron of architecture, led inevitably to Sophia, his alleged mistress and ruler of Russia during the period that Moscow Baroque culture began to flourish. It quickly became evident that assessments of Sophia tended to be squeezed into the beginning of biographies of Peter the Great, where she usually got short and sensationalised shrift. I decided that she deserved, if not rehabilitation, at least reappraisal, especially as the age in which she lived has hitherto received comparatively little attention from Western scholars.

Many people and institutions have helped me to carry out this exercise in reappraisal. On the academic side, special thanks are due to Professor Paul Dukes of the University of Aberdeen, who has given much-needed help and advice on a number of matters, as well as making available material from the original of Patrick Gordon's diary. Robert Frost of King's College London read the sections on foreign policy, excising several howlers. Professor Isabel de Madariaga has taken a personal interest in the project, and very kindly supplied a microfilm of the manuscript of La Neuville's key work. Dr James Cutshall gave invaluable advice on French materials. Colleagues attending sessions of the Study Group on Eighteenth-Century Russia and the Russian and East European Medieval Study Group have made many helpful suggestions at papers I have given to the Groups, and spurred me on by making tactful enquiries about Sophia's progress. In this respect, Professor A.G. Cross of the University of Cambridge deserves a special mention. Grants enabling me to visit the USSR and the USA were provided by the British Council and British Academy respectively. In the USSR I had consultations with Professor V.I. Buganov of the USSR Institute of History and Irina Gavrilovna Borisenko of the Novodevichy Convent museum, whilst in the USA the library staff of the Slavic reading room at the University of Champaign-Urbana were especially helpful. Additional financial support was forthcoming from the research funds of the University of Reading and SSEES. At Reading, Liz Bishop typed some of the earlier drafts, and her successor Ann Cade has pounded typewriter and word-processor to produce the final draft in record time. I am especially grateful to her. Finally, it should be mentioned that much of the work was done during the long-drawn-out and painful procedure of closing Reading University's Department of Russian, where I taught full-time from 1977 to 1987 and as visiting lecturer from 1987 to 1989. Those responsible for the short-sighted decision to terminate Russian teaching at Reading only helped to delay the completion of this book, but I should like to pay tribute to the moral support and friendship offered by my colleague Mike Pursglove and several generations of students of the former Department of Russian. This book is dedicated to them, and also to the memory of India, a cat who lived just long enough to see it completed.

Lindsey Hughes
School of Slavonic and East European Studies, University of London
November 1989

# Glossary of Russian Terms

The rendering of the terms for seventeenth-century Russian titles, ranks, functionaries and government departments into English is notoriously difficult, because there are rarely exact equivalents. In full awareness that there are no perfect solutions to this problem, I have opted for the renditions listed below. For a description of the workings of the 'boyar duma' or council (a modern term, for which there was no institutional title in the seventeenth century), see p. 6. On ranks and duties in general, see R. Hellie, *Enserfment and Military Change in Muscovy* (Chicago, 1971), p. 225 and *passim*. Sections 2–4 are listed in descending order of rank. No specific duties were attached to these ranks, which were conferred by the crown, although, as some of the terms suggest, office had once been linked to function. Members of sections 2 and 3 (the upper and middle Moscow-based service class) might be called upon to carry out the duties associated with the offices listed in sections 5 and 6, or to serve in the government offices (departments, chancelleries) listed in section 7. Their primary duties were, however, of a military nature.

## 1 The Royal Family

| | |
|---|---|
| autocrat | *samoderzhets* (fem. *samoderzhitsa*) |
| great prince | *velikii kniaz'* |
| great princess | *velikaia kniaginia* (wife of prince) |
| | *velikaia kniazhna* (daughter of prince) |
| sovereign | *gosudar'* |
| sovereign lady | *gosudarynia* |
| tsar | *tsar'* |
| tsaritsa | *tsaritsa* (wife of tsar) |
| tsarevich | *tsarevich* (son of tsar) |
| tsarevna | *tsarevich* (son of tsar) |
| | *titles of the Muscovite ruler |

## 2 Boyar Duma or Council

| | |
|---|---|
| boyar | *boiarin* |
| lord-in-waiting | *okol'nichii* |
| state councillor | *dumnyi dvorianin* |
| state secretary | *dumnyi d'iak* |

## 3 Moscow Service Nobility (Non-Boyar Grades)

| | |
|---|---|
| table attendant | *stol'nik* |
| crown agent | *striapchii* |
| Moscow servitor | *dvorianin moskovskii* |
| court attendant | *zhilets* (pl. *zhil'tsy*) |

## 4 Provincial Service Nobility

| | |
|---|---|
| military servitor | *dvorianin* (pl. *dvoriane*) |
| junior boyar | *syn boiarskii* (pl. *deti boiarskie*) |

## 5 Court Offices

| | |
|---|---|
| armourer | *oruzheinichii* |
| chamberlain | *postel'nichii* |
| personal attendant | *d'iadka* |
| privy councillors | *blizhnie liudi* |
| steward | *kaznachei* |

## 6 Provincial Offices

| | |
|---|---|
| military governor | *voevoda* |
| viceroy | *namestnik* |

## 7 Central Government Departments

(Variously referred to in the text as department, office or chancellery)

| | |
|---|---|
| Armoury | *oruzheinyi prikaz* (*oruzheinaia palata*) |
| Artillery | *pushkarskii prikaz* |
| Bondslaves | *kholopii prikaz* |
| Cavalry | *reitarskii prikaz* |
| Crown Appointments | *razriadnyi prikaz* (*Razriad*) |
| Foreign Office | *posol'skii prikaz* |
| Foreign Servicemen | *inozemskii prikaz* |
| High Court | *Vladimirskii prikaz* |
| Grain | *zhitnyi prikaz* |
| Investigations | *sysknoi prikaz* |
| Kazan | *Kazanskii prikaz* |

# GLOSSARY OF RUSSIAN TERMS

| | |
|---|---|
| Justice | *sudnyi prikaz* |
| Novgorod | *Novgorodskii prikaz* |
| Pharmacy | *aptekarskii prikaz (Apteka)* |
| Police | *zemskii prikaz* |
| Private | *tainyi prikaz (prikaz tainykh del)* |
| Royal Household | *bol'shoi dvorets* |
| Royal Justice | *dvortsovyi sudnyi prikaz* |
| Service Estates | *pomestnyi prikaz* |
| Strel'tsy | *streletskii prikaz* |
| Transport | *iamskoi prikaz* |
| Treasury | *bol'shaia kazna* and *bol'shoi prikhod* |
| Typography | *pechatnyi dvor* |

RUSSIAN ROYAL FAMILY TREE

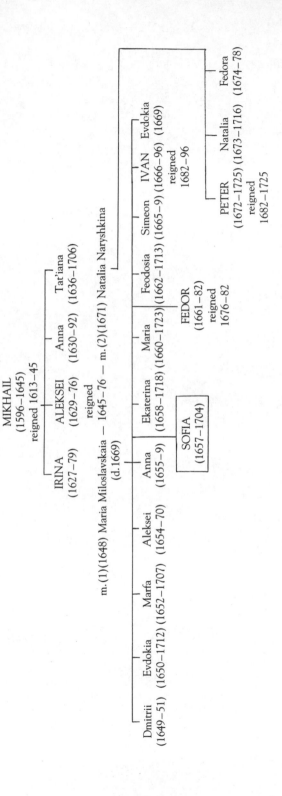

# Chronology of Events

xv

|      |      |      |
|------|------|------|
|      | May  | Chinese attack Albazin |
|      | Dec. | Election of Gedeon as Metropolitan of Kiev |
| 1686 | 26 Apr./6 May | Treaty of Eternal Peace with Poland |
|      | Nov. | Proclamation of first Crimean campaign |
| 1687 | Feb. | Troops depart for the Crimea |
|      | Feb.–Mar. | Envoys dispatched all over Europe |
|      | June | Golitsyn turns back from Crimea |
|      | July | Hetman Samoilovich deposed. Mazepa elected |
|      | Oct. | Slavonic-Greek-Latin Academy moves to permanent premises |
| 1688 | Sept. | Announcement of officers for second Crimean campaign |
| 1689 | Jan. | Treaties with Brandenburg, incl. offer of sanctuary to Huguenots |
|      | 27 Jan. | Peter marries Evdokia Lopukhina |
|      | Feb. | Troops depart for Crimea |
|      | May | Battles with Tatars |
|      | 21 May | Golitsyn decides to withdraw from Perekop |
|      | 8 Jul. | Clash between Sophia and Peter in Kazan Cathedral |
|      | 19 | Golitsyn and troops received back in Moscow |
|      | 7–8 Aug. | Peter flees from Moscow to Trinity Monastery Issues summons to strel'tsy and servitors |
|      | 27 Aug. | Treaty of Nerchinsk with China |
|      | 29 Aug. | Sophia turned back on road to Trinity Monastery |
|      | 7 Sept. | Sophia excluded from royal titles. Detained in Novodevichy Convent |
|      | 11 Sept. | Shaklovity executed |
| 1695–6 | Azov campaigns | |
| 1696 | Jan. | Death of Tsar Ivan |
| 1697 | Peter leaves for Europe on 'Grand Embassy' | |
| 1698 | Jun. | Rebellion of strel'tsy crushed |
|      | Aug. | Peter returns to Moscow |
|      | Sept. | Trial of strel'tsy rebels |
|      | Oct. | Sophia interrogated. |
|      | 21 Oct. | Takes the veil and name Susanna |
| 1700 | Beginning of Great Northern War with Sweden | |
| 1703 | Founding of St. Petersburg | |
| 1704 | 4 July | Sophia dies and is buried in the Novodevichy Convent |

# Introduction

Sophia Alekseevna was born in 1657, the sixth child of Tsar Aleksei of Russia and his first wife Maria. With three elder sisters and an elder brother, the heir apparent Aleksei, still living, and parents still young enough to add to the stock of male offspring, Sophia's prospects of coming to power in a country that did not recognise female succession was negligible. As it was, she seemed doomed almost literally to obscurity, for mid-seventeenth-century Muscovy held its upper-class and royal women in seclusion, and, in the case of the latter, also kept them unmarried. Thus the young Sophia could expect neither personal influence nor independence and was condemned to live out a spinsterish existence within the confines of the royal palaces. In the year 1682, however, the accumulated accidents of royal birth and death, rivalries between ruling court factions, and a rebellion of Moscow's armed guard, the strel'tsy, coupled with a strong dose of personal ambition, combined to raise Sophia to the role of regent and *de facto* ruler of Russia in the minority of her two younger brothers Ivan and Peter. The seven years of her rule saw a major expansion of Russia's foreign relations, as well as significant developments in cultural and religious affairs. In 1689 Sophia's rule was challenged, as was inevitable, by the young Peter the Great, who at the age of seventeen was capable of governing in his own right. Sophia was ousted after a defiant stand, when rumours of regicide plots flew thick and fast. She spent the last fifteen years of her life in a convent, although in 1698 she enjoyed another brief spell of public attention as a result of another rebellion. The pages that follow trace the rise, regency and fall of the first woman effectively to rule Russia, against the background of Russian culture and society in the latter half of the seventeenth century.

PART ONE

# Early Years 1657–1682

CHAPTER 1

# Russia in 1657

When Sophia Alekseevna, future regent of Russia, was born on 17 September 1657 it was less than a decade since the Peace of Westphalia had ended the Thirty Years' War in Europe and since Charles I has been executed in England. Louis XIV, still only nineteen, had been on the throne of France for fourteen years, whilst in Spain Philip IV was in the thirty-seventh year of his reign. In 1657 England and France were at war with Spain; Austria, Brandenburg, Denmark and Poland formed an alliance against Sweden; and the Turks captured Tenedos and Lemnos from the Venetian Republic. In Vienna Emperor Ferdinand III died and was succeeded by Leopold I (in the following year); in England the Lord Protector Oliver Cromwell was offered the crown and refused it. In Amsterdam, the commercial capital of Europe, Rembrandt was still painting and fighting off his creditors. Elsewhere in Europe, Molière and Racine were on the threshold of their careers, and Velasquez was nearing the end of his. Pascal was writing his *Pensées*, Spinoza was elaborating the idea of the Infinite, and Christopher Wren, already Professor of Astronomy at London University, was about to embark upon his architectural career, whilst Bernini was building the Piazza of St Peter's in Rome. At the same time, the political and economic interests of European states were being pursued not only in that continent but also overseas, in North and South America, the Caribbean, India, the Far East. It was an age in which scientific and cultural life was buoyant and inventive, but no less than its predecessors it was a century in which all classes continually fell victim to fire, famine and pestilence and in which millions still scraped a living from the soil using techniques little changed since medieval times.

The seventeenth century has acquired various blanket descriptions in historians' shorthand, of which the 'Age of the Baroque' is perhaps the most widespread and possibly the most elusive.[1] It has commonly been assumed that Russia, a slumbering giant on the edge of the 'civilised world', made little contribution to this 'Age'. She had, after all, been cut off from the West for more than 200 years by the Mongol occupation, formally ended only in 1480. The great ages of the Gothic

3

and Renaissance had passed her by. Indeed, the English claimed to have 'discovered' Muscovy as late as 1553. The Baltic German Jacob Reutenfels, who visited Moscow in 1670–2, wrote of the Russians: 'The colour of their skin is the same as that of Europeans thanks to the cold climate which corrected the original dark Asiatic tone,'[2] evidently unconvinced that the people he encountered were of the same race as himself.

But on a number of counts Russia could claim to be a European state and, although she often appeared 'exotic', even 'barbarous' to visiting foreigners, she was becoming increasingly involved in European affairs, and, in a limited sense, more 'modern'. Since 1654 she had been at war with Poland, a conflict which had been further complicated by the involvement of the Swedes under their King Charles X and which touched the interests of many European states, not least the Habsburg Empire, Prussia and Holland. In 1656 the Tsar of Russia had been promised the elective throne of Poland, occupied since 1648 by John Casimir. Russia was as yet not a central component in European power politics, but it was becoming increasingly difficult to ignore her.

What sort of country was Russia, or Muscovy, as foreigners most commonly called her, in the year of Sophia's birth?[3] In geographical terms the country was vast, stretching northwards to the White Sea and Arctic and eastwards to the Pacific, where the colonisation of Siberia was still in progress and bringing ever increasing danger of conflict with China. In the south she had a toehold on the Caspian, but still fell well short of the Black Sea, where access was barred by the Turks and their vassals the Tatars. In the north-west the Baltic still lay a tantalisingly short distance from the Old Russian lands of Novgorod and Pskov, whilst in the west lands still regarded as their 'patrimony' by the tsars of Russia because they had been part of Kievan Rus', including the city of Kiev itself, had since the fourteenth century formed part of the Polish-Lithuanian Commonwealth. Russia was not a contender in the rivalry for colonies overseas. These facts were to determine foreign policy for the next century and a half.

The population of Russia was in no way commensurate with her huge size. It has been estimated that by the middle of the seventeenth century it numbered about 10 million people, of whom about half a million lived in towns. In comparison Britain and Ireland had 7.5 million, France 19 million by 1700. The overwhelming majority of Russians were peasants, either state peasants, owing money and service obligations directly to the crown, or serfs, bound to the estates of individual landlords or the Church. In the towns, the largest of which, Moscow, had a population of about 200,000, inhabitants were divided into distinct estates (sosloviia), each owing defined tax obligations and duties to the state on a basis of collective responsibility. At the top of the pile were the chief merchants or gosti, in the middle numerous

4

tradespeople and artisans who lived in special settlements or *slobody*. The least privileged of the town population were the slaves (*kholopy*), who lived and worked in the households of richer folk, bound to them by contracts of bondage. The most exalted citizens, in theory, were the nobles, whose greatest privilege was the right to own land and serfs. But they, too, owed certain service obligations to the crown, and there were enormous differences in wealth and status between the top men in the sixty-strong boyar council or duma, and the service nobility, the so-called 'boyars' sons', in the provinces. Other sizeable groups of the population were the clerical estate (the married 'white' secular clergy and the 'black' monastic clergy), the strel'tsy or 'musketeers' who provided a permanent armed force, and numerous non-Russians, both tribespeople indigenous to the tsar's territories and foreign nationals in government service.

Apart from her daunting size, the other attribute of Muscovy best known to Europe was her form of government. The Holstein traveller and scholar Adam Olearius, the second edition of whose influential work on Russia appeared in 1656, described it as 'a dominating and despotic monarchy . . . closely related to tyranny'.[4] Reutenfels wrote: 'The power of the Tsar of Moscow is so unrestricted by any laws and so arbitrary, that one might rightly consider it equal to, if not greater than, the royal power of the ancient Assyrians and Greeks and the present-day Turks, Persians and Tatars.'[5] Since 1645 the Muscovite state had been ruled by Sophia's father Tsar Aleksei Mikhailovich, who styled himself 'Sovereign Tsar and Great Prince, Autocrat of All the Great and the Little and the White Russias'.[6] The precise meaning and optimal translation of the word 'autocrat' (*samoderzhets*) has been much debated,[7] but it is fair to say that it had no precise constitutional meaning and differed in its application at different periods of Russian history.

The term harked back to Russia's independent status, claimed by Ivan III from the Mongols in 1480; it echoed Byzantine precedent, and the efforts of Ivan IV, the 'Terrible' (1533–84), to subject even the loftiest of his subjects to his will. Ivan's line, however, died out with the death of his son Fedor in 1598. After the Time of Troubles (1598–1612), when nobles, pretenders and foreigners vied for the throne, in 1613 the monarchy had been revived in the person of Aleksei's father Mikhail Fedorovich, who, despite his youth and his family's fairly modest status, was elected to the vacant throne with full sovereign powers. Aleksei inherited this status in July 1645 at the age of sixteen. Even the members of the most ancient noble families, including those descended from the princes of Kiev and Lithuania, customarily referred to themselves as his 'slaves' and enjoyed no local titles or power whatsoever.

In practice, however, like all successful rulers who stop short of tyranny, Aleksei was obliged to co-operate with advisers and supporters, especially at the beginning of his reign. Autocracy was 'an aim rather than an achievement'.[8] Until 1653 Aleksei, like his father, frequently convoked the Assembly of the Land (*zemskii sobor*) to sound out opinion amongst various classes of the population. Throughout his reign he consulted members of the boyar duma, a body numbering between sixty and seventy members and consisting of the holders of the highest military and civil posts, mostly, but not invariably, drawn from about twenty top families. As Nancy Kollmann has demonstrated, in the fourteenth and fifteenth centuries the Muscovite government functioned on the basis of 'consensus and cooperation between boyars and sovereign', in which a self-perpetuating elite was virtually guaranteed entry into the boyar council in a regular sequence based on collateral succession.[9]

Clan honour was also regulated and protected by a system of precedence (*mestnichestvo*), over the mechanics of which the crown had no direct control. The court record books for April 1657 preserve a colourful instance of the working of the code, when Prince S.P. L'vov argued that he should have precedence over the 'upstart' I.D. Miloslavsky at a banquet. 'The sovereign was vexed by Prince Semyon L'vov . . . and told him to take his seat at the table and to petition later. But Lord-in-Waiting Prince L'vov challenged the sovereign against the boyar Il'ia Danilovich, so the sovereign ordered State Secretary Semyon Zaborsky to force Prince Semyon L'vov to take his place at table, which he had to do.'[10] In other words, L'vov had to be dragged kicking and screaming in protest at his slighted honour. Such incidents of individual wilfulness and disobedience hardly suggest a smoothly functioning despotism in which the 'slaves' kept meekly to their place. But the days of precedence and a self-perpetuating elite were numbered. By the mid-seventeenth century, as Robert Crummey notes, the 'elite within an elite' was increasingly supplemented by bureaucratic specialists, and the ruler exercised his prerogative to hand-pick worthy individuals from outside the inner circle. In certain respects, Aleksei's policy of appointments 'prefigures the Table of Ranks', introduced by Peter I.[11] In addition, from 1656 he operated through his own Private Office (*prikaz tainykh del*), which allowed him on occasions to bypass the official channel of the chancelleries (*prikazy*) and related institutions, which numbered over fifty.

Outside Moscow authority was maintained, often tenuously, on the Tsar's behalf by military governors (*voevody*) or, in the distant outposts, by armed garrisons. Autocracy, at its strongest in the awe-inspiring atmosphere of the Kremlin, was at its weakest in the outlying areas of the vast country. Here Cossacks, non-Russian tribesmen and fugitives from the obligations of serfdom and the towns, ranged further southwards and eastwards in an attempt to elude central authority. Yet the legitimacy of the concept of 'Tsar of all the Russias' seems to have taken deep root even amongst these dissident groups. Tsar Aleksei, like rulers before and after, was to experience challenges from pretenders to his throne (for example, a false Tsarevich Aleksei, posing as a son who had died in 1670), but no direct challenge to tsarism as an institution.

When Sophia was born, Aleksei was only twenty-eight. He had already survived one major rebellion, issued a new law code and led his armies on successful campaigns in Lithuania and Livonia. He has gone down in history as the 'most quiet', the 'pious one', but this is not a very accurate characterisation. Philip Longworth's biography portrays Aleksei as a 'manager of men'.[12] He was a 'severely practical as well as a spiritual man',[13] with both an eye for administrative detail and a broader vision of an expanded Russia, protector of true Christianity. He demonstrated that mixture of traditional and modern which was so characteristic of seventeenth-century Russia. Aleksei was suspended between two worlds, 'between isolationism and the lure of the West; between Byzantine exclusiveness and a yearning to be accepted on equal terms by his European peers; between Muscovite obscurantism and the more rational world of technology and science'.[14] These contradictions were evident in the environment in which Sophia was raised, and continued to be evident during her own rule.

In domestic terms 1657 was a quiet year, during the summer of which Aleksei was able to devote several days a week to his favourite pursuits of falconry and hunting. It was now nine years since he had been shocked by a major rebellion in Moscow and other towns, by people protesting against corrupt officials and unfair imposition of taxes. Lesser nobles were unhappy about their legal hold over their serfs and lands, merchants about growing foreign competition. So widespread were the disturbances of 1648–50 that many historians include Russia in their discussion of the general European 'crisis' of the era. One of Aleksei's responses to his own subjects' discontent and disobedience had been the publication of a new law code, the *Ulozhenie*, of 1649.[15]

This code is best known for the clauses confirming serfdom by terminating time-limits upon the return of fugitives to their rightful owners; but it was concerned with more than serfdom, its 800 clauses touching upon the status of the sovereign, obligations of townspeople, oaths of loyalty, maintenance of law and order, and customs duties, to name but a few. One may be surprised to read in the preamble the recommendation that 'the administration of justice in all cases be equal for all . . . ranks of people from the greatest to the least'. This was obviously a pious hope in a country which did not even acquire a legal profession until the 1860s, but it did reflect Aleksei's desire to establish 'good order', evident also in his campaign for 'spiritual rearmament' in the early years of his reign, and in his sponsorship of the programme, masterminded by Patriarch Nikon, to bring Russian religious practices into line with those of the modern Greek Church. One of the main aims of the 1649 law code was to 'convert the Russian classes into closed hereditary castes performing mutually exclusive functions'.[16] This may have been the ideal, but, as was the case with the efforts of seventeenth-century Russian monarchs to bring standardisation and compartmentalisation into other areas of life, the reality often fell far short of it. As we shall see, attempts to migrate from one 'class' or 'estate' to another, either to avoid obligations or to acquire privileges, were still a regular feature of Russia in the 1680s.

In foreign affairs 1657 found Russia in an uneasy truce with its erstwhile adversary Poland. In 1648 the Ukrainian Cossacks, under their leader Bogdan Khmel'nitsky, had rebelled against Polish rule, 'one of the greatest events of the age',[17] and in 1653 an Assembly of the Land had taken the momentous decision to accept the Cossack request for Muscovite protection. The Pereiaslav Act of Union of 1654 led to war between Russia and Poland. Aleksei left for the front in May of that year and by the end of it his armies had overrun much of what is now Byelorussia, and the long-disputed city of Smolensk had fallen to Muscovy.[18] In 1655 Vilna, the old capital of Lithuania, fell, and soon most of Lithuania was in Russian hands. In July 1656 Aleksei's armies reached the Baltic port of Riga, which since 1629 had been ruled by Sweden, but were forced to withdraw. In 1655 Sweden had entered the war to take advantage of Poland's weakness and to tighten her hold over the Baltic, and despite considerable gains the Russians were unable to consolidate their victories. Khmel'nitsky died in July 1657 and in the following year Ivan Vyhovsky, his successor as Hetman or Commander of the Ukrainian Cossack armies, signed a pact with the Poles which essentially liquidated the Union with Moscow. Khmel'nitsky's death is sometimes said to have inaugurated the period that Ukrainian historians refer to as 'the ruin'.

The war with Poland had several dimensions. On one level it reflected the traditional religious animosity between Catholic and Orthodox, whilst both the Kingdom of Poland and the Grand Duchy of Lithuania contained territories to which Russia nursed claims based on historical precedent dating back to the days of Kievan Rus'. Expansion southwards into the Ukraine was regarded by some Muscovites as part of a 'great crusade of liberation', a path to subjugated Orthodox peoples, perhaps to the 'second Rome', Constantinople itself. In the north there was the perennial lure of the Baltic, a foothold on which had eluded Aleksei's fifteenth-and sixteenth-century predecessors and which now seemed more vital than ever if Russia was to develop her economic and strategic potential. One may also detect a less obvious element – the distaste felt by Aleksei for the disintegration of government power in Poland and the anarchic authority of the great magnates, over which he might hope to impose his own notion of 'good order'.

War with Poland had a significant offshoot. Aleksei's biographer goes so far as to call it 'one of the significant turning points in the history of eastern Europe'.[19] Aleksei and his armies entered towns such as Polotsk, Vitiebsk and Vilna, with their heritage of Gothic, Renaissance and Baroque architecture so unlike anything in Russia and with living standards more sophisticated than those in Russian towns. In the words of Aleksei's English physician Samuel Collins: 'Since His Majesty has been in Poland and seen the manner of the Princes' houses there and ghess'd at the mode of their Kings, his thoughts are advanc'd and he begins to model his court and edifices more stately, to furnish his rooms with tapestry and to contrive houses of pleasure abroad.'[20] There is every indication that the Tsar's tastes were considerably influenced. In 1657 Aleksei's agents abroad, including the Englishman John Hebdon, were ordered to bring back a bewildering array of goods: optical equipment, tapestries and furniture, musical boxes, lace and tableware, singing birds, and carriages.[21] Most of these commissions duly arrived, and no doubt formed part of the surroundings in which Sophia was raised.

Western influence on the everyday details of court life was just one example of evidence of growing East–West contacts during Aleksei's reign. Such contacts were not new, but, in the words of B.H. Sumner: 'Ever since the late fifteenth century intercourse between Muscovy and the West had been increasing; between 1650 and 1700 intercourse began to grow into influence'.[22] One of the landmarks of such developments was the founding in 1652 of the Foreign or 'German' Quarter (*nemetskaia sloboda*) in the north-east section of Moscow.[23] This event illustrates two sides of the 'foreign question'. On the one hand, it testified to the number of foreigners resident in Moscow and to the government's success in recruiting much-needed specialists. A census of 1665 was to reveal merchants, silversmiths and goldsmiths, clock makers, tailors, gunsmiths, apothecaries, translators and pastors, and a preponderance of military men. On the other hand, the foundation of the quarter resulted initially from a wave of indignation *against* foreigners, which was rooted in religious intolerance and resentment about 'unfair' competition from foreign merchants and military personnel, a desire to eject foreigners and their contaminating influences from the heart of the city. There can be no question of the provision of foreigners with their own cordoned-off district indicating any desire to encourage cultural influence; in fact, the intention was just the opposite. The eventual outcome, however, was the creation of 'a small corner of Western Europe' with its own strong sense of identity, its own churches, shops, schools and taverns. It is a historical commonplace that Peter I acquired his first taste of the West within its walls.

As already indicated, the foreign specialists most in demand were military personnel to command the 'new model army' of regular troops organised on Western lines, which since the 1630s had supplemented the *ad hoc* mobilisation of the Russian service gentry.[24] Auxiliary specialists – weapon makers, explosives and fortification experts – were also much sought after. But, in the classic formulation of S.M. Solov'ev: 'Men of other beliefs did arrive in great numbers as hired officers, craftsmen of various kinds, industrialists and doctors. In the natural course of things the new had to appear in the guise of directly useful objects, it had to begin with craftsmanship'; then, almost unawares, Russians were made aware of less tangible aspects of Western culture 'like children tricked into learning by toys'.[25]

A small but influential category of Western experts, for example, were the painters who found their way to the main royal workshops in the Kremlin, the so-called Armoury Chamber (*oruzheinaia palata*).[26] Here one detects, from the 1650s onwards, the intrusion of secular devices and genres into a world of art hitherto dominated by the Church. Except for the First False Dmitry (reigned 1605–1606), Tsar Aleksei is the first Russian monarch of whom we have a true likeness.[27] One of the largest national contingents to enter the Armoury were Byelorussians, recruited in the Grand Duchy of Lithuania during the war against Poland. They brought new techniques of wood carving and decorative tilework. The 1650s saw small but significant changes in the royal household. In 1658, for example, Aleksei commissioned a German engineer to redesign his apartments 'in the new foreign manner'. Sparsely furnished chambers began to be equipped with chairs and cupboards from Germany, walls were hung with mirrors and engravings. Clocks became popular and a few foreign books appeared in the royal library.

It would be wrong, however, to conclude that this foreign influence was all-pervasive. It barely went beyond the walls of the royal palaces and a handful of noble mansions. In 1657 the most prominent stone edifices in the Russian town were still five-domed churches, richly decorated with Russian-style carved brickwork and limestone. The majority of domestic buildings were constructed of wood, in modes that had scarcely changed for hundreds of years. In workshops most artists laboured not over new-fangled portraits but over icons, manuscripts and an array of artefacts destined for churches and monasteries. In the countryside peasants produced age-old designs of colourful embroidery, painted wood and carvings, scarcely aware that Europe existed.

The Church itself seems to have made no protest about the interior design of the Kremlin palaces, but the authorities were very anxious lest 'heretical' influences penetrate religious art. Patriarch Joseph, the head of the Russian Orthodox Church from 1642–1652, wrote: 'The icons of the God–Man Jesus and of the Immaculate Virgin and of all the saints should not be depicted after the manner of the Latin and German deceivers, for it is not fitting that icons should reflect human lusts.'[28] The Greek cleric Paul of Aleppo records that Patriarch Nikon ordered the destruction of all icons painted in the 'German manner'.[29] Most graphic of all is the protest of Archpriest Avvakum, leader of the Old Believers (to be discussed below), who complained about the depiction of Christ 'with a plump face, red lips, curly hair, fat arms and muscles, thick fingers and likewise thick lips', making him look like 'a German, big-bellied and fat, except that no sword is painted on his hip'.[30]

The Orthodox Church constituted the main obstacle to more relaxed relations with foreigners. Foreign visitors to Russia frequently remarked on the 'obsessional' quality of the rites of the Russian brand of Orthodoxy, and there were even debates about whether the Russians were true Christians. Olearius concluded that although the *substance* of Russian religion was Christian, their *mode* of expressing it was 'questionable'.[31] The veneration of icons excited special disapproval, as did 'excessive' observance of saints' days and fasts, 'undue' reverence for church buildings, and apparent lack of attention to charity and good works.

Religiosity reached its height in the Kremlin itself, where the royal chapels, Patriarch's palace and chief cathedrals of all the realm stood in close proximity. A perusal of the palace records (*dvortsovye razriady*) of Aleksei's reign might well lead one to conclude that the Tsar's religious duties left him with little time for anything else. Even foreign Orthodox clerics complained of the excessive length of services. The Tsar and other members of his family made public appearances during celebrations of the thirteen major Church holidays, on family and national occasions, and countless saints' days. In the words of R. Wittram: 'If anything can be said to typify Old Russia it would be the sound of church bells, interminable services and fasting, the whole sacred inviolability of ecclesiastical formalities.'[32] These observances contained a strong political element, for the solemn rituals of Orthodoxy formed a vital part of the overall 'package' of autocracy. The Tsar had a sense of theatre and valued the exclusivity and aloofness that he attained during the more elaborate of the ceremonies, which underlined his role as head and protector of both Church and state. Sophia was to set similar store by the ritualistic side of religion.

Orthodoxy was both one of the main strengths and one of the main weaknesses of seventeenth-century Russia, but in the 1650s even this bedrock was being shaken by a schism within the Church. Aleksei had presided over a reform movement in the Church from the very beginning of his reign. In the 1640s this was limited to attempts to 'purify'

11

СОБРАЗ ВЕЛИКАГ
ГДРА ЦРА ИВЕЛИК
КНZА АЛЕZБА МІХ
ВZЕА ВЕЛІКІА ІМАЛ
ІБѢЛБА РОЗІІ ΣΑΜ

1    Portrait of Tsar Aleksei Mikhailovich: anonymous painting (1670s)

the Church by improving public morals and eliminating dubious practices such as *mnogoglasie* (the simultaneous incantion of different parts
of the liturgy), a movement associated with a group called the 'Zealots
of Piety'. With the accession of the strong-willed Patriarch Nikon in
1652, however, the reform movement expanded into a project for
bringing Russian practices and texts into line with those of the Greek

12

Church.[33] Controversial reforms included the abandonment of the traditional two-fingered sign of the cross in favour of the three fingers of Greek practice, and the revised spelling of the name Jesus. The service books were corrected by a team of learned monks imported from the Ukraine, Byelorussia and the Orthodox East.

Despite a huge wave of protest from a large body of the faithful – Old Believers or schismatics – Nikon's reforms were approved. Nikon himself, however, had only a year left in active office in 1657. He had alienated both clerical and lay figures by his arrogance and ambition, and by June 1658 even the Tsar, formerly his friend, had stopped attending services conducted by him. Throughout Aleksei's reign attempts were made to bring the Old Believers back into the fold, but by the 1660s verbal protests were to turn to acts of mass suicide and the state responded with exile and executions.

One of the issues indirectly raised by the schism was education. A historian of Russian science has claimed that 'Russian Orthodoxy . . . was dominated by a mystical acceptance of the Universe as an entity ruled by a miracle working Divine caprice, which could not be comprehended by an inquiring rational mind – only felt, through the medium of awe-inspiring ritual.'[34] Many of the dissidents rejected learning that emanated from foreign 'guile'. The conservative faithful were equally suspicious of foreign clerics imported to prepare translations and correct Slavonic texts, fearing (often with justification) that they might have been contaminated by contact with Catholic 'heretics' or Muslim 'infidels' in their lands of origin. The Church authorities could hardly be described as rationalists, but they were at least forced to have dealings with Greek and Ukrainian scholars in order to achieve reform objectives, contacts which may be regarded as a modest advancement in open-mindedness. A detailed knowledge of holy texts and Church history was now needed in order to refute the arguments of the dissenters, knowledge which in many cases could be obtained only from Orthodox foreigners.

This modest change in orientation was reflected in publishing activity. Throughout most of the seventeenth century Muscovite publishing was a state monopoly presided over by the Church. There were no private presses, a situation unique in Europe, and for most of the century only one publishing house was in operation, in the Printer's Yard Typography (*pechatnyi dvor*) on Moscow's Nikol'sky Street. The output was overwhelmingly religious, mostly liturgical books for use in church premises. This has led one investigator to the conclusion that 'pre-Petrine Russia did not know printing and publishing in the European sense of the word'.[35] Of the 480 or so books published in Russia between 1617 and 1700 only six could be described as wholly secular, whilst 80 percent were large-format liturgical books for use in church –

service book, psalter, book of hours, Gospels and so on. Between these two categories, however, were works which although religious in content still introduced new authors, ideas and influences. The patriarchate of Joseph saw the publication of Byzantine writers such as John Chrysostom, Ephrem the Syrian and Gregory the Theologian, of Ukrainians such as Metropolitan Peter Mohila and Archimandrite Zakhar Kopystensky, and even Patriarch Joseph himself. Another interesting category of publication were reading primers, which appeared in eight editions, even though their main purpose, to teach people to read religious works, was reflected in their content.

Landmarks in secular publication were few. They included the *Instruction on the organization of infantry* (a military manual translated from the German), the *Ulozhenie* (law code) and Melety Smotritsky's *Grammar*, all published between 1647 and 1649. There was still no place for works of fiction, drama, poetry, philosophy or history.[36] Foreigners may be forgiven for failing to notice the modest changes that were taking place. Olearius wrote:

> When you observe the spirit, the mores and the way of life of the Russians, you are bound to number them among the barbarians. Although they preen themselves on their connection with the Greeks, they have adopted neither their language nor their art. Indeed, they have little in common with the Greeks of which it was said in ancient times that they alone were intelligent and discerning, and the rest, the non-Greeks, were barbarians. For the Russians do not love the liberal arts and the lofty sciences, much less occupy themselves with them. And yet it has been said: 'Good instruction in the arts refines the customs and makes them secure against barbarianism.' Thus they remain untutored and uncouth.[37]

Olearius was a sophisticated Protestant man of science, a graduate of Leipzig University and court mathematician, librarian and councillor to the Duke of Holstein, qualifications which hardly inclined him to be lenient to Russian shortcomings in the educational sphere. But even a less erudite Westerner could hardly fail to notice that in the 1650s Muscovy still had no universities, no grammar or higher schools, no publications on science, philosophy, literature, scarcely any secular art or music, no theatre and no free professions. The publication of a few Byzantine Church fathers must have seemed like a drop in the ocean of ignorance.

One manifestation of 'ignorance' that struck foreigners particularly forcefully was the poor knowledge of languages. The Orthodox Church conducted services in Slavonic, a language close to the vernacular, hence there had never been any urgent incentive for Russians to master Greek, still less Latin, which had heretical connotations. Olearius writes: 'Since in the school the Russians learn to read and write only their own language, or at most Slavonic as well ... no Russian, whether ecclesiastic or layman, of high rank or low, understands a word of Greek or Latin.'[38] This was certainly a slight exaggeration, and Olearius himself was to observe in the 1656 edition of his book that a 'Latin and Greek' school had opened close to the Patriarch's palace.

Indeed, the period did see some broadening of educational perspective. In 1640 Metropolitan Peter Mohila of Kiev, himself the founder of the Kiev Academy, the foremost seat of learning in the Slavic Orthodox world had written to Tsar Mikhail urging him to establish a school. Nothing was accomplished, but in the late 1640s to early 1650s the Ukrainian monks who came to Moscow to start work on correcting texts also began to provide tuition on a small scale. The founding of a school has been linked with the name of Fedor Rtishchev, a pious Russian layman, but more recently it has been suggested that the first school was in the Miracles (Chudov) Monastery in the Kremlin, where the monks Arseny Satanovsky, Epifany Slavinetsky and Damaskin Ptitsky were based.[39] Eventually, a school to train chancellery officials also came into being, but it was not until Sophia's regency that an establishment of higher education, the Moscow Academy, was founded.

Despite these promising developments, it has to be conceded that institutionalised learning and publishing were, by Western standards, inadequate, and a more modern outlook, however tentative, was likely to develop only through unregularised contact with foreigners, for example amongst those Russian artists who rubbed shoulders with foreigners in the Armoury. Writes Samuel Collins:

> Such as have improved their parts by conversing with Strangers are more civiliz'd; yea those who have seen the Polish way of living, which though I cannot admire it, yet surely 'tis not so barbarous as the Russian; for they have a way to improve their wits by Learning, which they are debar'd in *Muscovia*; and may travel out of their own Country, a thing prohibited to the Russians.[40]

This has an uncannily modern ring to it and highlights another point: foreigners may have entered Russia in even greater numbers, but during Aleksei's reign and beyond any Russian wishing to travel abroad had to apply for permission to the Tsar himself or to the provincial governor. The Austrian envoy Augustin von Mayerburg, who visited Russia in 1661−2, wrote: 'It was no secret to us that the Tsar forbade any Muscovite to set foot outside his country or to practise any science at home, with the result that, through lack of knowledge of other peoples and countries, they prefer their motherland to all the countries of the world.'[41] This may be an exaggeration, for merchants and diplomats did manage to cross the borders, but it indicates the dilemma Aleksei encountered in the clash between his desire to uphold traditional values and his need to adopt modern technology.

In fact, one has to search beyond 'official' outlets to find new currents that were less susceptible to Church or government interference. The limited output of the solitary press, for example, needs to be seen in the context of a much wider availability of handwritten and oral materials, seemingly a perennial feature of the Russian cultural scene. Here we find signs of a lively secular tradition which did not shrink from satirising even the Church and the bureaucracy, for example in the tale of Ersh Ershovich, in which the bream brings a court case against the ruff, or *Shemiakin sud*, in which a poor man outwits both the judge and his accusers. Many popular tales were in circulation, some the traditional lives of Russian and Byzantine saints, others of foreign origin, for example moral tales from the *Gesta Romanorum* series, and *Speculum Magnum Exemplorum*, often translated from Polish versions. There were, moreover, examples of spicy, even risqué stories, characteristic of the crude, ribald side of Russian life which many foreigners were puzzled to see apparently happily coexisting with the solemn, rigid world of court ritual and religious observance.

Such developments heralded what Soviet literary historians often refer to as the 'emergence of the individual personality', a new interest in and respect for individual experience.[42] Just how far these developments had progressed by the late 1650s is difficult to say, given the problems of dating manuscript and oral tales. It is also hard to establish how much of this new 'popular' spirit penetrated the women's quarters of the palace which, as we shall now see, had their own special rules and regulations.

The status and role of Muscovite women have their roots in the political, religious and social features already examined. Sophia and her sisters were, of course, far from being ordinary women and their lives differed also in one very important respect from those of their upper-class sisters. In the words of the chancellery official Grigory Kotoshikhin:

> the sisters and daughters of the tsars, the *tsarevny*, have their own separate chambers and live like hermits, seeing little of people and being little seen, but are always at prayer and fasting, with their faces bathed in tears, since they do not enjoy the pleasure which God Almighty gives to mankind to join in wedlock and bear fruit. For it is forbidden that they be given in marriage to the princes and boyars of the sovereign, for the princes and boyars are his bondsmen, and in petitions they sign themselves as his bondsmen, and it would be an eternal disgrace to give a lady to a slave. And it is forbidden that they be married to the sons of kings and princes of other states since they are not of the same faith and must not change their faith or submit it to abuse, and also they do not know the language and politics of other states and this would cause them shame.[43]

Kotoshikhin, who defected to Lithuania in 1664, has been accused of exaggerating the negative side of Muscovite life, but there is much

evidence to confirm his picture of female celibacy and seclusion, although not, as we shall see, his interpretation of the reasons. Augustin
von Mayerburg wrote: 'To tell the truth, the female sex is not at all
venerated amongst the Muscovites as it is amongst the majority of the
nations of Europe. . . . In this country they are the slaves of men, who
esteem them little. And the worst condition of all is that of the sisters
and daughters of the Tsars.' He confirms the sanctions against marriage
to the Tsar's subjects or to 'heretics', adding that 'they suffer a perpetual
martyrdom in their involuntary virginity and spend their lives deprived
of endearments and of the most tender affections that exist in the
world'.[44]

There is substantiating evidence in the works of Adam Olearius,
Samuel Collins, Jacob Reutenfels and others, as well as in the dry
officialese of the court records. The Russian historian Ivan Zabelin,
whose detailed studies of the Muscovite court in the seventeenth century have still to be superseded, attributed the state of affairs described
above to Byzantine influence, characterising the latter half of the
century as 'a Byzantine era in our history'.[45] Others have regarded
female seclusion as a legacy of the Mongol occupation of Russia (1240–
1480), either as a result of the need for increased protection of women
or in direct imitation of Asiatic ways.

But the seclusion of Russian women reached its height long after the
most direct period of influence of both Byzantine and Mongol culture,
and in the seventeenth century enforced celibacy, as will be shown, was
both a comparatively new and also a short-lived phenomenon. In the
Kievan period, when Russia's links with Byzantium were at their closest,
Grand Prince Iaroslav the Wise (1019–1054) made political marriages
for his daughters, betrothing them to the Duke of Poland, the King of
Norway and the King of France. According to George Vernadsky:
'Russian women in that time enjoyed considerable freedom and independence, both legally and socially, and showed a spirit of self-reliance
in various aspects of life.'[46] The Mongol occupation held Russia back in
many ways, but in one sense indirectly enhanced the status of some
women by giving impetus to the unification of Russia, and thereby
promoting political marriages. Ivan III, the 'gatherer of the Russian
lands' (ruled 1462–1505), married his sister Anna to the Prince of
Riazan, whose lands he coveted. In 1497, far from being forced to hide
away in private, Anna was welcomed back to Moscow with public
festivities. The same Ivan, after considering several proposals, including
two from the son and nephew of the Holy Roman Emperor, finally
married his daughter Elena to Grand Prince Alexander of Lithuania,
again for overtly political reasons. Boris Godunov (reigned 1598–1605)
also planned to marry his daughter to a foreign prince.

The newness of the enforcement of celibacy is underlined by the experience of Sophia's aunt Irina, who died in 1679. Her father, Tsar Mikhail, conceived the plan of marrying her to Prince Waldemar of Denmark, not so much for reasons of foreign policy as to forestall a possibly dynastic crisis. In 1639 Mikhail's son Ivan had died, leaving only one male heir, Aleksei. It seemed unlikely that his wife Tsaritsa Evdokia would bear any more children, and so the continuation of the Romanov dynasty looked somewhat insecure. Under these circumstances Mikhail was obliged to look to his eldest daughter Irina not as his heir but as an instrument for securing the succession by marriage. In the event of Aleksei's death Waldemar might have been an acceptable candidate for the throne, and any issue from his marriage would have continued the Romanov line, albeit through the female branch. Such measures on Tsar Mikhail's part were prompted not merely by clannish pride but also by memories of the Time of Troubles, which had ended with his own accession in 1613, and of the chaos which could arise from the disappearance of a dynasty.

In the event, the proposed marriage foundered on religious grounds, for after arriving in Moscow the Lutheran Prince refused to convert to Orthodoxy and was kept a semi-prisoner in the Kremlin, released only after Mikhail's death in 1645. Even at this date, then, the tsarevny were not regarded as in principle 'unmarriageable', but it was deemed essential that the spouse convert to Orthodoxy. In addition, seclusion was already well established. Russian envoys sent to Copenhagen for Irina's marriage negotiations arrived without the customary portrait of the bride, on the grounds that only close relatives could look upon the face of a Russian princess and that the very process of portrait painting could be harmful to the sitter. Throughout the one and a half years of his detention Waldemar never once laid eyes on his intended.[47]

The ban on marriage for the tsarevny was clearly linked with developments in Russia's political structure and religious status. On the one hand, the unification of Muscovy and the establishment of autocratic rule gradually obliterated the need for the ruler to contract political marriage within the tsardom. In fact, the acquisition of Russian sons-in-law could be viewed as a positive inconvenience, adding troublesome candidates for privilege and favour around the throne. In the words of Nancy Kollmann: 'In the 17th century, grand-princely daughters were purposely not married in order to prevent the establishment of conflicting political alliances at court.'[48] As regards dynastic requirements, the only *necessary* marriages were those of the Tsar's sons, in order to propagate the royal line. Even if internal politics had not intruded, marriage to foreigners, very much the pattern in the ruling houses of Europe, was strongly challenged by Muscovite religious exclusiveness, as expressed in the doctrine of 'Moscow the Third Rome'. By the seventeenth century there were no independent Orthodox ruling families outside Russia who could aspire to a tsarevna's hand, and a Catholic or Protestant prince would have been required, as was the luckless Waldemar, to convert to Orthodoxy. It seems likely, too, that the daughters of the Tsar of Muscovy were not yet regarded as desirable matches by the ruling houses of Europe. No offers, as far as I know, were ever made for the hand of Sophia or her sisters.

By the reign of Tsar Aleksei, then, his daughters were politically redundant in all except perhaps one sense. To quote Susan McNally:

> The Muscovite tsars, whose efforts to differentiate themselves from the highest families of their realm was a major theme of Muscovite political history, used their daughters towards this end. . . . The private life of these women was utterly subsumed to the need of the public power to distinguish its central representative, the tsar, from every other person and family in the polity.[49]

In this sense the tsarevny may be regarded as the approximate equivalent of vestal virgins, around whom an exclusive air of mystery and sanctity was created. Ironically, this aura of exclusivity was probably to aid Sophia in her later quest for power, giving her a special authority in the eyes of ordinary Muscovites.

It is fairly easy to explain the evolution of the sanctions against marriage, but the practice of seclusion itself has more complex origins and was not confined only to royal women. Adam Olearius observed that 'generally, even the lesser nobles raise their daughters in closed-off rooms, hidden from other people'.[50] He reports that even the wives of Russian hosts would be brought out only occasionally after a meal to greet the guests as a special mark of honour. Mayerberg writes: 'The rich keep their women locked up in their chambers, where they engage in sewing and spinning, without being allowed to take any responsibility for household affairs. By the common law of their husbands' jealousy, they are forbidden to go out. This is revoked very rarely, either to permit them to visit their parents or to go to church.'[51] These journeys were accomplished in covered vehicles – sledges in winter, carriages at other times of year. In October 1634 Olearius witnessed a royal procession with women's carriages bringing up the rear. 'The carriages were tightly shut so that no one inside could be seen, unless by chance the wind raised one of the curtains.'[52] In church upper-class women were supposed to use closed boxes, and veils were the order of the day. Jacob Reutenfels wrote that 'no one can boast of having seen the Tsaritsa anywhere with her face uncovered'. He added, not entirely accurately as will be shown later, that 'they never appear at ceremonials, public prayers or meetings'.[53]

The apartments in which the women's lives were spent came to be known as the *terem*, the royal version of which was undoubtedly the strictest of all. 'Not in one of the convents of the day was there such strictness and restraint, so many fasts and prayers,' wrote one commentator.[54] The emphasis upon religion stemmed in part from the royal timetable described earlier. Whilst the Tsar carried out his duties at the endless public ceremonies for Church feastdays and national anniversaries, the women mirrored him in their private devotions. When they were not praying, they were busy with handicrafts, especially the embroidery of vestments and altar cloths which were bequeathed to the palace churches, convents and other religious establishments enjoying royal patronage. The dispensation of charity was regarded as the special prerogative of the Tsaritsa although, as a glance at the dates of birth of Tsar Aleksei's children will reveal,[55] pregnancy and childbirth must have been her overwhelming preoccupation.

The tsarevny were at least spared the rigours of bearing a child every one or two years. It has often been said that they pursued a 'monastic way of life';[56] in fact, some foreign commentators mistakenly reported that they were actually forced to take the veil; but if one interprets 'monastic' in the rather generous spirit of seventeenth-century Russia, where life in most monasteries and convents fell far short of ascetic ideals, then life for the royal women, although extremely restricted, contained much that was not strictly religious. They lived in an extended female household of ladies-in-waiting, seamstresses, chambermaids and female dwarves. As will be shown later, games and pastimes were not precluded, and at the very end of Aleksei's reign trips to the country and even attendance at the Tsar's private theatre became more frequent occurrences. One of the most responsible tasks allotted to the royal *terem* was the induction of royal brides into the Kremlin. This happened in 1648 when, according to Kotoshikhin, the strict supervision of Tsar Aleksei's intended by his sisters did not succeed in averting a poisoning attempt by rejected candidates.[57] In 1680 and 1682 Tsar Fedor's sisters also performed this duty, although they did not influence his choice. This remained the prerogative of male advisers.

Plenty of evidence survives for constructing a picture of the *terem* in the middle of the seventeenth century, but it is less easy to trace its origins. A major influence in forming the Muscovite ideal of passive womanhood was undoubtedly the sixteenth-century tract *Domostroi* or 'Book of Household Management', an 'instruction and exhortation to every Christian, husband, wife, children and male and female servants', attributed to the priest Silvester, an associate of Ivan IV.[58] It characterised the ideal woman as an efficient housewife, who scarcely slept in order to keep control of domestic affairs, and submitted to her husband in everything, including questions of 'how to save her soul, be pleasing to God and her husband and run the household well'. However, apart from stipulating that a wife should visit and entertain only those guests approved by her husband, should never get drunk and should discuss only domestic matters at table, the *Domostroi* did not specify avoidance of male company. The woman it idealised was far from being an idle creature hidden away behind closed curtains.

A late-sixteenth-century epitome of womanhood was Iuliania Laza-revskaia, whose life story was written by her son at the beginning of the seventeenth century.[59] The interesting thing about Iuliania, whose relics were said to have miraculous healing properties, is that she was not a nun or a hermit but a married woman, whose saintliness was expressed through devoutness, self-denial and good works. As a girl she was 'humble and obedient, assiduous in prayer and fasting'. She helped widows, orphans and the poor, and tended victims of plague and famine. Significantly, after the birth of her children, she renounced marital relations with her husband. Seclusion would have been incompatible with the life of service to the community which Iuliania, a noblewoman, adopted. On the other hand, her chastity in later life was evidently considered a saving grace. Female sexuality was clearly a thorny problem for the seventeenth-century Russian Church (which, incidentally, in the Orthodox tradition demanded that its parish priests be married), as it has been for many institutions and societies, but there is nothing in Orthodox Christianity to stipulate strict rules of seclusion.[60] The origins of the *terem* require further study, especially in order to establish the date of its appearance, but whatever its origins it could obviously function only on a very limited scale, dependent as it was on keeping women in idleness. For the vast majority of the female population of seventeenth-century Russia, actively engaged in subsistence agriculture, handicrafts and childrearing, such restrictions were out of the question.

Public behaviour was, in addition, sometimes diametrically opposed to the ideals of the *terem*, as some of the racier foreigners' accounts testify. Olearius' descriptions of public lewdness are well known. 'Women', he writes, 'do not consider it disgraceful to themselves to get intoxicated and collapse along with the men.'[61] Collins reports: 'To see Men, Women and Popes reeling in the streets is considered no dishonour' and tells of 'grand ladies' getting drunk in private.[62] Mayerberg both described and illustrated drunkenness, debauchery and mixed company in bathhouses. Bernard Tanner, a Czech who visited Moscow with a Polish embassy in 1678, saw many women on the streets and in carriages, and some amongst the crowds to greet his delegation, 'who had tried to beautify themselves for the arrival of the ambassadors, using white powder and rouge and attaching gold and silver ornaments to their foreheads'.[63] The use of thick make-up is remarked upon by several foreign writers. Tanner was also intrigued to see naked women in the bathhouse, 'running to and fro, quite unashamed'.[64] We should not be surprised if in seventeenth-century Russia private behaviour also often failed to maintain the standards required by public prudery. As will be shown later, by the 1680s rumour had it that even the untouchable tsarevny had found themselves 'gallants'.

The position of women in seventeenth-century Russia underlines the many paradoxes of that society: on the one hand the nun-like tsarevny cloistered from public view; on the other, nude bathers and female drunkards. One may point to further contradictions, such as the official xenophobia which necessitated ritualistic hand-washing ceremonies after the Tsar had been in contact with foreign envoys, and which evoked bitter denunciations of 'heretics', 'Germans' and 'Latins' from leading churchmen at the same time as the government was clearly anxious to attract the services of skilled craftsmen, mercenaries, doctors and other specialists. The Foreign Quarter, founded in 1652, was another such paradox. Many subsequent commentators have interpreted it as a sign of Russia's growing receptiveness towards the West, but in reality it represented an attempt by the authorities, especially the ecclesiastical ones, to isolate the 'Germans' and their corrupting influence.

With the advantage of historical hindsight it is possible to say that although many aspects of Muscovite life, such as serfdom and autocracy, appeared firm and unshakeable, by 1657 Russia was in the grip of what historians conventionally term its 'age of transition', even though modern developments – secular art and learning, contacts with foreigners – affected only a handful of people in the main towns, whilst in the countryside life continued much as it had done for centuries.

For the purposes of the present study, Sophia's future prospects in 1657 were especially paradoxical. On the one hand, palace protocol seemed to condemn her to a wasted life, a stultifying existence, more Oriental than European. On the other hand, she lived at the very centre of new currents, the Kremlin itself, where she could witness the arrival of foreign ambassadors and merchants, and experience an influx of books, portraits and other curiosities from abroad. The nineteenth-century historian D. Mordovtsev wrote of Sophia: 'She was the first to leave the *terem* and to open the doors of that *terem* for all Russian women who so desired it, just as her younger brother Peter later forged a window to Europe. . . . In a word, Tsarevna Sophia represents the transition from the women of pre-Petrine Russia to the women of contemporary Russia.'[65] And yet, as the present study will seek to show, the legacy of Old Russia never completely deserted her. The old and the new were to hold equal sway in her life and career.

# CHAPTER 2

# Childhood and Youth 1657–1682

The birth of a sixth child to Tsar Aleksei and his wife Maria is recorded in the court registers for the Russian year 7166 (1 September 1657 to 31 August 1658) without embellishment: 'On the 17th day of September was born to the Sovereign Tsar and Great Prince Aleksei Mikhailovich, Autocrat of all the Great and Little and White Russias, a daughter, the Sovereign Lady Tsarevna and Great Princess Sophia Alekseevna.'[1] The couple's first-born son, Dmitry, born 22 October 1648, had died before his second birthday, but four siblings survived – Evdokia (born 18 February 1650), Marfa (26 August 1652), Anna (23 January 1655) and one boy, Aleksei (5 February 1654).

As a sixth child and female to boot, it is perhaps not surprising that the infant Sophia left few traces either in official records or in the writings of contemporaries. Nor did she, like Catherine the Great, oblige her future biographers by leaving memoirs of the early years before her rise to power. The art of autobiography, indeed the art of individual self-expression in general, was still poorly developed in Russia even towards the end of Sophia's life, and, if personal papers had existed, Sophia's later disgrace, partial from 1689 and complete after 1698, must have discouraged their preservation. The drawing of a candid portrait is also limited by the private, enclosed nature of Sophia's childhood and young womanhood. When she emerged as *de facto* ruler of Russia in May 1682 few people beyond the immediate circle of family and palace clergy would ever have seen her, and even fewer would have been on intimate terms.

Several of her sisters, the closest companions of her youth, outlived her, but none seems to have left reminiscences of their more famous sister. Of her brothers, only Peter was in a position to recall her, but he was fifteen years younger and unhappy associations meant that he did all he could to expunge her from the public and perhaps his own memory. The most educated and articulate of her childhood acquaintances, her tutor Simeon Polotsky, left nothing but a few indirect and stylised glimpses of his royal pupil in his poetry, whilst two of the leading figures of her regency who might have been able to provide information about the earlier life, Prince Vasily Golitsyn and Silvester Medvedev, were exiled and executed respectively when the regency came to an end. Thus Sophia's biographer can expect to catch few personal glimpses of the girl behind a mature woman who herself remains something of a mystery. In the words of one investigator: 'The information for the history of Tsarevna Sophia before her appearance upon the political stage is fragmentary and incidental.'[2] This chapter will aim to amass and analyse the little evidence that survives.

Few precise details survive of the practicalities and rituals that accompanied Sophia's birth. According to Grigory Kotoshikhin, the usual practice was for the Tsaritsa to give birth in the palace bathhouse, assisted by a midwife and other female attendants. The Tsar would be notified, but, before he or anyone else was allowed to enter, a priest would be summoned to say prayers. The Patriarch usually conducted a service of thanksgiving in one of the Kremlin cathedrals, and the clergy of other Kremlin churches were instructed to do likewise.[3]

A celebratory banquet (rodil'nyi stol) was customarily held by the Tsar on or near the day, but in Sophia's case the celebrations were delayed by the Tsar's departure for the important Trinity Monastery forty miles to the north of Moscow to attend the feast of its founder, St Sergius of Radonezh, on 25 September. The banquet took place only on 1 October, in the Golden Chamber of the Kremlin palace, attended by the Patriarch, the Princes of Georgia, Kasimov and Siberia, boyars, lords-in-waiting and other courtiers.[4] Additional celebrations and rituals described by Kotoshikhin, which may or may not have been organized for Sophia, included the distribution of food and money to monasteries, almshouses and prisons, sometimes delivered by the Tsar in person, and the provision of drink from the royal cellars to the strel'tsy and other servitors. Envoys with rescripts announcing a royal birth were dispatched to metropolitans, bishops and governors all over Russia and returned bearing gifts, the size of which, according to Kotoshikhin, was carefully noted in case any failed to register sufficient satisfaction.

Kotoshikhin also tells us that it was customary to name the child after the saint whose feast fell eight days after the birth, but this was evidently not strictly adhered to as a suitable name could not thus be guaranteed. Sophia was named after Sophia the Martyr whose day, 17 September, coincided with that of her birth. Sophia's 'measuring' icon', the image customarily made of an infant's patron saint on the day of its birth, is preserved in the Novodevichy Convent, where she evidently brought it when she was detained there in 1689. It depicts the saint in a red robe, and measures just over 18 inches, the baby's length at birth.[5] The name Sophia also denoted Divine Wisdom (Greek sophos; Russian Premudrost' bozhiia), and the epithet 'wise' was to be conven-

2 'Measuring' icon of St Sophia

tionally applied to the Tsaverna in courtly verses. There was no fixed day for the baptism which, according to Orthodox custom, was carried out as soon after the birth as convenience and the baby's health allowed. Sophia was baptised in the Cathedral of the Dormition on 4 October, with Patriarch Nikon officiating. The occasion was marked by a banquet (*krestil'nyi stol*) in the Kremlin[6] A godmother and godfather would have been present (according to Kotoshikhin, often a monk from the Trinity–St Sergius Monastery and a senior female relative) but the names are not recorded in Sophia's case. It is possible that one of them was her aunt Irina, the eldest of Tsar Aleksei's sisters.

The birth of daughters was celebrated with less pomp than that of the male heirs. As Kotoshikhin, whose information about procedure relates mostly to the birth of tsarevichi, adds: 'But when a tsarevna is born, then her birth and baptism and prayers are conducted like those for a tsarevich, but according to other domestic rules, and the distribution of money is reduced in comparison.'[7] Once the relative excitement of the birth was over, the celebration of her nameday was to be one of the few official signs of Sophia's continued existence. It was marked by a night service, usually in one of the Kremlin churches, and a daytime mass in the Kremlin cathedral or an adjoining monastery on the day itself.[8] A banquet attended by the Patriarch, church hierarchs and members of the boyar council was customary, before which the Tsar distributed special nameday cakes (*imeninnye pirogi* or *kalachi*) to clergy, courtiers and members of the public. Kotoshikhin adds that these days were holidays, with a ban on the opening of shops and the celebration of weddings and funerals.[9] In the case of a royal daughter, these public ceremonies were conducted in her absence. The cakes were distributed by menfolk on her behalf, although when she was older she might conduct a parallel ceremony in which gifts were distributed to female attendants.

Sophia's first nameday was celebrated in 1658, when a banquet was held in the ante-chamber of the palace. The guests included Prince A.N. Trubetskoi, one of Aleksei's leading generals, I.D. Miloslavsky, Sophia's maternal grandfather, and Prince D.A. Dolgoruky. The Tsar evidently used the occasion to commend the nobles P.M. Saltykov and F.I. Matiushkin for their services during the military campaign in Lithuania, and sent food from the table as a mark of honour to the Prince of Georgia.[10] On 16 September in the following year Tsar Aleksei attended a night service, on the 17th went to mass in the Cathedral of the Annunciation and distributed nameday cakes to boyars, lords-in-waiting, men of the council and chamberlains on the palace steps. For some reason there was no banquet.[11] In 1660 he attended a night service in the palace chapel of the Raising of Lazarus.[12] In subsequent years the 17 September rituals followed a similar pattern.[13]

In the absence of individual records, one must turn to general information about palace protocol in order to reconstruct Sophia's infancy. Initially, closest contact would have been with the wet nurse, who was employed for a year then rewarded 'according to rank'.[14] A brief reference in Zabelin established that Sophia's was one Marfa Kuz'mina, who later became a chambermaid.[15] An extensive household of servants would be assembled, attached exclusively to an individual infant in its own apartments. After the departure of the wet nurse, a nursemaid was appointed. From 1659 Sophia was attended by Princess Anna Nikiforovna Lobanova-Rostovskaia who, according to Zabelin, received a salary of fifty roubles per year.[16] Supervision of the royal children was a task to be entrusted only to the well-born. Princess

Anna had married into a clan which regularly placed its members in the boyar council, and her presence in the palace was no doubt viewed as a potential channel of influence by her kinsmen, even if she was only attached to the househould of the Tsar's fourth daughter. She still appears under the same title (*mamka*) in records for 1680–2 and evidently survived her charge's disgrace, as her name appears in staff records for 1691.

Other members of Sophia's household included a mistress of the royal coffers (*kaznacheia*) (in 1667 this was Praskovia Skrypitsyna),[17] seamstresses, chambermaids and washerwomen. Unlike the Tsaritsa, who was attended in addition by the sons of noblemen, selected at the age of ten and transferred to the male quarters when they reached the age of fifteen, the tsarevny were tended only by women. An exception was made for travel arrangements outside the Kremlin when the tsarevny were always accompanied by male bodyguards drawn from families of boyar rank as a mark of favour. In the 1660s and 1670s the names that appear most frequently in this role are Peter Ivanovich Matiushkin, Boris Gavrilovich Iushkov, Ivan Fedorovich Streshnev and Avram Nikitich Lopukhin.

Sophia did not retain the centre of interest as 'baby' of the royal household for very long. On 27 November 1658 a sister, Ekaterina, was born, and on 18 January 1660 another girl, Maria. There was also a death, that of four-year-old Anna in May 1659. Attention must have receded even further from Sophia when on 30 May 1661 Tsaritsa Maria gave birth to another son, the future Tsar Fedor. August von Mayerberg, who arrived in Moscow in May 1661, reported: 'Since Aleksei wished passionately to preserve for his descendants the sceptre of Moscow and to establish his dominion by the number of his children and even to give Poland a king of his race, he was aggrieved to see his wife so often delivered of girls instead of the boys for which he hoped.'[18] There were even rumours that Tsaritsa Maria would be sent to a convent (as a means of divorcing her) if she failed to produce a boy. Mayerberg, incidentally, reported that Sophia was dead, no doubt in mistake for Anna. Dr Samuel Collins, who was employed at the Muscovite court from 1659 to 1669, wrote: 'If the Empress had not brought a second *Czaroidg* [sic] or Prince, born June 2nd 1661 after four Girls together, 'tis thought she would have been sent to her Devotions.'[19] Maria survived to bear yet more children. A further two brothers and a sister were added to the family before Sophia's tenth birthday – Feodosia (28 May 1662), Simeon (3 April 1665) and Ivan (26 August 1666).

In view of her frequent pregnancies and numerous offspring it is unlikely that Tsaritsa Maria gave much personal attention to Sophia. Still, Sophia's nursery was part of the extended *terem* over which her mother presided and as such must have merited regular visits. Whatever the relationship between mother and daughter (and we have no reason to doubt that it was a loving one), it was certainly not Maria Miloslavskaia who provided a role model for the independence, determination and neglect of convention that Sophia later displayed. Born in 1625, she was married to Aleksei in January 1648 and gave birth to her first child later the same year. She was thirty-two years old when Sophia was born. Maria, according to the few records that survive, possessed qualities well suited to life in the *terem*, notably modesty and piety, and was renowned for her charitable works, as the benefactress of several Moscow convents, but then these were the stereotyped virtues required of a tsaritsa. Otherwise little is known about her.

Contact between Sophia and her father Tsar Aleksei was probably even more sporadic. Mayerberg, for example, tells us that 'neither his wife nor his sons, still less his sisters and daughters ever eat with him',[20] a state of affairs perhaps reflecting the strictness of palace protocol, where much of the Tsar's time had to be devoted to public duties. Samuel Collins, however, who was able to observe the family at closer quarters than Mayerberg, left the following portrait of his employer:

> His Imperial Majesty is a goodly person, two months older than King Charles the Second, of a sanguine complexion, light brown hair, his beard uncut, he is tall and fat, of a majestical Deportment, severe in his anger, bountiful, charitable, chastly uxorious, very kind to his Sisters and Children, of a strong memory, strict in his Devotions, and a favourer of his Religion, and had he not such a cloud of Sycophants and jealous nobility upon him, who blind his good intentions, no doubt he might be numbred [sic] amongst the best and wisest of Princes.[21]

When he was resident in the Kremlin, most of Aleksei's day and often part of the night was occupied by the lengthy church services in which the Tsar played an integral part. Late mornings and afternoons might be spent in session with the boyar council, or receiving envoys and petitioners. Perhaps only in the evening could a period be set aside for the family, although the time spent an official duties was reduced somewhat towards the end of Aleksei's reign.[22] The Tsar was frequently absent from the Kremlin, either on military campaigns (the war with Poland ended only in 1667) or on pilgrimages to monasteries in the Moscow region. Aleksei was passionately fond of hunting and falconry, which also took him away from home. One must repeat that the Tsar of Muscovy was essentially a public personage, the centrepiece of innumerable religious and civic ceremonies and rituals, whereas the royal women occupied a world behind closed doors which rarely excited the interest of commentators. For this reason it is impossible to gain an accurate idea of how much time Aleksei spent with his daughters, but one may suppose it to have been insubstantial.

28

Not surprisingly, in the large royal household Sophia aroused little interest as an individual. More often than not her name appears in documents in strict order of hierarchy according to sex and date of birth, sandwiched between those of her closest siblings, Marfa and Ekaterina, for example in rescripts of blessing issued to each member of the royal family by Patriarch Macarius of Antioch on 5 June 1668.[23] Occasionally slightly more personal evidence survives, for example a list of 1673 itemising Sophia's wardrobe – furs, hats, caftans, outer- and under-garments.[24] The robes were of rich fabrics, for example:

> a warm overdress [telegreia] made of silk with a silver background with gold tracery; sewn in gold and silver thread and silk ribbon, with 15 buttons, fastenings of rubies and lined in ermine . . . a light satin underdress on a red background with brocade in white and yellow silk; with panels in cherry-coloured velvet with gold and silver thread and stars; the lower part in yellow silk, the lining of light green taffeta.

These descriptions not only bear witness to the wealth of the Muscovite royal family, but also show that the conventions which required female seclusion did not extend to any demand for 'sackcloth and ashes' asceticism, despite the heavily religious overtones of everyday life, with its never-ending alternation of feastdays and fasts. Male clothing, it should be added, was equally colourful. The seventeenth century was generally a period of great decorativeness and colourfulness in both secular and sacred art. Glowing colours, which still shine out of the icons and frescoes of the period, were the order of the day and one is not surprised to learn that the seventeenth-century Russian language abounds in terms for colours, especially reds and purples. Peter the Great's preference for dour, simple military-style clothing was just one of his many personal breaks with the traditions of his Muscovite predecessors.

Similarly, there is much evidence for the fact that life in the Kremlin was far from uniformly solemn for the royal children. In June 1669, for example, we read that one Nikifor Eremeev was ordered to make five painted wooden lions on metal chains in wooden cages for the eight-year-old Tsarevich Fedor.[25] In November 1670 six painted drums were delivered and the 'toy Germans that stand in a black wooden box and play' were sent to the Foreign Quarter to be repaired. Other items delivered to the palace included chess sets, toy soldiers, dolls, carts, sledges, cymbals, cards, maps and books, often made by the best craftsmen from the palace workshops in the Armoury. Another aspect of play were the numerous dwarves, both male and female, who lived in the royal apartments. In 1679, for example, there were four attached to Tsarevich Peter's household alone.[26] Jacob Reutenfels, writing in the 1670s, recorded the introduction of more robust pastimes, for example horse-riding, archery and tobogganning, although it is not made clear whether girls took part.[27] Their lives were bound to be more restricted even if their clothing and environment were far from 'monastic'. At the age of seven the boys moved from the *terem* to male quarters, whilst sanctions on male company and being seen in public could only increase as the girls matured. One is reminded of the purdah practised in some Eastern societies where rich adornments and relaxation are allowed, indeed encouraged, only behind closed doors.

As a counterweight to the pleasures of play there were the duties of religion. Unlike those of the Tsar, the devotions of the royal women were not public property and palace records do not provide a day-to-day account of the family's private worship. This was usually conducted in a network of chapels which could be entered without setting foot outside the palace. The most important was the Church of the Saviour 'Not made by hands' (*spas nerukotvornyi*), which was constructed at the same time as the Terem Palace in 1635–6.[28] Situated on the third floor of the palace, it was also linked by a stairway to the public square below – the *postel'noe kryl'tso* – where courtiers gathered. In 1670 an ornate metal screen was fitted to the public entrance, giving the church the popular name of 'behind the golden grille'.

Next to the Church of the Saviour, divided from it by a corridor, was the Church of the Resurrection, which contained a chapel dedicated to St Evdokia, in memory of Tsar Aleksei's mother Evdokia Luk'ianovna, which was in turn linked to the church below, on the second floor of the Terem Palace, the Church of St Catherine the Martyr, which was apparently much frequented by Tsaritsa Maria. In 1664 she commissioned an iconostasis modelled on that in the Kremlin Dormition Cathedral,[29] and in the 1680s Sophia herself was to order its renovation and the painting of new icons. Above the Church of the Resurrection was a chapel dedicated to the Crucifixion and the Stations of the Cross where, rumour has it, were deposited cloth icons embroidered by the tsarevny. Tsar Aleksei favoured this church as a private chapel.[30] There were many other churches situated in the vicinity of the palace, including the ancient Church of the Saviour (*na boru*), the Church of the Deposition of the Robe, and the Church of the Nativity of the Virgin.

A few yards from the palace and linked to it in some cases by covered galleries, stood the main Kremlin cathedrals, a legacy of the reign of Ivan III (1462–1505) and the hub of the ceremonial life of the Muscovite state. Next to them was the Patriarch's palace with the Cathedral of the Twelve Apostles. These cathedrals were the domain of men, both the extensive clergy and the numerous courtiers, and women entered them infrequently. When they did, they were shielded from

3 Kremlin Palace: view of the royal apartments in the Terem Palace (1630s): 19th-century photograph

public gaze by veils and curtained recesses. Sophia was baptised in the grandest of them, the Cathedral of the Dormition of the Virgin, built by an Italian in 1475–9, but is is unlikely that she was often there again until her regency when, as will be shown, open attendance in the cathedral was one of her boldest breaks with convention.

The Cathedral of the Archangel Michael, containing the tombs of the Muscovite Great Princes and Tsars, was even less frequented by women, except by widows at royal funerals. The Cathedral of the Annunciation, where weddings and baptisms were often held, completed the trio. Much closer to the lives of the royal women was the Convent of the Ascension (demolished in Soviet times), which stood in the north-west part of the Kremlin, next to the Spassky Tower. Its main cathedral contained the tombs of many of Sophia's female ancestors.

Her mother was buried there in 1669 and, had events turned out differently, it might also have been Sophia's resting place. Adjoining it was the Monastery of the Miracles (Chudov), which was often used for royal baptisms.

It is unlikely that Sophia would have ventured much beyond these confines during residence in the Kremlin, for example to the Cathedrals of St Basil the Blessed (or the Intercession) and Our Lady of Kazan on Red Square, both of which merited visits by the Tsar on special days in the Church calendar. More accessible to the tsarevny, in fact, were churches and chapels in the Tsar's out-of-town estates, which could be visited in the relative privacy of a closed carriage. According to Reutenfels, when a female party left town, they were wrapped up in veils. It was usually arranged that they complete their journeys either early in the morning or late at night to avoid the risk of being observed, and they were guarded by units of strel'tsy. Ladies-in-waiting followed in separate carriages.[31] Their destination might be any of several royal estates – Kolomenskoe, Izmailovo, Preobrazhenskoe, Vorob'evo – all of which had chapels. A frequent place of pilgrimage was to be the Novodevichy Convent, just a few miles to the south of the Kremlin, to which Sophia made generous endowments in the 1680s and where she was to live out the last years of her life. Others included the Moscow Donskoi Monastery, the Monastery of St Sabbas at Zvenigorod, and the great Trinity–St Sergius Monastery at what is now Zagorsk. Patronage of convents was regarded as one of the special spheres of the tsarevny, a habit cultivated early in life, and Sophia never abandoned the practice.

It has to be admitted that, despite certain diversions, even relaxations, introduced towards the end of Tsar Aleksei's reign, it was an enclosed and static life even by the standards of the seventeenth century and one from which Sophia never entirely escaped. Even during the years of her regency, she rarely ventured beyond a roughly forty-mile radius from her birthplace. Not only did she never visit a foreign country, but as far as we know she never set foot in such historic Russian towns as Vladimir, Suzdal', Iaroslavl' and Novgorod, not to mention such far-flung points of the Tsar's domains as Kiev, Archangel, Kazan and Astrakhan.

A subject of special interest is that of Sophia's education. As was shown in the preceding chapter, provision for any kind of formal, secular education was still poorly developed, even for men, and one notes with little surprise Susan McNally's comment that 'embroidery and morals were the normal subject of women's education in the terem'.[32] Kotoshikhin writes only of the education of the tsarevichi, remarking that a boyar and assistant were appointed to them at about the age of five and that later qualified tutors were chosen. Providing no information on the curriculum, he adds that 'apart from Russian no other languages – Latin, Greek, German and others – are taught in the Russian state.'[33] Reutenfels wrote disparagingly that the education given to the Tsar's children was 'very similar to that of all Asiatic peoples. . . . They do not study the generally educative sciences even in a superficial manner, except for a general short political survey, since their tutors teach them only to read and count, and acquaint them with the condition of their own country and of those neighbouring powers of which they should be wary.'[34] Particular attention was paid to knowing the language and manners of their various subjects, observing 'ancient customs' and defending the faith.[35] Reutenfels gave no indication that even this 'simple education to equip them for life' was extended to girls. Kotoshikhin left Russia too soon, and Reutenfels, as a foreigner, was too remote from the inner workings of the royal household to know that in the 1660s significant changes were taking place.

In 1656, passing through the town of Polotsk in the Grand Duchy of Lithuania on his way to the Swedish campaign, Tsar Aleksei had been treated to verses of welcome by a young scholar and monk named Simeon. Simeon Polotsky, as he is usually known, transferred permanently to Moscow in 1664 or 1665, establishing a small school for government clerks in 1665 and becoming tutor to the heir to the throne, Tsarevich Aleksei, in 1667.[36] After the Tsarevich's death in 1670 he transferred his attentions to Fedor and, apparently alone of the girls, to Sophia. This is a feature of Sophia's biography which is included in even the briefest of surveys, an element which is naturally considered a formative influence on the character of a woman whom everyone, her enemies included, regarded as intelligent.[37] Unfortunately, the evidence for Sophia's schooling with Polotsky is at best indirect. We do not know, for example, which year her studies commenced, although a recent monograph on Polotsky assumes it to have been 1667, when she was ten, and when he also undertook the schooling of Tsarevich Aleksei.[38]

Indirect evidence of Polotsky's relationship with Sophia includes the much quoted dedication to her of a manuscript copy of his work *The Crown of the Catholic Faith* (*Venets very katolicheskoi*), written in 1670. The verses, which survive in a single copy in Polotsky's anthology *Rifmologion* (compiled 1678–80) and without any indication of the year when the dedication was made, run:

> O most noble Tsarevna Sophia, you always seek heavenly wisdom. You live your life according to your name, wise in word, wise in deed. You are wont to read the Church books and to seek wisdom in the Holy Fathers. Seeing that a new book, called the Crown of Faith, was written, you desired to see it for yourself and to read it in draft form and so, conscious of its usefulness for the spiritual life, you ordered a fresh copy to be made.[39]

4    Simeon Polotsky, *Psalter in Verse* (1680): frontispiece by Simon Ushakov

*The Crown of Faith*, a controversial religious tract that expounded the Apostolic creed and drew on authorities of the Western Church and the Vulgate Bible, could scarcely be described as light reading, even by the standards of the time. Sophia's wish to read it indicates a seriousness of mind and dedication to matters of faith beyond her years. It may, in addition, indicate a personal admiration for Polotsky himself, given an environment in which male company was such a rarity. She owned other works by the poet, for example his anthology *The Many-flowered Garden* (*Vertograd Mnogotsvetnyi*), a collection of verses arranged alphabetically in themes and apparently compiled for the royal children. During the regency a specially bound copy of Polotsky's *Psalter in Verse* (*Psaltir' rifmotvornaia*, 1680) was presented to 'the wise Tsarevna Sophia' by the secretary V.I. Titov.[40]

There is thus ample evidence of Sophia's knowledge and admiration of Polotsky's writings. Unfortunately, no record of her lessons has survived and a notion of what she learned must be gleaned from other sources. She apparently knew Polish (according to a Polish source she enjoyed reading the works of modern clerics such as Lazar Baranovich), but we do not know whether she learned Latin, another of Polotsky's specialities. She undoubtedly took a keen interest in theological matters

34

and is said to have written an elegant hand and even to have composed verses (although no examples survive).[41] Any one of these accomplishments would have distinguished her from her Russian female contemporaries and go some way to explaining why she came to the fore in May 1682.

What of Sophia's knowledge of events in Russia during her youth? Despite the practice of seclusion, it is scarcely credible that news did not penetrate the *terem*, especially as most of the female attendants were the wives and daughters of prominent courtiers. Sophia would have been too young to appreciate the furore surrounding the retirement of Nikon from the patriarchate in 1658 or the 'Copper Coin' rebellion of 1662 when Moscow was in turmoil,[42] but she may have devoted some speculation to the Peace of Andrusovo, drawn up between Poland and Muscovy in 1667.[43] This treaty divided the disputed Ukraine, lands to the east of the River Dniepr (the Left Bank) going to Moscow, to the west (the Right Bank) to Poland, with Kiev retained under Russian governorship for a further two years. It established an uneasy peace after thirteen years of warfare, but the Ukraine continued to be an object of tension and dispute, in which Russia's quarrels with her Polish, Tatar and Turkish neighbours were complicated by internal rivalries and disturbances amongst the Cossack population. The region was to be at the heart of foreign policy during Sophia's regency.

A little closer to home, and an event which must have filled the *terem* with horror stories, was the Stenka Razin rebellion.[44] Razin, a Cossack adventurer, came to public notice in 1669 when he seized the town of Astrakhan at the mouth of the Volga, then gathered an army to march on Moscow, proclaiming the freedom of the common people from landlords and officials as he went. He was defeated at Simbirsk in October 1670 and executed in June 1671. There was an aftermath of punitive expeditions.

This rebellion, the leader of which has become a part of Russian folklore, corresponded with a series of private upheavals at court. On 3 March 1669 Tsaritsa Maria, now forty-three years old, died after giving birth to her thirteenth child, a daughter, Evdokia, who predeceased her by just a few days. (It will be recalled that Maria already had a daughter by the name of Evdokia, but repetition of first names amongst siblings sometimes occurred as a result of parents' adopting the name of the saint whose day fell closest to the child's date of birth, in this case St Evdokia on 1 March). The funeral, which took place on 4 March in the Convent of the Ascension, was attended by Tsar Aleksei. The daughters probably expressed their grief in private. In June of that year four-year-old Simeon died, followed, on 17 January 1670, by perhaps the most serious loss of all, the unexpected death of the heir-apparent, sixteen-year-old Aleksei,[45] who had apparently been a boy of some promise. If we accept that he and Sophia were educated together, we can imagine what her own feelings were.

Now only two sons survived – the elder, eight-year-old Fedor was bright but frail, whilst the younger, Ivan, aged three, was mentally and physically handicapped. Such disabilities in a person of the royal blood could not be admitted publicly but a large body of evidence, mostly from foreigners' accounts, makes it plain that by the time was an adolescent Ivan had a visual handicap and speech impediment, as well as other ailments.[46] The daughters, on the other hand, were relatively robust. All six of them outlived their brothers, surviving into the first decades of the eighteenth century. And yet, despite the lack of any law specifically banning female succession, it is most unlikely that Tsar Aleksei ever regarded his daughters as the potential salvation of his dynasty, taking a warning, no doubt, from his father's unsuccessful attempt to marry off Irina. Male succession was a part of Muscovite tradition, and by the 1670s the presupposition of male rule had been confirmed, as it were, by the practice of secluding the women.

The frailty of his two remaining sons was undoubtedly one of the main reasons why, on 22 January 1671, Tsar Aleksei remarried. His bride was nineteen-year-old Natalia, daughter of Kirill Poluektovich Naryshkin, a fairly minor servitor. The Tsar probably met her at the home of one of his closest advisers, the up-and-coming official Artamon Sergeevich Matveev, who was acting as her guardian.[47] Those who feared the 'upstart' Matveev's growing influence spread rumours that the Tsar had been tricked into the marriage by witchcraft, but the truth seems to have been that Aleksei loved his young bride. He himself was still only forty-one.

Sophia's reaction to her father's remarriage so soon after her own mother's death is not recorded. She and her sisters were certainly absent from the wedding itself and probably excluded from the accompanying celebrations.[48] For subsequent commentators, however, the events of January 1671 appeared as a crucial turning point when fourteen-year-old Sophia may have become dimly aware of her own potential role as protector of the interests of the Miloslavsky clan now that a new tsaritsa and new permutations of clan rivalries had entered the Kremlin. One of the most influential interpretations of the crisis belongs to the nineteenth-century historian S.M. Solov'ev, who tried to visualise Sophia's feelings: 'A new tsaritsa and her kinsfolk and close advisers, Matveev ruling the roost in the palace! A dreadful clash of interests and a dreadful hatred!'[49] D. Mordovtsev followed Solov'ev's lead in regarding bitter stepmother–stepdaughter rivalry as the chief stimulus to Sophia's rise to power. According to him Sophia regarded all the women at court as potential rivals.[50] However, despite the dramatic appeal of this version of events and even the psychological likelihood of Sophia's dislike of her father's new wife, who was only five years her senior, there is not a scrap of direct evidence. Similarly, it is mere speculation that Sophia was 'horrified' by the birth, on 30 May 1672, of a half-brother, the future Peter the Great. Those who had enjoyed power as a result of Miloslavsky ascendancy, especially the Miloslavskys themselves, may well have felt considerable anxiety at his consolidation of the Naryshkin position, for the relatives of a royal bride always formed part of a revised power network, yet Sophia and her sisters had no reason to harbour such fears on their own behalf because they could normally have no expectation of political power in their own right but were assured of respect and protection by virtue of their royal blood, especially while their father was still very much alive. It is most unlikely that Tsaritsa Natalia in any way persecuted her stepdaughters. On the contrary, there are strong indications that the arrival of Natalia Naryshkina had a liberating effect on Kremlin life. She had been raised in the home of Matveev, one of the most 'Westernised' Muscovites of his era, who boasted of a russified Scottish wife not subjected to the rigours of the *terem*, and of a mansion packed with foreign books, prints, clocks, furniture, portraits and other curiosities. Jacob Reutenfels reports that on her first public outing Natalia opened the window of her carriage slightly, thereby creating public consternation. Reutenfels added that 'although she never flouts tradition, she is evidently inclined to tread another path to a freer way of life since, being of strong character and lively disposition, she tries bravely to spread gaiety everywhere'. Reutenfels was able to supply a portrait of the Tsaritsa, 'a woman in the prime of life, of greater than average height, with dark, wide eyes, a rounded pleasant face, large and high forehead; her whole figure is beautiful, the individual members very well proportioned and, finally, her voice is pleasant to the ear and all her mannerisms graceful'.[51]

Amongst the unconventional events that Natalia had witnessed at 'semi-Westernised' Matveev's house were private theatricals, and no doubt she passed on her enthusiasm to Aleksei. Shortly after Peter's birth, on 4 June 1672, the Tsar ordered preparations for the first court theatrical performance in Russian history. The very first play, according to Dr Laurent Rinhuber from Saxony, who was a participant, was staged at the palace of Preobrazhenskoe on 17 October 1672, when the 'tragi-comedy of Ahasuerus and Esther', otherwise known as *The Drama of Artaxerxes*, was directed by Pastor Johann Gottfried Gregory of the Foreign Quarter's Lutheran parish and performed in German by boys from the same colony.[52] Apparently the Tsar watched transfixed for ten hours. Reutenfels provides a second-hand report of the first, or one of the first, performances which, he writes, would anywhere else be regarded as rather second-rate, 'but to the Russians it appeared something extraordinarily artistic in which everything – the new, unheard-of costumes, the unfamiliar sight of the stage, even the foreign idiom and elegant bursts of music – all these things easily aroused amazement'. The Tsar, he reported, watched from a seat, and the Tsaritsa and children 'through a grille, or rather through chinks in specially boarded-off premises'.[53]

Official records do not make it clear on how many occasions Sophia herself was present at court theatricals, although performances took place regularly until Tsar Aleksei's death. On only one occasion is the presence of the tsarevny specifically noted, at the performance on 11 November 1674 of the comedy 'how Artaxerxes ordered the hanging of Haman by the petition of the queen and at the instigation of Mordecai', in other words a repeat performance of the very first 'Russian' play. Organs, viols and other instruments were played and there was dancing.[54] Altogether in the three and a half years of the court theatre's existence nine different plays and one ballet were presented, some on several occasions. Although the majority were based on Biblical themes, the religious subjects were often treated nominally and were accompanied by preludes and epilogues, music, dancing and lavish costumes, and interspersed with comic interludes, creating a baroque spectacle that was quite unprecedented in the history of Russian culture. Thus the early history of the Russian theatre, to which Sophia was a witness, provides further evidence of the fresh currents of secularisation and Westernisation that were infiltrating the rigid conventions of Muscovite life. There are, incidentally, many unconfirmed rumours about Sophia's own attempts at dramaturgy, a topic that will be tackled below.[55]

The theatre was potentially a vision-broadening experience, but much better documented and arguably more important for determining Sophia's emergence as regent was the increasingly mobile lifestyle which was inaugurated by the arrival of Tsaritsa Natalia. Court records show that the Tsar, accompanied by his whole family, made frequent trips out of town. Their destinations included Alekseevskoe and Vozdvizhenskoe to the north, on the road to the Trinity–St Sergius Monastery; to the north-east, the palaces at Preobrazhenskoe and Izmailovo; to the south-west there was Pavlovskoe, on the road to the Monastery of St Sabbas at Zvenigorod, which Tsar Aleksei regarded with special favour; to the south lay the palaces at Vorob'evo and Kolomenskoe.

In the latter royal village a magnificent wooden palace had been completed in 1671, decorated inside and out by the best artists and craftsmen from the royal workshops. The palace had more than 200 rooms, with the state apartments arranged as an interconnecting series in the Western manner, and annexes built round a series of courtyards. The exterior was a compendium of wooden architectural devices – domes, 'tent' roofs, galleries, 'kokoshnik' gables, carved window surrounds and portals. Simeon Polotsky dedicated an ode to this 'most cunningly fashioned building', describing it as the eighth wonder of the world.[56] Even Reutenfels was impressed (foreigners were often disparaging about Russian architecture), declaring the palace to be 'well worth seeing', even though it was made of wood. 'It looks as though it has just been taken out of a jewel box, with its amazing shapes, skilfully executed with carved ornament and glittering gilt.'[57]

Records for the Russian year 7183 (1 September 1674 to 31 August 1675) offer some interesting insights into the pace and pattern of life.[58] On 1 September, the first day of the Old Russian New Year, in addition to the normal festivities Tsarevich Fedor, now thirteen years old, was presented to the people in confirmation of his status as heir-apparent. On 4 September there were celebrations for Tsarevna Marfa's nameday, the same day on which Tsaritsa Natalia gave birth to her third child in so many years, a daughter named Fedora. On Thursday 17 September Tsar Aleksei 'celebrated the nameday of the Sovereign Lady, Tsarevna Great Princess Sophia Alekseevna'. He did not attend mass in the cathedral, but ordered a private service in the palace chapel of St Evdokia and treated various nobles, clergymen and officials to nameday cakes. Sophia herself distributed cakes to nursemaids, ladies-in-waiting and mistresses of the wardrobe and on the same day 'the boyar and armourer Bogdan Matveevich Khitrovo brought a feast and a cup of wine from the Great Sovereign to the Sovereign Lady . . . Sophia'. At the age of seventeen Sophia was taking a less passive role than hitherto. On 23 September Aleksei left for his annual pilgrimage to the Trinity Monastery, leaving Peter Matiushkin and Boris Iushkov in charge of the tsarevny, an arrangement which was repeated on 6 October when the Tsar left for Sokolovo. On 4 October Fedora Alekseevna was baptised, with Tsarevich Fedor and Tsarevna Irina acting as godparents.

Although there was still no question of the complete desegregation of male and female company, the *terem* seems to have become more active on its own behalf. On 7 October, for example, while the Tsar attended an all-male baptismal banquet, the Tsaritsa presided over her own table, attended by the wives of boyars and the princesses of Georgia and Siberia, whilst on 24 October, after the Tsar and Fedor had made a tour of Kremlin cathedrals, the Ascension and Miracles Monasteries and other churches, the Tsaritsa and tsarevny made the same tour, accompanied by Natalia's father Kirill Naryshkin. On this occasion, however, it was still deemed necessary to protect the women from prying eyes by posting detachments of strel'tsy at strategic points.

The next day the court left the Kremlin for Preobrazhenskoe in a procession headed by the Tsar, followed by Fedor, Ivan, then Tsaritsa Natalia with her three children and the tsarevny bringing up the rear, accompanied by boyars, a strel'tsy escort and a retinue of ladies-in-waiting, dwarves and chambermaids. Diversions during this outing, which ended on 13 December, included the celebration of Tsarevna Ekaterina's nameday on 24 November and a visit to the model estate at Izmailovo to inspect new building work. The estate boasted a summer house, zoological and herb gardens, experimental windmills and glass-works and was in every way redolent of the more adventurous spirit of inventiveness, curiosity and even fun which permeated the last years of Tsar Aleksei's reign.[59]

There were several theatrical performances in 1674, although the records do not always specify the dates. In November, for example, the family attended *The Drama of Artaxerxes*, referred to earlier, and there was also a repeat staging of *The Drama of Judith and Holofernes*, first performed in February 1673.[60] It may be noted that the first two plays of the early Russian theatre featured the female protagonists Judith and Esther, to both of whom Sophia was to be likened during her regency. One can only speculate, of course, on their possible influence on the adolescent Sophia. The year of Our Lord 1674 ended for the Russian royal family with the celebration of Christmas, a festival which the Orthodox Church marked with much less pomp than Easter. The Tsar attended services in the cathedral, but the royal women remained in the palace.[61]

Sixteen-seventy-five was to be the last full year of the Tsar's life, and also one of the liveliest in terms of family outings and entertainments. On 11 February another theatrical performance was staged. Although the records do not give the title, the play may be identified as *The Tearful Comedy of Adam and Eve*, a topic deemed suitable for marking the beginning of Lent.[62] On 13 February the Tsaritsa, accompanied by Ivan, Peter and the tsarevny, visited the Ascension and Miracles Monasteries. Again, one must be careful not to exaggerate new 'free-doms' for 'while the Tsaritsa was going round the monasteries, the Great Sovereign commanded the State Secretary of the strel'tsy chan-cellery Larion Ivanov to lock up the Kremlin and not to admit any-body.'[63] The following day Tsaritsa Natalia distributed sturgeon and salmon to courtiers, and gifts of fish from the palace kitchens were distributed on behalf of the tsarevny.

On 26–27 February services of remembrance were conducted in the Ascension Convent in memory of Maria Miloslavskaia, who was buried there. These were attended by the Tsar and even certain ladies of the court, but the tsarevny did not participate openly, even though it was their mother who was being honoured. One is aware at the same time that women's occasions claim the attention of the official record keepers more often than previously, as on 1 March when, as part of her nameday celebrations, Tsarevna Evdokia distributed cakes to nurse-maids, ladies-in-waiting and mistresses of the wardrobe. The female sex was also remembered on 25 March, the Feast of the Annunciation, when drinking cups were blessed and sent to the Tsaritsa and tsarevny.

Easter Week, the greatest festival in the Orthodox calendar, began on 28 March. This was primarily a time of male ritual, opening with the colourful Palm Sunday celebrations when the Tsar customarily led a donkey bearing the Patriarch across Red Square. The women were not entirely forgotten, however, the Patriarch sending gifts of food from his banquet that evening. The rest of the week was taken up with services night and day, culminating in the joyful celebration of Easter Sunday. The royal women did not merit a mention, but a few days later, on 8 April, the Tsaritsa's carriage, accompanied by the royal bodyguard of strel'tsy, departed for an unspecified destination. On 11 April Tsaritsa Natalia was again leading a 'women's pilgrimage', taking in the Ascension and Miracles Monasteries and the Novodevichy, Conception and Passion Convents, the last three, it should be noted, situated outside the Kremlin walls.[64]

On 23 May a major expedition was planned to Vorob'evo, the royal estate to the south of Moscow (on the present-day Lenin Hills). The lady-in-waiting Matrena Blokhina was dispatched in advance with ten chambermaids and ten pages to ensure 'that everything was properly arranged in the apartments of the sovereign Tsaritsa, tsarevny and tsarevichi, and to await their arrival'. It is worth describing in some detail the elaborate cortège in which the whole royal family embarked upon the seven-mile journey from the Kremlin. The Tsar rode ahead with Fedor, followed by a huge retinue of courtiers and strel'tsy and the baggage train, after which carriages followed containing Tsarevich Ivan and his personal attendant P.I. Prozorovsky, then Tsaritsa Natalia, her son and two daughters, mother and sister-in-law (Anna Leont'evna and Praskovia Alekseevna Naryshkina), then the elder tsarevny (Irina, Anna and Tat'iana) accompanied by P.I. Matiushkin, and finally the Miloslavsky daughters with bodyguards Avram Lopukhin and Boris Iushkov. Some thirty wagons of baggage and attendants brought up the rear. The boyar Ivan Alekseevich Vorotynsky and permanent officials in the chancelleries were left behind in the Kremlin 'to attend to all matters' and report regularly to the Tsar.

The time spent away from Moscow was crammed with events, including the usual crop of namedays (Feodosia on 29 May, Fedor on 8 June, Peter on 29 June, Anna Mikhailovna on 25 July, both Natalias on 26 August, Ivan on 29 August, and Marfa on 1 September), all of which entailed religious services, banquets and distribution of gifts. There was a constant stream of visitors – officials from Moscow, envoys from the Ukraine, clergymen, the Tatar Prince Kasbulat Mutsalovich Cherkassky, an official from the Nogai Tatars. News of all sorts of events reached them, for example a scandal involving Prince F.F. Kurakin, who was accused of harbouring a blind witch (the latter died under torture), and reports of fires in Moscow on 11 and 12 June. On 14–15 June 'by the will of God there was great thunder and lightning' and a number of people and buildings were struck. Shortly after this, on 19 June, the whole royal party set off for Preobrazhenskoe, the Tsar riding in the same carriage as the Tsaritsa (a sign of relaxed protocol), and the tsarevny processing in order of hierarchy, Irina, Tsar Mikhail's eldest daughter, supervising her sisters, and Evdokia, Tsar Aleksei's eldest, in charge of hers. Sophia, a mere third in seniority to Evdokia, is not mentioned by name. The week spent at Preobrazhenskoe, which housed the new theatre, included pleasure trips to Izmailovo and another village, Pokrovskoe. On 28 June after a meal the party prepared to return to their quarters at Vorob'evo.

The description of this cortège is particularly detailed.[65] It was composed of several hundred individuals, including over a hundred strel'tsy. The mistresses of the wardrobe of the various royal children occupied seven carriages, with an additional coach provided for the royal dwarves and some forty coaches for assorted servants. Further relaxation of protocol is indicated by the fact that Tsar Aleksei was joined in his carriage by thirteen-year-old Feodosia, the youngest Miloslavsky daughter. The next day was Peter's nameday, which was celebrated more lavishly than usual with the arrival of the Patriarch and Church dignitaries from Moscow. The Tsar gave thanks in the nearby Donskoi Monastery and that evening held a banquet in tents. Seating at this feast was, incidentally, informally arranged without regard to precedence, the system whereby seniority was computed in accordance with a clan's service record. This type of arrangement was common during Aleksei's reign and heralded the abolition of the code in 1682. On 1 July the Tsar went to open ground near the Novodevichy Convent for his favourite sport of falconry, this time accompanied by the Tsaritsa, Fedor and Peter. Fedor himself became a keen falconer but Peter never seems to have been attracted to the sport. Ivan missed this outing, as he did several others, no doubt on account of his poor health.

On 12 July the Tsar attended memorial services for his father in Moscow, and on the 14th the family moved to Kolomenskoe, where one of the diversions was the arrival of the Polish resident with a letter from King John Sobieski. On 26 July they were back at Vorob'evo, where a month later there were extensive celebrations for the nameday of the Tsaritsa and her daughter Natalia, born in 1673. This was a most lavish occasion, attended by huge numbers of guests and was followed within a week by celebrations for Ivan and Marfa. In general, the summer and autumn of 1675 were a time of merry-making, of dinners, drinking, music (even a ballet on the theme of Orpheus, of which little is known).[66] Towards the end of the year two new plays were in rehearsal, *The Drama of David and Goliath* and *The Comedy of Bacchus and Venus*, the latter featuring ten drunkards, ten maidens and performing bears, subject matter a far cry from the Holy Russia of the 'pious' Tsar sometimes evoked in conventional histories.[67] Published palace records break off on 31 August, the end of the Russian year 7183. Five months later, on 30 January 1676 Tsar Aleksei was dead, just short of his forty-seventh birthday.[68]

The names of Sophia and her sisters do not appear in official accounts of the funeral because, with the exception of the deceased's widow, these occasions were deemed all-male affairs.[69] It may be possible, however, that the conventions were relaxed, for Reutenfels (admittedly reporting second-hand) alleges that behind the heir Fedor and the widow Natalia, both borne in litters, there followed 'the five daughters of the Tsar from his first marriage and a huge number of courtiers, in dark garments'.[70] Given the error (five daughters instead of six?) it is difficult to know how seriously to take this piece of information.

There is no record of Sophia's reaction to the death of her father. The daughters' grief was expressed on their behalf in verses of lament written by Simeon Polotsky, in which each member of the Tsar's family was addressed by their deceased father and in turn grieved for him.[71]

Thus Fedor came to the throne at the age of fourteen. He was the eldest son and heir and had been 'shown' to the people of Moscow in 1674 in confirmation of his father's wishes. Contemporary sources record no opposition to his accession, even though it was a matter of tradition rather than a written law of succession. Nonetheless, rumours survive that Tsaritsa Natalia's guardian Artamon Matveev, by now head of the important Foreign Office, fearing for his own position if the Miloslavsky clan were restored to power as a result of Fedor's accession, attempted to represent Tsarevich Peter's claim to the throne. An anonymous Polish memoir, the so-called *Diariusz*, which focuses on the Moscow Rebellion of 1682 and was probably written in the summer of 1683, records that Matveev withheld news of Aleksei's death and his deathbed blessing of Fedor from courtiers and clergy assembled outside the bedchamber. He sat the three-year-old Peter on the throne and argued that 'Fedor was all swollen up and lay sick, and there was little hope of his living and even less that he would rule over them or fight with foreign enemies.'[72] Patriarch Joachim, however, proclaimed Aleksei's last wish. Meanwhile the new Tsar's aunts and sisters settled down to 'watch over his health'.[73]

Allegations that Matveev tried to intervene in the question of the succession also appear in a short memorandum in Latin sent to the Papal Legate in Poland in the autumn of 1682. The author claims that Matveev urged the Tsar on his deathbed to bypass both Fedor and Ivan on account of their ill-health in favour of Peter, a plan that was

5   Posthumous portrait of Tsar Fedor by Ivan Bezmin (?) (c.1685)

allegedly thwarted by the appeals of Fedor's aunts and sisters, notably Sophia, the only one to be mentioned by name, who appealed for the assistance of the assembled boyars 'with plaintive wailing and weeping'.[74] It will be noted that both these accounts postdate Sophia's actual rise to power in 1682, and may be said to form part of the 'legend' that dated her ambitious schemes for taking over the government to the very beginning of Fedor's reign. Contemporary sources contain no trace of factional struggles about the succession following Tsar Aleksei's death. Even if Aleksei himself had at any time contemplated bypassing the ailing Fedor in favour of the promising-looking son of his second marriage, he never expressed it publicly.[75]

One is reminded, however, by the wording of a document issued to the Don Cossacks on 3 February 1676, one of many announcing the new Tsar's accession, that allegiance was sworn to the whole royal family, whose names appear in hierarchy of sex and age, Sophia's, as ever, sandwiched between those of Marfa and Ekaterina.[76] In view of Fedor's apparently fragile health, Peter's youth and Ivan's permanent incapacity, it seemed possible that the wording of the royal rescripts would become more than mere formality and that a female of royal blood might have to step temporarily into the vacuum.

For the time being, though, Fedor was to rule without a regent, indeed to live for almost another six years before his health failed. He has generally been regarded as a weak interim ruler, moderately well educated, pious and cultured, but too enfeebled by illness to exert himself against his advisers. Foreign commentators at the Muscovite court credited Fedor with some strength of character, however. H.E. Ellersiek's reading of Scandinavian sources for the period suggests that Fedor 'given half a chance – would have been a strong, perhaps even a great ruler'.[77] Moreover, official records make it clear that far from being a permanent invalid, confined to his sickbed, Fedor enjoyed at least intervals of more robust health. In the autumn of 1676, for example, he led expeditions to Kolomenskoe, Pokrovskoe, Kashin and the Trinity and St Sabbas Monasteries, a scale of activity which was to be the rule rather than the exception during his reign.[78] At the beginning of Easter Week 1678 he took part in the elaborate and exhausting Palm Sunday 'Entry into Jerusalem' ceremony, which entailed not only the usual lengthy services but also the ritual whereby the Tsar, on foot, led a donkey bearing the Patriarch from the so-called Place of Proclamations (lobnoe mesto) on Red Square to the Cathedral of the Dormition in the Kremlin. In the words of the record:

'And as the great lord, His Holiness Patriarch Joachim, Patriarch of Moscow and All Russia, mounted the ass at the lobnoe mesto and set off for the Cathedral Church in the Kremlin, the Great Sovereign, Tsar and Great Prince Fedor Alekseevich, Autocrat of all the Great and Little and White Russias, deigned at that time to take the ass's bridle by the end of the reins and to lead the way to the Cathedral.[79]

The rest of the week contained other lengthy ceremonials, culminating in Easter itself. There are indications that Fedor sometimes found the pace exhausting; for example, he did not attend the Saturday night liturgy in the cathedral but worshipped in the palace Church of the Saviour. The next morning, however, he was holding audience for courtiers and went to matins in the Dormition Cathedral, again celebrating the evening service in private.[80] Daily ceremonies continued for the next few weeks, including formal audiences for courtiers and servitors and visits to the Novodevichy Convent (13 April), the Convent of St John (16 April) and other religious establishments in Moscow. On 6 January 1680 Fedor took part in another lavish ritual, the Epiphany blessing of the waters of the Moscow river, which entailed attending early-morning mass, donning full regalia, including the Crown of Monomach, and walking down to the special canopy by the river, attended by a huge procession of clergy, courtiers and strel'tsy.[81]

Whilst records of Fedor's activities are fairly full and belie his standard image as a helpless invalid, the tsarevny, including Sophia, all but disappear from court records after their father's death. If the sisters' namedays were celebrated, as was patently the case during Aleksei's reign, the records no longer make note of it. For example, Fedor is the only member of the royal family mentioned in the description of the funeral cortège of Tsarevna Irina Mikhailovna, which took place on 8 February 1679. This involved a long walk from the Kremlin to the Novospassky Monastery, where Irina was laid to rest near her paternal grandmother Marfa Ivanovna.[82] Irina was the senior member of the *terem* and the one, it will be recalled, who in 1645 had narrowly missed being married off to the Danish Prince Waldemar. Her position was now assumed by Tsarevna Tat'iana Mikhailovna.

Another example of changes in court procedure is indicated by the record for 10 June 1680, when Fedor 'was pleased to visit the village of Vorob'evo and other villages',[83] but there is no indication that the whole family went with him as they would have done at the end of Tsar Aleksei's reign. Could it be that the conservative Patriarch Joachim was taking the opportunity to clamp down on excess merrymaking? He undoubtedly influenced Fedor in his decision to curtail the activities of the court theatre. But attempts to discourage the relaxation of seclusion would not explain why Ivan and Peter also virtually disappear from the records. Not surprisingly in these circumstances, Sophia herself all but vanishes from view. Even her nameday no longer commands any attention in the court records. We may assume her presence at the dedication of a private chapel for the tsarevny in August 1680, and at the consecration of the Cathedral of the Intercession at Izmailovo in October, but we cannot be sure of her whereabouts.[84]

The dearth of evidence for this period contrasts sharply with the theory advanced by contemporary commentators, both foreign and Russian, and perpetuated by historians right up to the present day to the effect that Sophia's rise to power occurred not in the immediate circumstances of May 1682 but in Fedor's reign. The 'armchair' compiler J. Crull, writing in 1698, claimed that Fedor even reigned 'under the Protectorate of Sophia his sister' and that when Peter was crowned in 1682 'seeing herself thus excluded from the Management of the Government, of which she had enjoyed the *full Advantage* [my italics] during the Minority of her Brother Fedor' she fomented rebellion to retain power.[85] The most influential of all foreign commentators was the Frenchman Foy de la Neuville, whose account of his visit to Moscow in 1689 as the agent of the King of Poland was first published in 1698.[86] In it, La Neuville attempted to recount not only the crisis of Sophia's downfall, to which he was a witness, but also the circumstances that brought her to power in 1682. She was, he wrote, 'ambitious and daring above her sex', actually leaving a nunnery in order to tend her sick brother, 'for this clever Princess judged rightly that the more she did for him, the more she would win this Prince's affection and gratitude and at the same time the respect and esteem of everybody else'.[87] The notion that Sophia tended and 'kept watch' over her sick brother was, as we have indicated, contained in two anonymous accounts written in 1682–3, to which La Neuville with his Polish connections may have had access.

Palace records, however, indicate that contrary to the popular view Fedor did not spend most of his reign confined to his chambers. Moreover, the shifting patterns of influence at court suggest that despite enjoying some initial success in subduing the power of the Naryshkins, for example by securing the banishment of A.S. Matveev and Tsaritsa Natalia's brothers Ivan and Afanasy Naryshkin in 1676, the Miloslavskys failed to gain a permanent upper hand. Early on in his reign Fedor began to show preference for the company and advice of Ivan Maksimovich Iazykov, his chamberlain (postel'nichii) since 1675, and for Aleksei Timofeevich Likhachev and his brother Mikhail. Iazykov entered the boyar council in 1680 with the rank of lord-in-waiting, and was promoted to boyar in the following year. As he rose to favour, so Ivan Mikhailovich Miloslavsky, who had been prominent in the first few years of Fedor's reign, receded into the background again.[88] There is evidence that the influence of Fedor's new advisers was promoted by the seasoned courtiers Bogdan Khitrovo and Prince Iury Dolgoruky, who were anxious to counteract Miloslavsky power.

Clear evidence of the balance of power at court can also be seen in Fedor's choice of brides, traditionally a matter in which the *terem* would have some say. In 1680 his fancy was taken by Agafia Semenovna Grushetskaia, the daughter of a minor nobleman of part-Polish descent, whom he married in July despite the protests of Ivan Bogdanovich Miloslavsky, who detected Iazykov's influence in the choice.[89] His second wife, Marfa Matveevna Apraksina, whom he married in February 1682, was a relative of Iazykov and a goddaughter of A.S. Matveev, whose partial release from exile she succeeded in obtaining, and hence even less acceptable to the Miloslavskys than Grushetskaia. An intriguing entry in the so-called 'Mazurinsky Chronicle' for 15 February 1681 (an account compiled in the Patriarch's chancellery in 1682) states that Fedor 'speaking with his sisters, the sovereign tsarevny, wished to join in a second lawful marriage', an indication that the chronicler conventionally assumed a formal consultation, even if the actual choice was influenced from elsewhere.[90] By the end of the reign, lists of servitors, promotions, attendance at functions and so on give no indication of any preference for the Miloslavskys.

Another popular theory that goes hand in hand with the suggestion that Sophia accumulated power during Fedor's reign is that from the beginning she had a friend and collaborator in the boyar Prince Vasily Vasil'evich Golitsyn.[91] Golitsyn, a member of one of Moscow's most distinguished families, was born in 1643. He rose to prominence during Fedor's reign, acting as co-ordinator of Russian operations in the Ukraine against the Turks and Tatars in the years 1676–8, directing several government chancelleries, including the Artillery Office and a division of the Moscow High Court, and in January 1682 heading the commission which proposed the abolition of the Code of Precedence. Judging by contemporary reports, the confidence that Golitsyn enjoyed was well deserved: 'The first Minister of State, who was of the Illustrious Race of the Jagellons, was undoubtedly the most accomplish'd, and most knowing Lord at the Court of Moscow, he lov'd Strangers, and particularly the French, because the Noble Sentiments he had observ'd in them, were very consonant to his own,' wrote Philippe Avril, a Jesuit father who met Golitsyn in 1689.[92] La Neuville pronounced him to be 'without contradiction one of the most spirited, most refined and most liberal men this country has ever seen'.[93] Even La Neuville, however, ascribes the Prince's promotion to Sophia's machinations. According to him, Sophia, 'being unable to succeed in her grand design without large support, began to form a party and having examined those around her decided that Prince Golitsyn was the most capable of leading it'.[94]

According to La Neuville, moreover, the alliance between the Tsarevna and the Prince was not just a political one. The writer of a recent popular history of the Romanovs expressed it graphically: 'In an act of supreme self-liberation, Sophia took Golitsyn to her bed and made him her lover.'[95] This 'self-liberation' would have been made doubly bold by the fact that Golitsyn was married with several children. This version of events with its admixture of sexual and political intrigue is the stuff on which historical novelists thrive, and indeed it forms the basis of a number of fictional accounts of Sophia's life, for example volume 1 of Aleksei Tolstol's novel *Peter the First*.[96] It perpetuates one of the common notions about female rule, namely that few women are willing or able to wield power without a man to support and inspire them.

La Neuville is also responsible for inserting another vital piece into the jigsaw of Sophia's complex political profile: she was ugly. In a much-quoted comment (which, incidentally, appears only as a marginal note in the manuscript of his account) the Frenchman described her thus: 'of a monstrous size, with a head as big as as a bushel, with hair on her face, growths on her legs, and at least forty years old'.[97] La Neuville probably never saw Sophia himself. She was only thirty-two in 1689, the year he was describing, and no other contemporary left such an unappealing portrait, but because no one else bothered to describe her

6   Engraved portrait of Prince Vasily Golitsyn by Leonty Tarasevich (c.1687)

at all, it is his description which has been most quoted. He adds one more piece: 'although her stature is broad, short and coarse, her mind is subtle, nimble and shrewd'.[98] The psychological profile is complete. As the biographer of the Romanovs concludes: 'She was obliged to rely primarily upon her intellect to gain victory . . . because she had none of the physical charms to seduce men to her cause.'[99]

Faced with the silence of Russian sources for the period 1676–82 on virtually all matters pertaining to Sophia – her activities, personality, appearance – the biographer cannot be blamed for clutching at the straw of foreign accounts, even those written many years after the events which they described. Needless to say, such works, and foreigners' accounts in general, need to be treated with caution and scepticism. Circumstantial evidence does not preclude a meeting between Sophia and Golitsyn before 1682. Golitsyn served at court from 1658. He was, for example, amongst those in attendance when Tsar Aleksei and his family visited Vorob'evo in the summer of 1675 and was frequently in attendance upon Tsar Fedor in 1678–9.[100] His mother was one of Tsarevich Peter's attendants. One may even subscribe to the view that Fedor's bouts of sickness necessitated consultations with servitors in his bedchamber and that Sophia, tending him, may have had the chance to make Golitsyn's acquaintance in fairly intimate surroundings. But to go a step further and suppose amorous intrigue is to be influenced by the morals and conventions of the courts of Europe, with which the foreigners who propagated the rumours were naturally more familiar, than with those of Moscow in the 1670 and 1680s.

It seems highly unlikely that Sophia, before her rise to power, could have embarked upon a relationship so much in conflict with the Muscovite ideal of pious virginity in an environment where even the smallest indiscretion could be observed not only by family, servants and courtiers, but also by the ubiquitous palace clergy. It is unlikely, but not, of course, impossible. One should never assume that lack of explicit reference to sexual activity indicates its absence. In the meantime, whatever Sophia's private anxieties about Fedor's health and the likely outcome in the event of his death, there is absolutely no substantiating evidence for any political action on her part until after his death on 27 April 1682.

In 1676–82, then, court politics were a good deal more complex than the two-sided Miloslavsky – Naryshkin rivalry to which they have been reduced by some commentators, but fate seemed determined to rekindle the feud between the clans. Fedor's first marriage ended in tragedy when on 14 and 21 July 1681 respectively Tsaritsa Agafia and her new-born son Ilia both died after a difficult birth. In a poignant entry in the Court Procession Records it is noted that Fedor accompanied the coffins as far as the Red Porch of the Palace but that there was no Tsar's procession, an indication that he may have been succumbing to illness.[101]

After this, however, he must have rallied somewhat, for on 1 September he attended the New Year festivities in the Cathedral of the Dormition, delivering a speech from the royal box.[102] He may also have been well enough to take an interest in the discussions leading up to the abolition, on 12 January 1682, of the Code of Precedence. In a speech he denounced the evils of a system that 'harms blessed love and destroys peace and brotherly concord'.[103] The records of precedence were burned in order to discourage future disputes. We cannot be sure, of course, of the extent of Fedor's personal contribution (official records referred even to infant and mentally handicapped rulers as 'deciding', 'decreeing' and so on), just as we cannot be sure that he personally devised the recommendations to the Church Council of 1681–2, which included proposals for the creation of more eparchies and the intensification of sanctions against the Old Believers.[104] One may certainly detect the hand of the Patriarch in both documents. On 15 February Fedor was still well enough to contract a marriage with fifteen-year-old Marfa Matveevna Apraksina. Some two months later, however, he was dead, and the stage was set for Sophia's emergence as *de facto* ruler of Russia.

CHAPTER 3

# The Rebellion of 1682

Although Fedor had always been sickly, if not the utterly helpless invalid imagined by some historians, there can be little doubt that his death on 27 April at the age of twenty came as a shock to his relatives. His second marriage just two months previously showed that there were still hopes that he would rally and produce an heir. The more practically minded members of court circles, however, must have already given some thought to the eventuality of his dying without issue.

Johann van Keller, the well-informed Dutch Ambassador in Moscow, had referred in a letter of 21 February 1682 to Peter's right to occupy the throne in the absence of a fixed law of succession, and reported that 'Tsarevich Ivan is acknowledged to be incapable of ruling on account of his feeble-mindedness and other mental and corporal handicaps.'[1] Less reliable sources, as we have seen, suggested that the possiblity of Peter's accession had been raised even earlier, when Tsar Aleksei was on his death bed in 1676,[2] but official sources fail to indicate that Aleksei ever contemplated passing over Fedor and Ivan in favour of his youngest son, or that Fedor himself named Peter as his heir, still less that Sophia and her 'party' had been plotting for years against the eventuality of Peter's relatives seizing the throne on his behalf. On the contrary, there is every indication that in April 1682 all parties had to improvise in a situation that quickly passed beyond their control.

In the event, the Miloslavsky clan was to be confronted with an unpalatable development. On the very day of Fedor's death Patriarch Joachim assembled the Church hierarchs, boyars, lords-in-waiting, men of the council and privy councillors, to quote from the careful listing in the account, who in turn 'summoned the table attendants, crown agents, servitors, clerks, court attendants, town servitors, junior boyars, chief merchants, tradespeople of the second rank, and artisans, and people of other ranks' to the Kremlin and asked which of the two surviving tsarevichi should rule.[3] Decision-making of this type had its roots in the zemskii sobor or Assembly of the Land, the last example of which had been summoned in 1653. Unlike its predecessors, however, this hastily convoked 'assembly' drew its members only from the immediate vicinity of the Kremlin.[4] This crowd was apparently unanimous in its preference for Peter.

In some accounts, Ivan's 'multifarious afflictions' were cited as the reason for bypassing him. It was even said that Ivan himself urged Peter to take the crown 'because his mother was alive'.[5] Others detected a plot. The Polish *Diariusz* reports, quite erroneously, that Peter was proclaimed tsar by Artamon Matveev, whom, as we saw earlier, this account accused of plotting to place Peter on the throne in 1676.[6] Matveev was not even in Moscow on 27 April. The finger has also been pointed at the Patriarch, who may have wished to counteract the 'Latinising' tendencies associated with the circle of the late Simeon Polotsky, who had exercised a considerable influence over Fedor and Sophia. Many of Fedor's advisers, such as Ivan Iazykov, had broken with the Miloslavskys and also preferred to throw in their lot with Peter's camp. Other boyars may have had no particular allegiance to the Naryshkin clan as such, but were aware of Ivan's disabilities and preferred a tsar who at least had a good chance of growing up and ruling in his own right.

Later histories have tended to exaggerate the foresight of the general mass of electors, however. 'The Russian heart beat strongly and was aflutter with joy at the thought of Peter,' enthused a work published in 1837, 'his high brow and frank glance were redolent of something majestic, his aquiline, penetrating gaze forced all upon whom it was directed to tremble. . . . The people saw something great in him.'[7] No clairvoyant predictions of future 'greatness' were needed, however, to see that Peter's election was probably, to use a modern concept, in the national interest. Such considerations were soon to be subjugated to two elements which were willy-nilly to join forces and overturn this preliminary 'sensible' decison – a factional struggle in court circles and the fears and prejudices of Moscow's armed guard, the strel'tsy.

Soviet historians are well nigh unanimous in placing the focus of their analysis upon the latter element. In the words of V.I. Buganov, the leading Soviet specialist on the period: 'The Moscow uprisings of 1682 and 1698, in spite of their specific nature, are part of the single chain of the class struggle of the Russian people in the seventeenth century.'[8] This interpretation, for all its ideological bias, has a solid basis in contemporary sources. The memoir of the German Heinrich Butenant, commercial agent to the King of Denmark and one of the most reliable of witnesses, begins thus:

> This bloody tragedy occured mainly as a result of the great dissatisfaction to which the strel'tsy gave frequent expression because of the great excess and heavy burden of work (from which there was no exemption even on Sundays and holidays) which they had to do for their colonels and which they were forced to perform by pitiless blows.[9]

Butenant's account, the first part of which is dated 16 May, makes the vital point that the troubles predated Tsar Fedor's death.

This fact is ratified by the influential account of Silvester Medvedev, a pupil of Simeon Polotsky who, although a member of Sophia's inner circle, had no reason to sympathise with the strel'tsy. He relates 'grievances' from 1681 onwards, many of them associated with 'favourites' of Fedor's regime. In February 1682 the regiment of Bogdan Pyzhov had accused their colonel of pocketing their wages, and were punished for daring to complain, apparently because Pyzhov enjoyed the protection of the Tsar's favourite, Iazykov.[10]

On 23 April strel'tsy complained against another colonel, Simeon Griboedov.[11] The charges against him, which are verified in a number of sources, were that he had forced his men to carry out building work on his own estate during Holy Week, made illegal deductions from their wages, forced them to clean ponds, excavate trenches and sew uniforms, and generally heaped 'burdens and insults' upon them.[12] A representative delivered their petition to lord-in-waiting Pavel Pavlovich Iazykov, a kinsman of the Tsar's favourite, who promised to take it to the palace, but reported instead to Iu.A. Dolgoruky, the unpopular director of the Strel'tsy Department, that the petitioner had been drunk. When the latter returned for an answer the next day he was told that he was to be beaten with the knout (a heavy whip) for 'insubordination', but he appealed to his comrades for help and was released before sentence could be carried out.

According to Butenant, the planned punishment greatly upset the strel'tsy of Griboedov's regiment, who appealed to other regiments to denounce their own officers who had committed similar abuses against their men. 'Thereupon the strel'tsy banded together, demanding that justice be done to them, otherwise it would cost their colonels their necks.'[13] This was the state of affairs when Fedor died on Thursday 27 April.

Now is perhaps the moment to pause a while to look in more detail at the body of men which was to play such a vital role in bringing Sophia to power.[14] In 1682 the corps of strel'tsy or musketeers, founded in the reign of Ivan IV, in the middle of the sixteenth century, numbered about 55,000 men. Service in the corps was hereditary, terminating only with sickness, injury or death. Obligations extended to both war and peacetime, including garrison and sentry duties, the manning of customs posts, provision of bodyguards and escorts for dignitaries and precious cargoes, the building and repairing of fortifications and firefighting. The bulk of the strel'tsy were footsoldiers, with the exception of the elite mounted or 'stirrup' regiment, which provided a royal bodyguard.

Although the troops were liable for service in foreign wars (they had, for example, fought in the war against Turkey at Chigirin in 1678), by the middle of the century their time was devoted more and more to internal policing duties, and they were being superseded as troops in the field by the 'new model army'.[15] Slightly less than half the strel'tsy were stationed in Moscow in regiments of 1,000 men. They were allocated their own settlements or suburbs, where they legally engaged in crafts and trades to supplement their income from the state.

In terms of wealth, education and lifestyle the strel'tsy could be classified along with the middling elements of the urban population. Some rose to be non-commissioned officers but the officer class was drawn from the nobility. The affairs of the corps were administered by a state chancellery, the Strel'tsy Department (*streletskii prikaz*) which in 1682 was directed, as already noted, by Prince Iury Alekseevich Dolgoruky, an aged and infirm member of one of Russia's ancient clans. 'Class antagonism' was aggravated by a substantial drop in living standards, according to Soviet statistics. V.I. Buganov writes that the corps suffered from a 'sharp deterioration of their material and legal position, and from ill-treatment by the authorities and their direct superiors.'[16]

It should also be added that many of the strel'tsy were Old Believers, were intensely suspicious of foreigners, and cherished a superstitious attachment to the person of the 'true Tsar'. Their legitimate complaints against their colonels were compounded by the dynastic crisis which aroused fears that 'wicked advisers' might persuade the new ruler to downgrade the strel'tsy even further and allow the boyars permanently to gain the upper hand.

This 'social' interpretation of the rebellion of 1682, which places it firmly within the series of 'crises' which shook seventeenth-century Russia, including the rebellions of 1648 and 1661 and the Razin revolt of 1667–71, is too lacking in colour for many historians and commentators, who have preferred to pin the blame on personalities in ruling circles. They were encouraged in this by the ultimately victorious Naryshkin party, which was naturally anxious to denigrate Sophia and her supporters, and by the overwhelming reputation of Peter himself, which tended to cast all his predecessors in the role of advocates of Muscovite obscurantism and barbarity.

Sophia's reputation as the mastermind of a plot was already well established by the time Peter first visited the West in 1697. The German Georg Adam Schleissing, for example, who visited Moscow in 1684–6, described her as 'the originator of all the internal unrest and tumults' in a revised edition of an account first written in 1687 which had contained no references to Sophia's 'obsession' with power.[17] La Neuville, who, as we have seen, dated Sophia's rise to prominence to Fedor's reign, wrote: 'Without ever having read Machiavelli, she has a natural command of all his maxims, and especially this, that there is nothing which may not be undertaken and no crime which may not be committed when ruling is at stake.'[18] By the time the Austrian Johann Georg Korb visited Russia in 1698–9, Sophia's reputation for intrigue was already confirmed by her alleged complicity in the strel'tsy rebellion of 1698. 'In the year 1682,' he wrote, 'civil unrest, supported by an ambitious woman, stirred up frightful internecine cruelties of rapine, carnage and pillage. They attribute these great disasters to the cunning wiles of Princess Sophia.'[19] By the 1720s the English pastor Thomas Consett, one of the first scholarly observers of Russia, was firmly convinced that the rebellion of 1682 'was carried out with such Circumstance of Barbarity and Cruelty as reflect heavily on the Memory of that Princess.'[20]

Most pre-revolutionary Russian and nearly all Western historians have taken the lead set primarily, although not exclusively, by foreign observers. One of the most influential accounts is still that in S.M. Solov'ev's monumental *History of Russia from Ancient Times*, which formed the basis for many subsequent interpretations of the early years of Peter I's reign. 'The hated stepmother was to be regent: this thought stifled Sophia,' who proceeded to form a conspiracy.[21] Weight is added to this interpretation if one accepts, as did Solov'ev himself, that Sophia enjoyed power during Fedor's reign. In terms of drama, of course, the 'cunning wiles' theory has much to recommend it over the dry analyses of 'class struggle' and 'material deprivation' favoured by Soviet historians. The French historian and novelist Henri Troyat provides a recent reworking of the story:

> But the massive and terrible Sophia was still to be reckoned with. Having tasted the life of a free woman at her brother Feodor's side, caring for him and advising him, she refused to contemplate a return to the *terem*, that gynaeceum of another age. . . . Sophia wanted to live, to love, to dominate. Especially because she now had at her side a man who satisfied her physically and intellectually: Basil Golizin. With him she devised a plan for revenge.[22]

If we return to contemporary sources, from which the likes of Troyat have generally strayed, however, it quickly becomes clear not only that evidence for a 'plot' devised by Sophia and supporters in the immediate aftermath of Fedor's death is very thin, but also that dissatisfaction with Peter's election was not confined to a narrow Miloslavsky 'clique'. At the very least, Peter's elevation offended feelings of natural justice, for Ivan, despite his incapacity, was the senior claimant to the throne. There are indications from the very beginning that some regarded Peter's election with suspicion. Andrei Matveev, for example, reported that at least one nobleman, M.I. Sumbulov, spoke out in favour of Tsarevich Ivan.[23] Some of the strel'tsy, too, had objected to the 'elder brother being bypassed in favour of the younger', and the Karandeev regiment had even refused to take the oath of allegiance to Peter.

These faint rumblings of discontent are said to have been voiced loudly the following day, 28 April, in dramatic fashion. To quote again from the Polish *Diariusz*:

> Although it was not usual for female relatives of the Tsar, especially his sisters (whose faces are not seen by any living man), to attend the funeral, nevertheless one of Fedor's six sisters, Sophia, insisted upon following her brother's body to the church, and no matter how people tried to dissuade her from this unprecedented action, it proved quite impossible to deflect her from her purpose. And so she set off for the church with great wailings and sobbings.[24]

Peter and his mother are said to have enraged her by leaving the funeral without taking leave of the deceased, and Sophia, returning from the church,

> and regarding the action of Peter and Artamon[25] as a dishonour and an insult, shouted loudly to the crowd: 'Look, people, how unexpectedly our brother Tsar Fedor was dispatched from this world by enemies and ill-wishers. Be merciful to us orphans, who have neither mother nor father, nor our brother, the Tsar. Ivan our elder brother has not been chosen as tsar. If we have offended you or the boyars, release us alive to go to some foreign land and to Christian monarchs.

The author adds: 'After this the mutual antipathy between Tsarevna Sophia and Tsaritsa Natalia increased greatly.'[26]

This unambiguous challenge to the Naryshkins appears in many secondary accounts of the 1682 rebellion as the first battle cry of Sophia's campaign. Yet this crucial piece of evidence is found in only one contemporary source, which, given doubts about its authorship and provenance, needs to be treated with caution. Internal evidence suggests that it was not written before the middle of 1683, that is after the establishment of Sophia's rule, and that its author may not have been an eyewitness to the events of April–May 1682, even though he undoubtedly had Russian informants.[27]

Sophia's attendance at the funeral is attested only by one other contemporary source, an official record which states that 'behind him [Fedor] walked the Great Sovereign, and the Sovereign Tsaritsa and Great Princess Natalia Kirillovna, and the Sovereign Tsarevna and Great Princess Sophia Alekseevna', but contains no reference to any 'appeal' to the crowd.[28] Even any reference to attendance at the funeral is missing from the memoir of Andrei Matveev, one of the most influential of eyewitness commentators. As the son of Artamon Matveev, who was murdered in the rebellion, and an ardent supporter of Peter and his later reforms, it seems odd that he should have failed to utilise such an incriminating piece of evidence of Sophia's guilt. The funeral

incident is also absent from Butenant's version. Buganov, who admittedly underplays the role of individuals in the revolt, doubts that
Sophia was even present at the funeral.[29]

Even so, the notion that Sophia quickly protested against Peter's
election and enlisted the support of the strel'tsy and other popular
elements gained currency. The writer of the report sent to the Papal
Legate in Poland in the autumn of 1682 has her shouting from a
window that Peter had been elected by Artamon Matveev's treachery
and that the latter had poisoned not only Fedor but also Tsar Aleksei.[30]
Korb, writing almost two decades later, alleges that she summoned the
strel'tsy and claimed that Fedor had been poisoned by the boyars, whose
next victims were to be the strel'tsy themselves. These allegations of
boyar treachery were confirmed when some strel'tsy were poisoned by
brandy allegedly tampered with by the boyars, but in reality prepared by
Sophia herself.[31]

Later eighteenth-century accounts have a more rational Sophia summoning the Patriarch and boyars immediately after Peter's election and
arguing that 'all the strel'tsy regiments wish Tsar Ivan Alekseevich to
be on the throne because he is of age and Peter is only ten'.[32] (He was
not, in fact, ten until 30 May). Peter's election, she argued, was
'contrary to the laws' (*protivno zakonam*). She suggested that both boys
should rule, but the Patriarch rejected this on the grounds that 'multiple
rule is an evil. Let there be one tsar. God wills it so.' Thus thwarted
Sophia sent for her kinsman Ivan Miloslavsky to ask the strel'tsy for
their support and the plot was set in action.

Despite widely differing details, the accounts quoted above have one
thing in common – they point to Sophia as the initiator of the ensuing
troubles and they indicate that she was willing to flout convention in
defence of her family interests. In the words of Ivan Zabelin: 'This feat
was most bold and daring, even impudent, overturning old customs
and scorning the pious protocol of life at the royal court.'[33] It may
never be possible to establish the role played by Sophia at Fedor's funeral, still less the words she uttered. There is however, good documentary evidence that from the day of Peter's election, quite independent
of any intervention on Sophia's part, there was a continuation of the
trouble immediately preceding Fedor's death.

Butenant reports that on 29 April twelve regiments petitioned the
new government to arrest their colonels and force them to pay back
embezzled money.[34] This time the government was intimidated into
granting the request. On 1–2 May officers were duly beaten with
cudgels and forced to make financial recompense.[35] On 1 May favourites
of the previous regime, including I.M. and S.I. Iazykov, A.T. and
M.T. Likhachev, I.A. Iazykov and I.V. Dashkov, were banished.[36]
Butenant recorded an atmosphere of growing discontent and suspicion,

as the strel'tsy threatened to take the lives of 'traitors', those who 'were leading his Majesty the Tsar astray'.[37] Evidently the election of an under-aged tsar had aroused fears that they would be subjected to the same harassment by 'advisers' as in Fedor's reign. These fears sprang from the personal experiences of a body of men, ill-educated and susceptible to superstition and rumour, who were encouraged by the new government's show of weakness to hope for radical improvements in their own status, but at the same time feared and even expected retribution for any concessions that they managed to obtain.

But how did resentment directed against specific officers and vague fears about having an 'under-aged' tsar grow into a thirst for the blood of the Naryshkins and their associates? One factor was undoubtedly the phenomenon that Soviet historians refer to as 'naive monarchism', which entails a belief that the 'true Tsar' is by nature benevolent, but is sometimes prevented from ameliorating his people's lot by the intervention of 'wicked advisers', or even by the substitution of a 'false' monarch.[38] Butenant writes: 'The strel'tsy kept on indicating that the election of the new Tsar had been improperly conducted. They could not believe that the elder Prince, Ivan Alekseevich, was unfit to rule because of his poor eyesight and other accidents of fate.'[39] They refused to believe that he had declined the crown, suspecting the hand of 'traitors'. In a country where the *urodivyi* – the 'holy fool' or 'fool in Christ' – was credited with special gifts of perception and insight, deemed superior by common folk to the products of schooling and reason, support and sympathy for a 'simple-minded' tsar is perfectly understandable. If Ivan were the 'true Tsar' by seniority, then his handicaps were of little consequence, and if the under-aged Peter was a usurper, then suspicion must naturally fall upon the Naryshkins, the 'wicked advisers' of tradition, who had much to gain from their candidate's accession.

Butenant writes: 'The strel'tsy and common people too were most dissatisfied that the Naryshkins had become so powerful so quickly.'[40] Tactless behaviour on the part of the Naryshkins themselves may in turn have fanned such fears. One chronicler records the rumour that on the very day of Fedor's funeral the Naryshkins, so long denied a share in power, left the cathedral jumping for joy: 'All the world was grieving and weeping, but they were joyful and merry.'[41] On 7 May Ivan Naryshkin was made a boyar at the age of twenty-three, an honour usually reserved for men in their thirties and forties.[42] It was rumoured that he had tried on royal regalia, had sat on the throne and had insulted Tsarevich Ivan and other members of the royal family.[43] Even some of the boyars complained that he had pulled their beards and Sophia herself is said to have reprimanded him for an attack on Tsarevich Ivan,[44] whilst the Polish account records that he impudently offered to rule until Peter's coming of age. Later during his interrogation on 17 May the strel'tsy are said to have demanded: 'How could you dare to take the royal regalia and try it on? Did you want to become tsar?'[45] It was feared that the under-aged Peter would be a mere puppet in the hands of unscrupulous relatives. In addition, the Naryshkins were closely associated with Artamon Matveev, and it may not have escaped the memories of some that Matveev and Ivan and Afanasy Naryshkin had been exiled in 1676 on charges of sorcery and attempted poisoning. The air must have been thick with rumours of poison plots and regicide.

Particularly disturbing to the strel'tsy rank and file were rumours that, despite initial concessions, the Naryshkins were planning to ruin them. The whole of the boyar duma had approved Peter's election, so it must be assumed that they too, unchecked by a mature and benevolent tsar, would inflict damage on the corps. In the words of the chronicler:

> In our land there remain two sovereign tsarevichi, Great Princes Ivan Alekseevich and Peter Alekseevich of all Russia. One Tsarevich . . . Ivan Alekseevich is of age, he can rule, but the other Tsarevich . . . Peter Alekseevich is very young, only nine years and eleven months, how is he to rule the kingdom without the boyars enriching themselves?[46]

In a version of events sent to Bernard Tanner from Moscow's Foreign Quarter, there emerges the view that there were two tsars, one from the people (Ivan) and one from the aristocrats (Peter).[47] Thus was the incapacitated Ivan transformed into the potential champion of ordinary folk, and by association the Miloslavsky circle came to be seen as 'good', Peter's faction as 'evil', in both cases quite undeservedly. Matveev and other writers hostile to Sophia accuse her and her circle of initiating such rumours and fanning discontent, but clearly these views could have developed under their own momentum, whilst at least one influential person was operating independently of Sophia's control.

Prince Ivan Andreevich Khovansky, who lent his name to the popular title for the troubles of 1682, 'Khovanshchina', is said to have delivered the following inflammatory speech to the strel'tsy:

> You yourselves can see what a heavy yoke the boyars have laid upon you and that they have chosen God knows what kind of tsar. You'll see – not only won't they give you money and provisions, but you will have to do heavy labour as before and your children will be eternal slaves. What's worse, they will give you and us over to the bondage of a foreign foe, Moscow will be destroyed and the Orthodox faith eradicated.[48]

Khovansky, as we shall see, was pursuing personal interests and ambitions which coincided only briefly with the Miloslavsky cause. The speech attributed to him indicates the level of scare-mongering that the strel'tsy were subjected to. Their response was to run wild. The Dutch envoy Keller reports, from the beginning of May, attacks on the carriages of boyars fleeing the city and on their servants.[49] Matveev writes that the strel'tsy were taking advantage of the situation to 'laze around in perpetual drunkenness'. They were afraid that Peter's 'wise advisers' would put a stop to their fun. Those officers who tried to reimpose discipline were thrown from the tops of high buildings by their men.[50]

In the midst of chaos the new government placed their hopes in one man, Artamon Matveev. Exiled in 1676, he had already been pardoned in February 1682 thanks to Tsar Fedor's second wife Marfa; his property had been restored and he had been allowed to move to the town of Lukh. Immediately upon Peter's election Tsaritsa Natalia had recalled him to Moscow,[51] and he entered the city on 11 or 12 May, to general rejoicing, according to Butenant,[52] although his son Andrei alleges that some regiments presented him with traditional offering of bread and salt whilst cursing him behind his back.[53] Most damaging to Matveev's cause were rumours that strel'tsy ringleaders were to be executed and that others would be banished to remote regions.[54]

Amongst the Miloslavsky faction one man in particular must have viewed Matveev's return with foreboding. This was I.M. Miloslavsky, who had been responsible for obtaining Matveev's exile. According to Andrei Matveev, Miloslavsky responded by forming a conspiracy. In anticipation of Artamon Matveev's arrival he enlisted the support of A.I. Miloslavsky (described by Matveev as a 'boor'), the brothers I.A. and P.A. Tolstoi ('imbued with great cunning and dark wickedness for conspiracy'), I.E. Tsykler and I.G. Ozerov, together with representatives from the strel'tsy regiments. Those who wavered were enticed with promises of rank and money. Matveev believed that Sophia gave her full backing to the plot, greeting news of the strel'tsy disturbances like 'the dove that brought the olive branch to Noah', but she was unable to operate openly, for example by visiting the strel'tsy, because of conventions regarding royal women. She is said to have sent money to the regiments via her chambermaid Fedora Rodimitsa. In the meantime, Miloslavsky compiled a list of targets for the moment when opportunity should arise for open rebellion.[55]

This version of events has been widely accepted, but should be treated with some caution. Andrei Matveev was only sixteen years old at the time of the 1682 rebellion, in which his father was brutally murdered and he himself narrowly escaped death. Subsequently he was to become a leading member of Peter I's reforming circle, serving as ambassador in England and France.[56] Writing his memoir in the 1720s, many years after events and after Sophia had been implicated in further rebellions in 1689 and 1698, he not unnaturally did his utmost to incriminate the Miloslavsky clan. Other contemporary witnesses, such as Butenant, Medvedev and official scribes, give no firm indication of

Sophia's complicity in a plot before the events of 15–17 May, although in all accounts she emerges as the main figure of authority during the three-day rebellion. As has been shown earlier, the interests of the strel'tsy and the deposed Miloslavskys began to converge on a number of issues. It was to take but a small spark to ignite the wrath of the already restive strel'tsy against the 'traitors' in the Kremlin, and Sophia and her party were to reap the benefits, quite possibly without having put in much preparatory spadework.

The spark that ignited the flame of revolt was to come in the form of a rumour that Tsarevich Ivan had been murdered. The date was significant: 15 May, the anniversary of the death in 1591 of Ivan IV's son Dmitry, allegedly at the instigation of Boris Godunov, who himself became tsar in 1598 when the Riurik dynasty expired.[57] There were a number of parallels between this event and the situation as perceived by the popular mood in 1682. Contemporaries refer to both periods, for example, as the 'troubled' or 'confused' time (*smutnoe vremia*), an appellation sometimes applied to the whole period from 1584 to 1613, when a new dynasty was installed. Monday 15 May 1682 is said to have dawned in a 'disturbed' fashion, as 'the air became still, then a great storm brewed up, and dark clouds came over'.[58] As in the early-seventeenth-century 'Time of Troubles', people were on the look-out for 'usurpers' and 'pretenders', as the Romanov dynasty seemed to hang on the thread of a nine-year old boy and a feeble adolescent who, for all his disabilities, was deemed by many to be the 'true Tsar'. That historical parallels were explicitly drawn is shown by the account in a contemporary chronicle, which records that the mob called for the blood of Ivan Naryshkin and his father, 'for they wish to eliminate the royal line just as Boris Gudunov did, and to be the heirs themselves and to throw the Muscovite state into confusion'.[59]

The response to news of Ivan's 'murder' was predictable, but where did the rumour originate? The Polish *Diariusz* assumed that it started with Sophia, 'who circulated it about town by dispatching her minions to shout on the streets that Ivan Naryshkin had murdered Tsarevich Ivan by strangling him'.[60] The 'minions' according to Matveev were Aleksei Miloslavsky and Peter Tolstoy.[61] Butenant, however, placed the source of the rumour as the 'strel'tsy' in the palace who guarded the royal chambers'.[62] Medvedev's version states that the strel'tsy had heard 'that certain boyars had turned traitor and tried to eliminate the royal line; they had killed Tsarevich Ivan Alekseevich and intended to carry out their evil intentions on Tsar Peter Alekseevich and deprive him of his throne'.[63] This is significant, for it portrays Peter, too, as a potential victim and focuses upon fears of general boyar treachery against the crown, rather than a straight Naryshkin – Miloslavsky feud.

As the rebellion escalated it was to become clear that the Naryshkins were far from being the sole targets of strel'tsy wrath. Although some of the victims of the riot were consistent with a plot originating in Miloslavsky circles, others were men against whom the strel'tsy held personal grudges, such as the directors of the Strel'tsy Department Iu.A. and M.Iu. Dolgoruky, Tsar Fedor's former favourite I.M. Iazykov and the military commander Prince G.G. Romodanovsky. As events were to show, any tenuous hold that Sophia and her party had over the strel'tsy was short-lived and for several months there was to be no real central authority in Russia.

The events of 15–17 May have been recounted in many versions.[64] Contemporary accounts are to be found in the writings of independent eyewitnesses, both Russian and foreign, in the records of Moscow chancelleries and in seventeenth-century chronicle compilations. Painstaking comparisons are required to reconcile numerous discrepancies of detail, and the role played by Sophia is just one of the many elements on which there is no consensus. As we have seen, writers fail to agree about the source of the rumour of Tsarevich Ivan's death, but there is some agreement about the strel'tsy response. They took up arms and marched to the Kremlin palace, where they demanded to see Ivan or, in some versions, his body. 'There were heard all over the royal palace from the Red Staircase shouts and cries from the strel'tsy, who came milling in with loud voices and brazen uncouthness and insubordination.'[65] The troops were thirsting for blood.

Initially they were stopped in their paces by the arrival of Ivan himself, brought in by his stepmother Natalia. According to Butenant he was accompanied by Tsarevna Sophia, 'a very clever lady', and Tsaritsa Marfa.[66] Peter was also brought out. The strel'tsy were dumbfounded. Several even mounted the staircase to take a closer look. When Ivan was asked whether he was really the Tsarevich and whether he had been mistreated, he is said to have replied: 'No one is mistreating me and I have no complaints against anybody.'[67]

It seemed for a moment that the sight of Ivan unharmed would defuse the mood of rebellion, but there were evidently extremist elements in the crowd still wishing to settle accounts with 'traitors and evil-doers' who at the very least had harboured evil intentions against the Tsarevich. The troops nonetheless hesitated to disperse and the crisis point was reached when certain courtiers went down to try to persuade them. In Matveev's account, his father Artamon Sergeevich attempted to talk to the troops but his efforts were sabotaged by M.Iu. Dolgoruky, the deputy head of the Strel'tsy Department, who reprimanded them for their insubordination.[68] Dolgoruky was killed, then Matveev, despite attempts by the courtier Prince Mikhail Cherkassky to shield him. (In some versions Matveev clutched at Peter for protection.) In Butenant's version, too, Dolgoruky and Matveev were the strel'tsy's first victims.[69]

The Polish account, which identifies Prince Ivan Khovansky as one of the ringleaders at this stage of the revolt, alleges that Khovansky went down with Matveev and signalled secretly to the strel'tsy that they should kill him.[70] In the official chancellery record known as *smutnoe vremia* the strel'tsy sent up a list of some twenty 'traitors' to the palace and when the authorities replied that 'they were not in the palace' the troops entered the building and searched through the royal apartments until they located some of their victims.[71] In this version Matveev was flung down from the Red Staircase on to their spears.

Accounts may differ in detail but they all point to the fact that despite the ferocity of the killings (most victims were chopped into small pieces), this was no indiscriminate bloodbath directed at all representatives of the 'ruling classes'. Prince Cherkassky, for example, escaped with no worse than a torn robe when he tried to protect Matveev. In the course of the next three days some sixteen pre-selected victims were killed.[72] Some of them were dragged from their hiding places in the palace itself, an area usually banned to all outsiders with the exception of the palace clergy and members of the boyar duma. Afanasy Kirillovich Naryshkin was actually dragged from the palace Church of the Resurrection, betrayed, according to Matveev, by one of the palace dwarves.[73] Others, like Andrei Matveev himself, were more fortunate. He found sanctuary in the apartments of Tsarevna Marfa Alekseevna, where he remained undetected.

On 15–16 May the strel'tsy claimed the following victims, in addition to those already listed: State Secretary Larion Ivanov and his son (a cuttlefish was discovered in his house, and it was concluded that he had wished to poison the Tsar and the strel'tsy);[74] Fedor Petrovich Saltykov (in mistake for Ivan Naryshkin);[75] Prince G.G. Romodanovsky ('You are a great traitor because you abandoned Chigirin, not allowing us to fight the Turks. And you starved us to death');[76] Prince Iu.A. Dolgoruky (who made a threatening remark which was overheard when the strel'tsy went to apologise for the murder of his son);[77] I.M. Iazykov, the former favourite of Tsar Fedor, who had made decisions in favour of the strel'tsy's colonels; Grigory Goriushkin and Andrei Dokhturov, particularly hated colonels. P.F. Naryshkin (mistakenly referred to as Vasily Fedorovich or Ivan Fomich in some sources)[78] was evidently murdered simply because he was a Naryshkin.

As mentioned earlier, motives for some of the killings lay outside Miloslavsky and strel'tsy circles. According to a later petition, State Secretary Averky Kirillov was killed because 'whilst in the sovereign's service he took huge bribes from men of all stations and inflicted taxes and all manner of injustice upon the people',[79] but he had also once had a dispute with Prince Ivan Khovansky's son Peter.[80] The Khovansky clan also bore a grudge against Prince G.G. Romodanovsky. It seems that various people were able to manipulate the troops to settle their own scores. In addition a number of unnamed victims met their end. Butenant records that about forty persons, including strel'tsy, were put to death for theft and plunder, and that some officials and clerks were killed.[81]

Three of the strel'tsy's victims in particular show how the massacre acquired its own momentum, rooted in deep-seated prejudices and superstition. Butenant records that the troops searched with particular earnestness for a Polish Jewish doctor named Daniel (in some versions Stepan) von Gaden, a convert to Orthodoxy.[82] He was suspected of having poisoned Tsar Fedor. Before he was discovered the strel'tsy killed his son Michael and his assistant Johann Gutmensch, who was said to have 'helped the doctor to prepare the medicines with which the Tsar was killed'.[83] Dr Daniel was arrested on the night of 16 May, having been apprehended sneaking back into the Foreign Quarter disguised as a beggar. His pleas were to no avail. The strel'tsy retorted that 'he had not only caused the death of His Majesty but was also a sorcerer'. 'Dried snakes' had been discovered in his house, with which he was alleged to have practised magic. Andrei Matveev considered that they were killed 'solely out of hatred and antipathy for foreigners'.[84] Sources indicate that members of both groupings in the palace pleaded in vain for the doctors' lives.

Dr Daniel met his end on 17 May, at the same time as the strel'tsy claimed their main victim, Ivan Naryshkin. In the rebels' view, Naryshkin had assumed the status of chief traitor, a man who had attempted to murder Tsarevich Ivan and had his sights set on nothing less than the crown, and whose reign would inaugurate a period of ruin and oppression for the strel'tsy. Since 15 May he had been concealed by the royal family in the palace but it fast became evident that only his death would appease the strel'tsy and avoid further killings. In the words of Butenant, the strel'tsy demanded: 'We know that you have got Ivan Kirillovich hidden in there. Hand him over amicably, or we will carry out the most thorough search until we find him, and then things may turn out very badly.'[85] Most accounts record how members of the royal family, foremost amongst them Tsaritsa Natalia, pleaded for Ivan's life.[86] In a desperate gesture they gave him an icon to hold in the hope that the rebels would respect it, but Ivan was dragged away, tortured and killed. That evening it was announced that the relatives of victims could bury their dead. The main massacres were over, although, as will be shown later, there were still many scores to settle.

What were Sophia's movements during the three-day rebellion? All accounts are united on the fact that by 17 May she was to emerge as the palace's chief spokeswoman and negotiator, one of the few people to keep their heads in the midst of chaos. Writers are deeply divided, however, on her motivation. Silvester Medvedev was in no doubt that Sophia was Russia's saviour and that her prompt and courageous action prevented an even greater disaster. 'For the Divine Wisdom of God has favoured her with more wisdom than others and except for her no one else was capable of ruling the Russian state.'[87] Matveev, predictably, depicted Sophia as playing a cunning game, awaiting the moment when she could emerge in public and take power. According to him this moment came on 17 May when Sophia persuaded other members of the family that Ivan Naryshkin must be sacrificed. She pretended to sympathise, but 'at the bottom of all this there lay the most profound Italian politics [politika ital'ianskaia]; for they say one thing, but think another and indeed carry it out.'[88] One is reminded of La Neuville's famous reference to Sophia and Machiavelli.[89]

In order to determine the nature of Sophia's authority it is as well to turn to authors with no particular axe to grind. Butenant, for example, writes that 'both empresses and the Princess Sophia Alekseevna fell down on their knees and begged for Ivan Naryshkin's life to be spared'.[90] In one chronicle version, the whole royal family came out to deny the charges against Naryshkin and reproached the strel'tsy for desecrating the palace.[91]

Butenant himself came face to face with Sophia on 16 May when he was brought to the Kremlin by a band of strel'tsy for interrogation about the whereabouts of Dr von Gaden. He records that he 'rode up to a stone staircase in the palace, then walked up as far as a step off to one side, where the younger widowed Empress and the Princess Sophia Alekseevna were gathered with several gentlemen.'[92] At this point Prince Ivan Khovansky came out to ask the strel'tsy assembled below whether they wished Tsaritsa Natalia to be banished from court. He asked Butenant (whom he recognised) why he was there and had a brief consultation with Sophia. Butenant continues: 'It cannot have been anything bad, because the Princess waved her hand to signal to me that I should simply leave.'[93] Butenant was told that he had been found 'innocent' and was escorted back to his home by a strel'tsy guard. This incident makes it clear that Sophia was already taking decisions. A woman who a short time previously had been secluded from human view was conversing freely with men in the midst of an extremely tense situation.

Khovansky's presence, incidentally, is explained by the fact that he had taken over as director of the Strel'tsy Department to replace the murdered Iury Dolgoruky.[94] Another appointment of that day, Prince Vasily Vasil'evich Golitsyn to the directorship of the important Foreign

Office (*posol'skii prikaz*), is thought by some to indicate that the com-
promised Naryshkins were no longer in command, even though Peter
was still Tsar, and that Sophia's party had taken over. Ivan Miloslavsky
was put in charge of the Mercenaries, Cavalry and Artillery Departments. As Robert Crummey points out in his recent study of the boyar
elite, however, a number of the men appointed on that day could not
positively be classified as members of the Miloslavsky 'faction'.[95] Men
like Vasily Semenov (Crown Appointments), Prince I.B. Troekurov
(Service Estates) and M.P. Golovin (Police) had served under previous
regimes and were members of the boyar duma that had elected Peter,
whilst the appointment of three Khovanskys to high office probably
reflects the influence which Prince Ivan Khovansky was seen to have
with the strel'tsy and which the emerging authorities could not do
without. Golitsyn himself had been a boyar since 1676 and was well
qualified for his new post. In no way do the appointments of 16 May
suggest a triumphant party rewarding its supporters, but they do show
that power had shifted away from the Naryshkins.

Like the Naryshkins, the Miloslavskys lacked a male personage of
royal blood to act as their spokesman, but they could at least boast a
formidable contingent of Romanov women, all of whom enjoyed the
sanctity of royal blood. The two senior members of the *terem*, Sophia's
aunts Anna and Tatiana, were aged fifty-two and forty-six respectively,
and were almost certainly too steeped in convention to take public
action. Sophia's two elder sisters Evdokia and Marfa, according to the
Polish writer, 'kept themselves apart from politics.'[96] Bearing in mind
the fact that Sophia is said to have been singled out amongst her sisters
for an education, one is bound to conclude that Medvedev approaches
closest to the truth when he claims that only she was able to rule.

Her willingness to appear in public was confirmed on 18 May when,
in the account of the Mazurinsky Chronicler, the strel'tsy came to the
Kremlin without their weapons and Sophia came out to meet them,
accompanied by Tsaritsa Natalia's father Kirill Naryshkin, whose banishment was demanded by the crowd. The Tsarevna spoke to the crowd
for a long time, but the writer was too far off to hear her words (*a chto, ne
slushat' izdali*).[97] Naryshkin was forced to take monastic vows in the
Monastery of St Cyril near Beloozero. The next day Sophia appeared in
public again to appease the strel'tsy by distributing pay arrears and to
give orders that all victims of the rebellion be buried.[98] The sum of
240,000 roubles, an enormous amount for those days, was somehow
collected.

The troubles had temporarily abated, although the ends still had to
be tied up in a satisfactory constitutional solution. The preceding pages
have sought to illustrate that the Moscow rebellion of 1682 sprang
primarily from the internal problems of the strel'tsy, which continued

from the previous reign; heightening of these grievances (the Pyzhov and Griboedov incidents) coincided with a dynastic crisis which brought to the fore the corps' naive attachment to monarchic legitimism. Butenant writes: 'Throughout the three days that this rebellion lasted they did everything in the name of Tsar Ivan Alekseevich, although of course the strel'tsy did not ask anyone, and they did everything according to their own will.'[99]

In a sense Ivan was an excuse, a mere symbol of a longed-for rule of justice by a 'good' monarch, just as the Naryshkins were convenient scapegoats for all the ills inflicted upon the long-suffering corps by the 'bosses'. As indicated by their monarchistic orientation, the strel'tsy were in no way revolutionaries. Even their much publicised ransacking of the Bondslaves Department (*kholopii prikaz*), where documents were destroyed, may be interpreted as an attempt to acquire allies and neutralise the men most likely to be used in battle against them, namely the boyars' bondslaves who served as armed retainers. As John Keep writes, their motives came to be seen as 'narrowly egotistic.'[100] Their continued interference in affairs of state after the main troubles had died down reflected a fear that if they relaxed their hold the new masters might turn against them and punish them.

With the ending of bloodshed, the stage was now set for constitutional developments, for one of the rebels' main complaints – the 'illegal' election of Peter and the bypassing of Ivan – was still to be rectified. According to Medvedev,[101] who provides the most detailed account, on 23 May representatives of the strel'tsy returned to the Kremlin and asked Ivan Khovansky to propose to the 'sovereign lady Tsarevny' that Peter and Ivan should rule jointly. The proposal, made on threat of further rebellion, was accepted by a makeshift assembly similar to the one that had elected Peter on 27 April, with the Patriarch again playing a prominent role. Justifications were found for this novel compromise, for example that while one Tsar went to war, the other could rule at home. Historical precedents were quoted – Pharaoh and Joseph, Basil and Constantine, Honorious and Arcadius.

That same day, Sophia summoned the strel'tsy, praised them for their loyal service and assured them of the Tsar's favour.[102] On 25 May representatives of the Moscow infantrymen, ever vigilant, returned to the Kremlin on the rumour, apparently started by Tsarevna Marfa's chambermaid, that Tsar Ivan 'was sick with anxiety about his realm' and that the tsarevny were 'lamenting'. Representatives were invited to an audience with Ivan, who assured them that there was no 'confusion' in the palace and that while Ivan was to 'rule' at home as first Tsar, Peter would receive ambassadors and go to war against Russia's enemies. The following day, 26 May, this arrangement was ratified by the taking of the oath of allegiance by kissing the cross and by a service in the Cathedral of the Dormition attended by both tsars.

The strel'tsy and infantrymen were to be admitted to the palace two regiments at a time to receive food and drink. At this point they presented a petition, 'that the government of the Russian realm be administered by the pious wise Sovereign Lady, the Tsarevna and Great Princess Sophia Alekseevna'.[103] The tsars considered this proposal and after consultations with their family, prelates of the Church and the boyar council 'were pleased to entrust the government of affairs of their great and renowned Russian realm to their sister the noble Sovereign Tsarevna and Great Princess Sophia Alekseevna', on the grounds of their 'tender years' and because their land 'was in great need of much governing.'[104] Sophia is said to have declined this honour, urged on her 'by all ranks of people of the whole Muscovite state', several times, but finally agreed 'to take upon herself that great labour. And with all her zeal, imitative of God, and merciful disposition, she deigned to govern all state affairs with that lofty judiciousness granted to her by God.'

Her rule was to be far from token. She decreed 'that the boyars and lords-in-waiting and gentlemen of the duma should always have audience with her and report to her on all affairs of state', for which purpose she was to 'sit with the boyars in the chamber'. The following formula was adopted for royal rescripts: 'the great sovereign tsars and great princes Ivan Alekseevich and Peter Alekseevich, autocrats of all the Great and Little and White Russias, and their sister the Great Pious Sovereign Tsarevna and Great Princess Sophia Alekseevna of all the Great and the Little and the White Russias have indicated and the boyars have assented.'[105] This formula was dated 29 May, which is generally taken to be the date of the establishment of the regency.

Medvedev's account of the creation of a diarchy and the establishment of Sophia's regency has been summarised in some detail as it is the fullest version of the events in question and was written by an eyewitness who was highly educated and close to ruling circles. It is clear even from a summary, however, that Medvedev rationalised and smoothed out proceedings which took place in the wake of a bloody massacre. The tsars, for example, quite clearly took no decisions. The consistent listing of 'all ranks' in order to denote consensus and popular support also arouses suspicions. Medvedev's aim is clearly to keep the focus of attention on Sophia and to show her in the most positive light.

More recently the Soviet historian A.P. Bogdanov has cast doubts on whether a regency as such was created at all in May 1682.[106] Although he does not dispute the fact that Sophia was *de facto* ruler, he believes that the assembly's appeal to Sophia and the triple formula for royal decrees were actually 'fabricated' in 1687–9 when Medvedev was writing his record of the regency, the *Short Account of the Years 7190, 91 and 92*, from which the above summary is extracted. This laudatory compilation, which was prepared in anticipation of Sophia's coronation,[107] was written on the basis of genuine and valuable documentary material (for example, on disturbances among the strel'tsy early in 1682), much of it supplied by Fedor Shaklovity, one of Sophia's most loyal supporters and, as the new Director of the Strel'tsy Department, by then one of the most powerful figures in her regime. According to Bogdanov's hypothesis, Medvedev had to invent a third decision by 'men of all ranks' as a complement to the decisions on joint rule and the 'subordination' of Peter to Ivan. Medvedev's concern was not with the fact of Sophia's authority, which by 1687 was self-evident, but with the legal basis of her rule.

Bogdanov's theory is consistent with the otherwise puzzling absence of contemporary evidence for the regularization of Sophia's status in May 1682. Many accounts record the establishment of joint rule on 26 May, but none mentions a regency. For example, the 'Mazurinsky Chronicle' and the 'Chronicle for the years 1619–91' leap straight from the creation of a diarchy on 26 May to events in June.[108] Chancellery papers, for example the records of the department of Crown Appointments and the account entitled 'the time of confusion', also pass over the establishment of a regency in silence.[109] Published accounts which mention it turn out to be based on Medvedev, for example documents included in the *Complete Collection of Russian Laws* and in the *Collection of State Decrees and Treaties*.[110] Andrei Matveev records 18 May as the day of the announcement 'that a third reigning person jointly wielding the sceptre of the Russian empire should be present at all palace conferences with a strong command of the monarchical orb',[111] but Matveev was writing in the 1720s and also, predictably, omits any reference to popular demands for the installation of Sophia as regent. Perhaps the most convincing confirmation of the lack of any formal arrangements for a regency is the fact that the formula for royal titles allegedly drawn up on 29 May was not used. Although there are many references to Sophia's hearing petitions in the council, decrees and rescripts for the early years of the regency are issued in the names of the tsars only.[112] Oaths of loyalty, for example the one taken by the Ukrainian Hetman and his Cossacks on 14 June 1682, were sworn to Ivan and Peter.[113] Only in 1686, as we shall see later, did Sophia consistently begin to add her name to those of her brothers in nearly all domestic documents, and then not in the 29 May formula but as autocrat (*samoderzhitsa*), equal in status to them.[114]

It must be emphasised that Sophia's emergence as a figure of authority in 1682 is not in dispute, but her constitutional position was anomalous. The reason for the failure formally to authorise a regency may stem from the fact that tradition demanded that Peter's mother assume this role, although political realities precluded it, whilst Ivan was already 'of age'. (It will be recalled that Fedor ruled without a regency from the age of fourteen.) Ivan, though, would be in need of tutelage for the rest of his life. Was Sophia to remain regent until his death, or step down when Peter came of age? It is unlikely that these questions were seriously considered at the time in the face of what was essentially an expedient to restore some semblance of order at court. It must be admitted that in May 1682 her ascendancy was far from complete. A few Naryshkins had been killed or banished and A.S. Matveev was dead, but the 'hated stepmother' was still at large, as were the majority of the boyars who had supported Peter's election on 27 April, and Patriarch Joachim, whose sympathies inclined towards the Naryshkins. Most significantly, in none of the sources is there any hint that anyone, least of all Sophia, demanded that Peter (who was the fatal flaw in any scheme for the extension and perpetuation of Sophia's power) be removed from the throne. At most she had rectified the 'injustice' of Ivan being passed over and stemmed a complete decline of Miloslavsky influence by playing 'a very clever political game.'[115]

The game was far from over, however, for the strel'tsy remained restive, eager to force more concessions out of a new government that seemed willing to accede to their demands. Nor was it only the strel'tsy that the new government had to contend with. On 5 June the alarm was sounded amongst the strel'tsy regiments, and several bondslaves were arrested. Under interrogation the latter admitted that they had gathered in preparation for an attack on the strel'tsy: 'And during the state of alarm there was shooting all over the place. And the next day they [the slaves] were tortured and executed for their crime.'[116] A slightly different version records that the alarm was raised when rumours reached the strel'tsy of a planned attack on the soldiers at Butyrky. Armed strel'tsy had marched to Butyrky, but had found no one but a couple of drunks, who admitted to having spread the rumour. The next day four men were executed for daring to boast that the strel'tsy would be 'chopped to pieces, just as the boyars had been.'[117] From the middle of June 'there were few days without shooting and gunfire in all the suburbs'.[118]

Meanwhile, the strel'tsy 'petitioned that a column should be built on Red Square. And the column was built in accordance with their petition.'[119] It commemorated the 'services' rendered to the crown by the strel'tsy during the rebellion of 15–17 May and listed on brass plaques the 'traitors' who had perished. The strel'tsy were renamed the 'infantry of the royal household' (*nadvornaia pekhota*).[120] A detailed list of strel'tsy requirements had been set out in a petition presented on or before 6 June, in which they joined their claims with those of the soldiers' regiments, merchants, artisans and other townspeople (although most of the demands were of little potential benefit to these other elements, whose 'support' was quoted probably only in order to add weight to the strel'tsy's own case). The victims of 15–17 May were listed and their murders justified. Princes Iury and Mikhail Dolgoruky, for example, were killed 'for their many crimes and boastful words, for beating many of our comrades with the knout for no good reason and without the sovereign's leave, and exiling them to far-off towns', as well as for embezzlement, and for 'enslaving and ill-treating the sovereigns'.[121] Of Ivan Iazykov it was said that 'in collusion with our former colonels he imposed huge taxes upon us and took huge bribes and incited our former colonels to beat our comrades with the knout and canes [*batogi*] to the point of death'.[122] Ivan and Afanasy Naryshkin were killed 'because they tried on the royal regalia and plotted all manner of evil against Tsarevich Ivan Alekseevich', and before that they had 'plotted all manner of evil against Tsar Fedor Alekseevich of Blessed memory'.[123]

The document illustrates the rebels' obsession with poison plots and foreign 'guile'. Artamon Matveev, Dr Daniel and his son, and Doctor Gutmensch were killed 'because in collusion they prepared a poisonous potion for your illustrious royal majesties'.[124] This section of the petition confirms what has been observed already: that a number of the victims of the May rebellion died not because they were identifiable members of the Naryshkin camp, earmarked for elimination in order to clear Sophia's path to power, but because the strel'tsy themselves harboured grudges and suspicions against them.

This petition could only have been a source of annoyance to Sophia, for in it the strel'tsy went on to demand that the notorious column be erected on Red Square and that courtiers and boyars desist from calling them 'traitors'. They denied any collusion between themselves and the bondslaves, and re-aired some of the grievances that had fuelled the rebellion in the first place, for example requesting relief from the financial burden of contributions to regimental expenses and protection from ill-treatment and exploitation by officers and state officials. They begged the sovereigns, in recognition of 'the many unworthy services and blood and wounds and imprisonment and sieges that we have endured, to issue a generous decree after the model of this petition. And order it that they who dare to call us, your slaves and orphans, by rude defamatory names, or rebels or criminals, be tried and subjected to your gracious and judicious decree without mercy'.[125]

The government's response was to issue a charter of privileges (*zhalovannaia gramota*) which repeated much of the strel'tsy petition word for word.[126] This charter ended on a warning note, however, reminding the strel'tsy and the other signatories 'to serve and obey in accordance with the oath you swore on the holy gospel, and to wish us well with true loyalty and without any guile, and to obey our royal will unfailingly in accordance with your oath without any contradiction, just as your grandfathers and fathers served. . . .'[127]

By raising the topics of service and obedience, the government was apparently merely echoing the troops' own avowals of loyalty, in full awareness of the fact that the men 'on the one hand proclaimed themselves the loyal servants of authority, whilst, on the other, their own sense of self-preservation prompted them to put that authority under constant pressure'.[128] At this stage, however, the new regime felt it wise to put the emphasis on the carrot rather than the stick in attempting to regularise its relations with the strel'tsy. There was an ostentatious show of exiling 'traitors' and redistributing their property. On 13 June, for example, the proceeds from the sale of horses formerly belonging to Stepan Ianov and other disgraced strel'tsy officers were transferred to the strel'tsy.[129] Valuable trading premises were also made over. For example, on 14 June market stalls belonging to the murdered State Secretary Averky Kirillov were transferred. Bogoiavlensky believes that these and other instances were a sign that 'the interests of the strel'tsy were limited to the acquisition of material wealth.'[130]

Relations with Sophia's government were complicated by the strong Old Believer element amongst the strel'tsy, who hoped to force the authorities into making religious concessions. Just a few days after the rebellion, members of the Titov regiment had discussed the possibility of drawing up a petition to force the Church authorities to explain 'why they hated the old service books and loved the new Latin – Roman faith'.[131] They made contact with some artisans from the Potters' district, who produced a dissident monk by the name of Sergei who agreed to compose the petition. These dissident elements were in turn exploited by the new director of the Strel'tsy Department, Prince Ivan Khovansky. There is evidence to indicate Khovansky's adherence to the Old Belief prior to 1682, for example, he is said to have offered protection to Archpriest Avvakum, who refers to him in his memoirs,[132] but it has generally been assumed that he supported the schismatics primarily for his own political ends, in order further to discomfit Sophia.

This was a particularly unwelcome development for Sophia. It will be recalled that although Patriarch Nikon had been ousted in 1666, the reforms initiated by him had received the full approval of Tsar Aleksei and were endorsed by the same Church Council that deposed the Patriarch. Tsar Fedor had upheld the reforms, and the entire royal family followed the revised service books and rituals. Any concessions to the strel'tsy in this area would be tantamount to questioning the Orthodoxy of Sophia's father and brother, whose memory she revered. Her dilemma was increased by Prince Khovansky's sponsorship of the dissident movement and the danger that he might turn the strel'tsy

73

against her. According to the dissident Savva Romanov, Khovansky gave his backing to the monk Sergei's petition from the very beginning and undertook to negotiate with the palace on the strel'tsy's behalf.[133]

The dissenters' sense of urgency was increased by the fact that the coronation of the two tsars was due to take place on Sunday 25 June. They hoped that the government might be persuaded to have the tsars crowned 'in the true Orthodox faith and not in the new Latin heresy'. On 23 June a group of them went to the Kremlin where they were admitted by Khovansky, who conveyed their request for a 'debate' on matters of faith to the royal family. The dissenters were asked to return on the following Wednesday, that is after the coronation. In the meantime it became clear that the strel'tsy were divided on the issue and many refused to sign the petition, but dissenters continued to arrive in Moscow in the expectation of a change of policy. Wednesday 5 July was appointed as the date for the formal disputation.

Sophia must have followed developments with keen interest. The dissenters' complaint about the coronation could only have added to her anxiety about the occasion, which was a delicate one from the Regent's point of view. For a start, the accession of two tsars meant that the ritual, dating back to the coronation of Ivan IV in 1547, had to be modified. An additional set of regalia was prepared and a double throne constructed. Peter's youth and Ivan's disabilities had to be taken into account, for the ceremonies were long and exhausting.

Sophia's own role in the proceedings posed a problem. Russian coronations were all-male affairs. There had been only two occasions since 1547 when the Tsar being crowned already had a female consort, and at the coronation of Boris Godunov in 1598 it seems likely that Tsaritsa Maria Skuratova was mentioned only in prayers, but was not present at the ceremony itself.[134] The combined wedding and coronation ceremony of False Tsar Dmitry and Marina Mniszech in May 1605 is hardly likely to have been regarded as a suitable precedent given that the bride was a Polish Catholic. Even then Marina did not receive the sceptre and orb.[135] None of the previous three Romanov tsars had been married at the time of his coronation. The practice of seclusion had limited the participation of other female relatives on major state occasions, although a widow was allowed to join the funeral procession of her deceased spouse. As for Sophia's right to accompany the tsars to the Cathedral of the Dormition for their coronation, there was no precedent. During the Moscow rebellion she had abandoned many of the conventions of seclusion and on 11 June she appeared in a public parade of icons carried by troops departing to Kazan.'[136] But it appears that Sophia decided against flouting the coronation conventions. There could at this stage be no question of her being crowned, nor even of her taking on one of the ceremonial tasks usually carried out by the Tsar's male attendants and members of the duma. In instructions for the formulation of prayers for the tsars' accession issued on 24 June there is no special mention of Sophia.[137] Her name simply appeared in the chronological listing of the whole royal family, to whom the oath of allegiance was collectively sworn.

Even if Sophia was unable to make an impact in public, however, she could make her political presence felt by the allocation of ceremonial duties and the order of the coronation procession.[138] The leading role was taken by Vasily Golitsyn, who had overall charge of arrangements, with Emel'ian Ukraintsev as his deputy. Golitsyn accompanied the regalia to the cathedral and went to summon the tsars to the service. In church he stood on the raised platform next to the monarchs and took Tsar Ivan's sceptre at the appropriate moments. Yet the fact that Peter's sceptre was held by Prince Vasily's cousin Prince Boris Alekseevich Golitsyn, one of the chief adherents of the Naryshkin clan, underlines the Miloslavskys' failure to achieve any clear predominance over their rivals. As has already been noted, certain clans were still accorded honours on the hereditary principle regardless of the abilities or affiliations of individuals. Of the boyars who stood on the dais during the crowning, two – P.I. Prozorovsky and B.G. Iushkov – were tutors (d'iadki) to Tsar Ivan and one – R.M. Streshnev – to Peter. Two Odoevskys (nearer to Peter's camp than Sophia's) stood next to two Khovanskys (Sophia's erstwhile supporters, but soon to branch out on their own).[139] It has been noted, however, that no Khovansky was honoured with a specific ceremonial task.

Another indication of the political balance at this stage of the regency is provided by the promotions and appointments to the duma made between 25 and 29 June.[140] There are some signs of Miloslavsky ascendancy, for example the promotions of M.B. Miloslavsky from lord-in-waiting to boyar, and L.S. Miloslavsky's entry into the duma as lord-in-waiting. Khovansky fortunes are less easy to gauge. A.I. Khovansky entered the duma with the rank of boyar, but it has been pointed out that on 24 June Sophia blatantly omitted the Khovanskys from a distribution of costly presents, recipients of which included several of Khovansky's enemies, including Ivan Miloslavsky's brother-in-law, P.I. Prozorovsky.[141] The simultaneous promotion to boyar of M.L. Pleshcheev, a man of less distinguished family than the Khovanskys, who in 1655 had been banished for slandering one of the latter, may also have been intended as a slight.[142] The ceremonies for the promotions of members of the higher aristocracy were conducted a few days later, on 26–27 June.

Sophia and her party did not have it all their own way, however. Appointments made on Peter's nameday, 29 June, show that the younger Tsar had not been deprived of his right to bestow personal promotions.

75

With the obvious exception of the Naryshkins, there is still little evidence that his party had been badly damaged.

Sophia was not much in evidence during coronation week, but she was soon to make a dramatic reappearance at the confrontation between the Old Believers and the Church authorities scheduled for 5 July. It was made clear to the dissidents that those female members of the royal family who wished to attend had appointed the Kremlin Palace of Facets as the meeting place 'since they, being women, were reluctant to appear on the square before all the people'. No doubt modesty was not the only consideration that prompted the insistence upon a closed session well away from the threat of public disturbances with possible armed intervention by the strel'tsy. Some of the crowd protested: 'This has nothing to do with the tsarevny. It is the tsars who should be here,'[143] and Khovansky tried to insist upon a public meeting, but Sophia refused.

In the end she went to the confrontation accompanied by several of her female relatives, although different sources identify them variously, maybe because the writers are still unfamiliar with the individual women. Savva Romanov, for example, identified Tsaritsa (sic) Sophia Alekseevna seated on one royal throne, Tat'iana Mikhailovna on the other, to the right Natalia Kirillovna, to her right Tsarevna Marfa Alekseevna and between the thrones, Anna Mikhailovna.[144] Archbishop Afanasy of Kholmogory identified Natalia Kirillovna, Tat'iana Mikhailovna and Maria Alekseevna as Sophia's companions.[145] In Medvedev's account, Sophia and Tat'iana occupied the thrones whilst Natalia and Maria sat on chairs at a lower level.[146] Whatever the composition of the royal party, the appearance of the women before an unruly crowd which had already clashed with the palace clergy prompted S.M. Solov'ev to write:

> Despite the fact that they were there to affirm the Old Belief and denounce all *novelties*, the dissenters failed to notice the unprecedented sight that greeted them in the palace: the tsars' place was occupied by women! The maiden tsarevny were showing themselves to the people and one of them was in charge of proceedings, but the dissenters failed to see this novelty as a sign of the times.[147]

The subsequent dialogue between the Patriarch and Nikita, the dissidents' spokesman, consisted mainly of demands for obedience by the former and for justification of Nikon's reforms by the latter. As one point there was a scuffle between Nikita and Archbishop Afanasy, after which Sophia intervened and asked Nikita why he had revoked a recantation that he had made during her father's reign. When the dissenters' petition was read out, Sophia leaped to her feet at the passage where her father was accused of having been 'perverted' by

Nikon and his associates. 'If Arseny and Nikon were heretics, then so were our father and brother. This means that the reigning tsars are not tsars, the patriarchs not patriarchs and the prelates are not prelates. We refuse to listen to such blasphemy and to hear our father and brother referred to as heretics. We shall all leave the country.' It was not the first nor the last time that Sophia used the threat of abandoning the capital in order to make her point. Some of the strel'tsy asked her to change her mind, but others were heard to mutter, 'It's high time you went to a convent, lady; you've caused the realm enough trouble already. May the sovereign tsars prosper, but we'll get on well enough without *you*.'[148] Sophia, in turn, rebuked the strel'tsy for lending their support to 'rebellious blockheads' and repeated her threat of leaving Moscow 'in order to tell all the people about this insubordination and chaos'.[149] These words made an impact on the strel'tsy. They assured Sophia that they were 'ready to lay down their lives for the Orthodox faith, the Church and your royal majesties, and to do everything you command'.

The meeting broke up without either side having made any concessions. Like much of the controversry over Nikon's reforms, this was a 'debate' between two sets of deeply conservative opponents: those who rejected out of hand anything 'new' and 'foreign', and those who deemed the reasons behind the Church's reforms to be no concern of the ordinary believer. The irony is that Patriarch Joachim was perhaps the most conservative of all, with a deeply ingrained mistrust of foreigners; but for him the reformed religion was the true version, for it had been ratified by Church Councils and accepted by monarchs. As for Sophia, the attitude that she displayed during the 'debate' set the tone for future dealings with the dissenters. It was only her anxiety about the allegiance of the strel'tsy which had prompted her to give permission for the meeting in the first place, but subsequently no mercy was to be shown to dissenters. Many of the harsh penalties instituted during the reign of Tsar Aleksei were revived during her regency and consistently imposed, and 5 July was to be commemorated by an annual service of thanksgiving.

Romanov records that after the meeting Sophia summoned representatives of the strel'tsy and offered them rewards for breaking with the dissenters. Entertainment in the royal cellars was provided as an incentive. Nikita was executed and other ringleaders banished. Khovansky appeared to have burned his boats by his patronage of the unsuccessful event, but Sophia could still not afford to oust him as long as he remained a popular figure amongst the strel'tsy. Even so, she had already taken steps to limit the clan's power, for example by transferring the Bondslaves Department (*kholopii prikaz*) from the jurisdiction of the Justice (*sudnyi*) Department, the Director of which was Prince Andrei

Khovansky, and declaring it an independent institution under the management of F.F. Volkonsky, a man whose loyalty Sophia had less reason to doubt.[150]

After the failure of the dissident venture, Khovansky seems to have re-employed tactics that had proved successful during the May rebellion, insinuating that the boyars and other officials had 'evil intentions' and were preparing to destroy the strel'tsy with the help of their private armies. On 12 July the government was confronted with the demand that all the boyars should be handed over to be dealt with by the strel'tsy. The government was also deluged with rumours about the Khovanskys' schemes. It was said the Prince Ivan Khovansky had set his heart on the crown and even hoped to marry his son to Tsarevna Ekaterina, or even to Sophia herself.[151] The Polish observer records the story that Sophia summoned the son to take a look at him, but found him 'too young and too ugly' for her tastes.[152] Variations on this story survive. Alexander Gordon, who first visited Russia in the 1690s and gleaned his information from sources hostile to Sophia, alleges that Ekaterina was Khovansky's choice, but 'if Prince Havansky [sic] had proposed his son to the Princess Sophia herself, he might have succeeded; but the making choice of the younger sister was the occasion of their fall'.[153] In July, meanwhile, the elder Khovansky married the widow of the murdered State Secretary Larion Ivanov and had a large portion of the latter's estates made over to his name.[154]

Wounded pride as a result of being passed over in favour of her more attractive sister is unlikely to have figured strongly in Sophia's list of reasons for wanting to get rid of Khovansky. The memoir of Andrei Matveev, a witness who, as we know, was hostile to Sophia, adds another dimension to the conflict. He believes that there was a private quarrel between Khovansky and Ivan Miloslavsky, and that it was the latter, as much as Sophia, who wanted Prince Ivan removed. Matveev writes that Miloslavsky withdrew to his out-of-town estate, where he hid 'like a mole', seeking a suitable opportunity to 'destroy the princes Khovansky and repay them in kind.'[155] Miloslavsky, as we shall see, lost all his government posts before the end of May and may have been feeling particularly resentful. Matveev claims, too, that Sophia revived tactics that had proved successful during the May rebellion and infiltrated the strel'sy regiments, where 'secret meetings and negotiations and consultation were on the increase'. Although it was she who had raised the Khovanskys, in recognition of their 'prominence and special authority', she was confident that their power would be short-lived.[156]

No reliable evidence survives of secret negotiations between Sophia and the strel'tsy. On the contrary, the best evidence available – official accounts of the day-to-day activities of the court – shows that she used the ploy of distancing herself and the tsars from the corps in the hope of undermining their confidence. From 13 to 29 July the royal party visited the Trinity – St Sergius Monastery, calling at royal estates to the north of Moscow en route.[157] Bogoiavlensky considers the movements of the royal party during this expedition to be 'irregular', given that no special church festivals were being celebrated. They spent four days at Taininskoe, just to the north of Moscow, and on 17 July moved to Vozdvizhenskoe. From there they headed north to the Trinity Monastery, and beyond it to Aleksandrovskaia Sloboda, remembered as the place where Ivan IV withdrew in 1565 to deliver an ultimatum to his subjects. Perhaps Sophia had similar ideas and was reconnoitring the ground for the eventuality of a future withdrawal or even escape from Moscow. It appears that for some of the time before their return on 29 July the whereabouts of the party were unknown even to officials in Moscow.[158]

Meanwhile, Ivan Khovansky had been left in charge of a boyar 'commission' in Moscow, on the face of it a risky strategy on Sophia's part. But surviving correspondence between Vasily Golitsyn, who was away from Moscow, and his deputy Ukraintsev in the capital suggests that Khovansky was becoming increasingly isolated and had no body of support amongst the boyars. Ukraintsev's letters, for example, indicate that many boyars had left Moscow, either to join the royal party or to visit their estates. Much official business bypassed Khovansky.[159] For example on 25 July, in the absence of precise information about the tsars' whereabouts, he asked Tsarevna Tat'iana, who was in Moscow, to approve measures to deal with unrest on the Dvina, but when Ukraintsev received the order he applied to Golitsyn for authorisation.[160] In a letter of late July Golitsyn advised Ukraintsev to report to the 'Sovereign Lady' personally on urgent matters and not through intermediaries.[161] Sophia's own involvement in affairs of state is indicated by a revealing letter from Ukraintsev to Golitsyn, dated 30 July. She had made arrangements for dealing with the dispatch of Crimean envoys ('vile Hagarenes') from Moscow. Ukraintsev had been told to report to her on the return of Ambassador Peter Potemkin from England. She asked for copies of letters from England and asked whether Potemkin had completed the official report of his embassy, which was to be delivered to her. She had been involved in an argument with Khovansky about the appointment of officers to strel'tsy regiments serving in the Ukraine, and had ordered his wife to appear at a reception. Finally, Ukraintsev writes: 'She has taken away the copies of the Hetman's dispatches and the letters which Leonty Nepliuev wrote to you.'[162]

Fragmented court records for the middle of August show life in Moscow going on much as usual. On 14 and 15 August the tsars attended services to celebrate the feast of the Dormition, and on 16 August were present at a night service in the palace Church of the

Saviour. On 19 August, however, the traditional procession to the Cathedral of Our Lady of the Don in the Donskoi Monastery was cancelled and the next day the court departed for the royal estate of Kolomenskoe.[163] The tsars were attended by a formidable retinue of servitors, headed by Vasily Golitsyn. Chamberlains, masters of the wardrobe and table attendants alone numbered over a hundred. In Moscow meanwhile, Ivan Khovansky headed a party of seven officials left in charge of the palace.[164]

There was nothing unusual about the royal expedition. Tsar Aleksei had made a practice of being out of town (*v pokhode*) in the late summer and early autumn, as had Tsar Fedor. But in the special circumstances of 1682 this departure alarmed the strel'tsy. On 23 August a delegation arrived at Kolomenskoe to express anxiety that the tsars had left Moscow on account of 'false rumours' that they, the strel'tsy, were planning 'to march on the Kremlin as before' and were plotting mischief against the boyars.[165] The delegates were assured that the tsars harboured no suspicions and that this was a regular expedition. Indeed, the royal party appeared to be observing a normal programme of outings and churchgoing. On 29 August, Tsar Ivan's nameday, they attended services in the nearby Church of the Beheading of John the Baptist at D'iakovo.[166]

There were clearly tensions, however. Sophia had asked Khovansky to send the 600-strong royal bodyguard of mounted strel'tsy (the *stremianny* regiment) to attend the celebrations, but he had procrastinated.[167] Medvedev reports that Khovansky had been demanding that the strel'tsy be given substantial subsidies from the revenues of crown lands, and, when Sophia refused, announced to the strel'tsy: 'Children! You should know that now the boyars are threatening even me because I wished the best for you. There is nothing more I can do. Act as you see fit.'[168] Another attempt at intimidation on Khovansky's part was a report, apparently fabricated, that a mutiny was about to break out amongst servitors in Novgorod, but Khovansky backed down when Sophia challenged him to produce evidence.[169] Further examples of insubordination were provided by the events of 1 September, Muscovite New Year's Day. Normally the celebrations in the capital centred on the monarch, but this year the royal family attended mass at the Church of Our Lady of Kazan in Kolomenskoe, leaving the Patriarch to officiate in town, where there were so few courtiers present that the occasion fell flat. Khovansky had been ordered to attend the service in the Kremlin, but he failed to do so.[170]

Sophia already had substantial evidence of Khovansky's disobedience, which on 2 September was supplemented by an accusation of treason in the form of an anonymous letter of denunciation pinned to the gates of Kolomenskoe palace. The contents, however, were not made public for another two weeks. That same day the court left for the village of Vorob'evo and on 4 September moved on to Pavlovskoe. From here an order was issued for the transfer of four regiments of strel'tsy to Kiev, no doubt for the dual purpose of testing Khovansky's response and removing potential troublemakers from the capital.[171] This order had to be repeated on 9 September.[172] It signalled a change of tone in Sophia's treatment of the strel'tsy.

On 6 September the court resumed its journey eastwards to the Monastery of St Sabbas at Zvenigorod, one of the richest foundations in the Moscow region thanks largely to the special patronage of the late Tsar Aleksei. The feast of St Sabbas the Miracle Worker fell on 10 September and the customary services were attended, whilst political business continued simultaneously. A large number of instructions were dispatched to Khovansky and, a clear indication of growing tension, an order was drafted for distribution to military servitors in towns of the Moscow region to be ready to go to the capital to restore order. The document denounced Khovansky and the strel'tsy in no uncertain terms, stating, in contradiction to the message of reassurance given to the strel'tsy delegates on 23 August, that the tsars had left Moscow 'because we could not tolerate the many offences, unlawful and gross actions and violations committed by criminals and traitors.'[173] The kid gloves were also removed for dealings with Khovansky. On 10 September he was ordered to release Colonels M. Lupandin and A. Porosukov, who had been imprisoned by the strel'tsy and were being tortured in order to extract money.[174] The order to the military servitors, so out of keeping with the conciliatory tone hitherto adopted for communications with the rebels, was probably never sent, but it indicates that the decision had been taken to stop pandering to the rebels. In the words of the Mazurinsky Chronicle: 'In Moscow at this time there were great disturbances from the strel'tsy and the soldiers; the strel'tsy had seized the whole of the Muscovite state and did whatever they wanted.'[175] Even allowing for exaggeration, there was a state of emergency.

On 10 September the royal party returned to Pavlovskoe, on the 12th they stayed at Khliabovo, and on the 13th moved north to the village of Vozdvizhenskoe on the main road to the Trinity Monastery. On the 14th a series of *gramoty* was issued summoning servitors to Vozvizhenskoe by 18 September for the reception of the Ukrainian Hetman's son, Semyon. 'To our boyar Prince Ivan Andreevich Khovansky and his assistants', one of the documents read, 'we have instructed our boyars, lords-in-waiting and gentlemen of the duma, all those who are now in Moscow, to attend us here on our sojourn at the village of Vozdvizhenskoe by the 18th of September in the first hour of the day to see to our royal business and to receive our subject Semyon, son of Ivan Samoilovich, Hetman of the Zaporozhian Host of both sides of the Dniepr'.[176] Servitors below boyar rank received a similar summons, 'in order that there should be no shortage of table attendants, crown agents, servitors and court attendants for the reception of the Hetman's son'.[177] On 16 September Colonel Samoilovich arrived, 'and the great sovereigns were pleased to attend evensong and prayers in the Church of the Elevation of the Sacred Cross to celebrate the [eve of the] nameday of the great Sovereign Lady Tsarevna and Great Princess Sophia Alekseevna'. The following day, the feast of the holy martyrs Vera, Nadezhda and Liubov' and their mother Sophia, the tsars went to mass, attended by courtiers dressed in 'robes of coloured brocade' in honour of the nameday. Later Sophia herself appeared and treated them to vodka.[178]

At this point the customary celebration took a novel turn. A session of the duma was called and the following statement issued:

> The great sovereign tsars and great princes Ivan Alekseevich and Peter Alekseevich, autocrats of all the Great and Little and White Russias, and their sister the Great Sovereign Lady, Pious Tsarevna and Great Princess Sophia Alekseevna, having heard the letter [of denunciation] have indicated and the boyars have resolved that Prince Ivan Khovansky and his son Prince Andrei on account of their many crimes and treason and evil designs upon the health and authority of the great sovereigns and their attempt to take over the Muscovite state, in accordance with genuine investigation and patent testimony to the deeds which they have committed in their insubordination and on the evidence of the letter of denunciation, shall be condemned to death.[179]

We must look more closely at the crucial letter of denunciation found pinned to the gates of Kolomenskoe on 2 September.[180] Historians have mostly declared it to be a fake, cooked up by Sophia herself or one of her associates in order to secure the removal of the Khovanskys. Matveev, for example, attributed it to the 'intrigues' of Ivan Miloslavsky.[181] Whatever the identity of its author, it was evidently widely distributed. There is a copy, for example, in the papers of Englebert Kämpfer, who visited Moscow in 1683 and had dealings with many prominent officials.[182] The letter transcended the piecemeal evidence of insubordination, non-cooperation and self-aggrandisement on the part of the Khovanskys by revealing nothing less than a plot to subvert the state. In it a 'Moscow strelets and two artisans [*dva cheloveka posatskikh liudei*]' denounced the 'criminals and traitors' Prince Ivan and Prince Andrei Khovansky:

> they summoned nine of us strel'tsy and five artisans to their house and told us to help them to obtain the Muscovite throne and to persuade our brethren to eradicate your royal line and to march on town in a great mob and to denounce you as the sons of heretics and to kill both you sovereigns and

Tsaritsa Natalia Kirillovna and Tsarevna Sophia Alekseevna and the Patriarch and hierarchs of the Church; and Prince Andrei was to marry one Tsarevna and the other tsarevny were to take the veil and be sent to distant convents; and we were to kill three Odoevskys, two Cherkasskys, three Golitsyns, Ivan Mikhailovich Miloslavsky, three Sheremetevs and many more boyars, servitors and chief merchants, because they do not love the old faith and practise the new. And when this wicked deed was done we were to raise rebellion all over Moscow in the towns and villages so that the townspeople killed the governors and officials, and the peasants were to kill their boyars and the boyars' bondslaves. When the state was in turmoil he, Prince Ivan, would be elected to the throne of Muscovy and would appoint a patriarch and prelates chosen by the people, those who love the old service books. And the Khovanskys kissed the cross and the icon of St Nicholas the Miracle Worker and we kissed the same cross to show we were ready to do the evil deed. And he gave us each 200 roubles and they vowed before the icon that if they came to the throne of Moscow they would reward the strel'tsy who were in the conspiracy by making us privy councillors [*blizhnie liudi*] and we artisans would be made chief merchants [*gosti*] with the right to trade freely forever.

And we three men, fearful of God and remembering our oath of allegiance, are unwilling to do such an insolent deed and advise you, great sovereigns, to take great care of your health. And we, your slaves, have fled, we are in hiding and we tell you of this evil deed without regard for our own lives. And when your lives are saved and God has restored calm we, your slaves, shall declare ourselves to you, and you, sovereigns, may reward us, your slaves. We cannot write our names. But these are our distinguishing marks: one has a black wart on the right shoulder; one has a scar from a cut on the right leg across the shin, and the third has no marks.

The document ended: 'To be handed to the Sovereign Lady Sophia Alekseevna without making a copy.'[183]

The main doubt about the authenticity of this letter lies in the lack of corroboration elsewhere of the Khovanskys' plans for snatching the throne of Muscovy and eliminating the leading figures of Church and state. There is no evidence that the anonymous informers ever came forward to collect their 'reward' from the sovereigns, nor does there seem to have been any attempt to identify and arrest the other persons allegedly present at the meeting, who had presumably failed to inform the authorities of Khovansky's treason. In fact, the anonymous letter was to be used as the 'grand finale' to a list of lesser charges brought by the authorities, the clinching 'proof' that treason had been committed and the death sentence was justified. Prince Mikhail Lykov and his assistants, entrusted with the task of arresting the Khovanskys, are unlikely to have had any doubts about their guilt. They learned that the princes were on their way to Vozdvizhenskoe in response to Sophia's summons, doubtless unaware of the grave charges that had been made against them. The elder Khovansky was apprehended in the village of

Pushkino, his son at his estate a couple of miles away.[184] They were brought to the entrance of the royal residence, where the court had assembled and sentence was read out to them.[185]

There was no trial, nor was Khovansky granted his request to confront his accusers (the *ochnaia stavka* procedure), not surprisingly, since the latter were either 'in hiding' or non-existent. The accused were simply presented with the blunt fact that they were to be executed, 'for committing great wrongs and for their many crimes and treason'.[186] The anonymous letter was preceded by a list of lesser charges: the Khovansky had 'acted of their own accord' without informing the tsars; they had distributed funds from the royal Treasury without permission; they had allowed all sorts of people to wander round the palace 'in an arrogant and oafish manner which would be unseemly even in an ordinary home', had detained prisoners unlawfully and extorted money and goods from the innocent. Special mention was made of the illegal and exorbitant imposition of money contributions on monastery and crown estates. It was recalled that the Khovanskys had boasted of their services to the crown in the presence of the boyars, despite the fact that it was public knowledge that Prince Ivan had suffered humiliating defeats whilst on military service, 'thus earning the reproach of foreign nations and bringing nothing of benefit to the eternal glory of the great sovereign's name and the state'. He had flouted the tsars' authority, boasting that the security of the Muscovite state depended on him, 'and if he were to go, then not a soul would be spared and the people of Moscow would be knee-deep in blood'.

Both Khovanskys were accused of insubordination, disobeying the tsars and insulting the boyars. The events of 5 July were recalled, including and incident where Khovansky had failed to restrain Nikita when he had raised his hand to Archbishop Afanasy, 'in the presence of the Great Lady Tsaritsa and tsarevny'. He had shielded the dissenters from justice. Failure to send regiments to Kiev and to fight the Kalmyks and Bashkirs, and the detaining of the royal bodyguard in Moscow were listed, as was Khovansky's non-appearance at the New Year celebrations. He had wrongly accused the military servitors of Novgorod of plotting mutiny. He had detained commanders appointed by the tsars and replaced them with his own nominees. Finally, he had created a rift between the strel'tsy and the palace, on the one hand by misleading the tsars about the strel'tsy's intentions, on the other by making false statements and delivering 'inflammatory speeches' to the strel'tsy. The reading of the 'anonymous letter' rounded off proceedings.

Matveev reports that Khovansky 'tearfully' begged to be heard, promised to reveal the initiators and perpetrators of the strel'tsy rebellion and asked to confront his accusers. But Ivan Miloslavsky, 'fearing that he and his accomplices would be the first to be unmasked', made a sign to Sophia to bring proceedings to a close.[187] The Khovanskys were beheaded then and there by a strelets 'on the square by the main road to Moscow'.[188]

The document listing the charges against the Khovanskys offers a fascinating insight into seventeenth-century Muscovite judicial procedure. Some of the charges, it is true, are corroborated elsewhere, for example failure to attend the New Year celebrations and hesitation over the dispatch of troops. But others referred to duties in which Khovansky apparently had the endorsement of the palace, for example the distribution of money and goods to the strel'tsy. Khovansky had been appointed by Sophia to head the committee left in Moscow whilst the court was on its travels and, according to Bogoiavlensky, far from taking matters completely into his own hands, he had followed the established practice of referring to the rulers for important decisions.[189] The reference to Khovansky's association with the religious dissidents begs the question of why a man who had so openly patronised the 'accursed schismatics' should have been appointed to a position of such high responsibility. Discrepancies and illogicalities could be multiplied, as could omissions, for example the absence of any reference to Khovansky's dealings with the strel'tsy up to and including the May rebellion. The main conclusion to be drawn from the list of charges and the letter of denunciation is that the prosecution intended the sheer number and variety of crimes listed, ranging from the petty to the capital, to make it clear which way the verdict was to go.

What of Sophia's contribution to the proceedings? The postscript to the anonymous letter stated that it was for her eyes only in the first instance, and her name appears together with that of the tsars on the death sentence. She had confronted Khovansky head-on on several occasions, and it is hardly a coincidence that the execution took place on 17 September. In the words of S.M. Solov'ev: 'Thus was the Tsarevna – Regent's nameday celebrated!'[190] In the complex process of rallying the support of all parties, dealing with the strel'tsy and isolating and eliminating the Khovanskys she showed a more determined and ruthless face than she had done during the May rebellion. At least, official records give a clearer indication of her role during this period.

The next task facing her was to replace Khovansky in Moscow. The boyar Prince F.F. Kurakin, who like many others had retired to his estate, was ordered to take command, and M.P. Golovin, Director of the Police (zemskii) Department, took over in the interim.[191] Reports of the execution of the Khovanskys were sent to him, to the Patriarch and to the strel'tsy. The latter were told that the Khovanskys had made many false accusations against them to the tsars and in turn had twisted the tsars' words in order to arouse discontent. The strel'tsy should know of their:

blatant treason and evil intentions against the sovereigns' health and their designs on state power, and should give no credence to the deceptive and crafty words of Khovansky, his children and relatives, and you should have no fear that you, the strel'tsy, have incurred the sovereigns' disfavour or anger, because we are not angry with you, and you can rely on our favour without any doubt or anxiety.[192]

Further reassurance was to be required. News soon reached Sophia that Prince Ivan Ivanovich Khovansky had made his way to Moscow and spread the rumour that his father and brother had been killed without the tsars' permission and that the boyars were preparing to march on Moscow and kill the strel'tsy. The latter had armed themselves, taken guns and ammunition from the Kremlin, set up patrols and barricades at the city gates and walls and were stopping people from entering or leaving town. On 18 September another rescript was dispatched from Vozdvizhenskoe, reiterating the information already publicised and urging the strel'tsy to disbelieve Prince Ivan Ivanovich's lies. Ivan Sukhotin, M.P. Golovin's deputy, reported that he had been visited by a delegation of strel'tsy asking that some of their fellows attending the royal party should be allowed to come to Moscow 'to give information'. More alarm had been spread by rumours that units of bondslaves were being sent to deal with the strel'tsy.[193] On the night of 18 September the royal party left Vozdvizhenskoe for the greater security of the Trinity Monastery, which was placed in a state of siege. Military servitors from neighbouring towns were ordered there immediately to defend the tsars.[194] Despite the comparative ease with which she had dealt with the Khovanskys, Sophia had reason to be anxious. There were more than 14,000 strel'tsy stationed in Moscow, whereas she had only about 3,000 troops at her disposal until the military servitors appeared.[195]

Fears proved groundless. On 19 September a strel'tsy delegation visited the Patriarch and asked him to persuade the royal party to return to Moscow. In the absence of a positive response, on 22 September delegates asked M.P. Golovin for permission to send their representatives to the Trinity Monastery, 'for we dare not go without the sovereigns' leave'.[196] In the meantime a stream of *gramoty* was issued from the monastery in an attempt to stabilise the situation. On 21 September, for example, members of the trading and artisan community were cautioned against believing rumours about the Khovanskys' innocence and were praised for their 'loyal service'. A copy of the letter of denunciation was appended.[197] On 25 September the strel'tsy submitted a statement assuring the tsars that 'we have no evil intentions, nor shall we have'.[198] The Patriarch acted as intermediary, on 28 September receiving instructions concerning the conditions under which the tsars were willing to pardon the strel'tsy.[199]

On 2 October a delegation of strel'tsy was allowed to go to the Trinity Monastery, where the following day they 'made their pleas with much weeping' and begged the tsars' forgiveness.[200] Tsars Ivan and Peter and 'their sister the Great Sovereign Lady, Pious Tsarevna and Great Princess Sophia Alekseevna' were willing to forgive, but only on the condition that the strel'tsy took a solemn oath in the Cathedral of the Dormition. This they did on 8 October in the presence of Patriarch Joachim, kissing the Gospels and the hand of the apostle Andrew. (The latter had recently been discovered frozen into a three-fingered sign of the cross!)[201] The next day the strel'tsy came to the Patriarch's palace in the Kremlin to announce that they were 'truly grateful to God and the Saviour for their ineffable mercy to them, and to you, sovereigns, they give most humble thanks'.[202]

The eleven-point conditions to which the strel'tsy had agreed were comprehensive to the point of repetitiveness.[203] Clause 1 stated that they were to have:

> no evil thoughts, nor to have conference or council openly or secretly with anyone, nor to foment rebellion or persuade others to rebel, or to join with schismatics and other criminals, nor to hold assemblies or enter the city with weapons or have conferences Cossack-style, nor to compose criminal slogans or man watchtowers, and on no account to revive or commit again the deeds of late, or praise them or threaten anybody.

Other clauses prescribed that all traitors and slanderers were to be denounced at once, as was any abuse of state officials. Guns and ammunition taken during the troubles were to be returned. They were to obey orders on new postings without complaint and to desist from recruiting peasants, bondslaves and other categories of person into their ranks. A number or prescriptions for fit and proper behaviour towards the authorities were listed. Clause 11 read:

> But if any of them should scorn the sovereigns' lofty and lavish kindness and should speak approvingly of the deeds of late, or boast of committing murder or make up phrases inciting rebellion as before, or stir people up to commit criminal acts, and if anyone, knowing of this, should fail to report it or apprehend the criminal and show him indulgence, such people will be condemned to death for their crimes without mercy in order that criminals and rebels should be afraid even to think of, not to mention carry out, such deeds, and henceforth no one should contemplate such an undertaking.

On 25 October the authorities felt secure enough to issue a list of rewards to those servitors who had accompanied the tsars on their expedition or obeyed the summons to join them. Golitsyn received the largest, a sum of 150 roubles.[204] For additional security an order was issued instructing the strel'tsy to carry weapons only on guard duty. On 27 October the court set off for Moscow. Sophia was no doubt gratified the following day to receive a petition from the Ermolov regiment of strel'tsy requesting the removal of the column on Red Square, since 'for our sins we carried out a massacre of boyars and gentlemen of the duma and men of all ranks in the royal city of Moscow on Red Square and many other places, thereby enraging God and you. . . . Hear us, your guilty slaves, and order that the column on Red Square be destroyed lest it bring you shame in the eyes of other states.'[205] It is worth noting that in this, and in a memorandum issued on 29 October,[206] the initiative for erecting the column is said to have come from Khovansky. According to the Mazurinsky Chronicle, the column was removed the day before the royal party entered Moscow.[207]

This final token of strel'tsy repentance meant that the court could come home in triumph. On 2 November M.P. Golovin was ordered to organize a fitting reception,[208] and the next day the royal procession arrived, led by the mounted strel'tsy bodyguard, priests bearing crosses, and servitors. Behind the tsars came Vasily Golitsyn and one of his 'assistants' in the defence of the Trinity Monastery, A.I. Rzhevsky, accompanied by state secretaries Emel'ian Ukraintsev and Fedor Shaklovity, the latter newly emerged to prominence. Only then came the tsaritsy and the tsarevny and their attendants. Sophia was not singled out by name.[209] Evidently she had decided against celebrating her victory ostentatiously, perhaps fearing public disapproval, but secure in the knowledge that her role in the events of the past four months could leave the high officials of state and Church in little doubt about who was actually in charge. More peaceful times looked to be ahead.

PART TWO

# Regent of Russia 1682–89

CHAPTER 4

# The Inner Circle

At the outset of her regency Sophia had no claims to sole rule, still less did she enjoy the status of autocrat. Any assessment of her position in May 1682 must therefore begin with an examination of her inner circle, and where better to start than at the summit of power, with the boys in whose name she ruled.

Historians have tended to dismiss Ivan V, senior partner in the dual tsardom by virtue of his age. Almost any ruler risks looking pale in comparison with Peter the Great, and one who was mentally and physically handicapped could hardly begin to compete. The nineteenth-century historian M.I. Semevsky provided a characteristic profile when he described Ivan as 'congenitally simple-minded, a stutterer who suffered from scurvy and poor eyesight, weak and enfeebled in body and mind, an object of pity and even ridicule for the boyars who attended him'.[1] It would be pleasant to be able to revise this assessment, but the evidence is overwhelming. La Neuville, for example, writes: ''twoud be more to his Credit not to shew himself abroad so often, for he is a frightful sight, so very ugly that 'tis irksome to look upon him, tho he is but Twenty eight years old'.[2] La Neuville, as we know, offered a sensational version of events in the 1680s and his account was not published until two years after Ivan's death, but foreign observers with better credentials differ only in the more moderate tone of their comments. Heinrich Butenant, for example, recorded that Ivan's disabilities were common knowledge; Peter was elected 'because the elder prince, Ivan Alekseevich, is said to have been nearly blind and furthermore to be able to speak only with difficulty', although, as he noted later, Ivan's 'poor eyesight and other chance matters' were not deemed sufficient reason to debar him from the throne.[3] The account sent to the Papal Legate in Poland, it will be recalled, includes the rumour that in 1676 Artamon Matveev urged Tsar Aleksei to bypass Ivan, because he 'had a disease of the eyes, was short-sighted and incapable of ruling'.[4]

The German traveller Englebert Kämpfer saw both tsars during a reception for a Swedish delegation in July 1683. His first remarks touched on the characteristic pomp of the occasion:

7   Tsars Peter and Ivan from an engraving by Larmessen (c.1685)

Both [tsars] sat somewhat towards the right of the room, both on an elevated silver bishop's throne covered in red cloth. Above each hung a picture. Over their robes they wore cloaks of flowered yellow and white silver fabric and in their hands instead of a sceptre they held a long gold staff, bent at

92

the end like a bishop's crozier and set with precious stones. . . . Ivan sat motionless with downcast eyes which were, in addition, almost hidden by a cap pulled down over them.

After the Swedish King's letter had been handed over, both tsars rose, as etiquette demanded, to ask after his health. 'The hand of the elder Tsar had to be raised to his cap by his young attendant and the cap was thus touched. At the same time a babbling noise issued from his lips.'[5] The contrasting impression made by Peter is emphasised by the fact that Kämpfer took the eleven-year-old to be sixteen. 'The younger, his face held upright and open, made such an impression with his wonderful beauty and pleasant gestures, as the crimson of his royal blood kept rushing to his face, that if the bystanders had had a young maid and not a royal personage before them they would certainly have fallen in love with him.' The contrast was even greater when the boys rose to speak. 'The younger was a nimble fellow and so eager to ask questions and to stand up that he had to be restrained by his attendant until the elder Tsar was ready and they could speak simultaneously.'[6]

In February 1684 the Scottish mercenary Patrick Gordon had an audience with Ivan. 'I went and kissed the elder Empereur his hand who being a sickly and infirme prince, looked out sadly, he said nothing, the Boyar only in his name asked for my health and praised my services.'[7] A week or so later the Austrian envoy Johann Eberhardt Hövel was received, once more by Ivan alone. (On both occasions Peter was indisposed by an attack of the 'pox'.) Hövel remarked that when it came to the moment for the Tsar to rise and ask after the Emperor's health, 'he was so weak he could hardly stand up and had to be held under the arms by two attendants and spoke in a very weak, very unclear voice'. This and the two preceding 'sightings' confirm that Ivan was almost literally a 'puppet' ruler, whose movements had to be manipulated by attendants.

The astute Hövel went on to speculate on the political situation at court, guessing that a disagreement might have arisen between the two tsars (or rather their parties) over Ivan's wedding, which had taken place a few weeks earlier, 'for Ivan is a very weak feeble gentleman, in contrast to the younger, who is of great promise, intelligence and vigour'. The tsars' sister Sophia, he wrote,

has such a firm grip on the government and seems to wield such power that she arranged this wedding in the hope that Ivan would be the first to get an heir and thereby propagate the succession. But in my humble opinion this seems a lost cause insofar as Tsar Ivan is very infirm and congenitally blind, with a growth of skin right over his eyes. So one can well imagine that the dual monarchy [in duobus simul] will not last long. It's true that Peter has the greater support from the boyars and magnates but sister Sophia, who is about twenty-six and said to possess great wit and judgement, has promoted the elder brother. But is should be evident to anyone that such a feeble-minded and sickly man is by nature unfit to rule.[8]

Further confirmation, if any is needed, is provided by two visitors from Saxony. On 20 June 1684 Laurent Rinhuber had an audience. When the hand-kissing stage was reached Ivan Miloslavsky had to intervene to tell Ivan that it was 'the doctor', explaining that 'his Majesty cannot see too well'. Peter, on the other hand, 'with his mouth half formed into a laugh gave a friendly and gracious look, and scarcely had he seen me than he held out his hand himself. An exceedingly handsome gentleman on whom nature has amply proven her powers.'[9] Georg Adam Schleissing, present at the same audience, included an illustration in a book published in 1694 showing Ivan with a veil-like covering over his eyes.[10] He explains: 'The elder Tsar Ivan Alekseevich was not at all blessed by nature, as one may gather from the engraving, for he could neither see nor speak properly, nor could he ever hope to look in the least regal or authoritative. All the time he wears a green taffeta cloth to keep his face hidden because his eyes dart to and fro in his head. Otherwise, he is very pious and God-fearing.'[11]

Contemporary Russian sources are far more reticent about Ivan. To the official clerks and chroniclers he was 'Great Sovereign Tsar and Great Prince, Autocrat of all the Great and Little and White Russias' by virtue of his birthright and coronation, and physical and mental handicaps in no way detracted from his sovereign status. Indeed, as was suggested earlier, reverence for 'fools in Christ' may have endowed Ivan with a special aura of sanctity denied to his robust younger brother. Palace and chancellery scribes would have deemed it inappropriate to mention Ivan's shortcomings. The records of the Razriad (Crown Appointments Department) for 27 April to 25 October 1682, for example, describe Peter's election on 27 April without any discussion of the boys' rival qualifications.[12] Medvedev's account makes no mention of handicaps. Indeed, in his record of the Patriarch's speech on the advantages of dual monarchy, he notes, without a hint of a raised eyebrow: 'In the event of an enemy attack upon the pious Russian realm we shall be fully prepared for defence and administration, for if one Tsar goes out to meet the enemy the other can remain on the royal throne in his kingdom and the Russian state will enjoy every advantage of good rulership.'[13] The maintenance of the myth that even infant tsars made independent decisions had such a long tradition that contemporaries would have had no difficulty in accepting the 'rulership' of a handicapped teenager. One of the few contemporary Russian writers to make direct reference to Ivan's disabilities was the state official Ivan Zheliabuzhsky, who explained that 'the Great Sovereign was initially not elected to the tsardom because he had a serious ailment of the eyes'.[14]

By and large it fell to a later generation of writers to provide a franker description. Andrei Matveev writes (in the 1720s) that 'the Tsarevich's multifarious ailments, suffered since infancy, precluded his elevation to the throne', adding later that Sophia was well aware 'that Ivan would never be capable of assuming the crown, sceptre and burden of the great All-Russian Empire or to endure that heavy labour by reason of his various illnesses'.[15] Peter Krekshin, writing in the 1740s, claims that in his speech to the Assembly of the Land on 27 April 1682 Patriarch Joachim argued that Ivan was 'simple-minded and in poor health [skorben glavoiu i slab v zdravii]; he cannot rule the tsardom because he is afflicted, and on account of his corporal frailty'.[16]

Contemporary evidence and the consensus of later writers, then, seems to confirm that Ivan had a visual handicap (a staple ingredient of accounts, although details differ) and a speech impediment and was 'feeble'.[17] Slow-wittedness is also indicated, although it is probably impossible now to diagnose the precise nature of Ivan's handicap. W. Bruce Lincoln pronounced him to be a victim of Down's Syndrome, a diagnosis suggested, perhaps, by the fact that Ivan's mother was over forty when he was born.[18]

Do portraits offer any further clues to what was wrong with Ivan? In the 1680s the art of portrait painting in Russia was still in its infancy and the few images of Ivan produced during the regency are all of a stylised nature, focusing on the regalia and symbols of tsardom rather than the personal attributes of the ruler. One such was the miniature from the manuscript book The Coronation Ceremony of Tsars Ivan and Peter, completed in 1683, in which the artist followed the conventions of the 1672 Book of Titles.[19] Another is the 1685 L'Armessin engraving in which both tsars, wearing fur hats and cloaks, appear virtually identical, except that Peter is shown full face, Ivan in profile.[20] The allegorical engravings produced by the Ukrainian artist Ivan Shchirsky offer similarly stylised images.[21] The most frequently reproduced portrait of Ivan is a much later oil painting by an anonymous artist.[22] Although the pose is rigid, the picture is not obviously that of an 'imbecile', indeed it would have been astonishing if the artist had dared to convey such an impression. There is an eighteenth-century copy of this painting in the museum at Zagorsk. A Soviet commentator described the man portrayed as 'thick-lipped, languid, and weak-willed, with heavy-lidded eyes'.[23]

Ivan's disabilities did not prevent him from carrying out ceremonial duties right up to the year of his death, and during the regency he appeared in public more frequently than Peter. It was important for Sophia that Ivan should embody at least part of the image of the ideal Muscovite Tsar – the pious defender of the Orthodox faith. As long as he was mobile and in the public eye Sophia had a role as his substitute in those areas of rulership that he was unfit to undertake. By the end of the regency, as we shall see, Sophia was increasingly to duplicate and even to usurp Ivan's ceremonial role, too.

There was another role for Ivan to play that was even more essential to Sophia's political future – that of continuer of the Miloslavsky line. If contemporary Russian sources were unforthcoming on Ivan's physical and mental ailments, they are positively taciturn on matters of sexual prowess. Suffice it to say that a bride was found (the political benefits to her relatives of access to the inner circle of the court allowed the girl selected no say in the matter) and on 9 January 1684 Ivan was married to twenty year-old Praskovia Fedorovna Saltykova.[24] Her clan was already amongst the wealthiest in Russia, with a hereditary claim to membership of the boyar duma. Tsaritsa Praskovia was to outlive her husband by more than twenty-five years and to become a well-known character at the court of Peter the Great.

Not until March 1689 did the marriage produce a child, a daughter, which was a remarkably long wait for the time. Le Neuville, ever quick to sniff a scandal, claims that Sophia eventually gave up hope of Ivan doing the necessary and presented Praskovia with a lover. It was her plan, he writes, first to enjoy the political capital gained from a Miloslavsky heir, but then to force Ivan to repudiate his unfaithful wife and her bastard, giving Sophia a free hand to go on ruling.[25] There is no evidence to corroborate this illogical scheme, nor were any aspersions cast upon the legitimacy of Ivan's second daughter Anna, who became Empress of Russia in 1730. The ill-fated infant Emperor Ivan VI (the grandson of Ivan's elder daughter Ekaterina) was also a direct descendant of the marriage.

In contrast to the paucity of material available on Ivan, so much has been written about Peter's boyhood and youth that there seems little point in repeating it here except to warn that the subject is replete with myths and that most of the eulogies to the Great Tsar as adolescent were written in retrospect. To quote but one of the more extreme examples of the genre, P.N. Krekshin, writing his 'Short description of the blessed deeds of Peter the Great' long after the Tsar's death, included the story that on the morning after Peter's conception the court poet, Simeon Polotsky, predicted to the mother- and father-to-be that Peter would rule Russia and that 'there would be no ruler in the world to match him'.[26] Contemporary evidence from 1682, however, gives no grounds to suggest that the boyars regarded the nine-year-old as outstanding, still less as a future Reformer. He simply looked a better prospect than Ivan, and a means of counteracting Miloslavsky power. Still, let Peter be given his due. The descriptions provided by Kämpfer, Rinhuber and others show that Peter was handsome, lively, curious, and big for his age. From Sophia's point of view, these attributes gave him a good chance of growing up, reaching his majority and dispensing with her services. La Neuville expressed it succinctly: 'The Princess forsaw all along that the Tsar Peter's life would one day be the ruin of her authority, and a dangerous obstacle to her ambition.'[27] After her downfall most writers accepted not only the charge that she had plotted to murder Peter but also that she had ill-treated and isolated him during her regency.

The first charge will be dealt with later. As for the second, it may be dismissed in part by the evidence of the palace records, which meticulously noted attendance at religious and state occasions. These show that Peter went to his fair share of church services and processions. When he was absent, more often later in the regency, other sources show that he was indulging in preferred activities, such as drilling troops and sailing boats, but was certainly not being persecuted, far less incarcerated, by Sophia. There is no basis for the accusation that Sophia 'stifled Peter's natural light',[28] neither did Peter himself ever accuse her of ill-treating him. Clearly, however, the relationship between half-brother and sister was not an easy one, and although there are many instances of Sophia and Ivan presiding jointly at ceremonies there are virtually none where Sophia accompanied Peter alone.

The male royals were greatly outnumbered by the female contingent, consisting of Sophia's two aunts, Anna and Tat'iana, five sisters and one half-sister and the widows of her father and brother: Natalia Naryshkina and Marfa Apraksina. Later, their numbers were further swelled by the arrival of the wives of Ivan and Peter, in 1684 and 1689 respectively. All these women enjoyed a degree of token power insofar as they were listed in order of seniority in oaths of allegiance taken to the royal family collectively, but none wielded any power outside the confines of the palace except on occasions when the ruling members of the household were absent. In July 1682, for example, when the royal party was on a tour of monasteries and estates, Tsarevna Tat'iana, who remained in Moscow, was asked to authorise certain matters.[29] Mostly the sisters and aunts kept a low political profile. The Polish *Diariusz*, almost the only contemporary source to pay them any attention, noted that Evdokia 'kept apart from affairs of state' and that Marfa 'did not interfere either'. Ekaterina wore hats and dresses in the Polish style and had discarded the traditional Russian caftan and hair plaited in a single braid. Feodosia was 'as pious as a nun' and lived with her aunt Tat'iana.[30] None of them ever married, although rumour has it that several took lovers.[31] Palace records show that they enjoyed a degree of financial freedom and embellished their Kremlin apartments and favourite monasteries and estates outside the capital. The events of 1698, recorded below, show that her sisters remained loyal to Sophia, and there is every reason to believe that they acted as her confidantes during the regency, although no records of conversations or letters survive.

Sophia's relationship with the 'hated stepmother' was another matter altogether, for Natalia Naryshkina, as mother of the crowned Tsar, was the only women in the palace to whom tradition might have accorded a degree of authority. But as we have seen, during and immediately after the May 1682 rebellion murder and exile deprived Natalia of the leading members of her clan, without whom no woman could hope to wield power even behind the scenes. The Tsaritsa seems to have accepted the new balance of power and devoted herself to looking after the personal safety and upbringing of her son. If there were any disputes with Sophia in the early years of the regency they were not recorded for posterity.

The under-aged tsars and their female relatives all enjoyed the honours and status of monarchs, but the day-to-day business of making policy and governing the state took place where it had always done, amongst the 'boyar elite', a few dozen men elevated either by birthright or royal favour to act as privy councillors, to lead the Tsar's armies and to head the *prikazy*, the government offices. The level of participation by the 'autocrat' was directly related to age, health, ability and personality and we may conclude that in the case of Ivan it was nil, in the case of Peter negligible until he started taking an interest in government affairs around 1688.

Within the elite upon whom Sophia relied, several names stand out, but none more prominently than that of Prince Vasily Vasil'evich Golitsyn, the chief statesman of her regency.[32] He has barely figured so far for the reason that it is hard to ascertain how close he was to Sophia before and during the events of May 1682. Some later commentators, as was mentioned earlier, claimed that the two had met at Tsar Fedor's sickbed and had formed an amorous liaison.[33] That such a relationship would have been out of keeping with the mores of Fedor's court has already been pointed out, as has the comparatively brief period of time that Golitsyn spent in the capital in the years 1676–82. Likewise, the case for viewing Golitsyn as one of the chief conspirators in the May rebellion does not bear scrutiny. His name scarcely figures in the accounts of contemporaries, even those hostile to Sophia like Andrei Matveev.

For our purposes, then, Golitsyn's documented association with Sophia begins on 16/17 May 1682 when he was appointed Director of the Foreign Office. The new appointment was necessitated by the murder of former Director Larion Ivanov on 15 May. The choice of Golitsyn to replace him was entirely in keeping with the Prince's distinguished lineage and service record. Not only was the Golitsyn clan one of those which had hereditary claim to membership of the boyar duma, but Vasily Vasil'evich had himself been a boyar since 1676, had served in the Ukraine in 1672–8 and again in 1680–1 as co-ordinator of Russian and Cossack officials in the region, had seen action at the siege of Chigirin by the Turks in 1677 and also had experience of civic office in the Artillery and High Court (Vladimir) Departments.

Perhaps more significant, just a few months before Fedor's death Golitsyn had headed the commission that abolished the Code of Precedence. It has been suggested that this role had a double edge, for whilst his promotion of her brother's policy brought Golitsyn to Sophia's attention, his willingness to discard the practice of making appointments on the basis of the lineage and service records of a candidate's ancestors may have alienated him from certain members of the upper nobility to which he himself belonged.[34] The argument goes that many members of the old aristocracy favoured the election of Peter in the hope of seeing a reversal of some of the 'meritocratic' trends noted at the end of Fedor's reign. Thus Golitsyn, almost alone of their number, found himself in the Miloslavsky camp.

This argument lacks consistency, however. As Robert Crummey has pointed out, in the four months between the May rebellion and Sophia's final clash with Ivan Khovansky in September, there were twenty-six new appointments to the duma, most of whom were hereditary contenders for high office with no obvious allegiance to a Miloslavsky 'faction'.[35] In other words, an unofficial Code of Precedence was still deeply ingrained. This also applied to most of the new appointments to government offices, as will be shown later. And so, far from being the mere beneficiary of favouritism, Golitsyn was actually unusually well qualified for his new position in an era when professional aptitude was still barely considered. Not only had his postings during Fedor's reign brought him into touch with Ukrainian and Turkish affairs, which were to remain the centre of foreign policy during the regency, but he also enjoyed the reputation of being a 'friend of foreigners' and having a command of foreign languages.[36]

It would seem, then, that it was a lucky combination of ancestry, ability and past loyalties to Sophia's brother that won Golitsyn the directorship of the most important chancellery in the land. He was also, incidentally, through his marriage to Evdokia Ivanovna Streshneva, linked to one of the most powerful patronage and influence networks at court. (An earlier Evdokia Streshneva had been married to Tsar Mikhail.) More honours were to follow: the directorships of the chancelleries in charge of foreign servicemen and cavalry in December 1682 and the award of the title 'Guardian of the great royal seal and the state's great ambassadorial affairs.'[37] If further proof of Golitsyn's prominence is needed, one need only consult the listings of duma members in attendance on the tsars on state occasions to see how often his name figures. But although foreigners often referred to him as 'First Minister', no formal title existed in seventeenth-century Russia, nor were Golitsyn's duties neatly defined. Sophia may have proved herself a good judge of talent by exploiting his abilities in the field of foreign affairs, but he was to prove less adept at bringing home military honours or at providing the ruthless support that would have been needed to keep Sophia in power after 1689.

A rather different profile is presented by Ivan Miloslavsky, that 'most cunning of men with a great talent for intrigue', that 'scorpion' whom Andrei Matveev singled out as the ringleader of the May rebellion.[38] Despite the fact that he was Sophia's kinsman and was more active than Golitsyn in the events that brought her to power, Miloslavsky's influence diminished rather than increased once the unrest was quelled. In his study of the 'Khovanshchina', S.K. Bogoiavlensky suggests that 'Sophia's imperious character would not allow her to share power even with a close relative,'[39] but it is even more likely that Miloslavsky was forced to step into the background because of a personal feud with Prince Ivan Khovansky. At the end of Fedor's reign, Miloslavsky had been in charge of the Treasury departments, the *bol'shaia kazna* and *bol'shoi prikhod*, but on 17 May he relinquished his posts to Prince N.I. Odoevsky, taking up instead the directorship of the Artillery, Foreign Servicemen's and Cavalry Departments.[40] On 25 May he gave up even these posts to F.S. Urusov, who was by all accounts a supporter of Peter's camp. Can one detect the influence of Ivan Khovansky in this stripping of Miloslavsky's *prikaz* posts, or in the fact that he did not play a leading role in the coronation ceremonies on 25 June?

Whatever the case, Sophia did not restore Miloslavsky to a government post after the execution of Khovansky in September, but employed him in a ceremonial and perhaps advisory role. Numerous entries in the palace records confirm that he retained his position of honour in the royal household: on 18 August 1683 he headed the party of boyars accompanying Tsar Ivan to the Donskoi Monastery; on 2 September his name appears fourth in the entourage on a visit to Vladimir and Suzdal'; in May 1684 he attended Sophia during a reception of Swedish ambassadors.[41] In diary entries for 8 January and 25 April 1684 Patrick Gordon lists Miloslavsky amongst the persons whom he petitioned for leave to go to Scotland.[42] Miloslavsky evidently remained at the heart of the court circle, perhaps in honourable retirement. He died on 26 July 1685.

The greatest temporary gains from the May rebellion were undoubtedly made by the Khovanskys, none of whom had previously held high office, despite a lineage which could be traced to Prince Gedymin of Lithuania. Prince Ivan Andreevich (date of birth unknown) had been a boyar since 1659 but had spent most of his career since 1650 acting as military governor in the provinces, for example in Tula, Viazma, Mogilev, Pskov, Novgorod and Smolensk.[43] In 1663 and 1667–78 he had directed the *iamskoi prikaz*, the department responsible for transport and communications. Nicknamed Tararui – 'windbag' or 'braggart' – he had been described as 'courageous to the point of insanity', and was best remembered for some disastrous campaigns in the wars against Poland and Turkey. From 1669–1681 he had been almost permanently away from the capital and thus cut off from the sovereigns' ear and patronage networks at court. Solov'ev summed up Khovansky thus: 'He was displeased with this age of Nashchokins, Matveevs, Iazykovs, Likhachevs, Naryshkins and Apraksins, and he longed for a time when all these people that he hated so much would disappear and he would at last receive the position he deserved.'[44]

It is by no means clear how a man so long away from the capital and without special links with the strel'tsy should in the space of a few weeks be referred to as their 'father', but by 16 May, when Heinrich Butenant spotted him talking with Sophia in the Kremlin, he was already sufficiently influential to be appointed Director of the Strel'tsy Department. His son Andrei, who had previously held no office, was made head of the Justice Department – the *sudnyi prikaz* – and on 24/25 June entered the duma with the rank of boyar. Other Khovansky promotions were to follow, with Peter Ivanovich (8 July) and Ivan Ivanovich (29 August) being raised directly to boyar rank.[45]

With the notable exception of the Khovansky clan, almost all the other appointments made by Sophia in 1682 followed traditional lines, for there was no way she could afford to offend those clans who conventionally helped to rule Russia, even those who had openly supported Peter on 27 April. Matveev included the Odoevsky, Troekurov, Urusov and Sheremetev clans amongst those who had lent overt support to Tsaritsa Natalia,[46] but Odoevskys continued to hold the offices in which they had served before the May rebellion – namely the Pharmacy, Royal Household (*bol'shoi dvorets*), Royal Justice (*dvortsovyi sudnyi*), Kazan and Grain Departments – and N.I. Odoevsky briefly replaced Ivan Miloslavsky in the Treasury. Prince I.B. Troekurov became head of the important Service Estates Department (*pomestnyi prikaz*) on 17 May, and on 21 June P.V. Sheremetev took over in the Armoury (*oruzheinaia palata*), the royal workshop. By no stretch of the imagination could any of these individuals be numbered amongst the Miloslavsky 'faction'. On the contrary, as Bogoiavlensky comments: 'Never before had the upper echelons of the Muscovite bureaucracy had such a markedly aristocratic character, or included in its ranks so many representatives of the upper crust of the boyar elite as after the rebellion of the strel'tsy, which had been directed against the despotism of those very same boyars.'[47]

Appointments to and promotions within the boyar duma, which did not in themselves entail specific duties, tell a slightly different story, for here Sophia may have allowed herself a little more leeway in rewarding supporters. Between 25 June and 25 December 1682 there were thirty-five new appointments to the duma, which compared with ten and eleven for the whole of 1680 and 1681 respectively, as well as a number of promotions.[48] Alongside the conventional crop of candidates from Moscow's leading families, who would expect promotion in a coronation year, some less familiar names appeared, for example Maksim Isaevich Sumbulov (made a *dumnyi dvorianin* – state councillor – on 27 July), who was reputedly the only person to shout out in support of Tsarevich Ivan on 27 April; members of the Khitrovo clan, who were probably promoted thanks to links with the Miloslavskys;[49] and Prince V.P. Prozorovsky (boyar, 29 June), whose sister was married to Ivan Miloslavsky. On the other hand, it would be misleading to attribute the promotion of Golitsyns (for example, A.I. Golitsyn to boyar on 27 June) to narrowly factional motives as the clan had virtually automatic access to the duma.

Finally, one might single out the name of a man who was to rise to prominence and notoriety only later in the regency, Fedor Leont'evich Shaklovity, a 'bureaucratic specialist' (Crummey's term) who had begun his career in Tsar Aleksei's Secret Chancellery.[50] On 23 July he entered the duma with the rank of state secretary. In July he was V.G. Semenov's deputy in the Crown Appointments Department (Razriad), and by December 1682 was Director of the crucial Strel'tsy Department, one of a handful of non-aristocrats to hold such an office. The bureaucratic specialist corps was a growing band, brought into being by the increasingly complex requirements of government. Shaklovity had thus risen up through legitimate channels and only later in the regency did he attain the position of 'second favourite'.

Another stratum of the inner circle was the court, whose personnel overlapped to a considerable extent with the military commanders and bureaucrats of the boyar duma. Vasily Golitsyn, for example, was frequently required to play a role in state ceremonials. Others confined their duties exclusively to service in the royal household, for example Peter Ivanovich Prozorovsky and Boris Gavrilovich Iushkov, 'tutors' (*d'iadki*) to Tsar Ivan, and Rodion Matveevich Streshnev, (a member of Tsar Aleksei's mother's clan) who attended Peter. Ivan Miloslavsky, as was noted earlier, seems to have moved in 1682 from state to court duties. The influence of these and other 'privy councillors' (*blizhnie liudi*) is impossible to calculate, but in some cases it may have been considerable. Posts such as chamberlain (*postel'nichii*) and steward (*kaz-*

*nachei*) allowed access both to the royal ear and to useful information.

There was another important base of authority in Moscow. This was the Orthodox Church, whose current head, Patriarch Joachim, had personally initiated the election of Peter on 27 April. At the end of May he had acquiesced in the expedient of joint rule, quoting examples from scripture and Classical history to sanction the arrangement. On the face of it, Joachim should have wholly approved Sophia's devotion to the Church and her subsequent harsh treatment of religious dissidents. With the advantage of hindsight, it might even be said that in Peter he backed the wrong horse, from the Church's standpoint at least. But it seems possible that Joachim, an arch conservative, was offended by female rule. As the regency proceeded he was to be further alienated by Sophia's authorisation of the entry of Jesuits into Moscow and by the increasing reliance upon foreigners for military leadership.

Moreover, Sophia was a pupil of Simeon Polotsky, whose influence Joachim had resented and whose publications were later banned on suspicion of heresy.[51] After Polotsky's death in 1680 his place as Sophia's spiritual and theological mentor was taken by the monk Silvester Medvedev (1641–91).[52] Much better educated and more sophisticated than the Patriarch, Medvedev based his theological studies and arguments on knowledge of Western, mainly Polish Catholic sources. In addition, his mastery of poetics allowed him to laud Sophia's virtues as both a Christian and a secular ruler. Medvedev's adherence can only have served to alienate Joachim further from Sophia's camp, for Medvedev was regarded as the leader of 'Latinising' trends that the Patriarch's circle firmly opposed. Thus a woman who was irreproachably pious and devout failed to win over a crucial pillar of support.

What position did Sophia herself hold in the interlocking power structures of court, state and Church? Her legal status at the beginning of the regency, as noted earlier, was ill defined, indeed, if one accepts the theory of A.P. Bogdanov, there may even have been no formal declaration of a regency as such.[53] But contemporary evidence leaves little doubt that Sophia was the real source of authority in the palace: Butenant's sighting of her in the Kremlin on 16 May, her appearance at the dispute with the Old Believers on 5 July, the addressing of the anonymous letter denouncing the Khovanskys for her eyes only, these and other examples tend to confirm her pre-eminence. The anonymous Polish diarist, in his listing of the members of the royal family 'in the present year of 1683' writes: 'She rules in Moscow with the boyars, having raised her brother Ivan to the throne. . . . She guards Ivan so well that he never goes anywhere and no one visits him without her leave. The boyar councils likewise cannot be called without her, both on affairs of state and for private cases.'[54]

Sophia's regular attendance at the council is confirmed by a number of entries in state documents. On 2 March 1683, for example, at a session which formulated procedures for rounding up fugitive peasants, 'the great sovereign tsars [titles] and their sister the Sovereign Lady, Pious Tsarevna and Great Princess Sophia Alekseevna having listened to these articles, indicated and the boyars assented.'[55] Rescripts sent to foreign rulers abroad made no mention of Sophia.[56] but foreigners on the spot quickly became aware of her power. Georg Adam Schleissing, for example, in the earliest-known version (1687) of a work later published in many editions, wrote that, although Peter and Ivan occupied the throne, neither made any decisions. Everything was decided by the Tsarevna and the magnates. 'It is as clear as day to many people that she is gifted with a high degree of talent for governing.'[57] By the time Schleissing left Russia in 1686 Sophia was ruler not just in fact but in name also, as will be shown later. Until then, however, all rescripts were issued in the joint names of great sovereign tsars and great princes Ivan Alekseevich and Peter Alekseevich, even though it was recognised that Ivan could never take part in decision-making and Peter was still too young to do so.

Visitors to the Armoury Museum in the Kremlin can still see the double throne with its curtained window in the back, through which Sophia is said to have whispered instructions to the two tsars. It seems most unlikely that Sophia herself would have undertaken such as task (although attendants may on occasion have used the window to prompt the boys during diplomatic receptions), but this throne, occupied by under-aged 'puppet' rulers, is a marvellous symbol of the 'façade' of Muscovite autocracy. Behind the curtain lay a time-honoured and complex power structure based on personal relationships rather than institutions. The interconnecting and overlapping ruling elites of royal family, boyar council, bureaucracy, army and court, bound by patronage networks and marriage links, formed a formidable patriarchal power base which could not easily be undermined by any one individual, as the Khovansky incident had demonstrated, and which was little influenced by 'class' interests. Personal relationships had been one of the factors determining the course and outcome of the 1682 rebellion, and such relationships were to continue to be crucial to a government headed *de facto* by someone whose status – that of unmarried woman – had hitherto been one of the most powerless, given that women usually influenced and moderated power relations only through marrying, producing heirs or, occasionally, presiding as dowagers. That Sophia performed none of these roles makes the seven-year duration of the regency that was to follow doubly remarkable. The events and developments of those years, up to but excluding her overthrow, and the record of her government at home and abroad are the subject of the following four chapters.

CHAPTER 5

# Domestic Policy

Sophia's regency has enjoyed a mixed reputation. Prince Boris Kurakin, who lived through it, claimed that the government 'was administered with great energy and justice, and was much to the people's liking; never had there been such a wise regime in the Russian realm. And during the seven years of her rule the country reached a pinnacle of prosperity.'[1] Compare this opinion with that of the historian Nikolai Ustrialov, published in 1858: 'In the acts issued in the seven years of her rule we find nothing of any significance either for the benefit of society, or for the growth of the nation's industrial forces, or for its education; there is nothing to match those enactments which distinguished the reigns of Aleksei Mikhailovich and Fedor Alekseevich, and there can be no comparison with the far-sighted wisdom of Peter.'[2] C.B. O'Brien saw 'a government of unusual distinction and promise, which pursued with intelligence and imagination the interests of Russia abroad and introduced reforms at home which are usually believed to have originated in succeeding generations,'[3] in sharp contrast to the anonymous author who more than a hundred years previously had complained of 'seven years of unmitigated horrors.'[4] In the footsteps of O'Brien, Z. Schakovskoy agreed that Sophia's regime was distinguished by 'the spirit of logic that guided her reforms and the methodical manner in which she straightened out the country's tangled affairs.'[5] It is hard to believe that these critics and admirers are referring to the same era.

Few assessments of Sophia and her government, as we shall see later, can be read in isolation from the thought and philosophy of the eras which produced them, or without reference to attitudes to Peter the Great. The few Western historians who have tackled the period have tended to be over-dependent on secondary sources and too uncritical of contemporary writings, particularly foreigners' accounts. The reputation of Sophia's regency as an era of 'reform,' for example, has its roots in a single source, Foy de la Neuville's *Relation curieuse*, first published in 1698, with its much quoted tribute to Vasily Golitsyn as a man who longed to 'colonise deserts, enrich beggars, transform savages into men, cowards into heroes and herdsmen's huts into stone palaces.'[6]

Even a cursory glance at such printed primary sources as the *Complete Collection of Russian Laws* or *Historical Acts*, however, suggests that at home Sophia's regime was concerned with much the same issues as its predecessors, occupied with much the same national priorities as the compilers of the twenty-five chapters of Tsar Aleksei's law code (*Ulozhenie*) of 1649.[7] In other words, a good deal of the energy of the government and its officials was channelled into establishing and exacting service requirements and tax liabilities from the population, regulating the closely related areas of ownership of land, serfs and slaves, and maintaining law and order in respect of threats to the safety of sovereign and Church, if not to the person of the individual, who counted for little. In a decade when Russian was to enter the Holy League against the Turks, which involved two lengthy and costly campaigns in the south, military requirements were, as they had been throughout the century, the prime motive for all government action. If we add to this the 'caretaker' role of Sophia's regime, based as it was on the 'minority' of the two legitimate rulers, then the scope for radical social or political reform looks distinctly limited. Sophia came to power in May 1682 ostensibly to restore order, that is to maintain the status quo, not to reform it, and her record must be examined first and foremost in the context of traditional Muscovite needs and requirements.

Determining the boundaries, population and usage of the landed estates was one of the continuing, routine tasks which faced the new government. In 1676 a general survey had been initiated in order to update the land registers or cadastres (*pistsovye knigi*), which were last completed in the 1630s. The exercise got as far as taking a census of homesteads and inhabitants, statistics which in 1679 Tsar Fedor's government decreed would form the basis of tax assessment per peasant household until the survey was completed.[8] Attempts to finish the job continued throughout Sophia's regency, as evidenced by the long decree of April 1684 setting out procedures for the updating of the cadastres.[9] One of the methods for establishing boundaries was the deployment of land surveyors (*mezhevshchiki*), as laid down in articles 50–3 of Chapter XVII of the *Ulozhenie*, an exercise which cost much time and effort. In July 1682 surveyors had been sent out all over Russia by the Department of Service Estates,[10] which anticipated a degree of resistance by issuing on 7 July a list of penalties for anyone who destroyed or moved border markers.[11]

Evidently the arrival of the surveyors was not universally welcomed, least of all by those nobles who feared a decrease in their holdings or the discovery of undeclared assets, or who resented the liability to feed and lodge the agents. The government was torn between fears of loss of revenues and the desire not to alienate the service gentry. In May 1683 it issued a forty-five article decree on surveying, specifying penalties of the knout, prison and fines for those who impeded the surveyors' work, or for surveyors who were persuaded by bribes to cook the books.[12] Then in July of the same year the Estates Department was ordered to foot the bill for the surveyors' upkeep 'in order that landowners should not sustain great losses and nobody be offended.'[13] In June 1686 it was ordered that landowners who abused surveyors and stole their measuring tapes should be flogged in public,[14] and in Many 1688 local governors were ordered to intervene in cases of dispute and to carry out the measuring themselves.[15] The affair evidently dragged on beyond the regency and into the next century, when Peter the Great finally aban- doned cadastral surveys and the homestead taxation system, which was comparatively easy to abuse, in favour of the poll or head tax.

Acts dealing with the inheritance of landed estates abound in the documentation of the period, not surprisingly given the complications occasioned by the absence of primogeniture. Examples include settle- ment of relatives' claims to dowry estates after the death of a wife,[16] the division of estates between children of different wives,[17] the general question of married women's property rights,[18] of escheated estates,[19] and so on. There is evidence here and elsewhere that the nobles were coming more and more to regard the land as their own personal property, a trend encouraged by the tendency to elide the categories of hereditary (*votchina*) and service tenure (*pomest'ie*) estates. Although the crown continued in principle to regard the 'Russian land' as its own 'patrimonial' property (*otchina*), which subjects held conditionally, it, too, came to maintain only a formal distinction between hereditary and service tenure, and by the end of the seventeenth century the two had become indistinguishable. Service estates were being passed on to male heirs, left as provision for windows and unmarried daughters, even sold. In 1714 the legal distinction was abolished altogether.[20]

Even so, the link between service to the crown and tenure of land was not lost entirely, nor could it be as long as the liability of the provincial nobility to state service was based on the number of peasant households owned. Sophia's regime continued the time-honoured practice of distributing estates to servitors as rewards (after the 1682 'troubles', the 1686 peace with Poland, the Crimean campaigns), and the formal upgrading of *pomest'ia* into *votchiny*.[21] In reverse, confiscation of estates remained, along with banishment, a standard penalty for noble offenders, as such notable individuals as Artamon Matveev and Vasily Golitsyn found to their cost. It was to be another hundred years before Catherine II's Charter to the Nobility of 1785 awarded the Russian *dvorianstvo* and their heirs rights of tenure and exploitation of their land equivalent to those enjoyed by their Western peers.

From the government's point of view, the collection of tax revenues and the exaction of service requirments remained high-priority issues. Efficient assessment and discharging of liabilities depended to a large extent upon the accurate and hereditary categorisation of all the tsars' subjects into estates or classes (*sosloviia*), the components of the so-called 'service state', in order that no one should slip through the net. During Sophia's regency there was no change in the basic divisions of society, but on occasions the authorities had to arbitrate in cases of reclassification, as in the case of serfs who had fled to the towns and had succeeded in being counted with the town tax-paying community, members of which protested that if the newcomers were returned to their owners (as stipulated in Chapter 11, Article 2 of the *Ulozhenie*), the remaining town-dwellers would be unable to meet their collective tax demand. An act of December 1685 decided in favour of the towns-people, decreeing that 'the newcomers shall enjoy the immutable right of residence in the urban community [*posad*] and pay their taxes and render services on the same basis as the urban dwellers', but fugitives who arrived subsequently were to be prosecuted and returned forthwith in order to halt the trend.[22]

It would be wrong to regard this act as emancipatory. Russian towns were not havens of freedom. On the contrary, the townspeople enjoyed no rights of movement and were as securely tied to their urban estates and duties as were the peasants to their rural ones.[23] As the act of 1685 illustrates, liabilities were discharged communally, thus pressure to maintain full ability to pay by discouraging individuals from absconding was exerted not only by the government but also by fellow tax-payers. In a similar case in reverse, in October 1683 tradespeople who had adopted the status of rent-paying (*obrochnye*) peasants in order to escape the urban community tax were prosecuted.[24] A decree of August 1682 arbitrated in the case of a group of people who wavered between the status of agricultural labourers and artillerymen (*pushkari*), apparently as it suited them. It was decided that they were more usefully employed as labourers.[25] The taking out of voluntary contracts of bondage by persons attempting to avoid tax and service obligations to the state was also carefully supervised, for example in a case involving newly baptised tribute-paying natives.[26] Article 7 of instructions to land surveyors issued in 1686 specified that slaves living and farming outside their owners' households should be included in the cadastres of tax-payers.[27] There is a common principle at work in all these cases: the assignation of all subjects to immutable, hereditary estates, with defined service and monetary obligations, a trend which was further strengthened during the reign of Peter I when the service of the nobility was institutionalised in the Table of Ranks.

When it suited them, the authorities occasionally demonstrated some flexibility in the assignation of their subjects to estates, but, as in the case of the town-dwelling peasants mentioned above, this did not extend to 'emancipationist' sentiments. The rulers of the 1680s did not deviate from the vital articles in the 1649 *Ulozhenie* which had ended the peasants' rights to leave their owners and reduced them to the status of hereditary bondsmen. It would have been surprising if Sophia and her government had made concessions in the matter of serfdom, given the hostile environment created by the rebellion of 1682 and associated unrest in the countryside, which could be tackled only by reasserting common interests with the magnates and the provincial gentry.[28] In February 1683, for example, bondslaves who had claimed their freedom during the 'troubles' were sentenced to be flogged with the knout and restored to their rightful masters.[29] If the latter rejected them, they were to be sent to Siberia. In March 1683 a fifty-two article decree on the rounding up of fugitive serfs and slaves and their restoration to their owners was drawn up by I.B. Troekurov in the Service Estates Department. This act strengthened the powers of the sheriffs or 'bounty hunters' (*syshchiki*), and attempted to improve mechanisms for deciding claims and counterclaims to ownership of serfs.[30] The 1680s saw the issue of a number of decrees setting fines and penalties for those who lured or harboured runaways, equating such acts with theft or robbery.[31] Serf-owners were in general gaining more leeway in the sale, exchange, gift and bequeathal of peasants without land, as the peasants were more and more reduced to the level of moveable property, like cattle.[32]

Faced with such evidence, what are we to make of Foy de la Neuville's report that Vasily Golitsyn (himself a major serf-owner), in order to achieve his aim of 'setting this state on a par with all the others, had memoranda collected on all the countries of Europe and their governments; he wished to start by liberating the peasants and turning over to them the lands which they now cultivate for the profit of the Tsar in return for an annual tribute, which, according to the calculations he had made, would have augmented the annual revenue to these princes by more than a half'?[33] Some have taken this bold scheme to be simply another example of the exaggeration in which La Neuville's eulogy to the man who wished to 'transform savages into men' abounds, for example his description of Golitsyn's mansion, which was rather modest by Western standards, as 'one of the most magnificent in Europe'.[34] La Neuville's admiration for the Prince was prompted largely by Golitsyn's patronage of Jesuits in particular and Catholics in general. But the information on the emancipation scheme deserves serious consideration because it appears not with the stylised eulogy to Golitsyn but in the final section of La Neuville's work, which draws upon information supplied by the Foreign Office official Nikolai Spafarius (Milescu), a close associate of Golitsyn's.[35]

We know from other sources that Golitsyn did indeed consult and obtain 'memoranda' from foreigners, some of whom (Johann van Keller, Patrick Gordon and Laurent Rinhuber, for example) many well have pointed out the disadvantages of peasant bondage. Golitsyn's library had a copy of the sixteenth-century Polish writer Andrzej Modrzewski's *Commentariorium de republica emendata*, a work which includes arguments for the extension of rights of land ownership to categories other than the gentry (*szliachta.*)[36] The context in which La Neuville's information occurs also gives a further clue to its real meaning. It appears in a section on the exploitation of Siberia, an area in which serfdom had never taken root. This fact, and the reference to lands worked 'for the profit of the Tsar', suggests that the peasants Golitsyn had in mind were not the private serfs of the nobility, but peasants on crown and state lands. The proposal looks very much like an attempt to replace the corvée (*barshchina*) system, whereby the peasants worked the lord's land, with the more flexible quitrent or *obrok*, which entailed payment of dues in money and/or kind. Golitsyn's chief concern, as demonstrated by his involvement in the abolition of the Code of Precedence in 1682, was with Russia's defence needs, with improving the efficiency of the military machine. This priority took on personal overtones in the period 1687–9 when Golitsyn organised and led two major campaigns against the Turks. This preoccupation is confirmed by a piece of information which occurs earlier in La Neuville's work: 'his [Golitsyn's] design was to change into good soldiers the legions of peasants whose lands remain uncultivated when they are led away to war, and instead of this useless state service to impose on each head a reasonable sum'.[37]

What Golitsyn seems to have had in mind was the more efficient and systematic exploitation of the efforts not only of peasants but also of nobles through the further development of the professional army and the imposition of a poll tax, measures which formed the basis of Peter's reforms. During Fedor's reign Golitsyn had shown his commitment to ending the 'duality' which had existed in the Russian army since the 1630s when new-formation regular troops, mostly infantry led by foreign officers, began to fight alongside and with time predominate over the old-style gentry cavalry, who were mostly ill-trained, unsure of modern firearms, poorly-equipped and slow to mobilise.[38] The period 1680–2 had seen further attempts to regularise and professionalise military service and increase the merit principle, but the schemes were only partially successful. The Code of Precedence was abolished 'for all time', but clan disputes over slighted honour continued into the 1680s and beyond. A scheme mooted in 1681–2 for the division of duties between military, civil and court ranks, with a system of permanently appointed viceroys for provincial administration, never got off the ground, ostensibly because of the objections of the Patriarch, who feared the weakening of 'God-given' autocratic rule, but probably in reality because Golitsyn even then was politically isolated and the provincial gentry may have objected to the idea of permanently stationed, powerful local magnates interfering in their affairs.[39]

If there is little sign of abolitionist thinking during Sophia's regency, what of her admirers' claims that the government exercised a 'civilising' influence in the area of law and order? O'Brien, for example, believed that Sophia and Golitsyn encouraged the introduction of a 'milder' penal code, citing the abolition of the death penalty for 'seditious utterances' (*vozmutitel'nye slova*), and the mitigation of punishment by mutilation.[40] In March 1683 the knout and banishment were indeed substituted for the death penalty in the case of the former offence, possibly because there were so many instances of this particular crime in the wake of the 1682 rebellion,[41] but it is difficult to reach such a positive conclusion on the question of mutilation, which the *Ulozhenie* had prescribed for a number of offences. In an act of 28 November 1682, for example, it was specified that criminals who confessed (after torture) to one robbery, without accompanying murder or arson, were to be sentenced to flogging with the knout, the removal (as a tagging device) of the left ear and two little fingers on the left hand, and banishment to Siberia. The penalty for one theft (*tat'ba*: the code distinguished between this and *razboi*, robbery) was the same. For two thefts the penalty was in accordance with the *Ulozhenie* (XXI, article 10), for three – death.[42] In March 1983, however, it was specified that only ears were to be cut off, not fingers.[43] It is hard to put a 'humane' interpretation on a mere redesignation of the parts of the body to be removed. A famous case revised the practice (*Ulozhenie* XXII, article 14) of burying alive wives who had murdered their husbands. In February 1689 two women were sentenced to be beheaded instead of suffering the traditional punishment, 'and henceforward such women as murder their husbands should not be interred'.[44] The practice seems to have continued, however, until the 1740s,[45] when the Empress Elizabeth made genuine efforts to establish a milder code, including the abolition of the death penalty.

Notwithstanding a few such isolated instances, the case for the 'mildness' of Sophia's regime is undermined by the savage measures adopted against religious dissidents, the so-called Old Believers, which are discussed in the next chapter.[46] Torture remained the standard method of extracting both confessions from criminals and evidence from witnesses, and the documents of the period 1682–9 seem no less full of references to floggings, beatings, beheadings, racks, tongs and fire than those of its predecessors. One recalls Sophia's peremptory order for the executions of the Khovanskys in 1682. Even the allegedly 'mild' Golitsyn attended torture sessions of Old Believers in the Foreign Office. This was an age, in Russia as elsewhere, when squeamishness about such procedures would have been a distinct disadvantage.

Individual acts of clemency remained, as ever, within the tsar's gift. In April 1684, for example, a workman by the name of Stepan Kolosov killed a peasant during a fight. He was sentenced to death, after he had appealed on the grounds that the crime had not been premeditated, but on 29 June, Peter's nameday, the sentence was commuted to a fifty-rouble fine, to be paid to the widow and children of his victim, and a vow not to murder again.[47] The crown could also show clemency in financial matters. In August 1682 people in Novgorod, Tver, Pskov and other towns were let off payment of some 157,062 roubles of tax arrears in memory of Tsars Aleksei and Fedor,[48] a tacit recognition, one suspects, that the money was never likely to be paid.

Perhaps the most positive aspect of the legislation of the period were the attempts to speed up the cumbersome judicial process, by specifying, for example, that trials were to take place within a fixed period, and by rationalising the jurisdiction of the many state departments and the functions of their officials, who, in the absence of separate courts or lawyers, administered justice. An extensive act of November 1685 attempted to improve trial procedures,[49] followed by another the month after aimed at clarifying the position of plaintiffs and litigants.[50] Further acts in January and February 1686 attempted to speed up procedures, for example by limiting the delays caused by having business in more than one government department.[51] In August 1687, it was resolved that cases of theft and robbery be dealt with in the Police (*zemskii*) rather than the Investigations (*sysknoi*) Department.[52] None of this amounted to much more than patching up a system which made no distinction between judges and functionaries. Golitsyn's scheme of 1681–2 for dividing civic and military ranks apparently also envisaged a twelve-member consultative chamber, a sort of higher court of appeal based on the Polish model, which would have refined and institutionalised the boyar council. After 1682 Golitsyn evidently had neither the confidence nor the time to reintroduce such a scheme.[53] Thus in the 1680s justice continued to be a hit-and-miss affair, characterised by 'neglect of legal norms in public administration, carried on by predominantly irresponsible and corrupt functionaries.'[54]

Some of the most fascinating documents of the period allow a glimpse of the violence and chaos which lurked behind the façade of good order and godliness carefully maintained in the public statements and rituals of Church and state. The security of the royal person remained a prime concern, as it had been in the *Ulozhenie* (Chapter III). In February

1684, it was deemed necessary to remind courtiers that, when the sovereigns 'deigned' to enter or leave the Kremlin, gentlemen were to stand aside, doff their caps and dismount from their horses.[55] In December 1684 a set of rules and regulations on access to the palace was drawn up, no doubt with the violations of May 1682 in mind. For example 'boyars, lords-in-waiting, gentlemen of the duma and courtiers have no business whatsoever' unless on special missions to approach the 'front staircase by the Kureshny gates which leads up to the chambers of the pious sovereign tsarevny, and from those chambers to cross the courtyard which is opposite the newly built stone chambers of the sovereigns, towards the royal workshops and past the Sovereign Lady Tsaritsa's workshops'. Certain staircases were designated for the delivery of food and drink at assigned times or for the entry of priests to the royal chapels.[56] Evidently, on certain occasions respect for the royal person had to be enforced, especially in the case of Tsar Ivan. In October 1684, for example, a number of boyars were placed under house arrest and another demoted for their failure to attend the Tsar during a procession.[57] In December an even larger number of courtiers were demoted for not joining Ivan's retinue during his autumn and winter excursions to out-of-town estates and monasteries.[58] In December the nobleman I.V. Dashkov was cautioned for using 'impolite language' in the palace.[59] The manners of Muscovite courtiers were generally less than polished.

There were attempts to curb unruliness outside the palace, too. In January 1683 times were specified for the locking and unlocking of the city gates, the use of whips and long reins in town was restricted (a frequent cause for complaint), and guards were told 'to conduct their watch peaceably and not engage in any unruly behaviour amongst themselves or to create a din or swear'.[60] An instruction of March 1686 (in anticipation of the arrival of a major Polish delegation) admitted that in some parts of town 'day and night people of various ranks shoot from rifles and let off grenades and rockets, thereby causing dangerous fires, so that even the strel'tsy are afraid to apprehend such people in their premises'.[61]

In many cases involving law and order the interests of Church and state were contiguous, as for example in licensing legislation, in which the period abounds.[62] Sacred and secular interests united in the sentence of beating with canes (batogi) imposed in June 1684 on a scribe who got drunk playing dice and gambled away or lost some government funds.[63] In other cases the interests of commerce clashed with the demands of godliness. In December 1682, for example, a ban was placed on the holding of fairs and markets on Sunday, an extension of the restriction (Ulozhenie, Chapter X, article 26) on the opening of shops.[64] In August 1684 an act was issued forbidding the sale of foodstuffs during processions of the Cross, and people were ordered to refrain from 'din, shouting and jostling'.[65] The latter decree simply repeats one of the articles approved by the Church Council of 1681/2, whose deliberations had revealed much corruption and disreputable behaviour amongst members of the religious orders.[66] Apparently there had been little improvement: in August 1684 peasants lodged a complaint against the monk Leonty from the St Sabbas Monastery, who 'in his lawlessness and naughtiness, forgetting the fear of God, ravished the wives of us men, your orphans. And this monk also insulted us by taking maidens from their fathers for his own immoral ends, corrupting them by fornication, then marrying them off against their will.' An enquiry was ordered.[67]

Patriarch Joachim carried on his own private battle with immorality and corruption both within the Church and without. On 24 December 1684 he issued a ban on entertainments during the Yuletide (*sviatki*) period, in particular the singing of 'devilish and diabolical songs', all forms of dancing, swearing and 'lustful improprieties'.[68] Joachim's strictures hark back to the puritanical campaign of the 'Zealots of Piety' during the early part of Tsar Aleksei's reign. As we shall see, with regard to the question of religious and cultural policy, there were a number of signs that the Church tried to make up for moral ground lost during the more relaxed later years of Aleksei's reign after his marriage to Natalia Naryshkina, which, it will be recalled, was celebrated with dancing and drinking in a 'Restoration' atmosphere.

We should not expect too much from this period in the way of social or welfare measure, although the Church ran some small-scale relief operations. In October 1682, for example, Patriarch Joachim ordered his friend Archbishop Afanasy of Kholmogory to send the sum of one *grivna* (ten kopeks) for every church in his diocese for the upkeep of almshouses and retreats established during Tsar Fedor's reign.[69] In general, however, the Russian Orthodox Church of the seventeenth century lagged well behind its Protestant and Catholic counterparts in providing for the sick and needy, whilst the crown appears to have shown little concern for such matters except when dispensing charity directly from the palace to mark namedays and other festivals or providing shelter in the royal apartments for selected dwarves and elderly women. In this respect there was a 'moral chasm' between Eastern and Western Christianity, a difference which struck many Russian travellers of the period quite forcefully, for example the nobleman Peter Tolstoi, who on his first trip abroad in 1697–8 made a point of describing in some detail the well-functioning hospitals, almshouses and orphanages that he observed in Italy and Austria.[70] As a recent study has shown, the lack of welfare facilities in Russia was to some extent compensated for by the institution of contract slavery, entered into voluntarily by those who fell upon hard times,[71] and monasteries and nunneries also offered support and shelter to those who entered them, although it should be noted that most initiates were required to make an entrance payment and inmates continued to depend upon gifts of food and clothing from relatives in the outside world. Prayer, not charity, remained the prime function of the Russian convent.

On the subject of environmental concerns, the usual view, ratified by foreigners' accounts, is that in an age still far removed from the revolution in plumbing, sanitation and personal hygiene, Russians and their towns lagged behind even their malodorous Western counterparts. Georg Adam Schleissing was not the first to remark that Moscow looked magnificent from afar, but as you got closer you observed:

> squalid dwellings, built without any system of architecture. The streets are not paved with stone, but just covered with logs, like wooden lanes. When there is even a light shower of rain, on account of people going to and fro on horseback the wood often crumbles away and such a stream of mud shoots up that it is difficult to pass even on horseback, especially in winter. And sometimes in really bad weather you can end up head over heels in the mud.[72]

Schleissing did, however, take note of Tsar Fedor's decrees on the building of houses in stone. Sophia's regime, too, was to urge the inhabitants of the centre of town to build their dwellings of masonry and use non-flammable roofing materials.[73] Schleissing probably left Moscow too soon (1686) to observe the construction, albeit by a small elite, of churches and palaces in the new Moscow Baroque style, in which even he would have detected a 'system of architecture'.[74]

Legislation on stone building reflected concern with fire prevention. In November 1683 a huge fire, apparently starting in Peter's quarters, swept the Kremlin, destroying the wooden apartments of the tsarevny and the Tsaritsa, and damaging some of the churches, the Patriarch's palace and other buildings.[75] This necessitated a large-scale programme of rebuilding and renovations. There were also some attempts to clean up the city. In December 1683 the selling of fish on Red Square was banned.[76] An act of March 1686 ordered that 'in Moscow all the streets and alleys be cleaned of manure and carrion and all manner of rubbish, and that it be swept up and transported beyond Zemliany Gorod', that is to the outskirts.[77] In March 1688 patrols were told to look out for 'excrement and carrion and [dead] dogs and cats and suchlike', and to make house-owners clear up the offending mess.[78]

La Neuville confirms that Moscow became a somewhat safer and more orderly city under Golitsyn's direction. He credited the Prince with building new premises for the Foreign Office, a stone bridge over the Moskva river and some 3,000 masonry dwellings.[79] He also reported in detail, mainly in the section based on Spafarius' information, on the Prince's plans for improving commerce, which included the development of the fur trade, notably by selling more sables abroad in order to earn hard (silver) currency with which to pay officers of the regular army. Trade routes to Siberia, China and Persia were to be opened up, both by land and waterways. A specific scheme was the setting up of staging posts, manned by peasants rewarded with land, and the maintenance of teams to keep the routes open in winter.[80]

Muscovite trade, both foreign and domestic, traditionally suffered from the heavy involvement of the crown and relatively poor development of financial institutions and individual enterprise, even the chief merchants or *gosti* spending much of their time acting as crown agents and running state businesses. According to La Neuville, however, Golitsyn was well aware of these failings and planned to foster the spirit of free enterprise by turning over more businesses to individuals, for example the state-run liquor houses, and other sales and commodities, 'thereby rendering people laborious and industrious in the hope of self-enrichment'.[81] There is little evidence, however, of any major change of policy in these areas. On the contrary, an act of October 1687 confirmed the 1681 decree which replaced the franchise (*otkup*) system of liquor sales by the procedure of sworn duty (*vernaia sluzhba*), in which agents working under oath paid in all receipts from liquor duties in a given area to the crown.[82] The state maintained its monopoly on liquor, as it did in other areas.

Genuine progress, albeit on a modest scale, seems to have been made only in the area of foreign trade and industry. The activities of foreign merchants in Muscovy were still governed by the New Commercial Treaty of 1667, which limited their participation in retail trade and imposed high tariffs.[83] Despite these restrictions, the hostility of native merchants and the difficulties of getting to Russia, a number of foreigners were attracted by the profits to be made from exporting furs, leather, pitch, potash, hemp, masts, grain and more exotic products such as caviar and rhubarb. Imports included wines (on which there were heavy duties), cloth (especially costly fabrics), dyes and spices.

With no merchant fleet of its own, the Russian government relied largely upon the foreign middlemen to run this trade, and Golitsyn seems to have made genuine efforts to facilitate their task. In a document of June 1682, for example, the government responded to complaints from Dutch and English merchants in Archangel over high port charges and poor servicing facilities.[84] Archangel, it should be noted, was Moscow's only port open to sea-going vessels, and then only from June to September. Golitsyn, as we have seen, had plans for opening up more routes. La Neuville reports that in 1687 Dutch shipwrights were sent to Astrakhan to build two frigates on the Caspian Sea, but the boats were burned by Tatars and not replaced.[85]

Golitsyn was also anxious to speed up communications with the West. In June 1684 a royal letter to the Military Governor of Novgorod complained that the post to Riga was getting slower and slower. Governors were instructed to punish those post drivers who carried the mail 'sluggishly and blunderingly, and henceforth to ensure that they ride from staging post to staging post with great speed day and night on good horses, and that they reach the staging posts at the times specified'.[86] The 1680s saw a number of commercial treaties or clauses on trade inserted into general treaties with foreign states, for example with Sweden, Prussia, Poland and China.[87] In 1687 customs barriers between Muscovy and the Ukraine were removed. In some other respects the government remained inflexible, however, for example failing to respond to pleas from Charles II and James II for the restitution of the 'privileges' stripped from the merchants of the Muscovy Company following the execution of Charles I in 1649.[88]

One of the most interesting cases of collaboration between the regime and foreign merchants is that of Arnut (Zakhar) Paulsson, who in 1681 had petitioned Tsar Fedor for a loan of 2000 roubles to allow him to bring workmen, instruments and materials from Hamburg for the manufacture of silks and fine fabrics.[89] His guarantor was fellow Hamburger Heinrich Butenant, the shrewd observer of the 1682 rebellion. Paulsson arrived back in Russia in December 1681 with eighteen workmen. His enterprise was set up in the Foreign Quarter under the jurisdiction of the Pharmacy Department. In return for the loan, which was to be paid back in annual instalments beginning in 1684, and the right to duty-free trade, Paulsson was to undertake to train Russians and to supply the needs of the palace for silks, velvets and satins before selling off any surplus.

When Sophia came to power she extended the royal patronage of Paulsson's factory. In February 1683 she wrote off 1,000 roubles of the loan when Paulsson complained of being in debt as a result of building work and purchase of materials, on the condition that he sell goods to the palace at a cheaper price than the usual foreign rate. In 1684 another 500 roubles had to be written off, and it transpired that only two of the foreigners originally hired remained in service, and even they were complaining of unpaid wages. As a result of Paulsson's failure to run the factory as a private enterprise, in November 1684 the works were transferred to Vasily Golitsyn in the Foreign Office. Under a new agreement Paulsson was to receive a salary from the state in return for supplying the palace with plain and printed silks and training at least eight Russian apprentices. Raw materials were to be supplied from the

Department of the Royal Treasury. Under the direct supervision of Golitsyn, the enterprise began to flourish, delivering regular supplies of fabric to the palace. In June 1689, for example, nineteen arshin and two chetvert of shot silk (*baiberek*) were delivered to Sophia's own apartments.[90] Much of the silk was used as gifts, Ukrainian Hetmans Samoilovich and Mazepa, Patriarch Joachim, Silvester Medvedev and the Likhud brothers being amongst the recipients. Golitsyn kept a special eye on the progress of the apprentices, in June 1687 ordering Paulsson to report on them, and personally conducting an examination of their competence. On this occasion the apprentices complained that they could not work properly without translations of foreign textbooks kept in the workshop, which Golitsyn undertook to have done. Paulsson himself was to be allowed to return home once training was completed.

It is interesting to note that with the overthrow of Sophia and the removal of Golitsyn's strict supervision, the enterprise fell into decline. There were reports of silk stolen and apprentices running riot. E. Lermontova, who wrote a study of the factory, comments: 'The government of Sophia Alekseevna devoted much more care and attention to the needs of Muscovite industry than the Naryshkin regime. . . . Not the Naryshkin period but the period of Sophia's regime has the better claim to be regarded as the preparatory period for the epoch of reform, and even as an epoch of reform in its own right.'[91] Lermontova's negative assessment of the 'interregnum' between Sophia's overthrow in 1689 and Peter's personal rule from the middle of the 1690s echoes the view of La Neuville: 'Those who had expressed most joy at the disgrace of the Great Golitsyn are nowadays perfectly aware of the loss they have suffered, because the Naryshkins who govern them now are all equally ignorant and barbaric and are beginning to destroy everything which this great man had done for the glory and the good of the nation.'[92]

Another enterprise, less well documented, was the textile works run by Elias (Ilia) Tabert, who in 1683 returned from abroad with six workmen from Brandenburg, Hamburg and Austria. This factory, too, was run under government patronage, with the same obligation upon the owner to train Russian workers in return for ten years of duty-free operation, granted in 1684 when Tabert was issued with a subsidy and charter to make 'cloth, serge, and other woollens'.[93] Other examples of foreign enterprise in operation during the regency were the Marselis iron works (dating from the reign of Tsar Aleksei) in Tula and Kashira, which produced cannon shells for the war against the Crimea.[94] The government maintained the practice, established in Tsar Aleksei's day, of sending foreign merchants on missions abroad. In 1685, for example, Thomas Kellermann was issued with a laudatory charter inscribed with the legend 'the trusted agent of the Muscovite state and worthy of honour'.[95] He was just one of a number of merchants who enjoyed Golitsyn's personal confidence.

It would seem that Sophia's regime was at its most successful in areas where domestic policy overlapped with foreign relations, that is in the fostering of trade relations and the recruitment and exploitation of foreign expertise. As will be shown below, these developments were associated with a significant widening of relations with the West. Elsewhere achievements were more modest, but by no means as negligible as implied by Ustrialov's remarks quoted at the beginning of this chapter, which fail either to acknowledge the essential continuity of Sophia and Golitsyn's domestic policy with that of Tsars Aleksei and Fedor, or to detect the modest harbingers of Peter's reforms. O'Brien and Schakovskoy, on the other hand, exaggerated the government's 'imagination' and 'logic', no doubt under the influence of La Neuville. The latter, as we have seen, focused his admiration for the regime on Golitsyn rather than Sophia, whom he believed to be guided by 'ambition' rather than enlightened ideals. But regular references in the documents of the period to her presence 'in the chamber' during deliberations on many of the matters described above suggest that she took an active interest in formulating policy, even if much of what she presided over followed traditional lines.[96] As numerous examples to follow will illustrate, Sophia was more than a mere figurehead (that role was played by Tsar Ivan), but she was never a self-proclaimed reformer after the manner of her brother Peter.

CHAPTER 6

# Religious Affairs

Sophia's regency saw the continuation and intensification of religious conflicts dating from her father's reign. At their most fundamental, they sprang from the clash between tradition and innovation, from the growing incompatibility of the cherished ideals of 'Moscow the Third Rome' with the demands of living and, perhaps more important, making war in the modern world. On the face of it, Sophia and her court appeared to belong more to the old than to the new. In matters of religious observance the 'Pious Sovereign Tsarevna' was very much her father's daughter, maintaining that almost 'nightmarish' round of church services, festivals and fasts that dominated the everyday life of the royal family. During the regency, the number of special occasions in an already packed calendar seems actually to have increased, by the addition, for example, of the commemoration of the dispute with the Old Believers on 5 July 1682 and the increased prominence given to local festivals in such places as the Novodevichy Convent and the Donskoi Monastery, which enjoyed the special patronage of the royal women. In comparison with the more relaxed, even 'fun-filled' atmosphere of the final years of Tsar Aleksei's reign, the court may even appear to have retreated again from the 'modern world'. There was, for example, no revival of the palace theatricals, discontinued in Fedor's reign, but highly theatrical religious rituals like the blessing of the waters of the Moskva river on 6 January and the Palm Sunday procession with tsar and patriarch came back into their own and were celebrated with obvious enthusiasm.[1]

On the international stage, too, Russia found new opportunities for playing out her role as the 'Third Rome', as the formation of the Holy League and alliance with Poland in 1686 gave her a closer interest in the fate of Orthodox Christians under Turkish rule. The 1686 treaty spoke of the desire 'to set free from bondage the Christian peoples groaning under the infidel yoke and to establish the reign of the true faith in the hallowed shrines of Christendom'.[2] Constantinople itself seemed within reach to the more ambitious. Patriarch Dositheus of Jerusalem, himself a subject of the Sultan, referred to Sophia as a 'model of virtue . . . the guardian of the royal sceptre, defender and champion of the apostolic faith'.[3] Russia's role in what later was to be termed the 'Eastern Question' was taking definite shape, as was that clearcut predominance over a once strong Poland that culminated a century later with Catherine II's partitions of that country. In article 9 of the 1686 treaty the King of Poland guaranteed to uphold the liberties of the Commonwealth's Orthodox dioceses and individual worshippers, and not to permit forced conversion to the Catholic or Uniate faiths, a concession which was to facilitate Russia's interference in Poland's internal affairs.[4] Although the intention of liberating and protecting fellow Orthodox Christians was to remain mostly on paper and in pious pronouncements, Sophia's government undoubtedly benefited from Russia's position of prominence in the Orthodox world.

In this respect an important landmark was set by the creation, in 1685–6, of a new metropolitanate of Kiev, which was subordinated to the patriarchate of Moscow.[5] With this act Moscow not only amended to its own advantage the anomalous status of the Ukrainian Orthodox Church, which had been subject to the jurisdiction of the Patriarch of Constantinople, but also shifted the focus of the Orthodox under Polish rule more firmly in the direction of Moscow. The new Metropolitan Gedeon (in secular life Prince Sviatopolk Chetvertinsky) had been Bishop of Luck in Poland, but had emigrated to Left-Bank Ukraine to escape the Polish authorities' attempts to convert him to the Catholic or Uniate faith. Needless to say, Moscow was able to make political capital out of his 'persecution' by the Poles. The religious unification of Moscow and Kiev preceded by a year the consolidation of Moscow's political hold over the Ukraine, when Kiev and the Left Bank were ceded by Poland to the tsars in perpetuity.[6]

Although the Russian Orthodox Church benefited, if only vicariously, from developments in foreign policy, at home it found itself under renewed attack from the spread of the schism (*raskol*) and the more insidious threats of 'Latin heresy', 'foreign guile' and associated evils. As we shall see, Sophia and her associates employed two quite different approaches to these dual dangers, combatting the first with uncompromising ferocity, but adopting a positive, even lenient attitude to non-Orthodox foreigners on Russian soil.

In the words of Michael Cherniavsky, 'the early 1680s mark the beginning of the real *Raskol*.'[7] In this period the dissident movement spread from the priests and parish clergy who had been its initiators to elements of the lay population, who expressed their protest against the authoritarianism of the Church hierarchy and their fears about the imminent end of the world by acts of self-immolation on a scale that continually frustrated the efforts of Church and state to contain them. The protest concerned more than dissatisfaction with minor changes in rituals and texts. To quote Cherniavsky again: 'There was only one general conclusion possible: if Moscow, the Third Rome, had instituted religious changes which required the condemnation of itself in its own past, then Moscow had accepted heresy – and the end was at hand.'[8] To the authorities such a view smacked not only of religious dissidence but also of rebellion against the state.

The government's response was to declare war on the dissenters. The way for the harsh measures adopted by Sophia's regime had been paved by the Church Councils of 1666–7, which had excommunicated the dissidents and declared the old practices and texts heretical, and the Council of 1681–2, which advocated that dissidence and schism were matters for the civil courts as well as the ecclesiastical.[9] On the eve of the May rebellion (on 14 April, according to Old Believer legend) the dissident leader Archpriest Avvakum and his associates were burned at the stake in the penal colony at Pustozersk,[10] and just two months later Sophia herself was forced to confront the dissidents as a result of Prince Ivan Khovansky's championship of their cause. No doubt the imputation made during the dispute on 5 July that her father and brother had been heretics steeled Sophia's resolve to show the dissidents no mercy. The execution of Nikita and his associates in the wake of the July dispute made it clear that Sophia's government regarded such outbreaks as a threat to the civil order as well as to the well-being of the Church.

Numerous Old Believers were apprehended and punished during the regency. For example, in 1683 in the Novgorod region, where Khovansky had served as governor, his replacement, Prince I.V. Buturlin, carried out a series of investigations into dissident activities with the co-operation of Metropolitan Kornily of Novgorod.[11] They succeeded in uncovering a veritable nest of Old Believers, drawn from all classes of society. Many of the ringleaders were brought to Moscow, where investigations were supervised by Vasily Golitsyn. Over twenty people were eventually executed. The testimony of the accused reveals some characteristic attitudes, for example that of Katerina Palitsyna, the widow of a military servitor, who argued that she:

> accepted and held to the Christian faith into which she was baptised as a baby and in which she had been instructed since babyhood. But she did not hold with the present teachings on the faith and did not know the revised [service] books. And she knew the cross which she had been taught since babyhood, but did not recognise or honour the four-pointed cross.[12]

In September 1683 one of the leaders, Varlaam, was interrogated under torture in the Novgorod Department in Moscow, and subsequently burned at the stake in Klin on 22 October. Sophia heard the report on his case in person, and was present at the announcement of the death sentence on 19 October.[13] Her personal participation in such cases is further confirmed by a passage in the account of the German traveller Georg Adam Schleissing, who writes:

> While I was in Moscow [in 1684–6] not a single morning passed without someone being executed at the Place of Proclamations [on Red Square]. I saw one old man lay his grey head upon the block as though it were the most natural thing in the world. The Tsarevna made it known to him that all he had to do to be pardoned was publicly recant of his errors, but the old man replied: 'I don't need the Tsarevna's grace and favour; all I need is the grace of Almighty God.'[14]

In 1685 the government issued a decree prescribing savage penalties, including the use of the knout, torture and death by burning, for every variety of non-conformist behaviour. Adherence to the schism was declared a state crime. Bishops and priests were to make a special point of interrogating under torture all those who failed to attend church or take confession or communion on suspicion of dissidence, as well as those who made a public show of their non-conformity.[15] Those who 'incited the common people, their wives and children to burn themselves to death would themselves be burned', but this and other measures simply prompted a further round of self-immolation, as whole communities sought to save their souls before the world ended. In 1685, for example, thirty people committed suicide near the Khutynsky Monastery in Novgorod province. In 1689 another group set fire to the building in which they had assembled as government troops approached to arrest them.[16] A less drastic option was flight to regions remote from the long arm of Church and government. The Cossack lands of the Don region were a popular retreat, as were Siberia, the Urals and the far north. A report submitted to Golitsyn in the Foreign Office in September 1685 told of Old Believer Cossacks on the Don 'luring away' converts to remote communities and hermitages.[17] In May 1686 the Don Cossack commander Frol Minaev was ordered to root out and destroy such settlements.[18] Even the 'humane' Golitsyn supervised torture sessions of dissidents brought into departments under his control, for example the trial of the dissident priest Samoil in the Foreign Office in May 1688.[19] That year Golitsyn delivered in person texts of Old Believer confessions to Sophia at Preobrazhenskoe, yet another illustration of Sophia's personal interest in the campaign.[20]

The examples cited should suffice to prove that in regard to the Old Believers Sophia's regime did not live up to the 'mild' reputation accorded it by certain admirers. Her regency was one of the most gruesome chapters in a history of persecution that continues to the present day, albeit with interludes of relative tolerance, for example during the reigns of Catherine II and Alexander I. The savagery of the measures surpassed even those imposed by Peter, who adopted a more pragmatic approach by replacing physical penalties with the levy of double taxes and fines, and subjected non-conformists to reason and persuasion. But his measures were no more successful than Sophia's in eradicating the Old Belief.

At the same time as it gave its full backing to the battle with the dissidents, Sophia's regime maintained a vigilant approach to the non-Christian native peoples of the Muscovite state. Her predecessors had wavered between the carrot of rewards for those who converted and the stick of penalties for those who resisted, and Sophia's government tended towards a mildly tolerant approach, as characterised, for example, by an edict issued to the overzealous Metropolitan Paul of Tobolsk, who was cautioned to baptise only those local Tatars who requested baptism 'of their own free will'.[21] The retention of landed estates by non-Christians was not made conditional upon conversion to Christianity. At the same time, there were penalties for 'improprieties' by non-Christians, especially those who persuaded new converts to reject their faith. They were warned to watch parades of the cross 'respectfully' and to refrain from misbehaviour, shouting and laughing.[22] The authorities were to be on their guard against natives who accepted baptism in order to escape punishment for crimes or to evade other obligations.[23] Clearly, the government had to strike a balance between the universal pretensions of the true faith and the fiscal and service needs of the state, which derived considerable revenues from native tribute payments and in some cases had to call upon them for military service, for example in the lands bordering China.

In another important area of economic concern, the government, like its predecessors, failed to find a consistent policy for dealing with the wealth of the Church, whose vast ownership of land and peasants had long been viewed as an obstacle to the extension of service tenure and the maintenance of the servitor class. In 1683 the restriction on the further acquisition of land by the Church in the 1649 law code was reconfirmed,[24] but this did not stop the government itself from granting land, money and peasants to churches, monasteries and individual clerics. Sophia made many personal bequests to favourite convents, notably the Novodevichy. At the same time some of the Church's wealth was clawed back by imposing taxes on patriarchal, monastic and episcopal peasants,[25] and in 1686 there was a special levy on these same categories to held fund the coming campaign against the Crimean Tatars.[26] In general, however, during Sophia's regency the Church had no grounds for complaint, either on matters of taxation or about the level of aid provided by the state in its fight against the Old Believers. There were, as we have seen, even attempts to enhance the dignity of church services, for example the act of 29 August 1684, which banned the sale of foodstuffs in and just outside monasteries during religious processions.[27]

Why was it, then, that despite these apparently impeccable credentials Sophia and her circle ultimately clashed with the Patriarch and in 1689, during the inevitable confrontation with Peter, forfeited his support? The answer lies in those very same developments of foreign policy which had enhanced the status of the Russian Orthodox Church vis-à-vis fellow Orthodox Christians abroad. In short, Moscow's entry into the Holy League brought her not so much within sight of Constantinople as into alliance with Poland, a Catholic power, and into a closer identification of interests with Poland's allies, the Holy Roman Empire, the Venetian Republic and the Vatican, in the shape of the militant Pope Innocent XI, as well as increasing her dependency upon foreign 'heretics' to command her armies.

Conservative circles within the Russian Orthodox Church viewed these developments with alarm, especially at a time when the hierarchy was on its guard against 'Latinisers' in its own ranks, as will be discussed below. Their suspicions were not without foundation, for the Papacy did cherish hopes of making inroads into Russia. In 1677 Cardinal Cibo wrote to Cardinal Buonivisi: 'His Holiness is well aware of the difficulties involved in co-operating with the most hardened and arrogant of all schismatic peoples, a people that in its dealings with others observes only the rule of self-interest and necessity,'[28] but it was felt that there were rewards to be reaped.

In the negotiations leading to the 1686 treaty with Poland religious motives were often not far from the surface. In May 1684, for example, the Austrian ambassadors Zierowski and Blumberg came to Moscow to urge Russia to join the military alliance against the Turks.[29] Politically, the talks were inconclusive, but the Austrians made progress on the rights of foreign Catholics in Russia. (Needless to say, no Russian could convert with impunity to Catholicism.) Vasily Golitsyn had already given a hint of his willingness to consider concessions in a conversation with Patrick Gordon the previous January, when the Scot reminded him that the Foreign Quarter's small Catholic community (numbering 'little more than a few score')[30] did not enjoy the same privileges as the more numerous Protestants, who had their own resident priests and permanent prayer houses.[31] Concessions were finalised in talks with the Imperial Secretary Maurizio Vota SJ, who came to Moscow in June 1684 disguised as a layman. It was agreed that two Jesuits should reside in Moscow under the protection of the Viennese court.[32]

The first priest, the Prussian father Johannes Schmidt, arrived in the same year, and in May 1685 the Imperial envoy in Moscow was able to report that the father was 'freely and openly' conducting services in a house designated for the purpose (with the hope of receiving permission to build a permanent chapel) and even openly running a school 'for the education and instruction of youth'.[33] In 1686 Schmidt was replaced by the Bohemian priest Georgius (Jerzy) David, whose account of the 'present state' of Muscovy and his own expulsion from Moscow in 1689 is a valuable source for the regency.[34]

The arrival of Jesuits in Moscow was regarded with consternation by the Patriarch and his circle. David reports that after the arrival of his companion, Father Tobias Tichavsky, in 1689, 'the Patriarch did not utter one civil world to Prince Golitsyn, because he was convinced that we had been admitted to Moscow in order to bring about the union of the Churches. When my companion arrived the Patriarch is reported to have said with sighs and tears: After my death all Moscow will become Jesuit.'[35]

In order to understand this reaction to the arrival of the Jesuits, a response which had vital implications for the position of both Sophia and Golitsyn, it is necessary to take a closer look at Russian attitudes to Catholicism in general, and at the character of Patriarch Joachim in particular. As the Holstein envoy Adam Olearius wrote a few decades earlier, the religion of the 'Roman Catholics and Papists' was 'a kind of abomination in the Russians' eyes. . . . Even the name [Catholic] is detested.'[36] Such attitudes sprang from hostility inherited from the Greeks (the sack of Constantinople by the Crusaders in 1204 continued to rankle) and compounded by events such as the Council of Florence in 1439, when a section of the Greek hierarchy had been 'subverted' by the Catholics, and, more recently, the Time of Troubles, when in 1610 Polish troops had occupied the Kremlin itself. Prejudices and fears were directed not so much at persons of the Catholic faith (some of whom were employed on Russian service), as against proselytisation and the penetration of heresies into Orthodox dogma and ritual. Fears of conversions by Jesuits were particularly strong. In fairness, however, it must be said that the most xenophobic feared infiltration by *all* non-Orthodox foreigners. In the words of an anonymous tract against the 'Latins and the Lutherans' attributed to Sophia's regency:[37]

> It is not fitting that either stone or wooden Latin chapels [*kostel*] or Lutheran prayerhouses [*kerk*] should be built in the Muscovite state, just as it is not fitting that those corrupters of the Orthodox faith, those false teachers the Latin priests [*ksendz*] and the Lutheran and Calvinist pastors should be in Russia and teach their heresy with their secret cunning . . . for such heretical Lutheran and Latin buildings are impious and vile, an abomination of desolation standing on the holy soil of the holy Russian land.[38]

These lines have sometimes been ascribed to Patriarch Joachim, who was described by Georgius David as 'hominem rudissimum' (a most ignorant man).[39] His detractors claim that the Patriarch was barely literate, although he could boast of a number of published works.[40] What is indisputable is that Joachim was highly conservative, and xenophobic to the point of obsession. Patrick Gordon records a characteristic outburst: '26 October 1688. A great Council, nothing concluded, where the Patriarch inveighed against me said that their armes could not prosper nor have any good or progress, For said he a hertick hath the best people in our Empire under his command, but he was taken up smartly by all the Nobility, and even laught at.'[41]

Joachim expressed his philosophy most eloquently in his testament (he died on 17 March, 1690):

> Let the sovereign tsars not permit any Orthodox Christian in their realm to come into contact or co-operate with the heretics and men of other creeds, Latins and Lutherans and Calvinists and the godless Tatars whom God abhors and the Church of God curses for their impious cunning, but let them, as enemies of God and detractors of his Church, be removed; and may they, the tsars, issue a royal edict that henceforth these men of other faiths should not preach their faiths in our pious realm or speak disparagingly about our faith or introduce their foreign customs and trick Christians with their heresies.[42]

He went on to blame the failure of the Crimean campaigns of 1687 and 1689 upon the employment of foreign mercenaries. 'I pleaded with the authorities, in prayers and letters, that heretics and men of other creeds should not be in command of Christians in the army, but the Pious Sovereign Lady Tsarevna Sophia Alekseevna did not deign to listen to me in this matter, neither did Prince Vasily Golitsyn.'[43] It is said that shortly before his death Joachim refused to see German doctors sent to him by the tsars 'because they were of a different faith'.[44] The reasons for Joachim's quarrel with the 'pious' Tsarevna start to become clearer, especially if one accepts the likelihood that a traditionalist like Joachim found it hard to come to terms with a female ruler, and one who insisted on participating in ceremonies usually reserved for the tsars.

The main reason for Joachim's hostility to Sophia and Golitsyn, then, was his belief that by admitting Catholics to Russia they encouraged 'Latin heresy'. This fear was exacerbated by developments that predated the regency, centring on the activities of the court poet and tutor Simeon Polotsky and his disciple and successor Silvester Medvedev.[45] Joachim said of Polotsky: 'Although he was a scholarly and learned man, he had been trained by the Jesuits and subverted by them, therefore he read only Latin books.'[46] Joachim detected heresy even in works commissioned by the Church authorities in the 1660s as a riposte to the Old Belief, for example Polotsky's *Sceptre of Government* (1667), not to mention the works published by the Verkhovnia tipografiia

(Palace Press) in 1679–83, which was run by Polotsky and subsequently Medvedev without patriarchal sanction or supervision.[47]

In general, Joachim was suspicious of any independent opinion in matters of faith. When interrogated in 1664 on his own Orthodox convictions, he had replied: 'I, lord, do not know about any old or new belief, but only about what the authorities see fit to teach, and I am ready to act accordingly and obey them in all matters.'[48] As his confrontation with the Old Believers in 1682 demonstrated, he expected the same unquestioning obedience to himself as 'arch-pastor'. It is not surprising that he was concerned about the influence of Polotsky, who was not even a prelate of the Church, upon Tsar Fedor and the other royal children.

Many rumours survive, exclusively in foreigners accounts, concerning the Tsar's 'Catholic tendencies'. Georgius David reported that Fedor 'is said to have been inclined towards the Roman religion and especially our own', and that he planned to build a college and schools for the Jesuits. He goes on to say that Sophia and Golitsyn intended to honour Fedor's wish, which 'provided the occasion for their good will towards us'.[49] The anonymous Polish *Diariusz*, written in 1683, attributed Fedor's tendencies to the influence of his first wife, Agafia, who was said to be of Polish extraction. There were even fears that 'he might begin to introduce the Polish faith into Moscow and to ally himself with the Poles, just like Tsar Dmitry, who married the daughter of Mniszech'.[50] The account of the 1682 rebellion sent to the Papal Legate in Poland also contains the rumour that Fedor gave permission for the founding of a Catholic church and school, this time in Smolensk.[51]

Even if a good part of Fedor's 'Catholic sympathies' was wishful thinking on the part of Catholic commentators, the conservative Joachim saw grounds for concern. One of the Patriarch's motives in urging the election of Peter in 1682 was undoubtedly his fear of Catholic tendencies in the Miloslavsky camp, which was headed by Sophia, Fedor's favourite sister and a pupil of Polotsky's to boot.[52] Suspicions could only have been increased by the fact that Sophia's adviser on spiritual matters was Silvester Medvedev, who had inherited Polotsky's role as court poet (one of his first official tasks was to compose his master's obituary)[53] and completed the publication of some of his works on the Palace Press. Recent archival studies have shown how closely the two collaborated during Polotsky's lifetime.[54]

During the regency Medvedev was further to provoke the Patriarch's wrath by his alleged adherence to the heresy of artolatry (bread worship), adopting Catholic teaching and terminology on the moment of transubstantiation.[55] By and large, the Orthodox Church regarded the eucharist as a mystery and did not engage in scholastic hair-splitting between 'accidents' and 'substance', but in the 1680s the issue was forced into the open by ecclesiastical politics, as the 'Graecophiles' (led by the Patriarch) and the 'Latinists' (led by Medvedev) vied for influence at court and control over education and publishing. It is said that the topic became a subject for public debate, so that 'not only priests but also lay persons, even women, argued about the moment of transubstantiation'.[56] The controversy centred on whether the bread and wine became the body and blood of Christ with the uttering of the words of Institution, 'This is my body . . . this is my blood' (Catholic teaching) or with the Epiclesis, the priest's invocation of the Holy Spirit, 'Send down Thy Holy Spirit upon us . . .' (Orthodox teaching).

The debate really got underway with the arrival in Moscow in the spring of 1685 of two Greek monks, the brothers Ioanniky and Sofrony Likhud, summoned to Moscow on the recommendation of the ecumenical patriarchs to set up a school.[57] In March they made a statement of their view of transubstantiation, based on the latest teaching of the Greek Orthodox Church.[58] This prompted Medvedev to produce a reply in the form of a pamphlet entitled *The Bread of Life* in the summer of 1685.[59] This in turn prompted one of Joachim's collaborators, the monk Evfimy from the Kremlin Miracles Monastery, to write his *Refutation of the Latin Sophistry,* in which he alleged that Medvedev must be either a Jesuit or a Uniate.[60] A second tract from Evfimy's pen issued in the autumn of 1687 denounced Ukrainian books, starting with the works of Metropolitan Peter Mohila of Kiev dating from the 1640s, as the source of heresies. He complained that 'Latinist' opponents confused common folk by the 'blooms of rhetoric and devices of philosophy'.[61]

Medvedev's response was the weighty tract *Manna of the Bread of Life,* a presentation copy of which was given to Sophia in November 1687, dedicated to 'the most illustrious, most devout and Christ-loving daughter of a glorious tsar, most glorious, wise and gracious, our Great Sovereign Lady, Pious Tsarevna and Great Princess Sophia Alekseevna'.[62] Medvedev based his arguments on ancient texts and works of the fathers of the Church. The tome was too weighty for general distribution, but a digest of the arguments was made by a priest of one of the palace churches and issued in forty copies.[63] (All of these works, it should be noted, appeared in manuscript form.) The debate continued with the Likhuds' response, a work entitled *Akos, or the Antidote* (December 1687)[64] and with several works by Medvedev penned in 1688 in which he called for proper analysis of sources.[65] By now, however, Medvedev had obviously gone too far. In Joachim's eyes the very fact of expressing his independent opinion was enough to condemn him. Medvedev had already lost out against the Likhuds in the rivalry to establish a school in Moscow, and in March 1689 he was dismissed from his post as corrector in the Typography.

Sophia's role in these debates remains unclear. A.P. Bogdanov argues that 'the government was unwilling to interfere directly in this strug-gle',[66] and that Golitsyn was more inclined towards the Likhuds than towards Medvedev. As we shall see in the next chapter, despite the fact that Medvedev addressed Sophia with a special plea in verse for the establishment of an academy, her government did not back Medvedev against Joachim's preferred candidates, the Likhuds. The Likhuds for their part produced a series of eulogistic orations to Sophia, for example in March 1687 when they likened her to an 'indestructible wall' of defence for Christians.[67]

In the end the issue was decided not by theological but by political developments. When Sophia was ousted in September 1689, Medvedev fell with her on a series of charges that implicated not only him but also Sophia and Golitsyn in a major plot to subvert Orthodoxy.[68] Georgius David records that 'a certain monk or elder was arrested for holding and propagating certain Catholic sentiments contrary to the Greek'. It was said that Golitsyn intended to use him as a means of propagating union and the Catholic religion. Others said that he was destined by the other party to become Patriarch. When questioned about his association with the Jesuits, Medvedev denied it.[69] David's editor, A.V. Florovskij, claims that 'there is little evidence that Medvedev actually did establish relations with David and Tichavsky',[70] although he concedes that the Jesuits did have some success with the Georgian Tsar Archill, who lived under the protection of the Muscovite court, and in securing the conversion of two Russian priests Peter Artem'ev and Pallady Rogovsky.

The rumour cited by David, to the effect that Sophia and Golitsyn were planning union with Rome, appears in a number of foreign sources, for example, La Neuville, who reported that Sophia and Go-litsyn proposed union with Rome in the hope of obtaining the Pope's permission to be crowned. La Neuville, it should be noted, was sym-pathetic towards Golitsyn precisely because of his lenient attitude to-wards Catholics and Jesuits, branding the Naryshkin's 'ces brutaux' mainly because they chose to expel the same Jesuits immediately after Sophia's downfall.[71] David, the better-informed observer, makes it clear that union with Rome and associated schemes were mere rumours and that political issues were to the fore. 'The reasons for our expulsion', he wrote, 'were the fall from favour of Prince Golitsyn and the removal from power of Tsarevna Sophia, who, it is said, on hearing of [our expulsion] groaned out loud, the hatred of the Patriarch and the clergy, with whom we had no dealings, and the interference of the heretics [Protestants] to whom we did no wrong.'[72]

The Patriarch lost little time in taking advantage of the political reversal. On 2 October, less than a month after the removal of Sophia and Golitsyn, David and his companion were given two days to leave Moscow on the grounds that they had been 'the cause of much harm to the Holy Apostolic Church with their printed sheets and images on canvas and bone and other artful devices; and there is much dissension between the Holy Apostolic Eastern Church and the Western Church in Rome'.[73] David's own account of the speech read out to them by a clerk in the Foreign Office mentions that they were only admitted to Moscow with a temporary permit in 'deference' to the Emperor, but that now it 'pleased' the tsars to send them back; the clerk then confided that 'the only reason is our Patriarch, who persistently begged the tsars with all his clergy, since your faith does not conform with our Orthodox Church and is even repugnant and hostile to it'.[74]

Other enactments of the autumn of 1689 show that the Patriarch was given considerable leeway by Sophia's successors to indulge his xenophobic inclinations. Religious communities in the Foreign Quarter were asked to furnish proofs of permission to erect and maintain churches,[75] and governors in the border regions of Kiev, Novgorod, Pskov and Smolensk were ordered to tighten entrance formalities for foreigners.[76] On 30 September the Protestant mystic Quirinus Kuhlmann and his associate Norderman were burned at the stake for heresy, although it must be noted that the capture and trial of Kuhlmann had taken place during Sophia's regency, as a result of pressure from Germans in Moscow, and it was Sophia who condemned him for 'schism, heresy and false prophecy'.[77]

Joachim's fears about the Orthodoxy of Sophia and her inner circle stemmed from his earlier clashes with Polotsky and were fuelled by the apparently lenient attitude towards Catholics which resulted from closer political ties with Catholic powers. But aside from rumours and hearsay there is no evidence that Sophia's and Golitsyn's attitude to Catholics was anything more than pragmatic. They were well aware that concessions in matters of faith made in the interest of foreign relations would earn the disapproval of the conservative Patriarch and that a balance had to be struck between the needs of foreign policy and keeping the approval of the Church. They continued, for example, to discriminate between Catholics and Protestants. Although the latter were able to replace wooden churches with stone during the 1680s, the former were repeatedly denied permission to erect and maintain a permanent chapel. A charter for a stone church was not issued until 1696.[78] The 1686 treaty with Poland should also have earned the Patriarch's blessing. Article 9, under which, as we have seen, the King of Poland made considerable concessions as regards the status of the Orthodox in Poland, simply maintained the status quo in relation to Catholics on Russian soil. The latter must not be 'ill-treated' but would be free to practise their religion only *in their homes*.[79]

There was no question of Sophia yielding to Joachim's extreme demand for the expulsion of foreigners from Russian service, but on occasions the civil authorities bowed to conservative circles. In January 1686, for example, priests in the Archangel region complained to Archbishop Afanasy, a former pupil of the Patriarch, that Russians were being corrupted by foreign merchants, losing their faith and attending foreign churches. Moscow's response was to order that Russians in the service of foreigners should be properly registered, be on the alert against foreign 'guile' and refrain from attending Protestant services.[80]

On many other occasions the attempt to balance the requirements of foreign policy and religious tradition resulted in decisions that should have reconciled the Patriarch to Sophia and her circle. In January 1689, for example, the French Jesuit Philippe Avril and his companion Beauvollier were refused permission to cross Muscovite territory en route to China, a decision prompted by the bad treatment of Russian envoys at the hands of the French in 1687 and by the lobbying of the Brandenburg envoy Czaplitz, who was in Moscow at the time.[81] The success of the Prussians in winning Golitsyn's support led to a decline in the fortunes of the Catholics. Perhaps the most remarkable product of Protestant pressure, and a testimonial to the tolerance of Sophia's regime, was the decree of January 1689 offering sanctuary in Russia to the victims of Louis XIV's revocation of the Edict of Nantes, a measure which, unlike the expulsion of the French Jesuits, was not calculated to win the approval of the Patriarch.[82]

The religious policy of Sophia's regency presents an uneven, even paradoxical picture. On the one hand, the purity of the faith of the rank and file was supervised more closely than ever before as sanctions against non-conformity were strictly applied. Observation of the daily routine of the court would also suggest that the norms of 'holy Russia' still held sway. But the new requirements of foreign policy demanded a more flexible treatment of foreigners, an acceptance of the ideal of a united 'Christendom' against the onslaught of the infidel, even on occasion the playing off of Catholic against Protestant. Meanwhile, in the upper echelons of ecclesiastical circles the legacy of Polotsky reached fruition, with the backing of his royal pupils, but encountered the opposition of Joachim, who smelled 'Latinist' heresy. The Patriarch's desire to be rid of the 'friends of Jesuits' in the Kremlin coincided with the political if not the spiritual aims of Peter's party, and for a few months after Sophia's downfall the Patriarch was allowed a fairly free hand in cracking down on 'foreign guile'. But the coincidence of the needs of Church and state was to be short-lived, and 'Latinist' trends, especially those emanating from the Kiev Academy, were to make a comeback during Peter's reign.

What of Sophia's own religious beliefs? On the face of it the epithet 'pious' – *blagovernaia* – customarily attributed to her was no mere convention. She was an assiduous daughter of the Church in her attendance at services, commissioning of churches, bequests to monasteries and persecution of the Church's enemies. The author of the Polish *Diariusz* described her as 'clever and pious, spending her time praying and fasting'. But, he added, she read the *Lives of the Saints* in Polish, in the edition of the Bishop of Chernigov Lazar Baranovich.[83] The fact is that Sophia's Orthodoxy could hardly escape a strong dose of foreign input from the Orthodox writings of the Ukraine and Byelorussia, part of which lay within the territory of the Polish Commonwealth. Orthodox clerics in those regions, of whom Simeon Polotsky was the most famous example, had been obliged to assimilate the terminology and tenets of Catholicism, often from Catholic teachers through the medium of Latin, in order to defend Orthodoxy from a position of strength. A typical product of such training was Polotsky's *Crown of Faith* (1670), a copy of which the writer actually dedicated to Sophia with a set of verses.[84]

The sheer number of religious engagements carried out by Sophia, as listed in the palace records and other official documents, shows that she took the religious aspect of rulership very seriously, but this cannot be used as evidence of personal conviction. On a number of such occasions there is more than a hint that politics rather than piety were the motivating factor. On 14 August 1685, for example, in the Cathedral of the Dormition on the eve of the Feast of the Dormition of the Virgin, 'the archpriest first censed the Tsar [with incense] then the Patriarch, then the Tsarevna three times, then the orb and the crozier. . . . Then he censed the bishops and the whole church and the icons and the sovereign and the Patriarch, but not the Tsarevna. This caused anger [*Za to byl gnev*].'[85] On the first Friday in Lent the Patriarch blessed four ceremonial dishes of groats instead of the customary three – for himself and the tsars – in order to include Sophia.[86] From these and other examples of the adaptation of public services to take account of Sophia's position as a ruling sovereign it may be deduced that Sophia's approach to the role of the Church in the life of the state was much the same as her father's: the 'most Pious Tsar' regarded himself as 'an icon for Russians to revere', as the 'divinely crowned wearer of the imperial purple', whose 'public magnificence and public piety were intended to inspire awe, and hence obedience'.[87] That same pious Tsar was capable of conducting urgent business in church, and was also responsible for an unprecedented increase in Russia's contacts with the West. In reference to Sophia's personal piety, it is worth noting that she did not take the veil when she was confined in the Novodevichy Convent in September 1689. This step was actually *forced* upon her after the strel'tsy rebellion of 1698. For Sophia politics and religion were closely entwined but it seems likely that she was motivated more by the former than by the latter.

CHAPTER 7

# Culture

## (i) Art and Architecture

Sophia's regency saw the continuation of many aspects of that 'transitional' cultural era inaugurated in the reign of her father Tsar Aleksei, when a new art began to grow within the womb of Old Russian medieval religious culture. By the end of Aleksei's reign fundamental changes in lifestyle were already indicated, as demonstrated by a royal decree of 1675 forbidding courtiers to 'adopt the customs of the Germans and other foreigners, cut their hair, or to wear dress, robes or hats of foreign design'.[1] But the fact that such trends were deplored rather than encouraged and even enforced, as they were to be in Peter I's reign, illustrates the restraints that still existed. It would be wrong, however, to regard the art of the 1680s, standing on the threshhold of Peter's reforms, as a mere 'cultural corridor' between one age and another. Painting, applied art and architecture, even literature, all display to a greater or lesser degree elements of a distinctive style commonly referred to as 'Moscow Baroque', which heralded not only the death of Old Russian culture but also the beginning of a prolonged stylistic era which came to an end only with the turn to Classicism in the 1760s.[2]

Here is not the place to embark upon a detailed theoretical debate about the applicability of the term 'Baroque' to the art in question, except to emphasise that in Russia the style so termed served a quite different function from its counterparts in most Western countries, where the Baroque followed on the Renaissance and entailed adaptation of the Classical repertoire. Appeal to the emotions rather than to reason, movement, dynamism, illusionism, ambiguity, spacial complexity leading to dramatic culminations, a mixing of art forms, deployment of lighting effects – many have been the attempts to list the elements and define the essence of the European Baroque in its many national guises.[3] What distinguished Russia from virtually all the countries where the Baroque gained a foothold was that she had no real experience of the Gothic or Renaissance eras; only in the age of 'Moscow Baroque' did Russian architects first begin extensively to use

134

devices and motifs derived from the Classical order system of architectural proportions and devices, albeit in stylised, decorative form. In
painting, the early Russian Baroque is associated with the appearance
of elements of 'naive realism' – experiments in straight perspective,
naturalistic light and shade, inclusion of fragments of landscape and
still life – in religious art, and also with experiments with secular
genres, notably the portrait. In literature it signified the influence of
Polish Baroque, filtered through the Ukraine and Byelorussia, notably
in the syllabic verses of Simeon Polotsky, Silvester Medvedev and
Karion Istomin, and also the school drama. Scholars have spoken of the
'liberation of the individual personality', both in the creations of fiction
(especially secular and satirical tales) and in the emergence of the
'professional' author.

These and other phenomena led the eminent Soviet cultural historian
D.S. Likhachev to equate the seventeenth century with a delayed
Russian 'Renaissance', which served as a 'buffer' between the old and
new eras.[4] Two concepts much favoured by Soviet art historians in
reference to the later seventeenth century – *obmirshchenie* (secularisation) and *zhizneradostnost'* (joie de vivre) – underline this 'Renaissance'
theory. 'The notion that a thing of beauty must bring joy lies at the
basis of seventeenth-century Russian aesthetics . . . the joy of fusion
with a humanised and accessible world,' writes I.D. Davydova.[5] The
ingredients have been identified as 'loss of monumentality, increase in
dynamism, fragmentation and multiplication of parts, an accent on
colourfulness . . . more direct acquaintance with reality in order to
provide an accurate reflection of nature based on direct observation of
everyday life'.[6] There was a multiplicity of motifs, devices and subject
matter transcending the traditional: '"Breadth, not depth" became the
unwritten programme for the aesthetic and art of the second half of the
seventeenth century.'[7] By the 1680s the attitudes and approach of an
increasing number of artists, not only in the capital but also in the
provinces, were undergoing a transformation, and they were producing
a tantalisingly hybrid style which first-time observers often describe as
simultaneously Russian and Westernised, without being able to specify
foreign prototypes.

In the 1680s, as in the 1650s to 1670s, the strongest new trends
originated at court, where the major centre of artistic activity continued
to be the Armoury Chamber (*oruzheinaia palata*), that early 'academy of
arts' which produced a wide variety of objects, both useful and decorative, for the royal palaces and churches.[8] It was noted earlier that Tsar
Aleksei hired foreign artists to carry out secular commissions and to
train Russian pupils. By 1683 this aspect of the Armoury's work was so
important that a separate secular painting studio – *zhivopisnaia palata* –
was set up.[9] An account book for the year 7196 (1687–8) lists a total

of forty secular artists (*zhivopistsy*) and their pupils, headed by the Armenian artist Ivan Saltanov and the Russian Ivan Artemevich Bezmin.[10] The number of icon painters was only twenty-seven, although this does not reflect any drop in demand since most of the *zhivopistsy* also painted icons. It is evident from their names that some of the artists were foreigners: L. Smol'ianinov and E. Elin were from Byelorussia, V. Poznansky, K. Umbranovsky, G. Odol'sky from Poland or the Ukraine.[11] Artists from the West were also represented in the Armoury, although their contribution has been little studied. One such was Peter Engels, 'master of perspective', from Hamburg. Arriving in Moscow c.1670, he had been involved in painting scenery for Tsar Aleksei's court theatre, and executing murals in royal palaces, for example scenes of 'King David enthroned', 'The wedding of King Solomon' and the 'Tale of the Prophet Ezekiel' for Tsar Fedor in 1679–80.[12] In 1686 he was officially attached to the staff of the Armoury, and in that year painted a series of 'perspective scenes' in Sophia's new Kremlin apartments.[13] Ivan Walter, another painter from Hamburg about whom less is known, is said to have painted the portrait of Prince Vasily Golitsyn.[14] In 1688 the diplomat Prince Iakov Dolgoruky hired the painter Otto (Artemy) Genin in Amsterdam.[15] Nothing survives to allow us to assess the nature and quality of their work. Their main contribution may have been in training the new generation of Armoury artists in such technical skills as the preparation of canvas and the mixing of oil colours.

An interesting case study of the 'new artist' is provided by the *curriculum vitae* of Ivan Bezmin.[16] In the 1660s he had studied in the Armoury with the Pole Stefan Lopucki and the Dutchman Daniel Wuchters, painting portraits, frescoes and icons, carving cabinets and iconostases. He was often commissioned to paint portraits, for example Patriarch Joachim's in 1678, and two of the most striking examples of 1680s art – the tomb portrait of Tsar Fedor (c.1686) and the painting of Patriarch Nikon with members of his clergy (c.1685–6) – have been attributed to him.[17]

In the 1680s Bezmin was employed almost continuously by Sophia and other members of the royal family, notably in the decoration of their new apartments in the Kremlin, built to replace wooden chambers demolished in the fire of November 1682.[18] Armoury account books for December 1684 to August 1685 record that the walls, ceilings and pillars of the 'newly built stone chambers' of Sophia, Ekaterina, Maria, Feodosia and Natalia were to be decorated with various paintings on Biblical themes at a cost of more than 730 roubles, and with 240 coins (*zolotye*) supplied for conversion into gold leaf for decoration. The work was supervised by Bezmin.[19] Although these apartments were refur-

bished many times after the 1680s, and at the beginning of the nineteenth century were demolished altogether,[20] contemporary descriptions
allow a tentative reconstruction.

Documents published by the Soviet art historian V.G. Briusova, for
example, show that in November 1684 a scheme was drawn up for the
decoration of Sophia's apartments, which was to include scenes from
the Passion of Christ, such as the Kiss of Judas, the Trial before Pontius
Pilate, the Crowning with Thorns and the Crucifixion, a somewhat
dour selection which prompted Briusova to suggest that the subject
matter reflected the taste of Tsaritsa Natalia rather than of Sophia
herself.[21] Briusova even suggests that these paintings were never executed, on the basis of a line in the same document stating: 'There is
no gold, paint or money in the Armoury.'[22] Descriptions published by
Ivan Zabelin in the nineteenth century, however, show that the Passion
cycle was indeed completed, and that the decoration of the apartments
of all the tsarevny bore a predominantly religious stamp. Alongside the
scenes from Holy Week already indicated (and supplemented by the
Garden of Gethsemane, Christ bearing the Cross, the Entombment,
the Resurrection, et al.), were portraits of prophets, apostles and evangelists (John the Baptist, Andrew, Matthew, Peter and Paul, David and
Solomon), iconographic subjects executed as frescoes (Christ Not Made
by Hands, the Virgin of the Sign, the Old Testament Trinity) and
scenes from the life of the Virgin. Smaller spaces – arches, alcoves,
columns – were filled with cherubim and seraphim. Of special interest
are the subjects flanking the doors leading to Sophia's bedroom. On one
side was an illustration of the text from Psalms 6:6: 'I water my couch
with my tears', on the other the Pure Soul, a maiden in royal regalia
decked with flowers.[23]

If the decor of Sophia's apartments maintained a strictly pious tone,
the rooms of her sister Ekaterina which adjoined them indicated slightly
different tastes. Ekaterina's rooms were adorned with fresco portraits of
her mother and father, her late brothers Fedor and Aleksei, the reigning
tsars, Sophia and Ekaterina herself. In the next room a further personal
touch was added by depictions of the holy martyrs Sophia and Ekaterina,
and figures from early Russian history, including Prince Vladimir, Princess Olga, and the martyrs Boris and Gleb.[24] The painting in both sets
of rooms included pictures of fruits, flowers and lenchafty: scroll or
ribbon motifs. The palace complex was under renovation throughout
the regency. In 1688, for example, the painter Anton Baikovsky was
ordered to paint a mural of the prophets Moses and Abraham, 'and
beneath them scrolls, and in the nearby window pictures of various
fruits'.[25] In December 1685 Ivan Bezmin was commissioned to paint a
canvas of the heavenly bodies and signs of the Zodiac for one of the

ceilings in Sophia's rooms,[26] a subject which also appeared on one of the ceilings in Vasily Golitsyn's palace, and in the chambers of Tsarevna Tat'iana Mikhailovna and of Tsarevna Maria Alekseevna.[27]

The study of seventeenth-century mural painting in secular buildings, especially of the Biblical scenes known as 'parables' or *pritchi*, is fraught with difficulties because virtually no examples have survived. As the Soviet art historian Evangulova has pointed out, this 'little-studied, complex and transitional' genre allowed artists working on domestic premises to break away from iconographic canons without departing from religious subject matter.[28] In composing Biblical scenes, especially those taken from the Old Testament, they were able to experiment with the depiction of scenery, architecture, costumes and horses, as well as with life-size studies of the human figure. Foreigners had given the lead. Ivan Bezmin's teacher Daniel Wuchters when applying for work in the Armoury had described his *forte* as the painting of 'portraits and various Biblical stories, life-size'.[29]

Wall paintings of deceased Russian rulers in churches were not in themselves a striking innovation, as anyone who has seen the interior of the Kremlin Archangel Cathedral will know.[30] What was new was the growing popularity of the depiction of living secular subjects in the easel portrait or *parsuna*, the first secular genre to make any significant impact upon the overwhelmingly religious world of Old Russian art.[31] It was not a big step from the art of the icon, with its focus upon the human, albeit idealised and transfigured forms of Christ, the Virgin and the saints, to the art of depicting earthly personalities in an idealised way. The icon painter believed himself to be painting a true likeness of his subjects, which had been handed down by the artists of antiquity, for example by St Luke the Evangelist, who is said by tradition to have painted the Virgin Mary. Thus, when Simon Ushakov, himself one of the pioneers of the 'transitional' style, wrote that a portrait represented 'the life of the memory, the memory of those who once lived, a witness to times past, a testimony to virtue, an expression of might, a revival of the dead, providing immortality in praise and glory and an incentive to the living to emulate, a remembrance of the heroic feats of old',[32] he might have been referring either to religious or secular art as they were conceived in late-seventeeth-century Russia.

The first portraits of non-saintly subjects appear to have been painted precisely with the aim of 'reviving' the dead, one of the very earliest being the posthumous portrait of the popular hero of the Time of Troubles, Prince M.V. Skopin-Shuisky.[33] During the reigns of Tsar Aleksei and his successors this trend continued alongside the more 'modern' demand for live subjects.[34] In 1678 Tsar Fedor, for example, commissioned Ivan Bezmin to paint pictures of his late father, mother and brother Aleksei.[35] In 1685 a portrait of Fedor himself was ordered in the names of Tsars Ivan and Peter, a full-length image on wood to be placed over his tomb in the Cathedral of the Archangel.[36] Everything about this picture demonstrates the still hazy boundaries between icon painting and secular painting, for although it is not an icon (Fedor had not been canonized), the materials (tempera on board), composition (full faced, stiff pose) and technique of applying paint (folds of robes, moulding of face, gold ornamentation) are all characteristic of icon-painting. This is decidedly the idealised portrait of a dead rather than a living subject, suggestive of the Tsar's life in heaven rather than his short illness-dogged life on earth. When turning to secular subjects Russian painters were still not comfortable with notions of change. Just as the images of saints were deemed fixed for all time outside time, so artists strove to 'fix' an eternal human image, ruthlessly expunging any transient features such as emotion (except piety) or ageing.[37]

A rather different work is the portrait of Patriarch Nikon accompanied by a group of Orthodox clergy. This is now thought to have been commissioned in connection with the completion and dedication of the Cathedral of the Resurrection at New Jerusalem in 1685 (begun by Nikon in 1656); in other words its purpose was to 'revive' the dead. The portrait of Nikon himself is based on contemporary images 'from life'. His face, and those of the clergy, are depicted in a lifelike manner. The poses are far from naturalistic, however, and the use of perspective is inconsistent. The rich decorative detailing of robes and carpet also recall icon-painting techniques. The work is very much a hybrid, one might say a typical product of the 'transitional' era.[38] Sophia and her family commissioned many portraits of Fedor and other deceased relatives during the regency, but it is in the realm of living subjects that the 1680s display their most interesting developments.

For our purposes the most striking examples of the new art of portraiture feature Sophia herself.[39] Hitherto, the female secular portrait was even rarer than its male counterpart, which given the conventions of seclusion was hardly surprising. (It will be recalled that couriers conducting preliminary negotiations for the marriage of Sophia's Aunt Irina in the 1640s had gone to Denmark without the customary portrait of the bride, on the grounds that such a likeness would be 'unseemly'.) There is good reason, in fact, for regarding Sophia's as the first realistic female portraits in the history of Russian culture. Her mother Maria (died 1669) was certainly painted on several occasions after her death, and a depiction of her whilst living appears on the bottom right-hand corner of Simon Ushakov's icon 'The Tree of the Muscovite State' (1668),[40] but this miniature rendering is clearly stylised, and belongs to the iconographic convention of earthly rulers in poses of supplication, in this case before the icon of Our Lady of Vladimir. Likewise, the production of icons of patron saints of the royal women, for example in the icon (c.1666) of the Elected Saints of Tsar Aleksei's family in the Novodevichy Convent, belongs firmly to the religious sphere.[41] Portraits of Sophia were to transcend these conventions.

The first-known pictorial reference to her produced during the regency, although not actually a likeness, already suggested a new point of departure. This was an engraving accompanying the text of Archbishop Lazar Baranovich's book *Grace and Truth* (Chernigov, 1683).[42] Baranovich belonged to the pro-Moscow party of Ukrainian clergy, and his work was a eulogy in illustration of the text (inscribed on ribbons at the sides of the tsars) 'It is good and seemly when two brothers rule jointly'. The engraving, by the Ukrainian Ivan Shchirsky, shows the two tsars being blessed by Christ, and above them a maiden with eagle's wings being crowned from heaven. The composition is a variation on the iconographic subject of the Holy Wisdom, *Sofiia – premudrost' bozhiia*.[43] In the centre of the composition is a columned shrine containing a double-headed eagle with a double heart, illustrating the text 'Wisdom hath builded her house, she hath hewn out her seven pillars' (Proverbs 9:1).

The implication was clear: the Holy Wisdom influences and protects the two under-aged tsars, just as their sister Sophia (the *de facto* ruler) was deemed to do in real life. Seen in political terms, the picture offered a rebuff to the Polish propaganda, then rife in the Left-Bank Ukraine, that the new regime in Moscow was weak and unstable. Artistically, it pointed to an important new source for the art of the Muscovite court, and one which had already been exploited verbally in the work of Simeon Polotsky: the Baroque eulogy or panegyric, combining a mixture of Biblical and Classical imagery and emblematic devices, usually composed in syllabic verse based on the Polish model.[44] The graphic counterparts, panegyric engravings (*pokhval'nye listy*) or *conclusiones*, themselves usually included texts on ribbons or in cartouches, alongside figures in a scenery of Classical architecture, clouds and flower motifs. It appears that the first Russian artist to master this style was Simon Ushakov,[45] but he died in 1686 and evidently left no sufficiently experienced successor, which is why the growing demand for such work in Moscow court circles had initially to be met by foreign artists.

The first overtly secular portraits of Sophia as regent are part of this trend and postdate the Treaty of Eternal Peace with Poland of May 1686 when, as will be shown, Sophia began consistently to adopt the titles and trappings of rulership.[46] Her portraits must be viewed in a political light, as testimonials for public and foreign consumption to the fact that Sophia was a ruler in her own right with a legitimate claim to royal titles, regalia and dignity. From 1687 she even began to consider the possibility of being crowned as a sovereign equal in status to her

8   Allegorical portrait of Tsars Ivan and Peter by I. Shchirsky: frontispiece to Baranovich's *Grace and Truth* (1683)

brothers, and portraits of her with crown and sceptre were evidently intended to prepare public opinion for this eventuality.

As it turned out, this illegitimate aspiration was to be deemed the gravest of Sophia's provable offences, and evidence of 'coronation' portraits figured prominently in proceedings against Fedor Shaklovity and her other adherents who were arrested and banished or executed after her downfall in 1689.[47] In the autumn of 1687, for example, we learn that two Ukrainian colonels delivered on oration to the tsars. Fedor Shaklovity, anxious that Sophia should receive equal praise, commissioned a similar oration for her, and also an engraved portrait to accompany the panegyric.[48] The artwork was commissioned from the Ukrainian engraver Leonty Tarasevich, then employed in Lazar Baranovich's press in Chernigov.[49] In the spring of 1689 an engraved metal block was delivered to the palace. It was said to have depicted the Father, the Son and the Holy Spirit, and beneath them the tsars and Sophia, the latter accompanied by seven 'virtues'. Prince Vasily Golitsyn and Hetman Mazepa are also said to have figured on the engraving, which evidently belonged to the same genre and style as the

141

1683 print by Shchirsky described above.[50] Although there have been many attempts to identify this work, of which 100 sheets are said to have been run off, with surviving engravings of the period, for example Shchirsky's 'Thesis of I. Obidovsky' (1691),[51] it is now generally accepted that no examples survived, even though the written panegyric, produced by Ivan Bogdanovsky in the form of the book *The Gift of the Holy Spirit* (1688), did.[52] One wonders, too, whether a work which depicted Sophia alongside her brothers would have satisfied the expanded aspirations of her party in 1689.

As it happens, another of Tarasevich's prints that did survive was a work of quite a different order. This is the so-called 'eagle' portrait, first published in 1895, which shows Sophia alone, crowned and bearing orb and sceptre, framed in an oval bearing on its rim the legend 'The most illustrious and sovereign, by the grace of God, Great Sovereign Lady, Pious Tsarevna and Great Princess Sophia Alekseevna, Autocrat of all the Great and Little and White Russias'.[53] The oval is set on the breast of a double-headed eagle. Between the eagle's heads is a medallion containing a lighted candle symbolising wisdom, surmounted by a crown similar to the one on Sophia's head. Each wing bears three medallions containing the symbols of other 'gifts' or 'virtues': virginity, justice, mildness (right wing) and piety, graciousness, firmness (left wing).[54] The eagle has a sword in its right claw and a feather in its left. The use of the oval frame and the pose with orb and sceptre are derived from the *Book of Crowned Heads* or *Titles* (*Tituliarnik*), compiled in the Foreign Office in 1672, which in turn provided the model for the 1682 coronation images of Ivan and Peter.[55] Sophia thus had herself depicted in a pose hitherto reserved for Russian tsars, holding a sceptre in her right hand and an orb in her left. Part of the Kremlin appears behind her. There are important differences, however. The crown, notwithstanding the remarks of some previous investigators, is decidedly not the crown of Monomach, which is a cap with a fur rim. Nor does Sophia wear the pectoral cross, which usually features in the portraits of the tsars.[56] She wears her hair loose in the style of the unmarried woman, but the features, suggestive of a heavy jaw, are far from girlish.

All the surviving portraits of Sophia that have any claim to being contemporary resemble the image in the eagle portrait, and although no documentary evidence of her sitting for artists has so far come to light, we must assume that this is the closest thing we have to a true likeness of Sophia Alekseevna. Clearly this is no 'bridal' portrait. There is no attempt to flatter in the sphere of physical attributes. Rather, the flattery is confined to the realms of piety and politics. In the words of A.P. Bogdanov, 'The very creation and distribution of these portraits must be regarded as a political act.'[57] This is underlined by the listing of all the lands ruled by the 'heiress, sovereign lady and possessor' and by

9  'Eagle' portrait of Sophia: anonymous oil painting (c. 1689)

the verses accompanying the portrait contained in cartouches at the base, in which Sophia's political accomplishments are lauded.[58]

The political purpose of the portraits is further confirmed by the well-known Bloteling engraving.[59] There is still some disagreement over the dating of this particular work. For the moment we might accept A.P. Bogdanov's suggestion, based on the early 1689 date for the eagle engraving, that Tarasevich's oval portrait minus its eagle surround was taken to Holland in 1689 by the Foreign Office Secretary Andrei Vinius, who passed it on to Burgermeister Nicholas Witsen of Amsterdam, who in turn commissioned a reworked version from the artist Abraham Bloteling 'in order that the great sovereign lady should enjoy fame overseas'.[60] The portrait itself differs little from the Tarasevich version, but the surround is entirely Westernised, the eagle being replaced by trumpeting victories, laurels and palms, and the virtues translated into Latin equivalents. The verses are also new.[61] The 100 prints which were sent back to Russia could barely have arrived before Sophia was overthrown. Most were destroyed by order of Peter, only copies abroad surviving. There could be no clearer attestation of Sophia's political image. In 1777 the Bloteling engraving served as a model for a russified copy by A. Afanas'ev, executed in the Academy with the approval of Catherine the Great.[62]

Surviving paintings are less well documented. E.S. Ovchinnikova, the author of a pioneering monograph on the seventeenth-century portrait, lists three extant paintings of Sophia that she believes to be contemporary.[63] The most interesting, an oil painting on canvas from the Novodevichy collection (exhibited intermittently in the main cathedral), is thought to have belonged to Sophia herself. It bears a strong resemblance to Tarasevich's 'eagle' but it is unfinished; the oval medallions on the wings remain blank, and there are no texts, perhaps an indication that work was in progress when Sophia was overthrown. This would suggest that the oil painting was based on the engraving, but there is no documentary evidence to link the two.[64] Ovchinnikova believes that the work may have been commissioned by Shaklovity from an unknown artist in the Armoury. Certainly, the workmanship is more reminiscent of the Russian *parsuna* than of contemporary Western portraiture. There are also undated, unsigned 'eagle' portraits on canvas in the Historical Museum in Moscow and the Russian Museum in Leningrad.[65] There may have been other contemporary works that disappeared. It is usually assumed that no images postdate 1689, yet a reference survives to a painting of Sophia in a nun's habit which was kept in the Monastery of St Sabbas at Zvenigorod, one of the foundations that received frequent endowments from the Tsarevna.[66]

It should be noted that some of the 'portraits' of Sophia sometimes reproduced by historians are either not contemporary or of dubious attribution. These include the picture of a pretty young girl wearing a crown printed in Massie's *Peter the Great*, on the basis of which he seeks to refute La Neuville's assertion that Sophia was 'hideous'.[67] This is evidently an eighteenth- or even nineteenth-century work, which bears no resemblance to contemporary images. This is likewise true of the print with the caption 'La Grande Duchesse de Moscovie' reproduced by Rovinsky alongside the series of ambassadors from the mission of Dolgoruky and Myshetsky to Paris in 1687.[68] If it is meant to be Sophia at all, it is clearly an imagined likeness. The costume looks more French than Muscovite. Also, the face and style bear a distinct resemblance to an engraving of Catherine I, no. 63 in the same work, which casts further doubts upon Rovinsky's attribution. Another engraving is undoubtedly contemporary, but unlikely to have been made directly from life. This is the unflattering full-length profile printed in Schleissing's memoir on Russia, and also reproduced by Rovinsky.[69]

Closely related to the oval portraits of Sophia is the contemporary half-length engraving of Vasily Golitsyn, accompanied by a coat of arms and verses, the latter sometimes attributed to Sophia herself.[70] The work, which depicts the Prince holding a hetman's *bulava* or mace, is in the manner of the Polish 'gala' portrait, very popular since the beginning of the century amongst the nobility of the Commonwealth. The oval is set off by a framework of Baroque scrolls and volutes. The artist was almost certainly Leonty Tarasevich, from whom the work was probably commissioned in 1687 in the wake of the first Crimean campaign.[71] The State Historical Museum in Moscow has an oil painting of Golitsyn, thought to be by a contemporary Russian artist.[72] Here he is depicted holding a book bearing the legend 'Treaty of Eternal Peace'.

Golitsyn was himself a collector of portraits, over forty-three of which were listed amongst the contents of his Moscow mansion, catalogued after his exile in 1689. They included, predictably enough, Tsars Aleksei, Fedor, Ivan and Peter, as well as earlier rulers such as Vladimir of Kiev. Patriarchs Nikon and Joachim were represented, as were the King and Queen of Poland and some unspecified 'German' rulers.[73] Golitsyn's own portrait hung in the dining room, but there is no mention in the catalogues of any images of Sophia. The Prince was one of the first recipients of the engraved portraits described above, but it is quite understandable that he would have hesitated to put Sophia's 'coronation' portraits on public display in a building that was much frequented by both government officials and foreign envoys.

Unfortunately, very few contemporary descriptions of interiors have come down to us and it is therefore difficult to assess just how typical Golitsyn's 'portrait gallery' was of the households of his era. Other documented examples include the house of A.S. Matveev, which contained portraits of his sons Ivan and Andrei and two of Matveev himself.[74] The russified Vinius family, originally from Holland, owned a collection of family portraits, as did presumably many of the inhabitants of Moscow's Foreign Quarter, but in view of the very few examples of Russian portraits surviving from the 1680s it seems reasonable to assume that Golitsyn was slightly in advance of his contemporaries in his taste for portraits, as he was in other areas, and that the habit remained confined to a narrow circle of courtiers and Church hierarchs. Interesting examples include the oil painting of Natalia Naryshkina, thought to date from the 1680s,[75] the engraving (again by Leonty Tarasevich) of St Theodore Stratilates in the garb of a warrior, thought to be an allusion to Fedor Shaklovity, of whom no authenticated likeness survives,[76] and the oil painting of G.P. Godunov, dated c.1686 on the evidence of the subjects's age on an inscription.[77] The latter shows Polish influence.

Fascinating though they are, the secular portrait and frescoes for the domestic interior formed only a small part of a cultural scene which continued to be dominated by religious art. The icon retained its role as an object of veneration, an essential component of even the humblest household, as well as royal churches and palaces. But the icon itself was not immune from fundamental changes in both function and form. It could be treated, for example, as a 'symbol of wealth', a function which was emphasised by the lavish application of gold paint and covers of precious metals encrusted with jewels, or a testimony to artistic virtuosity and ingenuity, as more and more artists began to sign their work. Increasingly, a 'Western' manner (even if not all patrons would have recognised it as such) was deemed desirable: use of perspective, 'naturalistic' faces, realistic landscapes, architectural details and objects. In church a sumptuous setting was provided by the new-style iconostases, composed of columns carved in high relief and gilded. The icon had 'begun to acquire the significance of a work of art in its own right. . . . The imagination with which the artist composed his subject, the ingenuity and skill with which he inserted details – these were the qualities which came to be admired.'[78]

In the court and inner circle of the nobility icons also took on an additional function as the bearers of dynastic or political messages. In 1682, for example, the icon of Alexis Man of God, John the Baptist and the Apostle Peter was inserted into the local tier of the iconostasis of the Cathedral of the Annunciation.[79] Icons of the Holy Wisdom and of St Sophia, mother of Faith, Hope and Charity, also appeared more frequently. In 1685, for example, the Armoury painter Fedor Zubov was commissioned to paint several icons of the Holy Wisdom for Sophia's rooms, and also an icon of Saint Sophia for the eponymous chapel in the main Cathedral of the Novodevichy Convent.[80] The Deisis row of the chapel's iconostasis included female supplicants: Efrosinia of Suzdal', Efrosinia of Polotsk, Eupraxia and Sosipatria.[81] An interesting example of the political interpretation of icons is provided by Archimandrite Ignaty Rimsky-Korsakov's exegesis, written for Dormition Day 1689, of the Holy Wisdom composition.[82] Wisdom, depicted as a winged maiden enthroned, was of course Tsarevna Sophia, 'who bears the sceptre of sovereign rule and sits on the patrimonial throne of the Russian realm along with the great sovereigns'. The wings were her aunts Tat'iana and Anna; the seven pillars – the seven ecumenical councils; John the Baptist – Ivan; the rock at Wisdom's feet – Peter; the six angels – the six sisters ('who like God's holy angels spend their lives in virginity, in fasts and prayers and praise of God, in psalms and singing, and the reading of Holy Writ, and in various holy good works pleasing to God, standing prayerfully and courageously before the throne of the Lord God, and praying for their sovereign patrimonial legacy, the pious Christian Russian realm.') The clouds and shining stars were the boyars and councillors. This work demonstrates that peculiar blend of the pious and the political which was so characteristic of the literature of Sophia's era.[83]

The 'political' icon did not, of course, originate in Sophia's regency.

One of the first and most successful exponents was the best known of all seventeenth-century Russian artists, Simon Ushakov, whose allegorical 'Tree of the Muscovite State' has already been mentioned.[84] Ushakov continued to work in the Armoury and to direct the work of its icon painters until his death in 1686, but the most productive years of his career predate the regency. Even so, he set trends which came into their own in the 1680s, for example by working in both sacred and secular genres, and also as a draughtsman. (See, for example, his fine engravings for Simeon Polotsky's *Psalter in Verse* and *Tale of Varlaam and Josaphat*, both published in 1680.)[85] An icon of 'The Last Supper', dated 1685 and probably one of Ushakov's last works, illustrates some of the devices that were now commonplace in the Armoury: 'naturalistic' moulding of faces with light and shade, use of perspective in an accurately depicted interior, attention to detailed delineation of objects and robes.[86] In the year just before his death we find Ushakov supervising the preparation of paints for the decoration of the new royal apartments, and 'drawing and preparing images on cypress boards, and portraits of the blessed princes and great sovereigns', a clear indication that he continued to divide his time between genres.[87] His enormous influence can be seen in the work of the artists of his 'school', including Kirill Ulanov, Tikhon Filat'ev, Mikhail Miliutin and Georgy Zinov'ev.

Another influential artist whose career reached its climax in Sophia's regency was Fedor Evtikh'evich Zubov (died 1689), who had been on the staff of the Armoury since 1662.[88] Works of the 1680s included the images of female saints in the Novodevichy Convent mentioned above, and 'Our Lady of Smolensk' (1685) for the same cathedral, a characteristic work with mild, softly moulded features; the 'Nativity of the Virgin' (1688), in which the artist was able to display his skill in conveying a sense of depth and in the intricate insertion of architectural features; icons for the newly built Church of Prince Josaphat at Izmailovo[89] and for the Donskoi Monastery; frescoes in the Cathedral of the Transfiguration in the Novospassky Monastery (1689), which included scenes from Russian religious history, portraits of Classical philosophers and of Tsars Mikhail and Aleksei, the monastery's former patrons. Perhaps the most striking of Zubov's numerous works is his 'Crucifixion' icon, also in the St Sophia chapel of the Novodevichy Cathedral.[90] The composition is altogether Western in the naturalistic depiction of the crown of thorns and the blood flowing from Christ's wounds, and in the untraditional choice of colours and treatment of the landscape. A foreign prototype is clearly indicated. Zubov, like Ushakov, kept a foot in both artistic camps. His son Aleksei was to emerge as one of the foremost secular artists of the new Petrine era.

Another talented artist of the period was Karp Zolotar'ev, whose career began not in the Armoury but in the workshops of the Foreign

10  'Crucifixion' icon by Fedor Zubov (1685)

Office, which employed a large staff of artists and craftsmen to produce diplomatic charters, ambassadors' credentials and gifts for foreign envoys.[91] By the 1680s the team had considerably extended the scope of its activities, building and decorating churches on a number of royal estates. Zolotar'ev was a versatile artist. In 1678, for example, he was said to have painted the portrait of Patriarch Joachim. In the 1680s he worked in the Kremlin chapels, painting icons and carving and gilding iconostases in the Moscow Baroque style. His most spectacular work – the interior decoration of the Church of the Intercession at Fili – falls just outside Sophia's regency, but is worth mentioning briefly as a superb example of the ultimate expression of the style of that era. Zolotar'ev's signature appears on the splendidly ornate iconostasis, nine tiers of carved and gilded columns, embellished with leaves, fruit, festoons, volutes and scrolls. The overall conception of the iconostasis was evidently Zolotar'ev's although other artists, including Ushakov's pupil Kirill Ulanov, painted a number of the icons. Two of the images that bear Zolotar'ev's signature – 'The Apostles Peter and Paul' and 'John the Baptist and Alexis Man of God' (reference, of course, to the ruling tsars) – are particularly redolent of the new 'Western' manner. The saints, depicted three-dimensionally, carry the attributes of their passion and are clad in robes distinctly Catholic in style. The medium is tempera and oil. As in the case of Zubov's icon of the Crucifixion, foreign models are clearly indicated.[92]

The new manner in its most sumptuous and exuberant forms was nurtured by the tastes of an elite inner circle, but fine workmanship was by no means confined to the Armoury and Foreign Office workshops. Some of the best art of the 1680s may be found on the walls of churches in towns such as Iaroslavl', Kostroma and Vologda, where wealthy merchants and townspeople supplied the funds and a taste for the colourful and lavish, even if the requirement for a 'Western' manner was toned down away from the capital. The frescoes of the Trinity Cathedral of the Ipat'ev Monastery in Kostroma (1685) are full of lively battle scenes, crowds and architectural motifs.[93] In Dmitry Grigor'ev's fresco of the Last Judgement (1686–8) in the Cathedral of the Holy Wisdom in Vologda foreigners in accurately observed Western dress go down to Hell.[94] The wall paintings of the cathedrals in the town of Romanov-Borisoglebsk (1680s) and the Spaso-Evfimov Monastery in Suzdal' (1689) also bear witness to a thriving provincial art, one of the outstanding exponents of which was Gury Nikitin, whose mastery of composition and detail and eye for colour were on a par with any of his Moscow contemporaries. His frescoes in Iaroslavl' and Kostroma are amongst the best works of the era, and his icon of 'Christ Enthroned' (1686), from the Church of St Fedor in Iaroslavl', with its intricate brocade-like ornament and finely applied gold work is especially striking.[95] It is said that Nikitin was opposed to the 'Western' manner and to exaggerated manifestations of realism, but his art is typical of its era in its quest for perfect technique and festive colourfulness.

The 1680s, then, although still dominated by religious painting, saw changes in methods and techniques which have often been associated with a loss of specifically Orthodox spirituality. Even the Soviet art historian Briusova, who is little concerned with the theological aspects of icon painting, writes: 'In the art of the period, alongside a great upsurge of accomplishment one can sense the unmistakable signs of an imminent decline.'[96] As Leonid Ouspensky expressed it: 'In the XVII century the decline of church art sets in . . . with a mixing of church image and worldly image.'[97] This evidently came about to no small degree because of the dual role performed by many artists painting icons and secular subjects simultaneously until the two genres began to intermingle, and traditional materials and techniques were abandoned. Evangulova notes that in 1690 paintings of the 'Crucifixion', 'Taking down from the Cross' and 'Deposition in the Tomb' on canvas and painted 'in the secular manner' (zhivopisnym pis'mom) were ordered for the apartments of Tsaritsa Natalia.[98]

Already the descendants of Ushakov were spending more and more of their time on secular commissions, as the Armoury prepared to form the nucleus of Peter I's early artistic programme, and the painting of icons, once the glory of the royal workshops, was given second place to the production of maps, charts, historical scenes, banners, engravings and triumphal arches. What is interesting is that the Church voiced little protest. It will be recalled that in the 1650s and 1660s both Nikon and Avvakum had denounced icons painted uncanonically in the 'German manner'.[99] Patriarch Joachim, arch-conservative though he was, seems to have confined himself to banning in 1683 images printed on paper and cloth.[100] He was fiercely opposed to 'Latin and Lutheran' influences – stubbornly resisting Catholic requests to build a church in Moscow and questioning the advisability of allowing any 'heretics' to desecrate Holy Russian soil with their 'kirks and mosques', but it seems possible that he simply did not detect the more insidious signs of Western influence in the sphere of icon painting. What may have seemed daring and unorthodox in the 1650s had become a commonplace by the 1680s.

The painting of the 1680s cannot easily be separated from the most remarkable cultural phenomenon of Sophia's regency – the Moscow Baroque style of architecture, which blossomed and flourished under the patronage of court circles, headed by the Regent herself.[101] The regency witnessed a brisk tempo of building activity in general, as the number of stone buildings in the city centre proliferated. Decrees of 1685 and 1688 required that town houses be built of brick for reasons of fire prevention as well as appearance, an echo of decrees issued in Fedor's reign.[102] As recorded earlier, La Neuville noted with approval (and probably with a characteristic degree of exaggeration) that 'more than three thousand stone houses' had been erected under Vasily Golitsyn's supervision, as well as a new stone bridge over the Moskva river.[103]

The architecture of Sophia's regency was to show a marked affinity with that of the preceding decade, for example in choice of building materials, construction techniques and a taste for elaborately carved decoration, but there was also a more consistently rational and symmetrical approach to design and, above all, a preference for decorative devices derived from the Western order system. Classical orders were not unknown in Russia before the 1680s,[104] and were to be seen ever more frequently in the reigns of Aleksei and Fedor, for example in the stone gates of the palaces at Kolomenskoe (1672) and Izmailovo (1679– 82), but these primitive orders were generally swamped by native devices. From the mid-1680s this trend was reversed, as the façades of buildings, both churches and palaces, were articulated with engaged columns and pilasters (smooth, twisted, fluted, decorated with twisting plants and other motifs), equipped with bases and capitals, often of a modified Corinthian or Tuscan order. Window surrounds and bays were capped with pediments: plain, triangular or round, single or double, broken, with volutes or wedges. Scallop shells, volutes and festoons, 'Oeil de boeuf' windows, decorative 'strapwork' and 'cockscombs' made up the diverse repertoire of Moscow Baroque decoration.

Although the centre of the Kremlin was dominated by its fifteenth- and sixteenth-century cathedrals, the Moscow Baroque style made itself felt early on in the citadel of royal power, for example, in the carved window surrounds of the fifteenth-century Palace of Facets, added in 1684–5 by the architect Osip Startsev. The windows are flanked by columns adorned with twisting vine leaves, one of the hallmarks of the new style.[105] The device recalls (and may, indeed, be derived from) the high-relief carved wooden columns of the characteristic iconostases of the era. The new style can also be observed in the decorative parapets and spires added to the Kremlin towers. The most interesting example is the Kutaf'ia tower in front of the Trinity Gate, with its parapet of rounded broken pediments, added in 1685. An instruction of July 1686 notes that Karp Zolotar'ev (already encountered in reference to his work as an icon painter) was paid for painting woodwork on the Trinity tower itself, and for gilding an eagle (no doubt on the spire.)[106] Work was constantly in progress in the royal palace complex. In 1683, as already noted, a new three-storeyed building was erected to accommodate the tsarevny. In November 1684 the new Church of the Apostles Peter and Paul was consecrated, and in 1688 the Church of St Catherine, fitted out with a new iconastasis, was reconsecrated. The churches of the Saviour, Resurrection and Crucifixion were all refurbished.[107]

It was in out-of-town locations, however, that the most radical of Sophia's commissions were erected, notably the complex of new buildings in the Novodevichy Convent. In the words of poet Karion Istomin: 'The walls surrounding the convent were heightened with bricks, and the towers were given various fine embellishments. Holy churches were also built with magnificence and splendour within the Convent and over the gates on the walls, and were decorated inside with all manner of finery.'[108] It was probably this ensemble that inspired the author of verses to one of her portraits to remark:

Marble bears witness to munificence,
Churches glorify the generous hand of their creator.[109]

One of the first commissions was the five-tier iconostasis (1683–5) in the sixteenth-century Cathedral of Our Lady of Smolensk, carved and gilded by a team of Armoury artists led by Osip Andreev and Klim Mikhailov. Mikhailov was a Byelorussian, one of many craftsmen who crossed into Muscovy during Tsar Aleksei's war with Poland in 1654–67.[110] He had been employed on Patriarch Nikon's building projects, on Tsar Aleksei's wooden palace at Kolomenskoe, and at Izmailovo, where in 1679 he designed the iconostasis for the Cathedral of the Intercession. In 1681 he was made head of the Armoury's carving and joinery section. There is evidence that Mikhailov and fellow immigrants from the Grand Duchy of Lithuania not only influenced some of the decorative forms of Moscow Baroque, but also pioneered the use of new terminology. In a testimonial for a team hired to build choir stalls for the cathedral, for example, Mikhailov assured the authorities that they would be constructed 'with frames and columns and capitals of highest-quality workmanship'.[111]

The most striking of the buildings commissioned by Sophia in the Novodevichy Convent is the Church of the Transfiguration (1687–9) over the northern entrance, which provides a splendid example of the adaptation of traditional architectural forms in the new symmetrical 'Western' manner.[112] The original function of all the traditional elements is subordinated to this aim. For example, the *zakomary* (rounded arches over the bays) are there – two instead of the usual three because of the narrowness of the façade – but they are purely decorative, and do not correspond to the vaulting of the roof as would be the case in older churches. The church has the traditionally favoured five domes, but these have no connection with the interior. False 'windows' are painted on. The church is composed of the same basic elements as the Cathedral of Our Lady of Smolensk (itself based on the Kremlin Dormition Cathedral) opposite, but these elements have been miniaturised and enclosed within a framework derived from the order system. The

11   Novodevichy convent, church of the Transfiguration (1687 – 9), modern view

arches of the supporting gates are flanked by Corinthian-style columns, which are echoed in pilaster form in the carved window surrounds and portals, and in the double layer of paired half-columns at the edges of the building. Window surrounds and portals are capped with broken pediments. The decorative scallop-shell motifs in the bays and the ornate golden cupolas complete the playful and festive impression.

The devices and materials of this church – red brick decorated with white limestone – are repeated throughout the convent, although no two buildings are identical, either in structure or decoration. The Church of the Intercession over the southern gates (consecrated in August 1688 by Patriarch Joachim) is based on an Ukrainian-inspired design of three octagonal towers on an east-west axis.[113] The towers are blind, treated purely decoratively. Two tiers of carved window surrounds give the façade a storeyed effect, despite the small size of the interior. The Church of the Intercession could be reached by a covered walk from adjacent apartments, and was used by the tsarevny as a winter chapel. Just to the west of the centre of the convent stands the refectory, incorporating the Church of the Dormition (1685–7). The chapel of the Holy Spirit was consecrated in August 1686 in the presence of Sophia and Tsar Ivan.[114] The interior of this building, with its large airy hall, illustrates another feature of the Moscow Baroque era: a new concept of well-lit space achieved through the use of higher ceilings, elimination of internal piers and insertion of large window apertures.

The last structure to be erected in the convent during the regency was the two-hundred foot high bell tower, composed of receding octagons, each edged with columns and topped with decorative parapets. Domestic and administrative buildings – the Maria (1683–8, by the south gates) and Ekaterina (1687–9, by the north gates) chambers – and the upper parts of towers and walls were all executed in the same style. Unfortunately, the name of the architects have not reached us. Some scholars have detected the hand of Osip Startsev (employed in the Kremlin, it will be recalled in 1684).[115] but there is no documentary evidence to chart the history of construction, including communications between its patron and her craftsmen. Although there can be no grounds for crediting Sophia herself with designing the new buildings, we can safely assume that she approved of their overall design, given the frequency with which she visited the convent. It may also be assumed that the sheer scale of construction, which was in progress throughout the regency, and the central role played by the convent in the life of the court made the new architecture highly influential in shaping the tastes of court circles.

At the same time as the Novodevichy buildings were going up, work was in progress on another royal church, on the Izmailovo estate to the

12   Novodevichy convent, church of Intercession (1688), modern view

north-east of the Kremlin. The Church of Prince Josaphat of India (sadly demolished) was completed in 1688.[116] Like the Church of the Intercession in the convent, it was based on a Ukrainian model of three octagonal towers, except that whilst the central octagon was treated architectonically the two flanking annexes had blind drums. The decoration of window surrounds and side columns recalled that of the

Novodevichy churches. It is worth noting that this church was constructed by a team of Russian workmen under the direction of the Foreign Office, thus linking it not only with Sophia but also with Vasily Golitsyn. The iconostasis and icons were also manufactured by the Office's workshop, a indication that the Armoury did not have a monopoly in such matters.[117]

Ukrainian influence can also be detected in another royal commission of the era, the Cathedral of Our Lady of the Don in the Donskoi Monastery, which was begun in 1684 with funds supplied by 'the Christ-loving patroness and Pious Tsarevna and Great Princess' Ekaterina, Sophia's sister.[118] Work was halted in 1686 when only the domes and interior decoration awaited completion, ostensibly in anticipation of the forthcoming war against Turkey. The church was consecrated in 1698. The massive exterior of the brick-built cathedral is sparingly decorated, except for surrounds and columns in Moscow Baroque style. Its most remarkable feature is its ground plan and the arrangement of the domes, which follows the Ukrainian rather than the Russian pattern (in the latter, domes are set at the corners of the cube). Might Tsarevna Ekaterina, who is said to have taken to wearing her hair and dressing in the 'Polish' fashion, have personally influenced the design? In the absence of explanatory documentation, it is impossible to be sure of the source of the inspiration. The first recorded work by Ukrainian architects in Russia postdates Sophia's regency by a number of years.[119]

Another set of buildings associated with the royal family (although, as was the case with the Novodevichy convent, archival references to the architects have not survived) are in the Trinity–St Sergius Monastery, which played such an important role at both the beginning and the end of Sophia's regency.[120] The refectory, incorporating the Church of St Sergius (1686–92), is a large spacious hall like the one in the Novodevichy Convent, raised on a substructure and surrounded by a ballustraded terrace. The elaborate window surrounds, sculptured frieze and scallop-shell motifs also seem to derive from the Novodevichy repertoire, although the painting of the façade in blues and greens produces a quite different effect. The nearby Chambers (Chertogi) and the small chapel over the spring appear to have been erected by the same team.

Mention must not be omitted of another work completed under royal patronage during Sophia's regency. This was the Cathedral of the Resurrection in the Monastery at New Jerusalem (now Istra), begun by Patriarch Nikon in 1656. Work was interupted by Nikon's downfall in 1666, but restarted in 1679 during Fedor's reign as a result of the intervention of Tsarevna Tat'iana Mikhailovna.[121] The great cathedral

13   Novodevichy convent, bell-tower (1689), modern view

14   Church of Prince Josaphat at Izmailovo (1688): engraving from I. Snegirev, *Russkaia starina v pamiatnikakh tserkovnogo i grazhdanskogo zodchestva*, (1846)

was consecrated in January 1685 in the presence of Sophia, Golitsyn and a large delegation of courtiers.[122] The cathedral (recently restored after destruction in the last war) is a remarkable edifice, capped by a huge tent roof and decorated with tiled window surrounds and portals of Classical design. 'Many of the forms of its exterior decoration', wrote the Soviet art historian M.A. Il'in, 'not only anticipated but also served as models for the exponents of the subsequent Moscow Baroque.'[123]

In 1685 Vasily Golitsyn had a wooden model of the cathedral made, just one of many indications of his personal interest in architecture.[124] As I have argued elsewhere, there are reasons for believing that one of the major sources for the decorative devices of Moscow Baroque were

Western graphic materials and illustrated books, of which the Foreign Office had an impressive collection, including books confiscated from the library of A.S. Matveev in 1677.[125] A catalogue of holdings, compiled in 1696, records that in the years 7192–3 (that is, September 1683 to August 1685) 'of the books listed above, seventeen with models for gardens, palaces and town-planning, carving and fountains and sculptures, were taken from the Foreign Office by Prince Golitsyn to his home . . . and he did not return them to the chancellery'.[126] Golitsyn himself commissioned at least two buildings in the Moscow Baroque style, both, frustratingly, demolished in the 1930s. His mansion on Okhotnyi Riad (now Prospekt Marx) was probably completed by 1685, with the help of foreign craftsmen.[127] (A Swede constructed the metal-covered roof.)[128] The two-storeyed structure was capped with a simple triangular pediment and the façade was articulated with window surrounds of typical Moscow Baroque design. The Prince's semi-Westernised lifestyle was even more clearly reflected in the interior, to be discussed below. Adjacent to the mansion was the Church of St Paraskeva Piatnitsa (1687), which had a Ukrainian arrangement of domes, the four side-drums each supported on the arms of a Greek cross. The whole structure was raised on a high base. It seems likely that the external decoration would have matched that of the mansion.

Golitsyn was just one of the members of the inner circle who adopted the latest architectural fashion. Others included P.I. and B.I. Prozorovsky, regular attendants of the royal party, whose Church of the Dormition on their estate at Petrovskoe Durnevo was consecrated by Patriarch Joachim in the presence of Ivan and Sophia in 1688.[129] Demolished in the 1930s, it comprised a large central octagon surrounded by four equal annexes, anticipating the centralised 'Naryshkin' compositions of receding octagons that came to predominate in the 1690s. In 1688 B.I. Prozorovsky built the Church of Boris and Gleb on his Moscow estate at Ziuzino.[130] Built of red brick with white limestone details with three octagonal towers, it recalls Sophia's churches in the Novodevichy Convent and at Izmailovo. Another monument to the new style was the church built in 1681–7 by A.S. Shein on his estate at Kurovo.[131] Shein had served in the Ukraine in the early 1680s, and later accompanied Golitsyn on the Crimean campaigns. His church is an almost unadulterated copy of a Ukrainian prototype – three large octagonal towers on an east-west axis, and lacking the non-Ukrainian rectangular substructure usually found in Moscow Baroque churches of this type.

Churches in the colourful new style sprang up all over Moscow and beyond. Many patrons inclined towards the 'compromise' style of the Church of the Transfiguration in the Novodevichy Convent, favouring a traditional five-domed cube decorated with an assortment of Moscow

Baroque motifs. Generally the façades were articulated with half-columns and window surrounds, as, for example,, in the Church of St Nicholas of the Great Cross in Moscow's Kitaigorod (now demolished), which was consecrated in 1688 by the Patriarch.[132] Its builders were the Filat'evs, a merchant family, who, judging by the forms of the window surrounds and the use of scallop shells in the bays, were inspired by the architecture of the Novodevichy Convent. The same might be said of the Church of the Resurrection in Kadashi across the river in the Zamoskvarech'e district, also built by merchants, the Dobrynins, around 1687.[133] Here the verticality of the conventional cube is accentuated by a high substructure and slender pointed cupolas. The most striking feature is the exterior decoration, which could serve as a copybook of Moscow Baroque design.

An indication of how the style might have been transmitted to the provinces is found in a contract for a new monastery near Nizhny Novgorod, which stipulates that items of ornamentation should be modelled on the Church in Kadashi,[134] By and large, however, Moscow Baroque made significant inroads into the provinces only in the 1690s, and once there lasted well into the first decades of the new century. Two particularly early examples of the spread of the style are the Cathedral of the Vvedensky Monastery in Sol'vychegodsk, commissioned by the Stroganov family,[135] and the Church of the Holy Spirit in the Solotchinsky Monastery near Riazan' commissioned by Archimandrite Ignaty.[136] Both were begun in 1689, the first a conventional five-domed model, the second incorporating a large octagonal drum. Elsewhere in the provinces, however, the 'decorated' style of the 1660s and 1670s clung on tenaciously, and in some cases there were even attempts to return to the purer, more monumental forms of an earlier era, for example in the impressive complex of the Kremlin at Rostov Veliky. In 1689 Peter's party rejected Sophia, but not her architectural style, which was to reach its apogee in the 1690s, in such buildings as the Church of the Intercession at Fili (1690–3), the Church of the Trinity at Troitskoe Lykov (1690–1704) and, perhaps the ultimate expression of the 'hybrid' style, the Church of the Sign at Dubrovitsy (1690–1704), an octagonal church capped by an openwork crown device, flanked by free-standing statues and embellished with Latin inscriptions.[137]

These buildings were commissioned by Peter's relatives and associates, Fili by the Naryshkins, Dubrovitsy by B.A. Golitsyn, but there is no reason to believe that they accurately reflected Peter's own tastes. Moscow Baroque undoubtedly demonstrated 'a striving for something new'[138] amongst the Muscovite elite, as did their new portraiture and naturalistic icons, but a wholly European idiom was not yet within the grasp of Moscow-trained architects and artists, and mostly beyond the imagination of patrons who had never travelled outside Russia, Sophia and Golitsyn included. The essential training ground both for the skills of craftsmen and the sensibilities of patrons was to be the brand new city of St Petersburg, designed and constructed by foreigners far from visual reminders of the Muscovite artistic heritage. We shall return to this theme at the end of the next section.

## (ii) Learning, Literature and Theatre

If the Moscow Baroque style signalled Russia's belated first step towards the mainstream of Western culture, then education must be regarded as the area in which she lagged furthest behind Western European nations. Few foreign visitors to Moscow let slip the chance to comment on the disparity, for example Tsar Aleksei's English doctor Samuel Collins, who declared the Russians to be 'wholly devoted to their own Ignorance'. Such education as existed was 'altogether illiterate and rude', and the Russians looked upon learning 'as a Monster, and fear it no less than a ship of wildfire'.[139] Russians were not insensitive to such criticism, which was customarily delivered with a liberal measure of foreign arrogance, and in Aleksei's reign, as already noted, some modest experiments in schooling had been instituted, notably under the direction of Simeon Polotsky, who ran a training school for government clerks.[140] Soviet scholars claim that basic literacy grew throughout the century,[141] but only a handful of Russians progressed beyond an elementary education. As the Saxon traveller Georg Adam Schleissing said of Vasily Golitsyn: 'He was a great lover of all manner of knowledge and learning, which makes him a very strange beast indeed in Russia.'[142] Yet even Golitsyn's accomplishments were probably modest by Western standards.

By the 1680s the point at issue was not *whether* education was needed, but what form it should take in order to extract the maximum useful knowledge whilst inflicting the minimum damage upon Orthodoxy and national customs. According to S.M. Solov'ev's classic formula in the introduction to his volume on the reign of Fedor:

> There was much talk of the need to find remedies to make the nation strong, win the respect of other countries, increase prosperity and raise moral standards. People spoke of the need for education and teachers arrived from foreign lands. Some came from Greece and, from Western Russia, monks and nobles schooled in Poland. Others arrived from the distant West, men of foreign race and creed, 'Germans', to give instruction in the military arts and other practical subjects. These new teachers clashed with the old, and strife and division ensued. In their alarm at the changes people began to clamour about the end of the world, about Doomsday and the reign of Antichrist. And in a way they were right to do so, for the old Russia was coming to an end and the new was beginning.[143]

In other words, the quest for education touched fundamental issues of national consciousness and orientation. It was no accident that the leading figures in the educational debates of the 1680s were also the spokesmen for the 'Latinist' and 'Graecophile' parties in the simultaneous religious controversy.

The debates and rivalries that were to come to a head in Sophia's regency had been developing during Fedor's reign. Simeon Polotsky had died in 1680, and his role as publisher, poet and educationalist had been assumed by his pupil Silvester Medvedev. In 1681 or 1682 Medvedev set up a school in the Zaikonospassky Monastery, Polotsky's former headquarters. Its curriculum included Latin, Greek and grammar, and presumably rhetoric, for in 1684 and 1685 boys from the school delivered orations in the presence of Patriarch Joachim. Numbers were small, however, no more than twenty-three.[144] A.P. Bogdanov believes that this school received a blessing and funds from Tsar Fedor himself, who intended it to 'form the basis for a future academy'.[145] He links its foundation with the curious Academic Privileges submitted to Tsar Fedor in 1682, which he attributed to Medvedev.[146]

The 'project' set out in the 'privileges' was an odd mixture. On the one hand, it proposed a broad curriculum that was sophisticated by Russian standards, to include 'civil and religious sciences': grammar, poetics, rhetoric, dialectics, rational, natural and legal philosophy, as well as languages. On the other hand, the staff of the Academy were to act as guardians of Orthodoxy, strictly vetting all teachers, administering censorship of books, handing over to the authorities pupils or teachers who lapsed from the faith. Solov'ev described it as 'a citadel to be erected by the Orthodox Church in preparation for its inevitable clash with the non-Orthodox West ... a frightful tribunal of the inquisition'.[147] It is difficult to reconcile the 'inquisitorial' aspects of the Privileges with Medveldev's 'progressive' views. Parts of the text read as though they could have come from the hand of Patriarch Joachim himself and, indeed, Bogdanov believes that the Patriarch amended them.[148] A.I. Rogov, however, believes that their author may have been Karion Istomin, who took a middle path between the 'Latinists' and 'Graecophiles' and, indeed, composed a series of appeals for the 'institution of learning' in the 1680s.[149]

Meanwhile, in 1681 the rival camp had set up a school in the Typography, sponsored by the Patriarch and run by the hieromonk Timothy. The 'Greek' school was intended to train editors and correctors. Starting with about thirty pupils, by 1686 it has 233; in other words it was much bigger than Medvedev's establishment.[150] This must have been the school visited by the German traveller Englebert Kämpfer in August 1683, when he reported seeing about fifty boys in the elementary class and remarked that 'the teacher himself was unable to explain anything. He was dressed in a torn robe.'[151] The Greek orientation of the Typography school was intended as a direct challenge to possible 'Latinist' tendencies in Medvedev's establishment. The Patriarch was supported in this aim by Patriarch Dositheus of Jerusalem, who early in 1682 wrote: 'Be sure to keep the flock of Christ pure from Latin writings and books, for they contain the teaching of Antichrist and they are full of novelties and full of blasphemy. . . . they are wheedling and enticing.'[152] This was just one of many such warnings. In the words of an anonymous tract of the period, it was essential to 'extinguish the smallest spark of Latin teaching, not to allow it to smoulder and catch light, with the result that the flame of pernicious Western sophistry might flare up and annihilate the truth of Eastern Orthodoxy'.[153]

In January 1685 Medvedev, still hopeful of improving the status of his own school, presented Sophia with a long appeal in verse in which he referred to the fact that Tsar Fedor, that 'lover of wisdom', had intended to found an academy but had not lived long enough to confirm his charter. This task was now to fall to Sophia:

Illustrious daughter of an illustrious tsar
The sovereign of many realms, principalities and lands
Most wise Sophia Alekseevna
Beloved of the Holy Trinity
Endowed with its Holy Gifts
You live your life in keeping with your name
Wondrous of speech, wise of deed . . .
Famed throughout the universe for wisdom
Praised for your graciousness to us all
The lover of the wise and good
The bestower of favour
Just as Olga revealed the light of faith
And thus lit up the heavens forever
So you intend to reveal to Russia
The light of learning, and thus live in heaven for eternity.[154]

The piece, which ran to over 230 lines, contained much play upon the polarities of light and dark, exhorting Sophia to 'drive away the darkness of ignorance from Moscow'. Many of the lines appear to be taken direct from Polotsky. Sophia was responsive to the appeal for an academy, but proved unable to support Medvedev's claim to implement the project. Bogdanov believes that in 1685–6 Sophia and the Patriarch had found a mutuality of interests over the subordination of the metropolitanate of Kiev to Moscow, and that Vasily Golitsyn may have been instrumental in the fate which ultimately befell Medvedev's school: its liquidation in favour of the Patriarch's project, which had the support of the ecumenical patriarchs.[155]

Shortly after Medvedev made his submission, in the spring of 1685, the two Greek brothers, Ioanniky and Sofrony Likhud, graduates of the

University of Padua, arrived in Moscow.[156] They immediately set up a school with about forty pupils in the Monastery of the Epiphany in Kitaigorod, just a stone's throw from Medvedev's school. They soon complained that the premises were unsuitable, and in October 1687 moved to newly built stone chambers in the Zaikonospassky Monastery, that is next to the premises of Medvedev's school, which was then closed. The defeat of Medvedev in the educational sphere must be seen within the context of continuing religious debates, especially the dispute over the moment of transubstantiation discussed earlier. The main point is that the Likhuds enjoyed the backing of the Patriarch, who preferred to entrust the delicate matter of higher education to foreigners rather than to Medvedev, whom he associated with his mentor Polotsky, a man 'trained by the Jesuits'.

The Slavonic–Greek–Latin Academy as it came to be known took over the pupils of the Epiphany and Typography schools.[157] (What happened to Medvedev's pupils is not clear.) Tuition was given at three levels: primary (Slavonic and Greek), intermediary (Latin and grammar) and higher (rhetoric, dialectics, logics and physics). By 1689 the school had 182 pupils drawn from a cross-section of society. The Moscow Academy long remained the foremost educational establishment in Russia (Moscow University was founded only in 1755), the *alma mater* of figures such as the scientist and poet Mikhail Lomonosov and the architect V.I. Bazhenov. In the first years of its existence, however, it evidently left much to be desired. A.P. Bogdanov writes that 'neither in its programme nor in its status did it bear any resemblance to that university of which the advocates of enlightenment had dreamed'.[158]

The remarks of the Jesuit Georgius David, expelled from Moscow in October 1689, are instructive. In the section of his memoir on Russia entitled 'De studiis, typographiis et libris praecipuis' he observed, like so many foreigners before him, that learning did not flourish amongst the Russians, 'who have neither schools of humanities nor philosophy nor theology, and no academies [sic], seeing that when the true religion was extinguished and fell into the Greek schism, all such things languished. . . . Apart from reading and writing, and that in the local language, they study nothing, and only very few youths are studying.' The 'boyars' sons' had little use for learning. There was no Latin, he said, and only a little Greek (and that of a 'barbaric' variety). He knew of the arrival of the Likhuds, 'but they had negligible, or very little, success'.[159]

David's Soviet translator objects that the 'Catholic-oriented' author had either not seen or failed to understand the significance of new developments in education.[160] One must, of course, take into account David's personal animosity towards the Patriarch, who had engineered

164

his expulsion and whom he regarded as *hominem rudissimum*. Yet David's assertion about the 'boyars' sons' rings true. It seems likely that the majority of the boyar elite had still not acknowledged the need for any more than basic skills, a problem which was to continue to dog Peter the Great himself as he strove to drag his reluctant nobles into the schoolroom. The influence of the Likhud brothers turned out to be short-lived. In 1688 Ioanniky went to Venice as envoy for four years. In 1694, a final irony, both were removed from their teaching posts as a result of objections by Patriarch Dositheus of Jerusalem at the predominance of Latin in the curriculum.

Despite the inevitable association of Sophia herself with the introduction of 'wisdom' and the above-average erudition of a number of her adherents, her regency was to inaugurate educational progress in only a narrow area. Very soon the scholastic timetable of the academy had to be supplemented and then superseded by the Mathematical and Naval Academies of Peter's reforms. One senses the frustration of the Deacon Afanasy, who in 1687 complained that foreigners on the one hand impeded Russia's attempts to acquire education, and on the other denounced the Muscovites as 'beasts and swine, berating them with abusive words because God has not granted the establishment of school learning in our Muscovite realm'.[161] Yet a way had to be found to acquire learning from those very foreigners who did the 'berating'. And, as in other areas of cultural development, full assimilation of Western knowledge was possible only by removing religious fetters, swallowing national pride and braving the dangers to the soul of study abroad or tutoring at home from 'heretics'. Vasily Golitsyn, La Neuville tells us, had 'exhorted nobles to make their children study, and given them permission to send them to Latin colleges in Poland and recommended that they invite Polish governors for the others'.[162] Even this modest proposal could not be implemented in Sophia's regency, and when Peter sent abroad his first contingent of students, it was not to Poland but to Italy and Holland.

The question of education cannot be considered in isolation from developments in printing and literary activity in general, even if, in the words of N.P. Kisilev, 'Muscovite publishing failed to reflect either stormy political events, social life or developments in culture and literature.'[163] On the face of it, by the 1680s little had changed to amend this view. A.S. Zernova lists just forty-eight works published during the regency, the usual print-run of which was 1,200 copies. Some titles were published several times, the six editions of the *Psalter*, four of the *Book of Hours* and two of the *Service Book* accurately reflecting the 'top three' for the century as a whole.[164] Only one secular work was printed (and that cannot with certainty be dated to the regency): the *Multiplication Tables* (*Schitanie udobnoe*) of 1682,[165] one of only six secular titles, according to Kisilev's reckoning, to be published in the whole century.[166]

All but one of these works were produced by Moscow's sole press, the Typography (*pechatnyi dvor*), a state institution supervised directly by the Patriarch, in whose chambers all new books were supposed to be vetted.[167] In 1679 this monopoly had been broken by the establishment of the Palace Press (*verkhovnaia tipografiia*), the title pages of whose publications bore the names of the Tsar and Patriarch, but which was in reality directed by Simeon Polotsky.[168] Of the six works published during its short existence, Polotsky was the author of four: – *Slavonic Primer* (1680), *Psalter in Verse* (1680), *Spiritual Repast* (1681) and *Spiritual Supper* (1683) – and edited and wrote prefaces to the others: *The Testament of the Emperor Basil to his son Leo the Philosopher* and *The Tale of Varlaam and Josaphat*, both 1680.[169] There is every indication that Polotsky intended to publish some of his verses, but this project was halted by his death in 1680. *Spiritual Supper*, the last work to be published, a chronologically arranged collection of sermons for Church festivals, was seen through the press by Silvester Medvedev in 1683, but in February of that year the press was closed at the instigation of the Patriarch. This event provides a further example of Sophia's relative weakness in relation to Joachim, who had evidently held off attacking Polotsky's enterprise as long as Tsar Fedor was alive. Sophia's failure to prevent the closure of her late tutor's press suggests that she was unprepared to clash with Joachim, whose support had been so vital for dealing with the strel'tsy and the schismatics in the aftermath of the 1682 rebellion. Thus in Sophia's regency Muscovite publishing reverted wholly to the hands of the Patriarch.

The vast majority of works published were liturgical, but there were some exceptions, for example what might be termed 'occasional' publications by Church dignitaries. These include two works by Joachim himself: *Condemnation of Nikita Pustosviat* (two editions, 1682),[170] a response to the 1682 confrontation with the Old Believers, and *A Tract in Gratitude for the Deliverance of the Church from the Apostates* (1683),[171] in reference to the same. *Spiritual Admonition* (1682), by Joachim's acolyte Archbishop Afanasy of Kholmogory, was also a diatribe against the schismatics.[172] *Prayers for the Victory over the Hagarene* appeared in May and June 1687 as the Russian armies struggled against the Tatars in the south.[173] Thus political events were, to a small degree, reflected.

In general, however, the publications of the Moscow Typography were intended not for private reading but for liturgical use, and provide only a very partial indication of what the literate actually read. In order to begin to answer that question one must turn both to the great volume of manuscript literature, and to printed works originating from other parts of the tsars' realms, notably the Ukraine, and from abroad.[174]

Manuscript publications remained both cheaper and more accessible than printed books well into the eighteenth century,[175] offering a much wider range of subject matter than the limited output of the Typography. Many such works were officially commissioned. For example, the Foreign Office workshops remained one of the chief centres for the production of manuscripts, which were often illustrated with engravings and finely bound. Thus in 1685 the workshop team headed by Leonty Gross was instructed to translate from the German a work on the art of firearms from an original printed in Strassburg in 1603.[176] In 1688 the same team translated a book on trigonometry and surveying from the French.[177]

Works intended purely for entertainment also proliferated, notably tales, both translated and home-produced. The most striking example of the latter is the 'picaresque' tale of Frol Skobeev, the events of which in some versions are set in the year 1680.[178] It is the amoral story of an unscrupulous seducer. Frol succeeds in gatecrashing an all-female party disguised as a woman, but the storyteller expresses no moral outrage at this violation of the *terem*. Indeed, the nobleman's daughter Annushka, having been seduced by trickery, keeps Frol hidden in her house for three days in order to sample further 'delights'. A similar disregard for the proprieties observed in 'official' literature can be found in the many satirical tales in circulation, for example the *Liturgy to the Ale House*, in which the Orthodox mass is parodied.[179]

Such examples of 'democratic satire' appear to have coexisted with works of a more traditional nature like lives of saints, the *Brightest Star* anthology of miracles associated with the Virgin Mary, and moral literature like the tale of Savva Grudtsyn and the *Rimskie deianiia* derived from the thirteenth-century *Gesta Romanorum*. Especially popular were tales translated from the collection *Speculum magnum exemplorum*, generally via the Polish *Wielkie zwiercadło*. Silvester Medvedev's library held several copies, together with the *Facetiae* (*Facecye polskie*), which contained risqué material.[180] Two examples of chivalric romances – the tales of Ottone Emperor of Rome, and Brave Knight Peter and the Golden Keys, were listed in the collection of Prince Vasily Golitsyn.[181] Such works, however, became available and popular before the beginning of Sophia's regency, and we cannot with certainty trace the origins of any such works to the 1680s. The time and place of the composition, not to mention the authorship, of works that survive in many versions, often in eighteenth-century copies, are invariably difficult, if not impossible, to establish.

The court literature of the period, what some would regard as marking the modest beginnings of professional *belles lettres*, presents problems of a rather different order. Many of the works can be precisely attributed and dated, but the very limited and 'closed' character of these early literary experiments requires a cautious approach to assessing their place in the history of Russian literature. For a start, this branch of literature was initiated virtually singled-handedly by one man, Simeon Polotsky, who in his role as Russia's first (and for some years only) court poet produced some 80,000 lines of verse in the form of declamatory and emblematic poems, odes, epigrams, labyrinths, cryptographs and plays.[182] Much of this prolific output, however, was intended for the ears and eyes of an elite inner circle – occasional verses to mark royal births, deaths, namedays, weddings, the completion of a royal palace, a eulogy to the 'Russian eagle'. If we add to this the fact that only one of Polotsky's poetic works, the *Psalter in Verse*, was actually published in his lifetime, that many others survived only in lavishly decorated bound copies stored in the palace,[183] and that his posthumous anathematisation by the Church limited still further the dissemination of his writings, then the narrow scope of Polotsky's influence becomes clear.

Even so, the taste for literary composition was implanted in a small number of followers, notably Silvester Medvedev, who not only emulated the devices and techniques of his teacher but on occasions lifted whole lines and verses from his works. In Sophia's regency Medvedev continued the tradition of writing occasional verse, and his output was supplemented by the writings, both poetry and prose, of Karion Istomin (whom A.P. Bogdanov has described as the 'real court poet' of the era).[184] The demand for panegyrics was additionally met by foreigners, such as Ivan Bogdanovsky and the Likhud brothers, and ecclesiastical dignitaries such as Archimandrite Ignaty of the Novospassky Monastery.

A few tentative conclusions may be drawn about the literature of this 'school'.[185] Most surprising is the impression that, in comparison with the output of Polotsky, a narrowing of the range of devices and subject matter seems to have taken place. Most of what survives is declamatory or panegyric in nature. Classical references all but disappear, whilst religious imagery firmly re-establishes itself, even though Biblical references are interpreted and incorporated in varied and ingenious ways. In Medvedev's first eulogy to Sophia, presented in the summer of 1682, he alludes to the 'gifts' bestowed on her by the Divine Wisdom, describing her as God's 'vessel'. If the tsars are the heads of the Russian eagle the tsarevny are the wings, bearing them aloft.[186]

As we have seen, the association of Sophia with Wisdom was fully exploited by contemporaries, both in portraits and in works like Archimandrite Ignaty's interpretation of the 'Sofiia-Premudrost' Bozhiia' icon. Sophia is God's chosen one, but also his servant, the 'Pious Tsarevna'. In verses dedicated to the Regent to mark Easter 1685 the poet writes:

But you, great and glorious Tsarevna
Wise Sophia Alekseevna
Obey him, the arisen one, most assiduously

And carry out his will zealously
And follow the path commanded by him
And enter into the light desired by all
And for centuries you will not die
There you will shine like the sun[187]

The only secular element in this and similar verse is the political undertone. Even in the 1685 'Privileges of the Academy'[188] the appeal for an establishment of higher learning is firmly linked with the requirements of piously serving God. The references are to David and Solomon, to Olga of Kiev, the dedication to the 'noble and pious, beloved of God, wise and kind' Sophia Alekseevna.

The most secular and most quoted of the verses to survive from the period, the dedication to the Bloteling engraving c.1689, may not belong to Medvedev at all but to the Ukrainian writer Ivan Bogdanovsky. They appeared in Latin on the Bloteling engraving of Sophia:

Qualis in augusto fulget Sapientia vultu!
    Qantus Honos oculis, quantus in ore, sedet!
Haec est illa tuis promissa, Ruthenia, regnis,
    condita ab aeternis, quae tueatur, avis.
Nominis haec tutela tui est, quam barbarus hostis
    sensit in inculto, pertimuitque, solo.
Quae conjuratas acies ac perfida signa
    fregit et indomitis mollia corda dedit.
Cujus ab auspiciis terni coiere Monarchae,
    fortiaque Adriacus concutit arma Leo.
Quam Pietas, quam Spes divinae conscia dextrae,
    famaque Virgineo consecrat alta choro.
Justitiaeque tenax animus, rerumque Cupido
    magnarum, et forti bella movenda manu.
Ex victrix fati Prudentia, et aemula coelo
    dextera, muneribus prodigiosa suis.
Vivunt magnanimas testantia marmora curas,
    et tot ab Augusta templa dicata manu.
Talis ad Euphraten pharetrata Semiramis altum
    nobile perpetuae condidit urbis opus.
Talis erat sceptri decus Elisabetha Britanni.
    Pulcheriam tali mente fuisse ferunt.
Sic licet innumeris foecunda, Ruthenia, regnis –
    Augusta minor es inferiorque tua.[189]

For the most past, however, the imagery summoned up in praise of Sophia had a Biblical derivation, for example comparisons with women of the Old Testament, as in the following extract from an oration (in prose) delivered by the Likhud brothers for Easter 1687: 'O most wise Sophia, most valiant Judith, holy Susanna, chaste Deborah – be joyful and of good cheer, for a crown is being prepared for you in heaven, made not of perishable and temporal precious stones but from the grace of God. . . . A crown and sceptre have been made for you since you, Sophia, have made firm the sceptre of the realm with your wisdom and courage.'[190] The references to royal regalia, it should be added, were especially apposite in the year that Sophia first began to toy with the idea of a coronation. Like others of its kind, this oration contains a nice blend of the spiritual and temporal.

Available texts (of which very few have been published) suggest that the 'professional' literature of court circles in the 1680s developed one strand of Polotsky's heritage – the ode – whilst allowing others to lie dormant. Many genres already well established in the West remained unexplored: lyric and love poetry failed to make any impact, as did prose fiction; drama, as we shall see, after a flurry of activity in the 1670s, disappeared for another twenty years. In particular, poets had to wait for the verse reforms of the 1730s before the rich possibilities of the Russian language which, like English, has a variable and strongly emphasised stress on individual syllables could be fully exploited in syllabo-tonic verse. Syllabic verse, in which metre is based upon the number of syllables in a line without regard to the marked stresses, was more suited to Polish, from which the early Russian poets had borrowed it. In the absence of a comprehensive study, and with the exception of political and polemical writings, the 1680s resemble something of a literary dead-end, when little progress was made.

The most interesting, if not most typical, insights into what Russians actually read in the 1680s may be gained from the libraries of some of the leading figures of the period. One of the most impressive, by Muscovite standards at least, was that of Vasily Golitsyn, whose books were listed along with the rest of his property after his expulsion from Moscow in 1689. Two hundred and sixteen titles, both printed books and manuscripts, were listed, ninety-three of which were discovered in his Moscow mansion on Okhotny Riad.[191] Half of the works were secular in content and include titles on history and politics, such as Hiob Ludolph's *Historia Habissinica*,[192] Andrzej Modrzewski's *Commentariorium de republica emendata*,[193] Iury Krizhanich's *Politika*,[194] a Dutch military statute, and several chronicles. There was a 'book on the art of warfare' (perhaps the one published in Moscow in 1649),[195] a law code, calendars, grammars, medical primers, the 'Privileges of the Academy', works by Simeon Polotsky, Lazar Baranovich and Dmitry of Rostov, the translated tales referred to earlier. Seven of the works were in German, two in Polish, and there was a Polish – Latin grammar. At first sight this seems like a small selection of non-Russian works, but it should be remembered that Golitsyn also had access to the library of the Foreign Office, the most comprehensive collection of foreign books then available.

An even bigger collection was that of Silvester Medvedev, which was also catalogued as a result of its owner's arrest and, subsequently, execution.[196] Not only was Medvedev, as we know, closely concerned with matters of learning, but he had also worked in the Typography as a corrector since 1679 and had inherited the library of Simeon Polotsky on the latter's death in 1680. Medvedev knew Latin, Polish and Greek, as the books in his collection attest. There were some 651 items, representing 539 titles. Of these 133 were secular in content, including works on astronomy, medicine, geography, arithmetic, history and emblematics. Amongst the titles on history there were Polish chronicles by Kromer, Bielski and Stryjkowski, Dempster's *Antiquitatum Romanorum* and *Annales ecclesiastici* by the Catholic Church historian Baronius. Classical authors were well represented: Aristotle, Cato, Cicero, Ovid, Plautus, Pliny, Seneca and Virgil, to name but some. As one would expect, there were many dictionaries and grammars. One notes a copy of John Dee's *Monas hieroglyphica*, Alciatus' book on emblematics (along with several others on the same subject, evidently inherited from Polotsky), John Barclay's *Argenis*, a copy of the Quran in Polish, numerous editions of works by Lazar Baranovich, collections of tales and novellas. Alongside works of the Eastern Church fathers – John Chrysostom, John of Damascus, Athanasius the Great – one finds many works from the 'Latin' West, including Latin and Polish bibles. No doubt a look at this library would have confirmed Patriarch Joachim's belief that Medvedev had inherited Polotsky's 'Latinising' tendencies along with his books.

Finally, what did Sophia herself read? Is there any justification for assuming, as did one scholar, 'an unusual familiarity with poetry, sermons, saints' lives and folk songs'?[197] Unfortunately no consolidated library list survives (and it is unlikely that one could ever be compiled), but a number of the works that passed through her hands can be traced. In 1683, for example, part of Tsar Fedor's book collection was transferred. Peter received twelve titles and Sophia two: manuscript copies of Polotsky's *Many-Flowered Garden* and *Crown of Faith*, which were delivered to Sophia's chambers on 27 May by I.M. Miloslavsky.[198] Sophia's interest in Polotsky's writings is already well attested. The verse collection *The Many-Flowered Garden* is said to have been amassed for his royal pupils, Aleksei, Fedor and Sophia,[199] and, as previously noted, a personal dedication to Sophia of a copy of his *Crown of Faith* is included in the *Rifmologion* anthology.[200] In 1687 V.P. Titov presented Sophia with a specially bound copy of Polotsky's *Psalter in Verse*, accompanied by music and verses of dedication, a volume which appears subsequently to have been presented to Vasily Golitsyn.[201]

Sophia received numerous presentation copies of odes and orations, some of which were later transferred to Peter I's library. These include

Karion Istomin's *Book in Praise of Wisdom*, presented to her in 1683.[202] In March 1687 he arranged for the presentation of a copy of Pseudo-Augustin's *Divine Love*, accompanied by an oration for delivery by pupils of the Greek school.

> Most virtuous maiden, chosen of God, most Pious Tsarevna and Great Princess Sophia Alekseevna; your most illustrious majesty, by your persua-sive words, prudent wisdom, good sense and assiduous prayer to the All-Good deity, you are a source of great joy not only to all Russians and to all the countless peoples of the extensive and rich Russian realm, but also to many Christian peoples all over the world,

the dedication ran.[203] Another presentation volume made to Sophia was Karion Zaulonsky's (Kievsky's) *Panegyric or Praise*, offered on the occasion of the Tsarevna's nameday in 1687. Zaulonsky, who had studied at the Kiev Academy, described Sophia as the 'ornament' of the Muscovite realm.[204] Early in 1687 Osip Titov, a secretary from the Novodevichy Convent, presented Sophia with a copy of the book *The Brightest Star*, an anthology of miracles associated with the Virgin Mary, accompanied by the usual panegyric and a set of engravings.[205] We have already mentioned Medvedev's panegyric of 1682, appended to his 'Lament' for Tsar Fedor, and the 1685 'Privileges of the Academy'. Sophia also commissioned works from him, notably the theological tract 'Manna', of which a presentation copy was made in November 1687,[206] and an Acathistus to St Sergius of Radonezh, presented 29 May 1689.[207]

We may assume that laudatory works printed in the Ukraine in the 1680s also formed part of Sophia's collection, for example Baranovich's *Grace and Truth* (1683), Bogdanovsky's *Gift of the Holy Spirit* (1688), Ioanniky Goliatovsky's *Infidel Gods* (1686) and Varlaam Iasinky's *Three Crowns* (1688).[208] It is likely that she also owned other works by Baranovich. The anonymous Polish diarist of 1683, it will be recalled, remarked quite specifically that Sophia read the lives of the saints in Baranovich's Polish edition.[209] Very many of Sophia's books would have been religious, of course. A number bearing her inscription, including some with the religious name Susanna, survive in the Novo-devichy Convent, but others may have perished in the fire of 1812 when, according to the convent's nineteenth-century historian, most of the library was destroyed.[210]

One of the most intriguing legends is that Sophia was herself an author, with a particular penchant for the theatre. William Coxe, the English traveller, writing in 1784 claimed that 'she translated Molière's *Médecin malgré lui* and performed one of the roles herself, and composed a tragedy'.[211] Twenty years later Karamzin listed Sophia in his 'pantheon' of Russian writers on the grounds that 'she studied literature, wrote tragedies, and herself acted in them in a closed circle of friends. We read one of her dramas in manuscript and consider that the Tsarevna might have compared with the best writers of all times if enlightened taste had shaped her imagination.'[212] Sophia as writer, dramatist, even thespian, has been accepted as a matter of fact in many subsequent studies, for example by C.B. O'Brien, who states that she 'wrote verses and inscriptions' (she is most usually credited with the verse dedication to the engraved portrait of Vasily Golitsyn) and 'had a taste for theatricals'.[213] N. Moleva in her short study of Sophia quoted a certain 'Countess Golovina', who is said to have spent her girlhood in the *terem* and to have taken part in theatrical performances on Sophia's nameday, when they performed a play composed by Sophia herself entitled *The Betrothal of St Catherine*, in which Sophia played the leading role.[214] Schakovskoy maintains, without giving references, that Sophia translated Molière's *Médecin malgré lui* and wrote a 'tragedy called Catherine'.[215] And so on. Even a recent Soviet listing of 'writers of early Russia' notes that 'there are vague references to the fact that she wrote verse' and names her as the author of a play called *The Betrothal of St Catherine*.[216]

Sophia's alleged thespian activities have, unfortunately, failed to leave any trace in contemporary sources. The authoritative *History of the Russian Drama Theatre*, for example, claims that 'the court theatre of Tsar Aleksei Mikhailovich did not cease to function after his death', but produces only a few meagre snippets of 'evidence' of its continued existence, including the 'declamations', that is panegyric orations, delivered by Istomin, Medvedev and others, which can hardly be classified as 'theatre', and an engraved edition of Simeon Polotsky's *Comedy of the Parable of the Prodigal Son* inscribed with the year 1685.[217] There is some confusion about this latter work. The editors of the texts of early Russian plays suggest that 'it is possible that Polotsky's plays were staged at that time', but the only evidence offered of productions in the 1680s is a performance of 'Prince Josaphat of India' in the 'theatre of Tsaritsa Praskovia Fedorovna at Izmailovo in 1685.[218] In fact, the likelihood of a play by Polotsky being produced, not to mention published, in 1685, or of Tsar Ivan's new wife establishing a theatre in that year seems remote.

One is inclined rather to accept the opinion of S.K. Bogoiavlensky that the last play to be performed at court was the *Comedy of Bacchus and Venus*, which was in rehearsal just before Tsar Aleksei's death in 1676. Tsar Fedor, Bogoiavlensky guesses, had no taste for theatricals.[219] Indeed, in December 1676, it is recorded, Fedor 'ordered that the chambers of the Pharmacy Department, which had been used for plays, be cleared out and everything there, organs, scenery and other equipment, be transferred to the house that formerly belonged to the boyar Nikita Ivanovich Romanov'.[220] Further confirmation is provided by the remarks of Georg Adam Schleissing, who was in Russia in 1684–6. Tsar Aleksei, he writes, had maintained many German musicians and players at his court. But after his death this all came to an end at the instigation of the Patriarch, 'who believes that Russia will perish if any kind of novelty is introduced'.[221] Schleissing's informant was probably Laurent Rinhuber, who had actually taken part in staging court theatricals in the 1670s and was present at the same diplomatic reception as fellow Saxon Schleissing in 1684.[222] It would be surprising if Rinhuber had not enquired about the fate of the theatre upon his return to Moscow. Even without this piece of evidence, Joachim's banning of court drama, which towards the end of Aleksei's reign had become increasingly secular and even bawdy (the *Comedy of Bacchus* featured ten drunkards, ten maidens and performing bears),[223] is entirely in keeping with what we know of the Patriarch's character. Sophia as we know, was obliged to make a number of concessions in order to retain his support, including the closure of the late Polotsky's typography, and it seems unlikely that she would have risked antagonising Joachim by reviving the court theatre, even had she wished to. Bogoiavlensky does not rule out the possibility that Sophia staged plays in private, but he found no evidence.[224]

The apparent curtailment of the activities of the court theatre during the regency had implications for the history of Russian music, which until the 1670s had developed almost entirely within the sacred sphere. The advent of the theatre had necessitated the purchase of musical instruments, notably organs (excluded from the churches, where unaccompanied vocal singing was the rule), trumpets and percussion. Vocal arrangements, sometimes of psalms and cants, but also of secular music, were performed during interludes. The ballet *Orpheus* is even said to have been danced to the music of the German composer Heinrich Schütz. All this was a novelty and much appreciated by the Russian audience, as Reutenfels had pointed out, but the musical aspect was probably the one that most offended the Patriarch, as Schleissing's comments would suggest. In 1676 the musical instruments were cleared out along with the rest of the paraphernalia.

But it was too late to quash the new tastes that were developing, even if novelty in music, as in painting, often appeared in religious guise. In church choral concertos, which although religious in tone were not strictly liturgical, became popular. Attempts to correct errors in sacred chants meant turning to other Orthodox centres: Serbia, Greece, Jerusalem and, especially, the Ukraine and Byelorussia, which often ushered in new trends, including polyphonic part-song and the influence of folk music. Ukrainian choristers, with their mastery of new harmonies, were eagerly sought. (In 1686 Golitsyn invited Ukrainian singers to perform in his home.)[225] The Ukraine also provided a new system of linear notation, 'Kievan notes', closely resembling today's five staves. A landmark in Sophia's regency was Vasily Titov's setting of Simeon Polotsky's *Psalter in Verse*, a copy of which was presented to Sophia in 1687.[226] Titov was almost certainly influenced by Nikolai Diletsky, a musician who came to Moscow from Vilna in 1679 and shortly afterwards wrote a treatise entitled *Musical Grammar*, which advocated polyphonic composition and expounded Western musical terminology.

What of the legend of Sophia as dramatist? The last word on the subject may for the time being come from Simon Karlinsky's study of early Russian drama, in which he tracks down the legend to a slip of the pen by Jacob von Stählin, the Russian theatre's first chronicler. The royal thespian was, in fact, Peter's sister Natalia, whose activities are well chronicled.[227] The first public theatre in Russia was opened by Peter in 1701, but it was a failure, and Natalia took over some of the scripts and scenery for her own company. Works performed included Molière, and the *Comedy of St Catherine* was also on the repertoire, a subject inspired by Tsarevna Ekaterina Ivanovna, who lived with Natalia and was keen on the theatre.[228] What of the play that Karamzin claims to have read in manuscript? It could have been the *Play of the Holy Martyr Evdokia*, the text of which (now in Pushkinsky Dom in Leningrad) bears the inscription 'composed by Sophia Alekseevna'. As A.S. Eleonskaya has pointed out, this was probably another of Tsarevna Natalia's scripts. The subject matter, based on Dmitry Rostovsky's *Book of the Lives of Saints*, published in 1700, effectively rules out Sophia as its author.[229] The Bibliothèque Nationale also has an eighteenth-century manuscript of the *Tragedy of Nebuchadnezzar* with an inscription in a nineteenth-century hand: 'composée par la fameuse Princesse Sophia Alexievna, soeur de Pierre le Grand', no doubt added after the legend of Sophia's theatrical exploits was already established.[230] Evidently there are still a number of those ends to be tied in the history of the early Russian theatre, but Soviet historians' reluctance to admit to a long gap between 1676 and 1701 seems to have led to the inclusion of some bogus information.

Disappointing though it is to admit it, in the absence of hard evidence Sophia as the author of literary works must remain in the world of myth and imagination. In Evdokia Rostopchina's poem 'The Nun' Sophia tells the young novice to whom she makes her 'confession' that she wrote a memoir 'in order to bequeath to posterity and to the fatherland a truthful record', but that the said work was burned by 'enemies'.[231] Needless to say, no trace of such a work survives. Two letters to Golitsyn in cipher from the time of the second Crimean campaign appear to be the sum total of the 'literary heritage'.[232] An intriguing piece of evidence does survive, however. In 1878 S. Moropol'sky published a description of a manuscript of the Gospels preserved in the Saviour-Transfiguration Monastery in Kargopol, apparently copied in a 'clear and elegant hand' by Sophia herself, and inscribed with her signature. The manuscript also had pen and ink drawings of the evangelists, and decorative vignettes and letters.[233] This particular piece of handiwork seems more in keeping with what we already know of the lifestyle of the 'Pious Tsarevna' than acting in plays or translating Molière.

These observations lead inevitably to the question: in what sense, if any, can Sophia's cultural world be described as 'Westernised', taking into account not simply individual elements of that culture but the totality of surroundings and experience? In many respects Sophia's immediate vicinity represented a feminised version of that 'nightmare of religiosity' created at the court of her father. The backdrop to everyday life was the church altar and icon stand rather than the proscenium arch. Reading matter was more likely to be the psalter, Gospels and lives of saints than Molière. The walls of private apartments continued to be hung with icons and painted with scenes from the Old and New Testaments. As I.E. Zabelin wrote in his masterly study of the royal court: 'By dint of her position in society a Tsarevna was a nun, a keeper of fasts, a hermit.'[234] This, of course, was the official image, but to a considerable extent it corresponded with reality. Yet, as we have seen, Sophia was also a ruler, the 'wielder of the royal sceptre', whose 'munificence' was epitomised by the building of churches, whose stylised Classical orders and Baroque decorative devices suggested not asceticism but a love of colour and decorativeness. Nor did the 'eagle' portrait of Sophia have much hint of the cloister, nor the verses to the Bloteling portrait, comparing her to Elizabeth of England – the 'Virgin Queen', it is true, but also a powerful ruler in her own right. A list of items purchased by the merchant Elizar Izbrant in Hamburg and delivered to the palace in 1688 also suggests that in the privacy of their own quarters the tsarevny were far from nunlike: two hats with ostrich feathers, two round mirrors framed in tortoiseshell, notebooks, boxes and reticules in the same material, buttons, ribbons.[235]

The most striking evidence of the 'hybrid' lifestyle of the 1680s is provided by the description of the contents of Prince Vasily Golitsyn's Moscow mansion, on which we have already drawn extensively for this chapter. I.D. Davydova links its contents with a growing 'cult of objects', a revised perception of the physical environment not merely as a backdrop for religious observance and piety, as set out in the *Domostroi*, but as a setting to be enjoyed for its own sake, the richer, more colourful and varied the better.[236] The mansion had a fairly simple façade, articulated with typical Moscow Baroque window surrounds, but the contents and decoration of the fifty-three rooms testified to an 'eclectic, often fortuitous' combination of the traditional and the modern.[237]

In the main reception room alongside the icons hung portraits of Russian rulers. The room's ceiling was decorated with a fashionable astronomical subject: the sun, planets and signs of the Zodiac. An adjoining room had a portrait of Golitsyn himself, no doubt dressed in the new 'Polish' fashion noted by Georg Adam Schleissing.[238] We know from surviving portraits that Golitsyn sported a modish clipped beard and moustache. The house was stuffed with foreign furniture: cabinets and cupboards supplementing the chests in which items were traditionally stored, an elaborately carved German bed (a gift from Sophia herself) in the main bedroom. Walls were hung with fabric coverings or decorated with a mock marble effect. There were seventy-six mirrors and some rooms were lit by stained glass. There was china from Venice, prints and engravings from Germany, clocks, maps, Persian rugs. In the outhouses stood carriages manufactured in Poland, Holland, Austria and Germany, gifts from embassies. As we have seen, half of Golitsyn's books were secular in content, and he is said to have owned musical instruments and invited singers to perform in his home.[239] In London or Paris none of this would have been worthy of comment. In Moscow it signalled a man of advanced tastes.

It is not surprising that the Director of the Foreign Office should have assumed a semi-Westernised lifestyle, nor that a chosen few in court circles should also have succumbed. Neither is it surprising, given the enclosed lives that most Russians lived and the conservative character of a Patriarch and Church authorities who felt themselves to be under attack from both inside and outside the realm, that the new culture settled only in fragments and snatches, and then mostly behind closed doors. Real limitations on wholesale imitation remained: the Church's disapproval of the depiction of the human form in the round meant that sculpture made few inroads; the strict canons of icon-painting limited straight copying from Catholic or Protestant religious art, and the conventions of Russo-Byzantine church architecture like-wise hampered direct adoption of foreign models; the Church's near monopoly on printing meant that only religious literature was printed; the ban on musical instruments in church, and official disapproval of 'profane' music, dance and merrymaking, along with the temporary disappearance of the theatre, imposed other limitations. Such inhibitions, both practical and psychological, were in the end lifted by Peter I's decree and example, as he commissioned the Cathedral of SS Peter and Paul in St Petersburg with a Western-style spire instead of onion domes, filled the garden of his Summer Palace with nude Classical statues imported from Italy, commanded Russian painters to take up apprenticeships with foreigners or to go abroad to study, set up a secular press with its own 'civic' typeface, and cultivated a Western-style court in which men and women socialised and attended theatrical and musical performances.

It is immediately clear how greatly the court of Sophia Alekseevna differed both in atmosphere and detail. Her artists received no unambiguous directives for change from above, they were not encouraged to visit the West, and were neither technically nor psychologically prepared to work in a fully-fledged Western style, even though a handful of patrons were on the verge of demanding that they did. Not only do we find few direct imitations of Western style; we also search in vain for Muscovite rivals, be it in technique or psychological complexity, to the European masters of the Age of the Baroque. In order to set the achievements of 'Moscow Baroque' in their proper perspective we should recall the paintings of Rembrandt, Vermeer and Velasquez, the buildings of Bernini, Guarini and Wren, the music of Monteverdi, Purcell and Lully, the writings of Molière, Corneille, Racine and Boileau, Descartes and Pascal, Spinoza, Milton, Marvell, Dryden, in order to appreciate how far removed Russian artists still were from the European artistic and philosophical community. Yet, as Golitsyn's mansion suggests, the way had been paved. Russia's belated 'Renaissance', modest though its achievements may have been, heralded a violent and irreversible break with Old Russian cultural traditions. And one of the keys to that break lay in Russia's new role in the world, which forms the subject of the following chapter.

# CHAPTER 8

# Foreign Affairs

Russian diplomacy, like many other areas of Russia's modern history, is sometimes thought to have originated with Peter I. On the eve of Peter's independent rule Russia was no longer isolated, it is true, but she was still primarily concerned with those states that bordered her own territories and with those issues that touched her own immediate interests. Even when Russia's envoys ranged further afield they often seemed more concerned with the minutiae of etiquette, titles and subsistence allowances than with vital issues of foreign relations. The major powers of Europe, for their part, still tended to regard Russia as a barbaric and outsized state on the fringes of the continent's affairs which could be exploited for commercial gain, utilised as a path to the East and, on occasion, wooed as a counterweight to a more significant adversary, but she was scarcely seen as a civilized nation. Muscovy was, in the opinion of a traveller whom we shall encounter again later in this chapter, 'a wretched Empire, expos'd to all manner of Vices, Violence, Perfidiousness, and Treasons'.[1] In the words of a more recent commentator, the country was like a 'giant . . . condemned to passivity and ossification,' whose 'continuing existence appeared to be due less to its own vital energy than to its neighbours' weakness and disinterest'.[2]

Justified though such comments might seem when making a direct comparison between Russia and long-established major powers like France or Spain, or up-and-coming ones like England, however, one cannot simply dismiss the evidence, already accumulated from previous chapters, of the rapid and significant growth of Russia's links with the outside world. In the words of S.M. Solov'ev, whose *History of Russia* still provides one of the most detailed accounts of foreign affairs in the 1680s: 'Russia had long lived in the East, but now that she was forging a new path towards the West and preparing to enter the community of European nations, a series of events was taking place in Europe which was destined to transform her policies and give the new state of Russia a leading role in European affairs.'[3]

Arguably this transformation was already well underway by the 1680s. Not everyone will agree with the Soviet historians' contention that

Russia was fully involved in the Thirty Years' War, but few would deny that the Thirteen Years' War with Poland in the following decades brought her firmly on to the European stage as more than a mere bit-player.[4] The Polish historian Zbigniew Wójcik writes: 'The important new element was that the Polish – Lithuanian State, Sweden, Turkey, and eo ipso also the Tatar Khanate of Crimea, had lost status to Russia,' whose victory over Poland 'was tantamount to Russia winning hegemony among the Slavonic nations'.[5] Western historians have more recently recognised a 'crisis of seventeenth-century Europe', leading to a reorientation which sprang from both the expansion of the Habsburg Empire into non-German territory and the temporary withdrawal of France from the centre-stage of European politics.[6] Russia was now to assume a position of importance in European affairs that was never to be relinquished.

In order to understand Russia's international position at the beginning of Sophia's regency it is as well to begin with the three major 'question' inherited from the reigns of Aleksei and Fedor: relations with Poland, Turkey and Sweden. Links with all three were regulated by treaties – Andrusovo (1667), Bakhchisarai (1681) and Kardis (1661) respectively – but in no case had old conflicts been permanently resolved. Strictly speaking, China, a territorial rival in the Amur basin, should form a fourth 'question', but this new dispute in the Far East appeared both remote and distinct from European affairs. On a slightly lower level of priority came links with countries beyond Muscovy's borders, for example Holland, England, Denmark and the German states, with whom Russia had trade relations and, on occasion, a mutuality of political interests determined by adjustments in European rivalries and alliances. Generally speaking, contacts with the Protestant north were easier than those with the Catholic south, although, as we have seen, there was no ban on the entry of Catholics into Russia. At the beginning of Sophia's regency Russia's relations with the two major Catholic powers of Europe, the arch-rivals France and Austria, were somewhat hazily defined, but were soon to be thrown into sharper focus.

Moscow's foreign relations were as yet uncomplicated by dynastic marriage links, nor was she a contender for colonies overseas. There was no permanent Russian diplomatic representation in Europe, neither did any European states maintain accredited ambassadors in Moscow, although some (in the 1680s Holland, Sweden, Poland and Denmark) had permanent agents referred to as 'residents'. Communications with foreign states were effected by the irregular dispatch and reception of ambassadors and messengers, and up-to-date information was collected by producing digests from the German gazettes. In addition, the community in the Foreign Quarter (*nemetskaia sloboda*) provided an essential means of liaison and information. Men such as Patrick Gordon and

Paul Menzies, whilst primarily soldiers of fortune, were also sent on diplomatic errands. Merchants, too, were employed as messengers. It should be reiterated that much diplomatic exchange concerned not issues of international importance but the trivia (to modern eyes, at least) of titles and protocol. When Menzies went to Rome in 1673 in an attempt to enlist the aid of the Pope in a league against the Turks, sixteen days were wasted in disputes about the Tsar's titles.[7] A significant proportion of diplomatic business was taken up by lengthy and lavish rituals, many of which had scarcely changed since the late fifteenth century.

Russia's foreign affairs were administered by the Foreign Office or Ambassadorial Chancellery (*posol'skii prikaz*), the largest of more than fifty departments of state.[8] During Sophia's regency it was, as we know, directed by Prince Vasily Golitsyn, aided by E.I. Ukraintsev and, from 1687, Golitsyn's son Aleksei, and a team of clerks, scribes and translators. The lack of professional specialisation that continued to hamper Russia's development in a number of areas is epitomised by the wide range of business that came under the Office's jurisdiction. Not only did its officials carry out the normal business of diplomacy – dispatch and reception of envoys and negotiation of treaties – but they were also in charge of doctors and apothecaries, the postal service, foreign manufacturers, foreign churches and a number of large monasteries. In addition, the Office maintained its own team of artists and architects. The former devoted much of their attention to producing royal letters and ambassadors' credentials, elegantly adorned with gold leaf and plant motifs.

The overlap of functions was further complicated by the fact that the Office's Director was himself a multiple office-holder, and from February to September 1687 and again from February to July 1689 was away from the capital waging war. The title 'Guardian of the state's great ambassadorial affairs' elevated him to the status of First Minister, with a brief that went beyond formulating foreign policy. Despite this, the Office maintained continuity and even did a fairly efficient job with the help of 'career' staff, both Russians such as E.I. Ukraintsev and V.T. Postnikov, who originated from families of professional scribes, and foreigners, many of them initially employed as interpreters, like the Moldavian Nikolai Spafarius (Milescu), La Neuville's informant.

To return to the broad outlines of foreign policy, by 1682 the Polish and Turkish 'questions' were inextricably linked in the minds of Russia's diplomats, as the era of 'Ottoman militancy' that had harassed the fringes of Europe for the past decade threatened to drag Russia irrevocably into the centre of European affairs. In the seventeenth century statesmen were already using variations of the 'sick man' image to describe Turkey, but the invalid kept rallying and his near neighbours had to be ever vigilant. In the words of Wójcik, Turkish leaders 'saw war as a panacea for all internal ills',[9] perhaps even regarding themselves as the heirs to Byzantium in a bizarre variation on the 'Third Rome' theme. Polish territory was amongst the most vulnerable in the face of such aspirations. In 1672 Poland had invoked the terms of the Treaty of Andrusovo to request Russian assistance against an invasion led by Sultan Muhammad IV. Russia, for her part, had dispatched envoys all over Europe to seek aid, but to little effect. In 1676 the Turks renewed their attack on the Polish Ukraine, capturing Kamieniec. By the Treaty of Zórawno the Poles ceded much of Podolia to the Turks, and Russia found herself facing a Turkish-Tatar assault on the lower Dniepr. In 1677 the advance was repelled, but in 1678 Chigirin, the former capital of the Hetman of Right-Bank Ukraine, fell to the Turks. The Treaty of Bakhchisarai (January 1681) established a twenty-year truce between Muscovy and the Crimea, and confirmed the 1667 division of Left- and Right-Bank Ukraine. The Turks undertook not to maintain garrisons in the land between the Dniepr and the Bug. It was actually 1685 before the Sultan ratified the treaty, but not before he had installed janissaries in forts in some of the 'forbidden' zones and replenished the markets of Constantinople with Christian slaves.[10]

The lack of security on Russia's southern borders was underlined by the frequent raids made by the Tatars, despite the fact that Moscow was obliged to continue paying tribute. In 1682 the Tsar's envoy was even arrested, beaten and tortured by his Tatar hosts when he refused to hand over more than the stipulated sum. The natural desire to end such affronts was only one of the factors that governed Russia's relations with Turkey and the Crimea, however. Tsar Aleksei had once dreamed of becoming 'an all-conquering ecumenical Emperor who would one day drive the Turks out of the Christian lands they occupied and re-create Constantine's empire'.[11] Such aspirations may not have been voiced of late, but many of the Sultan's Orthodox subjects continued to regard the tsars of Muscovy as their potential champions against Ottoman and even Catholic persecution, a fact which Sophia's government exploited to the full. On the material plane, the Black Sea may not yet have acquired the lure of the Baltic 'window on the West', but for the far-sighted it offered strong inducements for Russia's advancement southwards. The arguments had been elaborated by the Serb Juraj Križanič (Iury Krizhanich) in the 1660s, and Vasily Golitsyn, as we know, owned a copy of his *Politika*.[12]

Russia's relations with Poland were also governed by both practical and ideological considerations. In 1682 territorial disputes were centred on the Ukraine, which in 1667 had been partitioned between Moscow and Warsaw. Kiev, on the Right Bank, was ceded to Moscow for a period of two years, and had not been relinquished despite Polish claims. It is a Soviet historian's commonplace that the 'fraternal' Orthodox peoples of the Ukraine regarded Moscow as their natural champion and as a more reliable defence than Poland against Tatar attacks. In fact, ever since the 1654 Treaty of Pereiaslavl', Cossack leaders had taken a pragmatic line, throwing in their lot with Turk, Pole or Muscovite as circumstances dictated. The Zaporozhians (the warriors of the Sech' encampment above the Dniepr rapids) were particularly jealous of their ancient 'freedoms' and lent their fighting power to whomsoever they saw fit, regardless of boundaries and treaties. In 1676 this wavering allegiance had swung back towards Moscow when the Turkish-oriented Hetman Peter Doroshenko was defeated by the Left-Bank Hetman Ivan Samoilovich, who laid claim to the Right Bank on behalf of the Tsar. The Poles were highly displeased by Russian interference but were in no position to enforce any demands.

Russia, in the meantime remained impervious to Polish requests for direct aid against the Turks, despite the alleged presence of a pro-Polish party at Tsar Fedor's court. In 1678 Moscow extended her truce with Poland for a further thirteen years and paid an indemnity for the retention of Kiev, but the anti-Polish faction at court would not countenance the joint operation against the Crimea which the Poles were pressing for, regarding Catholic Poland as Moscow's natural enemy and deploring any Polish encroachment into Turkish domains populated by Orthodox Christians. This group voiced deep-seated fears and prejudices against the Poles that dated back to the Time of Troubles.

Russia's third neighbour, Protestant Sweden, had long been regarded as the natural enemy in the north, barring the path to the Baltic.[13] The entry of Sweden into the war with Poland in 1655 had prevented Russia from consolidating victories won in 1654–5, thus underlining the difficulties of finding simultaneous solutions to the acquisition of lands on the Baltic and in Lithuania – Byelorussia. The Treaty of Kardis (June 1661) ratified the borders established by the Treaty of Stolbovo in 1617, and Sweden undertook not to aid Poland in a war against Russia, as had been the case in 1656–8, nor to attack the Grand Duchy of Lithuania. Kardis, in the words of Wójcik, 'signified Russia's temporary resignation from its long-cherished goal',[14] even though the Baltic remained an essential long-term aim. Golitsyn's predecessor Afanasy Ordin-Nashchokin favoured peace with Poland and war with Sweden, whilst one of the policies of Nashchokin's successor A.S. Matveev in the period 1671–6 had been to 'blackmail' Sweden by threatening to give military aid to her enemies Denmark, Holland and Brandenburg. Austria, who was particularly wary of a Paris-Constantinople-Stockholm 'axis', urged Russia to put diplomatic pressure on Sweden and even to send troops to the Livonian border, but open conflict was avoided.[15] Endemic territorial conflict was mitigated somewhat by good trading relations. Swedish merchants maintained warehouses and depots in several Russian towns and were allowed duty concessions. In the words of the British envoy John Hebdon, Tsar Fedor wanted peace with Sweden, 'being at present threatened on all sides not alone by the Pole but also by the Turk and Tatar'.[16] His immediate successors were to take the same line.

This, then, was the state of affairs inherited by Golitsyn and his colleagues in the Foreign Office in May 1682. It was fortunate for him that the strel'tsy rebellion had occured in peacetime, for Golitsyn was obliged to spend the first few months of his term of office, as we have seen, helping Sophia to quell domestic unrest. In July they left Moscow with the tsars and the court for the Trinity-St Sergius Monastery and after a short spell back in the capital departed again in August, not returning until November, when the Khovanskys had been executed and the strel'tsy brought to heel. Ukraintsev was left in Moscow to supervise the Foreign Office. A series of letters between him and his chief in July refer to routine matters, such as arrangements for the dispatch of tribute to the Crimea and the reception of Cossack and Tatar envoys. In a letter dated 22 July Ukraintsev reported that there was 'nothing new from other countries'.[17]

News was soon to arrive, however, of Polish attempts to take advantage of the 'novice' regime in Moscow by making incursions into the Ukraine. A letter from the Orthodox Bishop of Lwów was intercepted in which he assured the Cossacks that both the late King Michael and the ruling monarch John had tried consistently to defend the Ukraine against the Turks and to safeguard Cossack privileges.[18] King John Sobieski, meanwhile, sent a letter wishing the tsars 'the best of health and a happy reign in your realm'.[19] He was just one of the many recipients of rescripts delivered to all the major courts of Europe announcing the accession of the 'great sovereign tsars and great princes Ivan Alekseevich and Peter Alekseevich'.[20] There was no reference to Sophia in these official proclamations (or indeed in any formal diplomatic correspondence of the regency) and it was not until 1684 that the German newspapers, for example, began to report that Sophia ruled in reality, Ivan in name only.[21] In 1682 those states with representatives on the spot in Moscow, like the writer of the Polish Diariusz, were well aware of the novel ruling 'trinity', but etiquette demanded that their rulers' rescripts be addressed to the tsars.

Numerous missives arrived in Moscow offering condolences on the death of Tsar Fedor and congratulations on the accession of Tsars Ivan and Peter: from the King of Sweden, expressing the hope that the new tsars would abide 'unwaveringly' by the terms of the Treaty of Kardis as their predecessors had done; from the King of Denmark; from the Estates-General of the Netherlands;[22] and from Charles II of England (dated 24 November 1682), who confessed to being 'comforted' that the throne was filled by 'Princes of the like eminent Vertues'.[23] The Turkish Sultan wrote that 'from now and henceforth friendship and true love are fit and apposite, so that from day to day the goodly business of love and friendship and ancient neighbourliness may multiply'. His chief minister, the Grand Vizier, expressed similar hopes for the preservation of the peace.[24]

The Sultan had good reasons for wishing to maintain his truce with Moscow. Since 1681 Turkey had been using the pretext of offering protection to the Hungarian subjects of the Habsburg Emperor in order to further her own plans for expansion into Europe. The rebel leader Imre Thököly had appealed for Turkish aid in resisting the Emperor's infringement of Hungarian privileges, and in 1682 a huge Turkish army entered Hungary. In the face of the Turkish threat Emperor Leopold turned to the only available ally, John Sobieski of Poland. On 31 March 1683 they signed a pact undertaking to send each other military aid in the event of the Turks attacking either Vienna or Cracow, and resolved to invite other rulers, including the tsars of Muscovy, to join their alliance. Not long afterwards the terms of the pact were invoked when in July 1683 the Grand Vizier Kara Mustafa laid siege to Vienna. After holding out for sixty days, on 12 September the city was relieved by a joint force of the troops of Poland, the Empire, Saxony and Bavaria under the command of Sobieski. The success awakened hopes of a 'crusade' to drive the Ottoman from Europe. In March 1684 Austria, Poland and Venice, under the patronage of Pope Innocent XI, formed the Holy League, with an undertaking to make every effort to enlist the tsars of Muscovy in their venture.

Russia was not in principle opposed to an alliance with her old adversary Poland. Russo-Polish rapproachment, as already indicated, had been one of the cornerstones of the policy of the Foreign Minister Afanasy Ordin-Nashchokin in the 1660s, for the two countries had always had good reasons for co-operation against the common threat of Turkey and Sweden. Russia had to weigh up the implications of a separate Polish victory over the Turks for her own position in the Ukraine, take account of the dangers of further Turkish expansion, and estimate the costs, both financial and political, of a major military campaign. Traditional anti-Polish prejudice also had to be countered. The case for joining the alliance was certainly not so clearcut that consent could be given without demanding major concessions from Poland. Golitsyn was to be adamant and consistent on this point. In 1683 the Russian ambassadors to Warsaw, I.I. Chaadaev and L.T. Golosov, sent to ratify the Treaty of Andrusovo, insisted that 'without a permanent peace and without the surrender of the towns of Ukraine and Zaporozh'e it is impossible for us to make an alliance'.[25]

Claims naturally centred on Kiev, still only in Muscovy's temporary possession. In Left-Bank Ukraine, however, there was a strong anti-Polish lobby, headed by Hetman Samoilovich. He argued that the Poles were 'a deceitful and unreliable crew, inveterate enemies of the Muscovite and Cossack peoples'. Poland wished to lure Russia into an alliance in order to exhaust her resources. What guarantee could there be, he asked, that the Emperor and the King would not betray the tsars by making a separate peace? He referred to the King's attempts to sow dissension during the troubles of 1682. 'May the sacred and wise judgement of the tsars and their sister, the Sovereign Lady Tsarevna, and the sound advice of their illustrious council prevail, but you will not quickly find peace if you seek it by declaring war.'[26]

Other expert advice was sought. Patrick Gordon records a 'private conference' with Golitsyn on 16 January 1684 which they discussed the pros and cons of an alliance. In a written report submitted the next day Gordon confessed 'I find the present state of Russia, and the nature of their affaires and the tyme to be such that it is a very hard lesson to give a positive advice to live in peace, or engage in a warr.' Neverthe-less, he was able to set out nine arguments against the venture – the tsars' youth, the 'nonconcordance, jealousies, dissentions among the Nobility breeding confusion and irresolution in counsells', lack of funds, indiscipline amongst the troops, anti-war feeling, the benefits of the truce with Turkey and the immorality of being the first to break it, the dangers of the allies' making a separate peace and the fact that 'peace bringeth plenty, profitt, pleasure and ease' – but then countered each argument, reaching the conclusion that a campaign would allow Russia to eradicate the infidel 'nest' that had so long harassed Christendom, secure her own position in the Ukraine and guarantee the loyalty of the Cossack army. 'You will gaine to yourselves the greatest honour that any Nation hath done of a long tyme by not only freeing yourselves but Chrissendome of that dreadfull and cursed plague generation as also liberating yourselves of that . . . tribute which you pay them yearly, and so redeeme all former affronts and injuries.' Gordon was of the opinion that it would not be a difficult task to conquer the Crimea, advice that he may later have had cause to regret.[27]

At about the same time talks were taking place at Andrusovo between Russian envoys Iakov Odoevsky and Ivan Buturlin and the Poles Krzysztof Grzymułtowski and Marcjan Oginski. The Russians insisted that the terms of 1667 be made permanent, whilst the Poles argued that terri-torial disputes could be settled only after Russia had joined the alliance. The talks became bogged down in conventional quibbles over the spelling and formulation of royal titles and accusations of minor mis-demeanours by both sides. They ended without agreement, mainly over the topic of Kiev, in February after thirty-nine sessions.[28]

Austria also tried to put pressure on Russia. Already in September 1683 Emperor Leopold had dispatched a letter informing the tsars of the expulsion of the Turks from Vienna and adding, 'we most amicably wish that Your Excellencies might agree not to let slip this opportune moment now that the rage of the common foe has been quelled and constrained, to avenge past and present affronts committed by the Turks'.[29] At the beginning of 1684 the Imperial Secretary Johann Eberhardt Hövel arrived in Moscow bearing a letter from the Emperor dated 18 November, announcing the imminent arrival of a plenipotentiary delegation.[30] Hövel left some interesting observations on his mission, pertaining both to Muscovite diplomatic protocol and to some of the personalities of the period. He was received upon arrival by Tsar Ivan, 'who sat alone on the throne . . . a few steps away from which sat twelve boyars and senators on benches. Almost in the centre stood the Prime Minister and Director of all affairs, Prince Golitsyn, a most discreet and handsome man of middling years.'[31] Hövel had several meetings with Golitsyn, at which the Turkish war, the siege of Vienna and other topics of mutual interest were discussed. As we learned earlier, Hövel remarked on the fact that Tsar Ivan had to be supported by attendants when he rose to ask after the Emperor's health. The astute Austrian had good cause to speculate on the relationship between the two brothers – one sickly, the other full of 'primise and vigour' – and the political role played by their sister.[32]

Hövel's farewell audience with Ivan on 4 February was marred by one of those undignified squabbles that characterized many diplomatic encounters of the period. In the words of an official report, 'he wished that His Majesty the Tsar should present the royal rescript with his own hands and not pass it on via his privy councillor'.[33] When Hövel stepped towards the throne, upwards of forty boyars gathered round him as Golitsyn tried to thrust the letter into his hand. When he refused to accept it, Golitsyn said that the document would have to be sent by post. The failure of the Emperor to present *his* letters to Russian envoys in person was quoted. In the end Hövel got his own way and in another audience he took the letter from Ivan's own hand. The mission, which had done little more than prepare the ground for the arrival of the plenipotentiary delegation in May, was, like many of the period, an exercise in the niceties of diplomatic etiquette in which the aim of both sides was to preserve or if possible augment the honour and dignity of their respective sovereigns. The fact that Russia felt herself to be still struggling to achieve equal status often made her the more sensitive partner in such exchanges.

In May 1684 Sebastian von Blumberg and Johann Christian Zierowsky arrived from Vienna. They assured the Russians that they need do no more than constrain the Sultan's 'right arm', the Khan of the Crimea, but Golitsyn continued to insist: 'If the King of Poland relinquishes the city of Kiev to Their Majesties the tsars, the tsars will enter an alliance with the King and wage war against the Khan of the Crimea.'[34] It is unclear whether Golitsyn was aware of the opportunities for playing the allies off against one another. Poland and Austria were in dispute over the Balkans, and the Austrian war effort had recently suffered a setback when the Emperor failed to take Buda from the Turks. The Austrians, however, were unwilling to accept the Russian position on Kiev. They left Moscow in June without agreement having been reached. Close on their heels came the Imperial Secretary Carlo Maurizio Vota bearing congratulations on Tsar Ivan's marriage of some five months previously and requesting permission for two Jesuits to reside in Moscow under the sponsorship of the Viennese court.[35] Permission was granted. As was shown earlier, this was an unusually favourable period for Catholics in Moscow. Later in the year the tsars received a letter from the Pope himself, dated 5 August, urging them to join the coalition: 'We are in no doubt that in the recent conflict the strength of the aforementioned enemy has been broken and enfeebled and that he will be unable to resist the weight of such forces.'[36]

It turned out to be only a matter of time before Russia joined the League. The focus of attention on the south seemed to preclude anything more ambitious than maintaining the status quo in the north, and Sophia's regency was to see a complete halt to the quest for the Baltic. In April 1684 a Swedish delegation headed by Kerstin Gullenstierna, President of the Royal Council, arrived in Moscow.[37] This was a return visit in exchange for a Russian mission to Stockholm the previous October, which had expressed Russia's willingness to renew the current treaty. Despite the apparently routine nature of the exchange, Golitsyn conducted the talks in person, employing the conventional technique of endeavouring to wear down the opposite side by references to breaches of protocol and etiquette: in a rescript to the King of Poland in 1669 the King of Sweden had referred to the Tsar merely as 'Great Prince', Swedish accounts of the Razin rebellion had 'dishonoured' the Russian crown, libels of the Orthodox Church had been published in Revel, in 1676 the Governor-General of Riga had referred to Tsar Fedor by the patronymic 'Mikhailovich', and so on.[38] In compensation for Swedish 'errors', he demanded the return of 'Russian' towns on the Baltic, but this claim was not pressed and was probably made as a matter of form lest Moscow's traditional pretensions to lands under Swedish rule should appear to have lapsed. The Swedes, in turn, tried similar tactics, complaining that the Russians had used the form 'Carlus' instead of 'Carolus'. They asked for an agreement on permanent 'residents' in Moscow and Stockholm, the renewal of border markers and a reduction in taxes for Swedes living in Russia. On 22 May a treaty was signed confirming the border as established by the terms of Kardis, with additional clauses on royal titles, religious toleration, exchange of envoys and trade.[39]

Because Russia made no substantial gains from this treaty, Golitsyn has sometimes been criticised for 'caving in' at a time when Sweden was herself experiencing a period of military decline. The historian Ustrialov, who made no secret of his disapproval of Sophia, wrote: 'Our boyars were ashamed to relinquish so easily those ancient regions of Russia which Tsar Fedor so staunchly defended.'[40] More recently, an admirer of Peter I's foreign policy complains: 'The "Westerner" Golitsyn began by acknowledging and consolidating the disastrous separation of the Muscovite state from Western Europe.'[41] But by May 1684 the balance of Russia's diplomatic activity was tipped towards the south and the prize of Kiev, and, who could tell, perhaps the Black Sea and Balkans beyond. A venture in the north was incompatible with such plans. Peter I himself, it will be recalled, started his own independent military career in 1695 with a war against Turkey, rather than aiming immediately for the 'window on the West' via the Baltic.

The visit of the Swedish ambassadors provides some interesting material on diplomatic protocol, and sheds some light on Sophia's own contribution to the conduct of foreign affairs. The fact that Golitsyn was Sophia's chief adviser, that she herself attended meetings of the boyar council, knew Polish, was a fervent defender of the honour of her father and brothers and was later to give her unconditional support to the military expeditions that resulted from the treaty with Poland gives grounds for suggesting that she herself may have assisted in the formulation of Russia's foreign policy.

Direct evidence is lacking, however, and we must content ourselves with the proven fact that Sophia frequently chose to add dignity to diplomatic occasions by giving audiences to foreign envoys. Times had changed since that era, just a few years previously, when foreigners had expressed amazement at catching a mere glimpse of one of the royal women from behind a curtain. On 28 May 1684 Gullenstierna and his companions were received by the tsars, then escorted past a guard of strel'tsy in dress uniform to the doors of the Golden Chamber, where a speech of welcome from the Tsarevna was read out by a state secretary: 'The Great Sovereign Lady, Pious Tsarevna and Great Princess Sophia Alekseevna of all the Great and Little and White Russias, her royal majesty greets you the great and plenipotentiary ambassadors of the mighty and noble Prince and Sovereign Carolus, by the grace of God King of the Swedes and the Goths and the Vandals, Great Prince of Finland, Duke of Estonia and Karelia, Lord of Ingria. . . .'[42] The ambassadors proceeded through the entrance chamber, which was lined with strel'tsy, and beheld the Tsarevna, who was seated on her royal throne which was studded with diamonds, wearing a crown adorned with pearls, a cloak of gold-threaded samite lined with sables, and next to the sables an edging of lace. And the sovereign lady was attended by ladies-in-waiting, two on each side of the throne . . . and by female dwarves wearing embroidered sashes and gold sable-lined cloaks. And the lady was also attended in the chamber by several courtiers and at the sides there also stood Prince Vasily Vasil'evich Golitsyn and Ivan Mikhailovich Miloslavsky.[43]

The exchange that followed was highly formal. The ambassadors paid their respects to Sophia by bowing, and she asked after the health of King Charles, his mother and his wife. The ambassadors were allowed to kiss her hand and further enquiries about health were exchanged. In their speech the ambassadors passed on greetings to Sophia from their King, 'who wished the same long life and prosperity for your royal house as he might desire for himself', and they promised to report back about the great kindness and generosity they had been shown in Moscow. The interview concluded with the Swedes being invited to partake of food and drink, for which purpose they were ushered into an antechamber.

The year 1684 saw further useful exchanges with representatives from the Protestant north. In June the Saxon doctor Laurent Rinhuber, who was already well known in Moscow, arrived bearing letters from Johann Georg III, the Elector of Saxony, and his son Duke Friedrich, who endorsed the doctor's request for a safe passage to Persia and also urged the tsars to fight the Turks: 'We trust that your troops will be granted courage of strength and victory of arms against those common enemies of Christianity the Sultan of Turkey and the Khan of the Crimea, who even now are attacking the Holy Roman empire and other Christian sovereigns, our friends and brothers.'[44] In informal talks with Goltsyn, Rinhuber was able to supply further information about the attitude of the German princes to the war with Turkey, and also news of Holland and England. Even so, he was not spared a lengthy dressing down in the Foreign Office over an incorrect formulation of the tsars' titles.

Rinhuber paid little attention to Sophia during his visit, but there is one telling reference in his account. On 27 August he was present at a reception for the consecration of a new church on Golitsyn's country estate at Chernaia Griaz' and witnessed the arrival of coaches from Kolomenskoe bearing Tsar Ivan and his wife and a third containing Sophia, who upon catching sight of Rinhuber exclaimed, 'Look, a German!' and questioned an attendant about his identity.[45] This incident provides further confirmation of Golitsyn's pre-eminence; few members of the inner circle were honoured with home visits from the royal family. It is also evidence of the Prince's cordial treatment of foreigners, who found that their dealings with Russians were more open than formerly. At the dinner which was held later in the day Rinhuber was seated next to Golitsyn, who urged him to stay in Moscow because he could read and write Russian and had served loyally on previous occasions.[46] Apparently the offer was not taken up.

On 10 August a treaty was signed with Denmark. The contents seem trivial – regulating protocol for diplomatic receptions (no hats or swords to be worn) and stipulating subsistence payments, including rations of alcohol, for envoys. Along with generous allowances of meat, poultry, fish and bread the envoys were entitled each week to: 10 pounds of sugar, 1 pound of pepper, 1 pound of ginger, $\frac{1}{2}$ pound of cinnamon, $\frac{1}{4}$ pound of cloves, $\frac{1}{2}$ pound of nutmeg, $\frac{1}{2}$ pound of cardammon, 20 *zolotniks* (about 100 grams) of saffron, 1 pound of thyme, a pound of prunes, 10 pounds of raisins, 8 pounds of almonds in their shells, 10 pounds of currants, 10 pounds of rice, 2 pounds (*sic*) of olive oil, 10 lemons and 12 pounds of dried figs. The list offers interesting insights into Eastern influence on the eating habits of the time.[17]

If the treaty was inconsequential, the negotiations which preceded it raised some important issues. The Danish envoy Hildebrandt von Horn had been in Moscow since October 1682 and, in the words of Georg Adam Schleissing, a member of the same delegation as Rinhuber, 'it was said that he wanted to prevent Russia from making a permanent peace with the Swedish crown'.[48] He hoped to draw Russia into the Danish–French–Brandenburg coalition against Sweden, Holland and England, but had to admit defeat when Moscow renewed her treaty with the Swedes in May 1684. In 1689 the Danes were to put pressure on Russia to withdraw from the war against Turkey, again to no avail.

Meanwhile, events in the south were bringing closer the fulfilment of Golitsyn's demand for the permanent ratification of the Treaty of Andrusovo. In 1684 Poland had suffered defeat when Sobieski tried to recapture Kamieniec, and again when hetman Stanisław Jabłonowski had been forced to retreat from Moldavia with heavy losses. The Poles had sought aid from France, and had even proposed a truce with the Crimea, but to no avail. They then renewed their efforts to bring Russia into the alliance. The King was an indefatigable letter-writer. In January 1685 he reminded the tsars that 'the history books are full of occasions when banners with the image of the Holy Cross have been raised aloft and beneath them have gathered the armies of various peoples of various tongues, suffice it only that they call themselves Christians'.[49] In April Johann Kurz came to Moscow from Vienna, in August Jan Zembocki from Warsaw, both with the same message. The Turks administered counter-pressure against the Poles. When the envoy Nikita Alekseev went to Turkey late in 1685 to consult the Patriarch of Constantinople about the establishment of a new metropolitanate of Kiev, by which Moscow hoped to underline the permanence of her presence in the Ukraine in the establishment of a diocese subject to the authority of the Patriarch of Moscow, he met with a favourable response from the Grand Vizier, who begged that the 'great sovereigns should refrain from inflicting injury upon His Majesty the Sultan' and assured him of their 'love and friendship'. A number of conciliatory gestures were made, including the granting of permission for the rebuilding of an Orthodox church in Constantinople.[50]

Finally, in February 1686 Grzymułtowski and Oginski again arrived from Warsaw, accompanied by an impressive retinue of over 1,000 men and 1,500 horses.[51] In response to the Poles' insistence that Moscow undertake a campaign against the Crimea, Golitsyn set out the hazards of such a venture. He referred to the Treaty of Pereiaslavl' of 1654 and the surrender in 1676 of Podolia to the Turks, who in turn had recognised Russian claims to the Left Bank in 1681. He even used the presence of a Tatar envoy in Moscow and rumours of the imminent arrival of a Turkish one to put pressure on the Poles. The conventional controversy over titles was thrown in for good measure, for example the complaint that Tsar Aleksei had been referred to as Mikhail. At first it looked as though the Poles would not yield. Grzymultowski opposed the idea of a settlement and was horrified at Muscovite demands, writing to Sobieski: 'I would rather that my heart withered and my tongue was struck by paralysis before I signed a treaty so prejudicial to the Commonwealth.'[52] Oginski, however, favoured a swift conclusion, an attitude which reflected the Lithuanian viewpoint. On 27 March the ambassadors even made as though to leave, but then talks resumed and dragged on until the middle of April.

On 26 April (6 May, according to the Gregorian calendar) both sides agreed to a treaty of Eternal Peace (*vechnyi mir*), consisting of thirty-three articles. These included the permanent cession of Kiev and its immediate hinterland to Moscow, and ratification of Russian rule over Smolensk, Dorogobuzh, Roslavl', Zaporozh'e and their districts. Russia was to pay the Poles 146,000 roubles 'out of friendship', and was to sever relations with Turkey and the Crimea.

> The great sovereigns on account of the many wrongs committed by the Muslims, in the name of Christianity and to save many Christians held in servitude, have deigned to break the truce with them and forthwith upon the signing of the treaty to send their troops to the Sech' and to the Crimeans' customary crossing places for the defence of Poland against a Tatar attack; the Don Cossacks will be ordered to carry out military operations on the Black Sea; and in 1687 they will advance all their forces to the Crimea itself. In the meantime the Polish King will wage war against the Turks and the Belgorod Tatars to deflect their forces from Russia.

The treaty also contained clauses on royal titles, religious toleration and the encouragement of trade. The signatories were to seek the aid of 'other Christian monarchs'.[53]

There is no doubt that the Treaty of Moscow was regarded as a major triumph by Sophia and her party. 'How the Kremlin must have rocked with amazement at this free gift,' writes a recent historian of Poland, who believes that the Ukraine was 'needlessly abandoned.'[54] Another writes: 'The only gain it brought to the Republic was the presents that in accordance with custom the plenipotentiaries received from their hosts.'[55] 'The treaty was a major diplomatic defeat for Poland and her king,' writes Wójcik. 'It was the formal expression of the final capitulation of the Commonwealth to Russia, and of the ultimate failure of Poland's eastern policy.'[56] In Poland there were still hopes that the treaty might be revoked, and Sobieski did his utmost to postpone ratification. In July 1686 he set out for Moldavia but was forced to retreat from Jassy by shortages of water and provisions, a harbinger of Golitsyn's later experience in the southern steppe. In December at Lwów the King regretfully ratified the treaty that Grzymułtowski had negotiated some eight months earlier. Even then, negotiations to define and fix the boundaries of the two states were to drag on for many years.[57]

For Sophia the treaty of 1686 marked the high point of her regency. The permanent acquisition of Kiev, the 'mother of Russian cities', was doubly prized as the culmination of at least one part of her father's foreign policy. Her personal approval was amply demonstrated by attendance at the ceremonies marking the conclusion of negotiations. On 27 April 1686 the Polish ambassadors were received by the tsars, then treated to a separate reception by Sophia, who 'deigned to enter the chamber and seat herself upon the throne, dressed in a cloak of sables and a three-cornered cap'.[58] The Poles were summoned to kiss the Tsarevna's hand and she assured them that 'the great sovereigns will keep firmly to the terms of the eternal peace without any infringement'. She then offered them goblets of wine. The next day Oginski presented Sophia with a coach drawn by six horses, the vehicle 'richly decorated and painted with various colours and motifs and valued at 550 roubles'.[59] Another source records that 'at the reading of the clauses of the treaty of permanent peace between Russia and Poland signed in Moscow in April 1686 with the plenipotentiary ambassadors of Poland Tsarevna Sophia was present with the sovereigns, and when they had heard the clauses they ordered that a copy be made'.[60]

Sophia intended that her presence on such occasions should be taken seriously and that foreign envoys should regard her as a legitimate representative of the royal house. Later in 1687 there was an attempt to incorporate the 'female reception' into regular diplomatic practice, when the Poles were informed that their King should:

instruct that the great and plenipotentiary [Russian] ambassadors have an audience with the Queen and kiss her hand, because the Great Sovereign

Lady, Pious Tsarevna and Great Princess Sophia Alekseevna received the great and plenipotentiary ambassadors of His Majesty the King, Krzysztof Grzymułtowski, Governor of Poznan, and his companions and allowed them to kiss her hand, so it is appropriate that they, the . . . ambassadors, should in exchange follow this example.[61]

It is noteworthy that Sophia's 'equivalent' was deemed to be the Queen. There never seems to have been any suggestion that Tsar Ivan's consort, Tsaritsa Praskovia, should carry out public duties of this variety.

The extent of Sophia's satisfaction over the 1686 treaty may be further gauged from a laudatory charter issued to Golitsyn in the presence of the royal family on 29 June, Peter's nameday. It commenced: 'By the decree of the great sovereign tsars and great princes Ivan Alekseevich and Peter Alekseevich, and the Great Sovereign Lady the Pious Tsarevna and Great Princess Sophia Alekseevna, autocrats of all the Great and Little and White Russias'.[62] The formulation of titles in this document provides just one example, and by no means the first, of a slight but crucial adjustment in Sophia's status. By placing the word *samoderzhtsy* (autocrats) after her name instead of immediately after the names of the two tsars she was laying claim to an equal share in royal dignity. This formula was used sporadically before April 1686, but after the signing of the treaty it became standard form.[63] In rescripts issued in her sole name, Sophia was referred to as *samoderzhitsa*. It should be noted, however, that this formula does not appear to have been used in diplomatic correspondence or for the signing of treaties.

Sophia's attachment to titles is further illustrated by a passage in the 29 June document in which it is stated that 'according to that treaty of permanent peace, the Polish ambassadors conceded and agreed to write their royal majesties' and great sovereigns' titles in a form which is highly prized and famed among all Christian sovereigns'.[64] The use of the epithets *presvetleishie* (most illustrious) and *derzhavneishie* (most sovereign) were especially valued. The document ends: 'And the likes of that permanent peace, bringing profit and praise to the Russian realm, have not been seen before in the time of their royal forebears; it brings to their majesties' renowned dominion of the Russian realm great profit and eternal glory and praise throughout the whole world.'[65] Lewitter remarks that this statement 'was no vain boast'.[66] Golitsyn, incidentally, was rewarded not only with a charter from his sovereigns but also with a gold cup, a sable coat, a 250-rouble supplement to his salary and hereditary tenure of 3,000 peasant households.

One of the clauses of the treaty stipulated that aid should be sought from 'other Christian monarchs', but it was 1687 and the first Crimean campaign was underway before Russia carried out her obligation. V.T. Postnikov was dispatched to Brandenburg, Holland, England and Florence, B. Mikhailov to Sweden and Denmark, B.P. Sheremetev and

I.I. Chaadaev to Austria, Ia.F. Dolgoruky and Ia. Myshetsky to France and Spain, I. Volkov to Venice; none of these missions resulted in any substantial offers of aid. The King of Denmark agreed to make his fleet available in case of 'dire necessity'.[67] In Berlin in June 1687, meanwhile, Postnikov achieved no more than an agreement on diplomatic protocol, dealing with the usual niceties of titles, raising of hats, questions about the sovereign's health, reception of royal letters, bows and so on.[68]

The envoy proceeded to England, where he had two audiences with King James, on 8 November and 9 December. In a royal letter dated 4 December 1687, James (referred to in error as James VII in Postnikov's credentials) wrote:

> We cannot but heartily rejoice for that prudent and glorious resolution of Your Imperial Majesties' tending so apparently to the honor of the great God, and to the exaltation of the holy Christian religion wishing Your Imperial Majesties all the advantages and glories which may reasonably be expected from so renowned an engagement. We acknowledge ourself highly obliged by Your Imperial Majesties' for your Brotherly kindness in communicating to us that firme alliance made with those great Christian powers against their implacable adversaries the infidells, which we look upon as the best and strongest bulwark for the safety and glory of Christendome that could have been invented, and though we be so farr remote that we cannot have our desyred share in the honor of those laudable expeditions yet our prayers to the Mighty Lord of Hosts are never wanting for the successe of those eminent Princes that fight his battles.

James did not miss the opportunity to renew the plea for the restoration of the privileges of British merchants trading in Russia, as being 'the most effectual meanes to preserve and augment that full and perfect amity . . . which has in former times been maintained and cultivated between both our ancestors of glorious memory'.[69] James was too preoccupied with domestic problems and too hampered by the costs of enlarging his own army to provide the requested financial aid, even had he felt it politically expedient to do so. Postnikov, for his part, spent much of his time in England engaged in wrangles over subsistence allowances and transport, and in quibbles about the raising of hats during exchanges on the sovereigns' health.[70]

The allegedly 'rude' reception given to the envoy in London may also have had something to do with the fact that in the summer of 1686 Patrick Gordon on a visit home had been instructed to find out whether the English were in favour of an exchange of ambassadors, but he had returned to Moscow in August bearing a letter from King James requesting his own release from the tsars' service.[71] As Gordon wrote in his diary, the Russians 'had conceived an evil opinion of our King, as favouring the Turkes too much',[72] for interference in the terms of service of foreign mercenaries, especially one as experienced as Gordon, on the eve of the forthcoming Crimean campaign, did not go down well with Golitsyn or Sophia. They were also unwilling for Gordon's attention to be diverted from military affairs by having him appointed to the post of 'Envoy Extraordinary to their Czaarish Majesties' as proposed in a letter from the Earl of Middleton dated 25 October 1686.[73]

In Spain, Russia's request for a loan was politely turned down. Sheremetev's talks with Poland's ally the Emperor of Austria ended inconclusively when negotiations became bogged down in the apparently inevitable squabbles over titles instead of dealing with the crucial question of a Russo-Austrian agreement.[74] The Austrians, in confident mood after the capture of Buda in September 1686, probably saw little need for closer involvement with Russia.

Perhaps the most ill-advised of the missions of 1687 was the one to France.[75] Dolgoruky and Myshetsky arrived at a particularly inopportune moment for persuading Austria's arch-enemy to support a war against France's traditional friend, the Sultan. King Louis XIV, who had temporarily called a halt to his advance on the Rhine and was pursuing a policy of 'pressure without war', was happy enough to see the continuation of the war in the east if it brought discomfiture to the Emperor. He was annoyed by the fall of Buda in 1686 and the destruction of the Turkish field army the following year. When the Russian ambassadors arrived in July 1687 he did not even grant them an audience. There was a number of undignified scuffles between French officials and the Russian party. When they finally secured an interview with the Foreign Minister Colbert de Croissy in September, they learned that the King 'offered thanks for the alliance against the enemy of the Holy Cross and wished the Christian allies every success. But the King wished it to be known that he could not possibly enter an alliance with the Christian rulers at this juncture.' Various reasons were given – reluctance to be 'the last to win glory', ill-treatment of French troops by the Austrians in the past and, crucially, 'the world would see little wisdom or glory in the King's actions if he were to help an enemy to fight a friend'. The Russians were treated to an unceremonious farewell and put on boats at Le Havre.

One wonders how often, if at all, during this mission Dolgoruky found the opportunity to carry out the instructions issued to him on departure from Moscow in January 1687, namely that he should inform the French that 'their sister, the Great Sovereign Lady Pious Tsarevna and Great Princess Sophia Alekseevna rules jointly (*sotsarstvuet*) with the tsars'.[76] Certainly Louis showed no awareness of this fact.

The French 'fiasco' of 1687 has often been used as evidence of Russia's still rudimentary grasp of diplomacy and ignorance of international affairs. It has been argued that Louis XIV's wish to profit by the involvement of Austria in a war against the Turks was patent and obvious to all. He had already taken advantage by attacking the Spanish Netherlands in June 1684, and was hoping that Austria's destruction by the Turks would allow him to gain mastery of the German states and even the chance to become Emperor himself. But Russia had to set such considerations against the fact that the King of France was a Christian monarch, and that in January 1686 one of the documents brought to Moscow by Grzymultowski had been a letter from Louis himself encouraging Russia's participation in the alliance.[77] Meanwhile, a pamphlet issued in Paris in 1687 to mark the Muscovite mission shows that the French were as ignorant about Russia as were the Russians about the French, deriving their information from a compilation of out-dated sources.[78]

It is unlikely, all the same, that Russia's diplomats were entirely conversant with the intricate mechanics of an international situation which prompted France, a Catholic country, to support the 'infidel' Turk and sponsor Protestant Sweden, whilst the Pope in Rome refused to ratify bishops nominated by Louis, especially when even the most sophisticated statesmen of the era had difficulty in predicting the next move of a King who was 'foundering in the bog of his own contradictions'.[79] Maybe, in retrospect, Dolgoruky's mission was worth a try. As it was, the rebuff to the Russian ambassadors was to have serious repercussions for Franco-Russian relations, which remained sour until Peter I made fresh overtures to the French in 1716.

If Russian diplomacy enjoyed few tangible successes in the immediate wake of the Treaty of Moscow, what of Russian military might? On 5 September 1686, the forthcoming campaign against the Tatars was officially announced.[80] State servitors were ordered to join the colours. In November it was proclaimed that the purpose of the expedition was to rid Russia of unendurable abuses and humiliations. The decree referred to the 'destruction of God's churches, the defilement of holy icons and sanctified crosses, the trampling of sacred objects, the annual capture of Orthodox Christians of the Ukraine and their transport to Muslim lands to live in torment or be sold like cattle'.[81] Despite the annual tribute which the tsars were obliged to pay to the infidels, the Khan persisted in violating the truce, raiding Russia's territory and ill-treating her emissaries. There was virtually no reference to the international implications of Russia's participation in the war against the Turks.

Prince Vasily Golitsyn was to be field-marshal and commander of the first (bol'shoi) regiment. The other four regimental colonels were A.S. Shein, V.D. Dolgoruky, M.G. Romodanovsky and I.Iu. Leont'ev. The credentials of Golitsyn's associates as military commanders were no better and no worse than most of their predecessors. All were members of the boyar council (Leont'ev was admitted to membership on the eve of the campaign), and came from families that traditionally held high office. In the words of Robert Crummey: 'Throughout the seventeenth century, the tsars and their closest advisers proceeded on the assumption that the best commanders were to be found in the traditional military elite, the aristocratic families of the court.'[82] At a time when it was normal practice for aristocratic servitors to hold military and civic office alternately or even simultaneously, such *ad hoc* appointments raised no eyebrows.

Nor would the appointment of Golitsyn have seemed odd, as has sometimes been suggested. Golitsyn had seen military action in the Ukraine, was familiar with at least part of the terrain over which his armies would march, and had been an initiator of military reform. As chief signatory and negotiator of the treaty with Poland he had a direct personal interest in the implementation of its articles. Moreover, as Sophia's chief minister and favourite Golitsyn arguably had first claim to the 'glory' that the conquest of the Crimea was expected to bring. At the same time, acceptance of the 'honour' was clearly a gamble, not only because of the possibility of military failure but also because of the dangers of unfavourable political reorientation at court during his absence. La Neuville writes:

> The Choice of their General took up some time; Prince Galischin nominated several Lords fit for that Command; but he was told on all hands, that since he had made up the Peace with *Poland* he ought to give himself the trouble of trying whether the Conquest of *Precop* [the town of Perekop] was so easy as he imagin'd. He did all he could to excuse himself from this Employ; rightly conjecturing he should find great difficulties, and all the ill success would be laid at his door, notwithstanding his utmost Precaution and Prudence. That tho' the Army he commanded was formidable in Numbers, yet they were but a multitude of raw undisciplin'd Peasants, with whom he could never undertake any vigorous Action, and come off with Honour. Being a greater Statesman than Soldier, he foresaw that his Absence might do him more Prejudice than the Conquest of the *Crim* bring him Glory; and especially seeing he could not raise himself higher by it, nor have a greater Sway in the Government by commanding the Army: He saw besides that those who insisted most upon his taking this Charge, did it only out of the Jealousy they had of him, and with design to ruin him, under a specious shew of honouring him with the Title of *Generalissimo*.[83]

Who were those who 'insisted most'? Are we to identify them as members of Peter's camp, or as rivals for favour amongst Sophia's associates? What of Sophia herself? Was she torn between the desire to see her favourite win military honours and the wish to keep him in Moscow? It is difficult to know how much credence to give to La

Neuville's analysis, but the comment that Golitsyn was 'a greater Statesman than Soldier' rings true. Sophia seems to have involved her most loyal and able adviser in too many different areas of domestic and foreign policy and to have thus made his downfall entirely dependent upon her own. Letters written during the campaign by Golitsyn to Shaklovity (who evidently profited from the Prince's absence by enhancing his own political power)[84] confirm that the Prince was very anxious indeed about the political climate at court and a possible move by Peter's camp, although he could not have guessed just how few tangible results the campaigns would bring. It also seems likely that Golitsyn received no precise instructions on the conduct of the campaign before he left Moscow. Such was Sophia's confidence in him that he was obliged to shoulder the full responsibility. The task looked unenviable, although Gordon was to write, in a letter to the Earl of Middleton dated 7 January 1687, that 'I am confident that our Generallissimus [w]ho hath been the chieffe and almost only promoter of [t]hiss warr, and who is extreme-ambitious, will bring us [to] action.'[85] In a letter of December 1686 Gordon confirmed that 'no certaine resolution of any great business is lyke to be taken' in Golitsyn's absence.[86]

On 22 February 1687 the commanding officers prepared to depart for the south. In a ceremony conducted in the cathedral by the Patriarch and attended by Sophia and the tsars, prayers were offered up for victory over the enemy, and military personnel were blessed. Sophia prayed before the Royal Doors of the altar and listened to much of the ceremony standing in the place previously reserved for the Tsaritsa. Banners, icons and crosses which were to be carried into battle were consecrated.[87] Later Sophia accompanied the men as far as the Nikol'sky Gates. This ceremonial departure was only the beginning, however. With the exception of the foreign units and strel'tsy regiments, the bulk of the troops had to be mobilised by the call-up of military servitors, a slow and cumbersome process to which many failed to respond, despite the threat of stiff penalties. Almost three months were spent in mustering and equipping the army, and it was 2 May before they set off on the first leg of their journey by crossing the River Merlo at the Ukrainian town of Kolomak.[88] On 30 May at the River Samara they were joined by 50,000 Cossacks under the command of Hetman Samoilovich.

Progress was extremely slow. In the seven weeks after crossing the Merlo they covered only 300 versts (about 200 miles), an average of less than four miles a day. This was due mainly to the large amount of equipment being carried. Every man carried provisions for several months and there were several hundred pieces of heavy cannon to transport. There were also problems with runaway horses. In the middle of June they reached the watering place at Konskie Vody and made camp at Bol'shoi Lug. There had been no sign of the Tatars, and

Golitsyn hoped for news of their whereabouts from Polish messengers.

Then on 13 June they saw the first signs of an enemy scarcely less fearsome than the Tatars – fire on the steppe. There were rumours that it was the Tatars, as yet invisible, who had started the fire. Despite the danger and discomfort, it was decided to carry on, at an even slower pace. On 14 June, Patrick Gordon records, they covered only two miles. On the 15th:

> our march continued over the burnt-out steppe towards the small river Anchakrak, a distance of six versts. There was only a little grass and no wood whatsoever, but there was a herd of wild boars. The horses were visibly beginning to flag, the soldiers were falling ill; one could observe their distress and foresee what would happen if we were to march over the burnt-out steppe for several days more.[89]

On 16 June the fires were doused by torrential rain, but for miles around the grass had been scorched and blackened. La Neuville wrote: 'The armies could pass no further, being halted by the drought, which they learned to their amazement extended for 50 leagues around; the sun had burnt up all the Grass, and there was no hope of any forage.'[90] On the 16th they reached the River Karachakrak, and here they stopped.

Gordon further describes conditions that seemed to allow of only one possible decision:

> We were in a dreadful predicament, for it cost much pain and effort to procure enough grass to keep the horses alive, and it was reckoned that if the Tatars were to attack it would be impossible to obtain even that amount; the horses were already dropping and would be in no fit state to pull the guns, not to mention the provision wagons. . . . One could just not see how there could be any possibility of achieving the main goal of this expedition, the conquest of the Crimea, given that we could hardly escape the danger of a patent and inevitable destruction if we were to proceed further.[91]

To make matters worse many soldiers fell ill from drinking contaminated water. There were still 130 miles (200 versts) to travel to reach Perekop, which guarded the entrance to the Crimean isthmus, a distance which, at their previous slow pace, could be covered in no less than six weeks. On 17 June Golitsyn called a council of war and it was decided to turn back. A unit of over 20,000 troops under the command of L.R. Nepliuev was sent down the Dniepr. The Swiss soldier Franz Lefort, later companion to Peter the Great, reported that 'Our Generalissimus was beside himself and wept most bitterly, I can assure you.'[92]

There was little hint of disappointment, however, in Golitsyn's dispatch to Moscow, dated 18 June, which was to form the basis of official reports of the expedition to Russia's Polish allies, and appeared in a number of government decrees (for example that of 5 September

1687, reproduced below). He claimed that the Khan had been so intimidated by the size of the Russian armies that he had feared to show himself, deciding instead to set fire to the steppe in order to impede the enemy's progress while he made his escape.[93] The Russians had attempted to proceed, coming within ninety versts of Perekop, but in the end fodder and water shortages had got the better of them. There is a serious discrepancy between this account and that of Patrick Gordon, who records that when they halted they were still 200 versts from the Crimea.

Conclusions about the success or failure of the first Crimean campaign depend partly on one's perception of Moscow's aims. The Soviet scholar M.I. Belov, whose sources included the letters of Johann van Keller, the well-informed Dutch Resident in Moscow, believes that there were no plans for a full-scale invasion of the Crimea in 1687 and that the expedition was intended by Sophia's government as a reconnaissance mission in technical fulfilment of Russia's treaty with Poland.[94] There is evidence that opinion in Moscow had been prepared in advance for Golitsyn's withdrawal by rumours of hazards and difficulties. Sophia may had her own reasons for approving a short campaign with limited aims. She felt insecure at court with Golitsyn away, and there were fears of disturbances among non-Russian nationalities in the south, in particular those Muslim peoples, like the Kalmyk and Nogai, who had ties with the Crimean Tatars. The loyalty of the Cossacks also gave cause for concern, and resources were, as ever, limited.

In his first dispatches Golitsyn had blamed the Tatars for starting the fire on the steppe, but rumours soon began to circulate that the Cossacks were the real culprits. Hetman Samoilovich, it will be recalled, had held out against the alliance with Poland, and it was now being suggested that he was reluctant to risk the decline in Cossack bargaining power with Moscow that might result from a defeat of the Tatars. At the beginning of July a group of the Hetman's own officers presented a denunciation, accusing Samoilovich of arrogance, neglect of church-going, abuse of officers, nepotism and, crucial from Moscow's point of view, treason. As one of the Cossacks argued: 'The humiliations which the Hetman has inflicted upon the people and upon many of us are great indeed, but it is because treason is involved that we have decided to deal with him in this manner.'[95] Golitsyn sent a list of charges to Moscow, and received the reply that 'the great sovereigns, having read your indictment of Ivan Samoilovich and learning that he is unacceptable to the Cossack officers and the whole Little Russian Host, order that he be dismissed from office'. This order was carried out on 22 July. On 25 July Ivan Mazepa was elected hetman, with Moscow's approval.

La Neuville was to claim that 'the Prince, to excuse himself at Court for the ill success of his campaign, left no stone unturned to lay the blame for his failure upon the Hetman'.[96] But, if we accept Belov's interpretation of events, Golitsyn had no need of excuses. The eulogistic account of the campaign issued in Moscow on 5 September initially adheres to Golitsyn's first claim, that it was the Khan who burned the steppe in order to make his escape, referring only later to Samoilovich's 'treachery', a clear indication that there was no consistent or serious attempt to offer a scapegoat to critics at court.[97] Significantly, the Samoilovich affair was exploited not at home but abroad, for, as we shall see, it was Russia's allies who were most in need of convincing that Golitsyn had not reneged on his promises. The real reason for Samoilovich's dismissal was his unpopularity amongst his own people. Moscow could ill afford to jeopardize fragile Ukrainian loyalties by maintaining its backing for an unpopular hetman, despite the fact that Samoilovich had consistently demonstrated his own loyalty to Moscow. Golitsyn was later rewarded for conducting the case 'without detriment or hindrance to the great sovereigns, and without bloodshed or any loss of life'.[98]

By the time the Samoilovich affair had been resolved, Moscow had approved a version of the campaign deemed suitable for public consumption, with the result that a venture in which the non-appearance of the enemy had allowed little scope for heroics assumed an exaggeratedly dramatic colouring. On 13 July Fedor Shaklovity had arrived from Moscow bearing laudatory charters. In August messengers brought gold medallions as rewards for the officers. These bore portraits of the tsars on one side and Sophia on the reverse.[99] On 5 September the government issued a rescript addressed to Golitsyn:

> You went to the appointed places with great speed, and reaching those places the regiments of the great sovereigns' men-at-arms were mobilised with great speed and . . . you left those places to advance on the Muslim enemy in the very early springtime, and along the road with your baggage trains towards their Muslim encampments you hurried with commendable zeal and fervent endeavour and avid solicitude, and you were the whole time engaged in unceasing labours of war, carrying out the sovereigns' military operations with ceaseless and indefatigable diligence. You allowed yourself no rest in caring for the well-being of your regiments and organising defence from enemy attack, and in such a vigorous and resolute manner you crossed many steppe rivers and came within sight of the Crimean settlements. . . .
> And when you crossed the River Konskaia and marched towards the rivers Anchakrak and Karachakrak, the Crimean Khan, hearing of your skilful advance with so many troops and of your operations against him, realised his helplessness and burned all the steppe around Perekop and the Dniepr in order to escape from you and your regiments. And seeing you and the men-at-arms of the great sovereigns' regiments advancing, the Khan and his Tatars were seized by fear and terror and their customary boldness deserted them; he did not appear himself, nor did his Tatar warriors come out to

meet you; nowhere did they show themselves and they did not engage you in battle, but plunged into the depths of despair they departed for their distant settlements beyond Perekop and other places.[100]

The many discrepancies and inaccuracies in this document are all too evident: the alleged date of departure and the speed of the advance, the implied closeness of the 'Crimean settlements', the intensity of military encounters, are all at odds with more reliable accounts. Nonetheless, there are grounds for arguing that the 1687 expedition, limited though it was in scope, aided Russia's allies by depriving the Turks of Tatar reinforcements and keeping part of the Turkish army on the alert. This was the view of Patrick Gordon, who in a letter dated September 1687 referred to the diversion of Tatar forces and the stationing of a considerable part of the Turkish army on the Black Sea.[101] It may be an exaggeration to claim, as did a Soviet historian, that 'the entry of Russia into the League threw the Turkish command into disarray',[102] but at the very least fears of a Russian attack caused Turkish forces to be redeployed. Neither was the campaign entirely without practical results. It was decided to strengthen defence and supply lines in the Ukraine and to construct a fortress, to be named Novobogoroditskoe, at the confluence of the Samara and Dniepr rivers. Lessons had been learned about the terrain and the problems of managing horses and moving unwieldy baggage trains over barren steppeland.

Golitsyn returned to Moscow in early September, to be 'received by the princess with all the marks of favour that he could have hoped for, and resumed the management of affairs with as much authority as ever'.[103] More detailed confirmation of the political climate in the wake of the first Crimean campaign is provided by letters from the Swedish Resident Christopher von Kochen. In a letter to the Governor-General of Riga, dated 23 September, he wrote that Golitsyn had been welcomed by both tsars and the Tsarevna on his return. 'He still enjoys the same respect as before and stands at the helm of the government; what is more, Tsarevna Sophia Alekseevna, who wields almost complete command over the government of the realm, firmly supports him.' He repeated the rumour that 40,000–50,000 men had perished in the course of the campaign and described the medals presented to officers, bearing the 'image of the two tsars and the Regent, and also the initial letters of their names'.[104] He added:

Here there is great concern to publish abroad, in German and Dutch, a commendatory account of the campaign, setting out in detail the reasons for the unsuccessful withdrawal of the tsars' troops. There is already talk about new taxes being levied on the peasants and townspeople and about a plan to undertake a new expedition to the Crimea early in the spring of next year, following a different route. Prince Golitsyn will again take part, it is said.

Two days ago Tsar Ivan and the Regent, as is their habit every year, went on a pilgrimage to the Trinity Monastery. . . . They are expected back in ten days' time. Tsar Peter has stayed at home.[105]

Kochen confirms that the Crimean campaign had done nothing outwardly to shake Sophia's authority. Accounts of the campaign for foreign consumption were indeed prepared, with the help of Keller, who had Latin, German and French texts printed in Amsterdam.[106] It was about this time, as revealed in evidence presented after Sophia's overthrow in 1689, that the possibility of her coronation was first mooted. Engraved portraits depicting her with crown, orb and sceptre were commissioned, panegyric verses were penned and she appeared more and more frequently at public occasions. The inconclusive military exercise of 1687 was thus successfully exploited to provide a positive boost to Sophia and her party.[107]

Storms had been weathered at home, but Russia's allies were not so easily appeased. In a letter to the Italian Cardinal Francesco Barberini, dated 28 August 1687, John Sobieski complained tht the Russians had failed to honour their undertaking to invade the Crimea: 'Consider the villainy of these people who send us couriers to report on their military operations in letters full of fine phrases, but at the same time desert their posts and send us little or no real information.'[108] In an account of the campaign sent to the Poles Golitsyn emphasised the fact that the Khan had been too intimidated to engage in battle and that the 'treachery' of Samoilovich had also hampered operations. Minor forays, however, had been successful. A division had made reconnaissance as far as Kazikermen, and Cossack and Kalmyk troops had inflicted losses on the enemy. Turkish detachments had been repulsed by Don Cossack troops. The Poles were apparently not impressed.

In December 1687 Dominic D'Aumont came to Moscow in the capacity of Polish Resident and his opposite number P.B. Voznitsyn took up his duties in Warsaw. In a conference held shortly after his arrival D'Aumont claimed that the King had been astounded to be confronted by Crimean Tatars in his engagement with Tatars of the Belgorod horde, but Golitsyn denied their presence on the grounds that the Crimeans had been confined to the peninsula by the approach of the Russian army. He, in turn, complained that the Poles had done nothing to help the Russians.[109]

In March 1688 the two sides met again to discuss details of the next campaign, but it proved difficult to reach agreement. Keller wrote: 'The prejudice and old enmity between the Russian and Polish nations keeps reappearing, just like the sparks that leap up when you poke a glowing ember; they do not trust each other, and indulge in mutual recriminations about dereliction of duty.'[110] Russian suspicions were roused by news of secret talks between the Poles and the Tatars. Since the autumn of 1687 Moscow had been alarmed by rumours, originating in Poland, of a large-scale Tatar attack on the Ukraine, but in April the Tatars made a raid on southern Poland, thus prompting renewed Polish pleas for another Russian expedition to the Crimea. The Russians, however, refused to accept the blame for Polish losses as a result of the raid. A dispatch from Voznitsyn in Poland made it clear that the Polish parliament, the *sejm*, had not issued plans for further action that year, which made it look as though they expected the Russians to bear the full brunt of Tatar forces. Golitsyn thus decided against military operations for the time being and concentrated resources on building the fortress at Novobogoroditskoe. Perhaps there were even hopes that there would be no need for a second campaign. Patrick Gordon wrote in February 1688: 'Wee live in hopes that if it please God to bless the Christian arms with good success this summer, the Turkes will be necessitated to make a peace, for which I long as much as any, hopeing to gett my dismission from this service.'

Gordon may have anticipated further Christian victories with pleasure, but the case was not quite so clearcut for the government in Moscow. In September 1688 letters arrived from the former Patriarch of Constantinople, the Hospodar of Wallachia and the Patriarch of Serbia: 'All pious men – Serbs, Bulgarians, Moldavians, Wallachians – await your holy tsardom!'[111] They expressed the fear that further Austrian victories would lead to Catholic oppression and even to the eradication of the Orthodox faith. What they seemed to be asking was that Moscow should pre-empt an Austrian victory and march south-westwards for a combined attack on the Belgorod horde. In their reply the tsars assured their Orthodox brethren that an expedition to the Crimea was planned for the following spring. The conquest of the Crimea would allow them to cross the Dniepr and attack the Belgorod horde. But events were to prove that particular scheme wildly overambitious.

On 10 September Gordon recorded 'a generall intimation of service with a proclamation of all suits of law to cease against those who were ordered to service', and on 18 September there was an official announcement of the plans for a second campaign. It was less parochial than the proclamation of November 1686, referring, for example, to the weakened position of the Turks, following the defeat of the Grand Vizier at the Battle of Mohacs in August 1687, and Venetian gains in Greece and Dalmatia. 'The Lord God is inflicting severe punishment upon the Turkish state, and Muslim rule is about to meet its doom. The Turks have been rendered weak and impotent by the Christian armies and by internecine strife. Never before have they suffered such ruin and destruction, never was there such confusion.' At the same time, they continued to commit outrages against 'Orthodox Christians, men, women and innocent babes'.[112]

On 28 October the list of commanders for the campaign was published, with Golitsyn again named as field-marshal.[113] If he had been worried by his appointment in 1687, now he had even greater cause for concern. La Neuville reports that he tried surreptitiously to find a replacement, 'perceiving that Peter's party grew stronger every day, and fearing their power would increase during his absence . . . but finding it very difficult to accomplish his design, he adopted the tactic of offering himself, putting himself in the position of being able to rectify the mistakes which he had made in the last campaign'.[114]

There was now considerable anxiety that other members of the Holy League might make a separate peace, especially in view of Louis XIV's attack across the Rhine, which it was assumed would divert the Emperor's attention. Gordon reported on 27 October that they were:

> beginning to apprehend some danger by the makeing of a peace, which in this juncture of tyme the Rom Emperor would be forced to, by the French invadeing the Empire and breaking the truce and doubting that their actions and expeditions would not be well interpreted, as not done sincerely and cordially, which they perceiving, and reason prompting them to beleeve that at the makeing of a generall peace the allyes would not include them.[115]

Voznitsyn wrote from Poland: 'The Germans are terrified in case the Poles make a peace with the Tatars and I suspect that their fears will make each of them scramble to be the first to make a peace with the enemy.'[116]

Talks with the Poles, in which the Russians reiterated the need for a Polish operation in the west to support their campaign, remained inconclusive. On 8 November the tsars sent a letter to Sobieski, stating: 'If the King cannot send his troops at the time indicated and if there are delays, then our royal forces cannot undertake this venture.'[117] In January 1689 the King was to express his willingness to send troops 'as soon as the snow melts and the grass appears', but in the absence of confirmation by the *sejm* and against a background of suspicions that the Poles were having secret talks with the Crimean Khan, little trust was put in this promise.

By this time, as we shall see when we come to consider the events leading up to Sophia's downfall, Russia was already too heavily committed to a campaign to withdraw, and only the announcement of a treaty between her allies and Turkey could have allowed her to do so with dignity. On 19 April 1689, when the Russian army was already in the field, Keller was to write:

The pride, which predominates here over all other feelings, makes them reluctant that this matter [of a truce] should be mentioned. . . . On the contrary, at the imperial court they are encouraging open publicity for the considerable forces with which the tsars are preparing to mount an attack on the Turks and Tatars. But as the successes with which they delude themselves do not correspond to the brilliant promises, they are taking a more sober view. . . . If it should happen that the second campaign is no more successful than the first (God save this country from such misfortunes) one can say with confidence that a general uprising will break out here.[118]

Fears of a separate peace prompted Golitsyn to send the secretary Aleksei Vasil'ev to Vienna in January 1689 to keep an eye on developments there. In the event he was not admitted to negotiations between Austria and Turkey, and Golitsyn was obliged to channel Russian demands through the Dutch envoy in Vienna. Vasil'ev's mission eventually met with success when the Emperor undertook to form an alliance with Moscow on the same basis as with Warsaw, but by that time the second Crimean campaign had ended in failure and Sophia's government was in no position to take matters further.[119]

According to Keller, hopes of a truce with Turkey continued to be very much alive in Moscow, not least because Sophia and her party were beginning to experience pressure from Peter's camp. Golitsyn's experiences in 1687 may have persuaded them that peace gave marginally better hopes of political salvation than another costly and hazardous campaign. In March 1689 a project for the inclusion of Russian demands in a treaty was forwarded to Voznitsyn in Poland. They included the evacuation and surrender of the Crimea to Moscow, surrender of Azov and Turkish towns on the Dniepr, the return without compensation of prisoners of war and 2 million gold crowns of compensation.[120] These hopelessly extravagant claims could hardly have been taken seriously by Russia's allies. In any case, by the time they were submitted the second Crimean campaign was already underway and Austria had stopped short of signing a truce with the Turks.

In 1688 and 1689 attention was of necessity focused on the war with Turkey, but Russia's more sophisticated diplomats, notably Golitsyn, must have been more aware than ever before of the interdependence of European politics and the need to maintain communication even with those countries not directly involved in the Holy League. In May 1688 Golitsyn gave an audience to the Swedish envoy Christopher von Kochen, who reported that the prince:

was very pleased at the good reception given by his Royal Majesty to [the Russian envoy] Boris Mikhailov, and was full of praise for the preparation of the site for the Russian church in Reval. He expressed his desire to show the most friendly courtesy to the Swedish crown and assured me that he always represented everything concerning Sweden to their majesties the tsars in the best possible light.[121]

In the same letter Kochen reported the promotion of several members of Peter's party. Evidently Golitsyn was anxious to maintain cordial relations with Sweden, whose attention was currently distracted from Russian affairs. In 1686 the Swedes had abandoned their long-standing friendship with France and joined the League of Augsburg in coalition with Spain, Austria and Bavaria against Louis XIV. There had even been a suspension of traditional Swedish–Brandenburg hostilities when news of James II's accession to the English throne and fears for the Protestant cause prompted a secret pact between the two.

The Postnikov mission of 1687 had done little to improve Anglo-Russian relations. On 30 August 1688 Patrick Gordon dined with Golitsyn, one of many such occasions, and was told: 'We could agree well enough with your King's father and brother, but we cannot come to right with this, he is prowd beyond all measure.' He added 'moreover that the English could not subsist without their [the Russians'] commodities of Leather, hempe, potash, tallow and masts', to which Gordon gave 'a dubious complaying answer'.[122] Gordon reports that on 22 November, after the landing of William of Orange in England, he had talks with Fedor Shaklovity and other council members and was asked to elaborate on 'the Hollanders designe upon our King'. Gordon, a Catholic, was an ardent supporter of King James and was horrified by the proclamation, just a few months after these conversations, of the accession of William of Orange and his wife Mary. As he expressed it in an entry for 3 January 1689, the King was 'forced by the infidelity of his unnaturall English subjects to flee'.

In view of his own hostility towards Louis XIV, William would have welcomed the anti-French mood at the Russian court, which had been fanned by the news of the rude reception of Dolgoruky and Myshetsky in Paris in 1687. On 16 January 1689 two French Jesuits, Philippe Avril and Anthonie Beauvollier, arrived in Russia bearing a letter from Louis requesting that they be granted safe passage to China. The King's letter was addressed to the tsars, without reference to their co-ruler Sophia. Although the Jesuits had reason to expect favourable treatment from Golitsyn, and were confident that the Treaty of 1686 contained assurances 'that the Czars should grant a free passage through their Countries to such Religious as the King of Poland should be pleas'd to send for the future, to preach the Gospel among the Infidels',[123] it soon became clear that as envoys of the King of France their request would not be met.

Not only was Golitsyn experiencing a personal political crisis on the eve of the new campaign, but the Jesuits' visit to Moscow also happened to coincide with that of envoys from Protestant Brandenburg, which in October 1688 had joined a coalition of other German states in response to Louis XIV's attack across the Rhine. The envoys, who had been in Moscow since November, reminded Golitsyn of the ill-treatment of his ambassadors in France, and on 31 January the Jesuits were ordered to leave Moscow as tit for tat for the 'humiliation' of Dolgoruky's party and, for good measure, because of the incorrect formulation of the tsars' titles in the King's letter.[124] Avril found evidence of anti-Catholic feeling in Moscow's Foreign Quarter, reporting the execution of the Catholic officer Everand De Rouillé, who had killed a man in self-defence. Avril believed that the Brandenburg envoy Czaplitz had persuaded the Russian authorities to impose the death sentence.[125] The anti-French mood had still not abated in the summer of 1689 when the Frenchman La Neuville felt obliged to enter Russia in disguise, one of his errands being to report back to the King of Poland on Prussian activities in Moscow.

In the meantime, the Prussian envoy had induced the Russians to issue a decree offering protection to Huguenots expelled from France by the Revocation of the Edict of Nantes in October 1685. 'It has been revealed', reads the document,

> that His Majesty the King of France has begun to persecute his fellow countrymen and other adherents of the Evangelical faith. He has tormented many into fleeing the country. He has employed sundry cruelties in order to force them to convert to Catholicism and many have been put to death. He has separated husbands from their wives and children by imprisoning them. Others have managed to obtain their freedom by fleeing to neighbouring countries. A great number of these exiles have fled into the domains of His Highness the Elector [of Brandenburg] who expects the arrival of many more of these fugitives from France. There are also those who wish to come to our country, where they hope to find refuge from persecution and secure themselves with a livelihood. We have listened to their appeal and regard it with favour.[126]

This document is interesting not only for the light it throws on the poor standing of France in Russian eyes early in 1689, but also as evidence of the comparatively tolerant attitudes of Sophia's government. The 'exiles of the Evangelical faith' were to be offered work in keeping with their home service record, birth, honour and rank and the all-important right of return to their home country.

The Brandenburgers also secured two trade treaties, one on free access to the port of Archangel on the same basis as other foreign traders, and another granting Prussian merchants trading rights in Smolensk and Pskov.[127] Czaplitz even succeeded in persuading Golitsyn to take action against the Russian envoy Simonovsky, who back in

1682 had refused to kiss the hand of the Elector of Brandenburg because he was not a king, or even to drink to his health. Golitsyn agreed that the latter offence called for punishment and demotion.[128]

While Golitsyn was preparing to embark on a second campaign to the Crimea, another Russian diplomat was nearing the end of an even longer but less well-publicised journey. Since the 1630s the Russian conquest of Siberia and the Far East had followed the well-tried pattern of exploration and settlement, subjugation of local tribes and establishment of fortified posts (ostrogi) from which the valuable fur 'tribute' could be collected from the subject peoples. There were periodic local rebellions, but there seemed to be no stopping the eastward march of Muscovite civilisation – until, that is, it came face to face with another empire-building giant, China. From the town of Nerchinsk to the east of Lake Baikal Russian settlers had spread into the Amur valley, but in July 1685 a large detachment of Chinese captured the Russian fort at Albazin. The Russians were able to return later that same year, but in July 1686 the Chinese renewed their attack. In January of that year Moscow had reacted to news of the conflict by dispatching a plenipotentiary ambassador F.A. Golovin with an armed guard for peace talks with the Chinese. He was instructed to make territorial concessions if the Chinese proved obdurate, but on no account to lose valuable trading rights.

News of Golovin's approach led to a temporary Chinese retreat, but when he finally arrived in Nerchinsk in August 1689, three and a half years after he had set out, a Chinese delegation awaited him, accompanied by two Jesuit interpreters, a Portuguese and a Frenchman. The Chinese at first laid claim to all lands east of Lake Baikal, rejecting Golovin's proposal that the Amur should form the boundary between the two states. Golovin was eventually forced to make considerable concessions when he heard that the Chinese were preparing for war with the aid of rebel tribesmen.[129] After much quibbling the border was settled on the Gorbitsa and Argun rivers, with claims along the Ud to be decided at a later date. Much territory remained undesignated and there were discrepancies between Latin, Russian and Chinese texts, but the overall result of the Treaty of Nerchinsk (27 August, 1689)[130] was a Russian retreat from the Amur basin which was not made good for another 170 years. N.F. Demidova describes it as 'a major defeat for Russian diplomacy in the Far East'.[131]

For Sophia's critics, in retrospect, the treaty seemed an appropriate conclusion to the regency, but at the time of the signing its political impact was negligible, given the slow passage of news over the vast expanses of Siberia. Demidova believes that the decision to concede had been taken early on, probably by Fedor Shaklovity in the context of and during the first Crimean campaign, and that every attempt was made to keep the concessions as secret as possible. Agreement at virtually any price seems to have been the message, given the more pressing concerns of events nearer home.

In February 1689 the second Crimean campaign was launched. The plan was to make an earlier and speedier approach to the peninsula in order to avoid some of the hazards encountered during the first attempt. Golitsyn was to have some 112,000 troops under his command. In the middle of April he met up with the regiments of Sheremetev, Shein and Dolgoruky at the Orel river and on 20 April liaised with Hetman Mazepa and his Cossacks at the new fortress of Novobogoroditskoe on the Samara. By that date operations had already been hampered by the slow mobilisation of troops and the difficulties of transporting men, horses and supplies across swollen rivers and streams. Even so, they were more than a month ahead of the timetable of events in 1687. By 3 May they had reached the Karachakrak, the farthest point of the earlier campaign. According to La Neuville the Khan arrived back in the Crimea from his latest campaign just two days ahead of the Russian armies.[132] On 15 May the Tatars made their first attack, on Shein's regiment at the rear. There were further battles on 16 and 17 May.

The main source on the campaign is Golitsyn's dispatches, which contain detailed accounts of these encounters, and also formed the basis of laudatory charters later issued by Sophia's government. These dispatches, it will be noted, were addressed to 'the great sovereign tsars and great princes Ivan Alekseevich, Peter Alekseevich and the Great Sovereign Lady Pious Tsarevna and Great Princess Sophia Alekseevna, autocrats of all the Great and Little and White Russias', in recognition of the now established practice of according Sophia titles corresponding to those of her brothers. We can assume that the dispatches were intended for her eyes in the first instance.

Golitsyn reported that on 15 May the tsars' troops had:

> fought courageously and boldly with the infidel, and killed many nobles, murzas and fine commanders and many rank and file troops, and taken others alive and captured banners and horses and much equipment, and the prisoners reported under interrogation that a great many of their men had been killed and wounded. . . . And the infidel fought fiercely, not only with musket fire but also with artillery, and even catapults. Missiles rained down upon us, but by God's grace the only thing they achieved by their efforts was defeat.[133]

The Russians took refuge at Chernaia Dolina and the next day the Khan renewed his assault, apparently with similar lack of success. 'Your Majesties' men-at-arms courageously and boldly repelled the infidel in a bloody battle and drove them from the battlefield.'[134] The next day, according to Golitsyn's account, was much the same story: 'By the courage and valour of your men-at-arms, the infidel was repelled in a bloody battle, and throughout the day battles with the infidel raged right up to the River Kolonchak, as they now attacked, now retreated, and the enemy were forced to abandon their fierce assaults and fled across the Kolonchak in the direction of Perekop.'[135]

On 20 May Golitsyn's armies reached Perekop. 'There', wrote the Prince,

> we prepared to attack the town, and we made reconnaissance to find a place to make camp and to discover where we might find food and water for Your Majesties' men-at-arms; but our own investigation and that of your subject . . . Ivan Mazepa revealed that there was nowhere to get fodder for the horses. From the Kolonchak everything was trampled down and stamped out, and what was more, there was nowhere to get water, neither streams nor springs, on this side of Perekop. To the right the very walls of Perekop were washed by the Black Sea, and to the left by the Putrid Lake, which contains salt water, and between these seas we, your slaves, stood with the baggage trains. And the Crimean Khan did not come out of Perekop with his infidel hordes to meet us and did not join us in battle. In Perekop the suburbs and adjacent villages and hamlets had been burned to a cinder. And many times he sent out murza Suleshev to sue for peace on the terms [1681] that were made by State Secretary Tiapkin.[136]

After a council of war on 21 May Golitsyn decided to withdraw. 'The officers', he reports, 'were willing to serve faithfully and to spill their blood, but we were unable to go on the offensive for lack of water and horse fodder.' He refused to accept the Khan's peace terms because they were 'contrary to the Polish alliance'.[137] In a subsequent extended official proclamation he declared that 'he refused the Khan's offer of a truce because that truce would have been contrary to the eternal agreement of alliance made by us with His Majesty the King of Poland'.[138]

As the Russians withdrew they were harassed by units of the Belgorod horde and by troops from the 'Turkish towns', but there was no sign of the Khan. Gordon, whose diary entries break off on 15 May, resumes on 25 May with a detailed account of the retreat. 'The Tatars', he writes, 'appeared in greater numbers than before. They had burnt up the grass all around us, and marching was made arduous by the great quantities of sand, with the result that men and horses were exhausted and we had little hope of finding enough water for the night, which made many grave and downcast.'[139] Golitsyn made the point on several occasions that if the armies had stayed outside Perekop for more than a day there would have been considerable casualties as a result of water shortages. By 11 June they were back at the fortress of Novobogoroditskoe.

In a dispatch of 15 June Golitsyn transmitted some interesting information allegedly gleaned from Tatar captives. The Khan, they said, wished for peace with the great sovereigns. It was also reported that the

Poles had sent an envoy to Belgorod to make peace with the Khan, although it was suspected that this was a false rumour aimed at averting a Tatar attack on Poland. It was also said that the Sultan had not been engaged in military action because the King of France had diverted the Emperor's attention by his conquests in the west. The Sultan had allegedly summoned the Khan to invade Hungary, but the Khan protested that he was unable to do so because of the threat posed by the:

> numerous men-at-arms of their majesties the tsars. . . . And the Khan and the nobles and all the common folk of Tatary are saying that they have never seen the like of the numerous regiments of the tsars' men-at-arms; no other sovereigns had such forces, and those troops made their retreat from Perekop by God's will, not because of Muslim valour, but because the troops were short of water and horse fodder and there was nowhere to get water and the forage had all been trampled down.[140]

These latter comments arouse the suspicion that the intelligence already gathered from Tatar hostages had been embroidered or even fabricated in order to show Golitsyn's exploits in a more positive light. Just how accurate was the Prince's own account of the campaign and, more specifically, of the events outside Perekop? By and large, historians have taken a less enthusiastic view of the victory over the infidel than the one supplied by the 'victor' himself. It was impossible, after all, to gloss over the fact that once again the Crimea had not been captured or even penetrated. Less than four months after the retreat Golitsyn was sent into exile on a whole list of charges, including the one that:

> in this past year of 7197 [1689] you, Prince Vasily, were sent with the great sovereigns' men-at-arms to the Crimea and, reaching Perekop, you failed to carry out military operations and withdrew from that place and by your lack of enterprise great losses were inflicted on the Royal Treasury, ruin on the state and oppression on the people.[141]

Further perspective is added by Franz Lefort's estimate of 20,000 Russians killed and 15,000 captured.[142] Golitsyn's figures for 15–17 May of 441 injured and 61 killed in battle of course omit those who died of wounds, epidemic and starvation during the retreat.

Georgius David, writing less than a year after the event, records that Golitsyn reached the very approaches to Tavrida, but 'did nothing'. He records 'surprising rumours' to the effect than the Khan's horse was shot from under him, that his son was killed, that fourteen Tatar princes fell in battle and that many were taken prisoner, 'but all this remained a legend, for in the triumphal procession there was not one prisoner of war to be seen'.[143] He also lists the peace terms which Golitsyn is said to have proposed to the Khan's messenger: the Tatars were to promise not to attack Muscovy or Poland, not to aid the Turks against Christian rulers, to revoke their claim to tribute and to return all prisoners of war.

It was also reported that the actual battles had been on a small scale, with minimal casualties on both sides, even though Golitsyn had boasted at a reception for the Polish Ambassador, where David himself had been present, that the Muscovites 'had never achieved so much as in that campaign and for such a huge Muscovite army to reach the approaches to Tatary so quickly was unprecedented'.[144]

David's version of the peace terms offered by Golitsyn tallies with those recorded by La Neuville, whose source was reputedly the Polish Resident himself: 'That Russian slaves should be restored; that the Tatars should make no more incursions into the tsar's dominions; that they should renounce their claim to the 80,000 Crowns which they drew annually from the Muscovite treasury; that they should leave the Poles in peace, and not assist the Turks'. The Khan is said to have countered these proposals by insisting on a return to the terms of 1681 (as claimed by Golitsyn in his dispatch) and demanding 240,000 crowns in back payment of tribute.[145]

Both David and La Neuville were critical of Golitsyn's conduct of the campaign and subsequent account of it, but neither substantially refuted his version of events outside Perekop. There were to be more serious accusations, however. During the 'trial' of Fedor Shaklovity and his associates later in the year, a Cossack by the name of Evstafy Glistin alleged that Golitsyn had been persuaded to retreat by the gift of two barrels of gold, which turned out to contain just a thin gold layer on top of tar.[146] The story of Golitsyn's capitulation to the 'French' gold supplied by Louis XIV to facilitate his struggle with the Emperor was widely believed. Ivan Afanas'evich Zheliabuzhsky, a contemporary, wrote:

> Golitsyn took written reports from his officers, in which they were ordered to write that it had proved impossible to enter Perekop because there was not food or water there. But then the boyar Prince Vasily Golitsyn took two barrels of gold from the Tatars who were stationed at Perekop. And after the campaign those gold coins which went on sale in Moscow turned out to be brass, with just a thin layer of gold.[147]

Schleissing recorded a similar rumour.[148]

Of course, after Sophia's downfall many people had their reasons for discrediting Golitsyn, and charges of treachery and greed were much more damaging than accusations of mere incompetence. In fact, Golitsyn was probably beaten by a combination of bad luck, bad climate, inhospitable terrain and outmoded military practice. Yet another adverse factor, omitted by contemporary Russian critics, who generally lost sight of the international aspect of the Crimean campaigns, was the lack of co-ordination and co-operation from Russia's allies. It is significant that Golitsyn's own reason for not accepting the Khan's peace terms was that this would have been 'contrary to the alliance with Poland', but loyalty was undoubtedly strained by the isolation of Russia's war effort. Golitsyn's frustration is eloquently expressed in a letter to the Polish Hetman Jabłonowski, dated 2 June 1689, in which he wrote that the 'glorious victory' over the Tatars made it even more imperative that the Poles, 'our closest ally, should with all possible haste lend us a hand in these places against the sworn enemy of Christ and his Holy Mother'. Even though the Khan had sustained heavy losses, he was even now preparing to seek revenge: 'In order that we might avert God's punishment from us, we urge you to undertake military operations at the earliest juncture before time and opportunity desert you.'[149] He was probably also aware that peace talks in Vienna had freed Tatar units which had been operating in the Balkans and placed them at the disposal of the Crimean Khan. All in all, Russia had good reason to feel let down by her allies in her first venture into a European military alliance.

To focus all attention, as did his contemporaries, on Golitsyn's failure to capture the Crimea is to overlook the very substantial achievements of Sophia's regime in the sphere of foreign policy. The conquest of the peninsula was, in any case, unlikely to have been more than temporary, given the difficulties of maintaining a garrison and administering the area in the face of the Turkish threat. It was to elude Russia for another hundred years. The Crimean campaigns involved no loss of territorial status to Russia vis-à-vis Turkey, and, it has been argued, had a beneficial knock-on effect for Russia's allies, especially Austria. The combined efforts of the Holy League led to the further weakening of Turkey, which Peter I was to turn to his advantage when he captured Azov in 1696. Only the accommodation reached by the allies with the Turks in 1699 prevented Peter from consolidating his position.

As regards the 'Polish question', the tables had turned decisively in Moscow's favour. If 1667 was regarded as a victory 'tantamount to Russia's winning hegemony over the Slavonic nations', how much more impressive was the treaty of 1686, by which Russia consolidated long-cherished territorial claims, gained the right of interference in Poland's internal affairs on the pretext of religion, and entered the Holy League as the champion of Orthodox peoples languishing under Muslim rule. The weakening of Russia's traditional enemies Turkey and Poland meant that the conquest of a foothold on the Baltic, effectively shelved since the 1661 Treaty of Kardis, could be restored to the agenda. During Sophia's regency, in the meantime, the 'Swedish question' remained on ice. Relations were cordial and no further territory was conceded. Danish efforts to draw Russia into a coalition against Sweden during the 1680s were doomed to failure, but would fall on more fertile ground in the 1690s. Just fourteen years after Golitsyn returned empty-handed from the Crimea, Peter was founding a new capital on the Baltic.

The expansion of diplomatic activity in general, of which the multiple embassies of 1687 were the most impressive manifestation, also heralded developments of Peter's era, when the first permanent embassies were established, not to mention the Tsar's own 'Grand Embassy' of 1697–8'. A number of Peter's diplomatic specialists, men such as Golitsyn's deputy Emel'ian Ukraintsev and the envoy to England Vasily Postnikov, had received most of their training during the regency. One might also point to the regime's commitment, in the face of the Patriarch's objections, to the employment of foreign officers and technical experts, a policy more often associated with Peter, as well as Golitsyn's pursuit of the general reform of army organisation in the guise of the 'new model' forces. Foreigners such as Georgius David, who had benefited from the regime's enlightened policies towards Catholics, and other Catholic-oriented observers like La Neuville detected a marked increase in xenophobia, obscurantism and isolationism immediately after the overthrow of Sophia and Golitsyn and before Peter took a firm grip on power.

Such a generous view of the foreign policy of Sophia's regime can probably only be reached with the benefit of hindsight, and without reference to domestic politics. The court factions which opposed Sophia either did not see, or chose not to see, the matter in such a positive light. Back in Moscow, where Golitsyn was welcomed on 19 July by Tsar Ivan and Sophia but not, as we shall see, by Peter, his own version of the Crimean campaign was made public. A laudatory charter proclaimed:

> We, the great sovereigns, give our most gracious thanks to you, our own boyar and guardian . . . for your great and devoted service. By your efforts those savage and inveterate foes of the Holy Cross and all Christendom have been crushed and defeated and scattered by our royal armies in their infidel abode, an event quite unprecedented. They destroyed their own dwellings, their customary savage impudence deserted them, they were seized with terror and despair and set fire to the outlying villages and hamlets around Perekop. They did not venture out of Perekop with their infidel hordes to meet you . . . and did not engage you in battle as you retreated. And now you have returned unharmed to our frontiers with all the men-at-arms after winning the aforementioned victories, famed throughout the world.[150]

It is not hard to detect Sophia's hand in the eulogistic tone of this decree. Ivan probably had no personal view on events at all, whilst Peter, as we shall see, refused to treat the campaign as a 'victory'. The man who had most to lose by the undermining of Sophia's authority by a military disaster was the 'second favourite' Fedor Shaklovity, who undoubtedly played a major part in the elaborate 'cover up' campaign of receptions, prayers, rewards and eulogies that greeted Golitsyn's return. Other less partial people, including men like Patrick Gordon who had actually taken part in the inconclusive campaign, prepared to transfer their allegiance to Peter's camp once the expected repercussions came.

PART THREE

# Downfall 1689–1704

CHAPTER 9

# Overthrown 1689

*Tsar Peter has already grow taller than all the gentlemen of the court. We are convinced that this young prince will soon undertake the duties of a sovereign. If these changes do take place, then we shall see affairs taking a new direction.*
(Johann van Keller, 13 July 1688)[1]

Sophia had taken power in May 1682 in peculiar circumstances. It was understood at the time that she ruled during the tsars' 'minority', but in the case of Ivan 'incapacity' may have been a more appropriate term, for it was tacitly agreed that he would never be capable of ruling unaided even though, at sixteen, he could be deemed to be of age. His marriage in 1684 had done nothing to change the situation, his wife so far having failed to produce the heir that might have enhanced the Miloslavsky claim to ascendancy.

The case of Peter is more puzzling. His Romanov predecessors Mikhail, Aleksei and Fedor had come to the throne at the ages of sixteen, sixteen and fourteen respectively, with no formal arrangements for a regency, even though all three were backed by powerful male advisers. It appears that there was no official age of majority on which Peter's party might base a bid for power, but if a sickly Fedor could rule at fourteen, why not a robust Peter? The answer is, of course, that even if any special significance had been attached to Peter's fourteenth birthday on 30 May, 1686, this would have been a less than propitious time for Peter's supporters to press their claims, in the wake of celebrations for the permanent acquisition of Kiev. More significance might have been accorded to the fifteenth birthday, but this occurred too early for the Naryshkin party to exploit the inconclusive outcome of the first Crimean campaign. The sixteenth looked more promising, and there were indeed signs that Peter was now being groomed for power.

As early as December 1687 Christopher von Kochen had written: 'Tsar Peter is becoming better known, as the Prime Minister Prince Golitsyn is now obliged to report to His Royal Majesty on all important matters, which was not the case previously.'[2] He mentioned rumours that Peter was soon to be married. On 25 January 1688 Patrick Gordon noted in his diary: 'a Councill day wherein did sitt both the Tzaars & the Princess, the Youngest Tzaar the first tyme'.[3] Kochen wrote: 'Tsar Peter attends the council assiduously and, it is said, recently inspected all the chancelleries secretly at night. About eight days ago notes were found pinned to the gates making threats against certain people in power.'[4] Peter's inspection of the chancelleries included the Foreign Office. Scribes reported a visit to Golitsyn in the following terms:

> We wish to inform you that on this 16th day of March [1688] . . . in the fourth hour after sunset the Great Sovereign and Great Prince Peter Alekseevich paid a visit to the state ambassadorial chancellery and was pleased to pause at the table in the great reception chamber and to inspect the list of detainees and also to visit the secret treasure store and to inspect the icons.[5]

Peter's attendants on this occasion included Prince M.A. Cherkassky, one of Golitsyn's sworn enemies, and Prince B.A. Golitsyn, who was to be the mastermind behind Peter's eventual bid for power.

Appointments and promotions in the duma give further clues to the relative strength of the parties. Kochen interpreted the promotion of Peter's uncle, twenty-four-year-old L.K. Naryshkin, to the rank of boyar in April 1688 as a sign that 'the favourites and supporters of Tsar Peter will henceforth also be taking part in the ruling of the state'.[6] In June 1688 M.F. Naryshkin and K.F. Naryshkin entered the duma with the rank of lord-in-waiting (okol'nichi), and at the beginning of 1689 several Lopukhins, the relatives of the new Tsaritsa, were promoted.[7] Even if Sophia still hated the Naryshkin party as much as she did in 1682 she was evidently powerless to block their advancement.

Despite the evidence that Peter was being pushed into more active participation in affairs of state, his sixteenth birthday, 30 May 1688, came and went without any attempt to end the regency. Only on his nameday, 29 June, did Peter make any public show. He attended mass, then dispensed the customary liquid refreshments in the palace. Several promotions were made, as mentioned earlier.[8] There is every reason to believe that Peter had little appetite for the ceremonial aspect of his duties, for his adolescent enthusiasm was focused on matters military and naval. It was in 1688 that he discovered the decaying sailing boat that inaugurated a lifelong love affair with ships and the sea. This new interest was to displace for a while his passion of the past few years, the training and drilling of his so-called 'play' regiments (poteshnye), the Preobrazhensky and Semenovsky Guards.

It should be noted that Sophia never sought to limit or interfere with Peter's activities at Preobrazhenskoe, perhaps deeming them to be at worst adolescent nonsense, at best a useful means of delaying Peter's active participation in political life. Later writers interpreted Peter's frequent absences from court as part of Sophia's plan for extending her power. C.F. Weber, for example, writes that she

> did either out of Love to Ivan, or out of a boundless desire of governing try all Methods imaginable to remove out of the Way the present Czar her Brother ... or at least to get him some way or other excluded from the Succession. To compass which End she judged it the surest Method to deprive the young Czar Peter of all Education by letting him carelessly grow up among a Company of raw Youths, in Hopes that by an unbecoming Conduct he would in time render himself odious to the People, and that his promising Genius and the good sense of which he gave early Proofs, would be stifled by Debauches and Licentiousness, and consequently he be rendered unfit for Government and great Enterprizes.[9]

The fact is, as the palace records bear witness, Peter was never removed 'out of the Way'. He frequently participated in public ceremonials, and if he appeared less frequently than Ivan it was evidently of his own volition. Sophia had no need to banish Peter to Preobrazhenskoe. In the words of S.M. Solov'ev, it was his 'flamboyant passionate nature' that drove him out of the stuffy confines of the palace and Kremlin cathedrals.[10] Far from being contrived by Sophia and her party, the manoeuvres with 'raw Youths' were beginning to cause them concern. Patrick Gordon records that on 7 September 1688 Peter requisitioned five pipers and five drummers in Dutch uniform from his regiment, much to the displeasure of Vasily Golitsyn, who as head of the Foreign Servicemen's Office had to sanction the transfer.[11] There was every indication that Peter was going to exert himself as a military leader before he became a political one.

If Peter had little enthusiasm for the affairs of state in which his advisers were trying to involve him, he had even less for the next step in the programme for his 'coming of age'. On 7 January 1689 he was married to Evdokia Fedorovna Lopukhina, a girl from a family of middling status. The wedding was a quiet affair, conducted by Archpriest MerKury in the palace Church of SS Peter and Paul.[12] The selection was made by Peter's mother, who probably hoped to tempt her son away from his hazardous boyish pursuits, but, according to Boris Kurakin, her choice was influenced by T.N. Streshnev, who succeeded in eliminating Prince B.A. Golitsyn's candidate, a Princess Trubetskaia, in order to counter the growing power of Prince Boris (a cousin of Vasily Vasil'evich).[13] The Lopukhins, of course, had much to gain from a dynastic link with the Romanovs (Kurakin described the family as a large one, its members generally 'nasty, mean and underhand'), but unfortunately the modest and old-fashioned Evdokia turned out to be a less than suitable spouse for Peter. In Kurakin's words, she was 'fair of face, but mediocre of mind, and no match for her husband.'[14]

In April Peter was back on Lake Pleshcheev with his foreign instructors, supervising the construction of a small sailing fleet. He wrote several letters to his mother, mainly listing his excuses for not returning to Moscow, but none survives to his new wife. Despite this apparent lack of communication between the spouses, however, the hopes of Peter's supporters were more than justified. By the summer Tsaritsa Evdokia was pregnant, with the ill-fated Tsarevich Aleksei, yet another piece of good fortune for the Naryshkin party.

What was Sophia doing during this period of mounting political tension? As ever, we have little direct access to the state of her emotions, but we can suppose that she must have long been aware of the threat posed by Peter even before the recent manifestations of his growing maturity. Since 1686, as we know, Sophia had stressed her own status as legitimate ruler by including herself in the royal titles, having her image stamped on the coinage and appearing as often as possible at public ceremonies. Praise had been heaped upon her, in prose, poetry and engravings, as admirers, both false and genuine, likened her to heroines of the Old Testament – Judith, Deborah, Esther –, to the Byzantine Empress Pulcheria (she was, after all, the 'reviver of the Third Rome', 'the heir to Byzantium'), to Elizabeth of England, calling her most pious, virtuous, gracious, kind, judicious, Christ-loving and, above all most wise. She was the 'ornament of the Muscovite realm', the co-ruler of the pious tsars.

In the light of such hyperbole, it comes as no surprise to learn that she and her party began to explore the possibility of her coronation. In the investigation of the 'Shaklovity affair' in 1689 it emerged that in August 1687 there were attempts to persuade the strel'tsy to submit a petition on this very matter. Shaklovity recorded that Sophia summoned him to Kolomenskoe and asked him to sound out the likely strel'tsy response 'if the great sovereign lady should deign to be crowned with the royal crown'. Apparently in the end Sophia herself withdrew the proposal for fear of her brothers' 'anger',[15] but graphic evidence in the form of the 'coronation' engravings described in an earlier chapter survives to attest to the reality of her ambition. As we shall see, the coronation 'plot' was to be one of the main charges made against her.

In the meantime, entries in the palace records for 1688 show that Sophia continued to maintain her own court alongside that of Tsar Ivan, whilst the younger Tsar, with his own set of retainers, followed his own programme. That summer, for example, Ivan and Sophia made their customary visits to out-of-town estates and monasteries: Izmailovo on 24 June, the Novodevichy Convent on 2 July, Vorob'evo on 3 July, returning to Moscow for the celebration of the 'victory over the schismatics' on 5 July. Peter, in the meantime, having celebrated his nameday on 29 June, left on 30 June for a pilgrimage to the Trinity–St

Sergius Monastery accompanied by a sizeable retinue. On 25 July there were celebrations in Moscow for the nameday of Tsarevna Anna Mikhailovna. On the 28th Sophia again visited the Novodevichy Convent for the feast of Our Lady of Smolensk, the major local festival in the convent's calendar. A number of the buildings being erected there under her patronage were completed or nearing completion in 1688.

The fact that the two parties did occasionally join up is evidenced by entries for August. On 18–19 August Sophia and Ivan attended services in the Donskoi Monastery, then went on to Kolomenskoe where, on the 22nd, they were joined by Peter. The whole royal party celebrated Tsaritsa Natalia's nameday there on the 27th. One can imagine, in view of mounting political rivalries, that the occasion was less than relaxed.[16]

There is evidence that both parties sensed a crisis looming in the autumn of 1688, especially with the issue of the forthcoming Crimean campaign on which much of the prestige of Sophia's regime was to hang. Ill luck played its part. Keller in a dispatch of 22 September reported a major fire in Moscow which had given rise to public disturbances and mutterings that 'such misfortunes generally occur through the fault and mischief of certain persons in power'. On 2 October he reported another massive fire: 'At the moment Moscow presents a most sorry sight. One might think that it had recently been captured by an enemy and aggressor. These new misfortunes worsen the lamentable state of the capital.'[17] Sophia, it seems, was sensitive to the popular mood. Gordon records that on 3 October she treated firefighters to brandy.[18] Soon afterwards it was business as usual as Ivan and Sophia departed for Izmailovo, leaving Peter in the capital where, on 22 October, the younger Tsar took part in a lengthy religious ceremony in which he and the Patriarch processed through the Kremlin cathedrals, visited the Place of Proclamations on Red Square and entered the Cathedral of Our Lady of Kazan before returning to the Kremlin.[19]

Whatever Peter's own attitude to this formal ceremonial side of his duties there can be no doubt that his supporters, and his mother in particular, insisted that it should not be neglected. Such events not only underlined the Tsar's traditional role as protector of Orthodoxy but also pushed him into the public gaze. It would not be too cynical to imagine that his supporters were eager that the people of Moscow should make favourable comparison between the tall handsome young Tsar and his rather pathetic elder brother with his pushy female protector. The palace records, it may be noted, make specific reference to Ivan's absence from the ceremonies of 22 October. Both sides, it would seem, were anxious not to invade the other's territory.

The year 1689 opened, as we have seen, with Peter's marriage, as well as a flurry of diplomatic activity with the arrival of ambassadors from Brandenburg, Jesuits from France and the continuation of negotiations with China. A particularly useful summary of the atmosphere at court during this period was supplied by one of the Jesuits, Father Philippe Avril, who arrived in Moscow in January bearing a letter from Louis XIV asking for free passage to China and 'all manner of Protection and Assistance'.[20] As we have seen the request was not to be granted. It became clear that Vasily Golitsyn, to whom they directed their appeal, was no longer fully in control of affairs at court. Avril writes:

> It was no fault of his, that we did not receive all the satisfaction he made us hope for, the first time we had the honour to speak to him; and had he been absolute Master, and not oblig'd to keep great Measures with all the Boyars who were concern'd in the management of Affairs, he would willingly have granted us the Passage of Siberia. . . . But having already too many Enemies against him, he was oblig'd to sacrifice us, for fear of embroiling himself the more, and of being involv'd into more troubles than he daily met with already, notwithstanding the high Post he possess'd, which was not capable to secure him from the Shafts of Envy.[21]

Golitsyn's many 'troubles' included two 'vexatious incidents' reported by Avril, one an assassination attempt when he was driving to the palace in his sleigh. The assassin had time to shout before he was dragged away: 'Infamous Tyrant . . . since I have been so unfortunate as to fail in this attempt, to deliver my Country from the most horrid Monster, that ever bred in it, by making thee a Sacrifice, know that some happier hand than mine will be found. . . .'[22] In the second incident a coffin was found outside the gates of the Prince's house bearing the warning that 'unless the Campaign that art going to open, prove more successful than the former, thou can'st not avoid this'.[23] Such events, news of which Avril gleaned whilst staying in the gossip-prone Foreign Quarter, cannot have failed to disturb Sophia and her party. No doubt the expulsion of Avril and his companion on 31 January was regarded as a minor victory by her opponents.

The outcome of the new Crimean campaign was indeed regarded as crucial by both sides, even if the extent of the issues involved was appreciated only by a small circle in the Foreign Office. The troops set off southwards in the second week of February and those left at home could only wait and hope. Sophia buried her own anxieties in a frantic programme of visits to churches, monasteries and convents, whilst Peter escaped to his beloved boat building. An entry in the palace records gives a hint of atmosphere and priorities. On 26 April Peter arrived back in Moscow to attend a memorial service in the Archangel Cathedral for Tsar Fedor. He returned under protest, as we know from a surviving letter to his mother, and, in the laconic prose of the record, 'having heard the service he, the great sovereign, was pleased to depart from Moscow for the village'. The report continues: 'And then the Great Sovereign Lady and Pious Tsarevna and Great Princess Sophia Aekseevna, Autocrat of all the Great and Little and White Russias, was pleased to hear the liturgy in that same church.'[24] There can be little doubt that Sophia held back until the impatient young Tsar had left, both to avoid confrontation and to emphasise her own independent dignity as a *de facto* head of state. On 12 May she also presided alone over a service of prayers for victory in the Dormition Cathedral, collecting Ivan later that day for a visit to the Novodevichy Convent.[25]

Another event from which Peter was absent was the dinner, on 17 May, to celebrate the birth (on 21 March) of Tsar Ivan's first child, Tsarevna Maria. It was held in the Palace of Facets and was attended by Sophia, Ivan and the Patriarch.[26] Peter, the child's godfather, was not present. There could be no disguising the disappointment that must have been felt, after five years' waiting, at the child's sex. Peter's party breathed a sigh of relief.

On 19 May Sophia was again in the Novodevichy Convent, the following day in the St Aleksei Convent and on 21 May in the Miracles Monastery.[27] This intensive round of prayers coincided, although Sophia could not have known it at the time, with Golitsyn's arrival and withdrawal from Perekop. News of the campaign, and of the battles that preceded it, reached Moscow some three weeks later. Palace records for 14 June mention dispatches from the front which occasioned a service of thanksgiving in the Cathedral of the Dormition.[28] Sophia herself may have received news somewhat earlier. In a coded letter to Golitsyn, one of the very few pieces of personal correspondence to survive from her hand, she mentioned receiving dispatches on 11–12 June. It is worth quoting this letter and its companion at length, as they provide some of the only direct evidence of Sophia's relationship with her first minister.[29]

The first begins: 'My light, little brother Vasenka, be healthy for many years, my lord.' Besides the fact that the terms of endearment used (*moi svet*, *bratets*, *batiushka*, and others such as *moia dusha* and *nadezhda* which occur later) are virtually untranslatable, the letter must also be read in the context of the formal epistolary conventions of the era and the abundant religious references, all of which make it almost impossible to capture a suitable tone or register of language in English. She continued:

By the grace of God and the Holy Mother of God and your own good sense and good fortune you have defeated the Hagarene; may God grant you future victories over your enemies. I, my light, shall be unable to believe that you will return to us until I actually see you in my embrace. You write that I should pray, being a sinner and unworthy in the eyes of God; still, I dare to trust in his goodness, sinner though I be. I always pray that my light might be happy. Be healthy and prosper, my light, in Christ for countless ages, Amen.

The second letter is longer and more topical:

My lord and light and hope, may you have long life and prosperity. Joyful to me indeed is this day on which the Lord God has glorified his holy Name and the name of his mother the blessed Mother of God through you, my light, the like of which has not been heard throughout the ages, nor have our fathers recounted such divine mercy, for God has delivered you, as once he delivered the Israelites out of the land of Egypt by his prophet Moses; now praise be to God for the mercy he has shown us through you, my dear. My lord, how can you be repaid for your innumerable labours? My joy, my light, I can hardly believe that I shall ever see you again. Great indeed will be the day when I have you with me again, my dear. If it were possible, I would set you before me in a single day. Your letters from Perekop in God's safekeeping have all reached me safely. . . . On the 11th five dispatches arrived. I was coming on foot from Vozdvizhenskoe and had just reached the holy gates of the Monastery of St Sergius when I received your reports of the battles. I cannot remember how I entered. I read as I walked. How can I ever express my thanks to God for his mercy and to his mother the blessed Mother of God and to the gracious worker of miracles St Sergius?

The courier Zmeev has not yet been. Your instructions about visiting monasteries have all been carried out; I myself went around all the monasteries on foot. I shall soon send Vasily Narbekov to you with the delivery, but the gold pieces are not yet available. Do not fret on that account. It would be a pity to delay you. I shall send them as soon as they are ready. I am also collecting the strel'tsy money, which will be sent as soon as it is ready. Tell them that it is on its way. Your zeal, my dear, shall be made manifest. In the case of Shoshin, my lord, either pay the ransom or exchange him. You write, my dear, that I should pray for you. God knows how much I long to see you again, my dear, and I trust in his mercy that he will allow me to see you, my hope. Deal with the troops as you yourself have written, whether Boris should go to Belgorod, and also Obram, as you see fit. And I, my lord, am well, thanks to your prayers; we are all well. When, God willing, I see you again, I shall tell you everything that has happened. Do not tarry, continue your march; you have toiled so much. How can I ever repay you, my light, for the essential service that you have rendered? You have laboured more than all the others. If you had not done it, nobody would.

Given a dearth of similar letters from unmarried Russian women to men during this period with which to make comparisons, readers will have to decide for themselves whether these sole surviving letters, written in cipher, constitute proof of a love affair between Sophia and Golitsyn. What they undoubtedly show is the seriousness with which

Sophia viewed the Crimean expedition, and the genuine delight which she took in Golitsyn's 'victories'. They illustrate also the extent to which she relied on Golitsyn and the confidence she had in his abilities, although this trust did not preclude appeals to Divine Providence and a faith in the power of prayer.

As we know, the official story of the campaign presented it as a great victory, too. This is the version that Sophia would have liked to believe, but it is inconceivable that she was totally shielded from the news of errors and losses which soon began to arrive from the Crimea. There was no break in her devotions. On 15 June she presided alone over a service in the Dormition Cathedral and the next day attended the consecration of a new church not far from the Kremlin.[30] On the 20th we find her praying for rain in the Church of the Prophet Elijah, on the 21st in the Dormition Cathedral, on the 23rd following a procession of icons from the Kremlin to the Purification Monastery and back again.

On 24 June Peter arrived back in Moscow from Preobrazhenskoe, no doubt encouraged to do so by his advisers, for not only were two important anniversaries pending but the Naryshkin camp may also have sensed the imminent discrediting of Sophia and her regime. The 25th was the anniversary of the coronation in 1682 and for once Sophia was absent from the cathedral. The event must have reminded her only too clearly that she herself had never been crowned. On 26 June she left for the Novodevichy Convent and was joined there by Ivan on the 27th. Their departure again left Peter the centre-stage for the celebrations of his nameday on 29 June. The palace records specifically mention that Ivan was not present at the mass for the feast of SS Peter and Paul, and Peter officiated alone at the reception for courtiers, treating them to wine and vodka. Several men from Peter's camp – I.I. Naryshkin, F.A. Lopukhin and P.M. Apraksin – were promoted. The whole day gave Peter and his circle ample opportunity to assert themselves, but they were not ready to stage a formal takeover. On 2 July Peter went off to Kolomenskoe, which was the cue for Sophia to re-enter the spotlight. On 5 July she attended services in honour of St Sergius of Radonezh, then, in the Dormition Cathedral, a commemoration of the 'victory over the schismatics' of 1682, in which, of course, Sophia herself had been one of the leading players.

Keller's prediction of July 1688 was yet to be fulfilled, but the time could not be far off when Peter's supporters would force the issue of the Crimean campaign to discredit Sophia's government, confident for once that the militarily minded young Tsar would take an active interest in the matter. As the 'victorious' Golitsyn approached Moscow, an occasion was found for open confrontation. On 8 July fell the feast of the Icon of Our Lady of Kazan, at which the royal family traditionally attended mass in the Kremlin and followed icons to the Kazan Cathedral on Red Square. On this occasion both tsars and Sophia were present, Peter arriving in Moscow about an hour before the start of the service.

The palace records tell the following tale. In the fifth hour of the day the two tsars and Sophia left the palace Church of the Saviour and followed a procession of icons into the Annunciation Cathedral, thence to the Dormition Cathedral, where they were met by the Patriarch. Inside the cathedral whilst prayers were sung for the tsars' health they did obeisance to icons and relics. Then, we learn, for some reason the procession divided. Ivan and Sophia followed the icons and the crosses through the Spassky Gates and out on to Red Square. Peter, on the other hand, followed icons into the Archangel Cathedral and crossed himself by the relics of Tsarevich Dmitry, then 'was pleased to depart from Moscow for that aforementioned village of Kolomenskoe'.[31]

One might suspect a simple division of labour were it not for a passage in the memoirs of Andrei Matveev to the effect that when Sophia proceeded 'publicly' to accompany the icons out of the cathedral, she was accosted by Peter, who declared that 'it was not fitting and contrary to custom that her shameful person should be present at this ceremony'. When she refused to comply Peter left the ceremony abruptly and returned to Kolomenskoe.[32] Matveev, as we know, had good reason to dislike Sophia and show her in the worst possible light, but his version is fully in keeping with that of the far blander palace records. Sophia may have been puzzled by the outburst, for her participation in such ceremonies was by now a commonplace, but there is no sign that she took any notice of it. On 14–15 July she attended services in the Church of St Vladimir near the Convent of St John and on the 18th took a day trip to the village of Pokrovskoe.[33]

Golitsyn and his troops were now at the gates of Moscow. Sophia issued orders that they should enter the city and deposit icons, crosses and banners from the campaign in the Donskoi Monastery. The next day they continued as far as the Serpukhov city gates. Sophia, in the meantime, went to pray in the Church of St Tikhon, then came out to meet the procession. The record continues:

> She deigned to meet the Lifegiving Cross of Our Lord and the holy icons beyond Zemliany Gorod by the gates. And doing obeisance to the Cross of Our Lord and the holy icons, she, the sovereign lady, greeted the boyars and commanders, the guardian and palace commander Prince Vasily Vasil'evich and his comrades.[34]

The military procession, with Sophia and Golitsyn at its head, then made its way across the river and entered the Kremlin by the Predotechensky Gates, where they were met by Metropolitan Adrian of Moscow.

A little further on Tsar Ivan appeared to greet the commanders. Then they all entered the Dormition Cathedral, where Patriarch Joachim:

> offered prayers to God and the Virgin Mary and the miracle-workers of Moscow and to all the saints for the continuing good health of the sovereigns, and for their lofty sceptre and for peace and calm and prosperity and the extension of Their Majesties' great and glorious Russian realm and for every blessing and for victory and defeat of the enemies and foes of the Holy Cross and of the sovereigns.[35]

After the service Ivan and Sophia retired to their chambers, but appeared later to give a reception to Golitsyn and his fellow officers, at which a speech of praise was delivered by State Councillor V.G. Semenov.

One sovereign was prominent by his absence. Peter was still at Kolomenskoe whither he had stormed on 8 July. Palace records note that Golitsyn and his officers set off for Kolomenskoe on 20 July and were received (*byli u ruki*) by Peter.[36] Sophia, meanwhile, stubbornly clung to the myth of a glorious victory. On 23 July she staged a thanksgiving ceremony in the Novodevichy Convent for 'the victory over the sovereigns' enemies the damned Hagarene'. Golitsyn and his officers were in attendance and afterwards were treated to cups of Italian wine and vodka.[37] On 24 July a proclamation of rewards and honours for the campaign was drawn up. Golitsyn, 'for his loyal and zealous service and fervent and unceasing endeavour in that military encounter . . . for the glorious and splendid victory over the infidel', was awarded a gold cup, a sable-lined robe, a salary supplement of 300 roubles and a hereditary estate of 1,500 serfs.[38] Others were rewarded in keeping with their rank.

The decree, issued in the names of both tsars, proved too much for Peter. He refused to accept expressions of thanks from the commanding officers. Patrick Gordon records in a diary entry for 24 July:

> We were admitted to kiss the eldest Tzaar & the Princess Sophia Alexiovna their hands with the ordinary ceremonies & compliments, the Princess gave me particularly thanks for my good service. Our skasky [commendations] were delayed by reason that the youngest Tzaar would not give his consent to bestow so much on our Boyars as they had concluded without him.

On the 26th: 'with a great deale ado and entreaty the youngest Tzaar was brought to assent to the rewards which had been concluded to be given for our services'. The award ceremony took place the following day in the Kremlin. Gordon himself received a month's salary, twenty pairs of sables, a silver cup and 'rich stuffe to a coat'.[39]

Peter may have conceded on the question of rewards, but he was obviously unwilling to let the matter rest. The Jesuit David writes:

Peter refused to receive Golitsyn but summoned the State Treasurer and questioned him about the Tsarevna's expenses. During the interrogation he seized the Treasurer by the beard, threw him to the ground and trampled on him. When news of this disgrace reached the Tsarevna, her anger flared up. Many troops started to enter the town and nobody knew for what purpose.[40]

In the words of Patrick Gordon:

all did apparently see and know that his consent or rather assent was by great importunity extorted from him and this did more irritate him against our Generalissimus and the chieffe counsellours of the court of the other part, for now there was plainly to be seen an open eruption or breach which was like to turn to animosityes.

Attempts at concealment were, it seems, unsuccessful. In an entry for 31 July Gordon reported 'passions and humors increasing lyke to breake out with a Poroxismus'. In the palace there had been further indications of the 'breach'. The nameday of Tsarevna Anna Mikhailovna fell on 25 July but Peter, we learn from the palace records, arrived back in Moscow from Kolomenskoe that afternoon and almost immediately departed for Preobrazhenskoe without attending the celebrations. The reception of the gentlemen of the duma and other leading officials was organised by Sophia and Ivan.[41] The palace records, of course, maintained decorum at all costs. It was not the job of scribes to allude to gossip and scandal, even when the 'great sovereigns' acted in an impulsive or unpredictable way. On 6 August we find all three of them going about their separate business, Ivan attending a service in the palace Church of the Transfiguration, Sophia making a day trip to the Novodevichy Convent and returning with the customary bodyguard whose numbers were soon to give rise to anxieties, and Peter 'deigning to continue his sojourn at Preobrazhenskoe'.[42] That same day, in the face of apparent 'business as usual', Gordon reported 'rumers unsafe to be uttered'.

These rumours anticipated a move from either camp and were far from being confined simply to fears that Sophia was planning to extend her rule. Kurakin, for one, believed that both sides engaged in intrigues,[43] whilst E. Shmurlo, the author of one of the most careful analyses of the events of 1689, suggested that 'there was no plot in the sense of something organised, but the universal fear of such a plot put everyone on edge and turned heads. The tense anticipation of a crisis actually led to that very crisis.'[44] Many rumours circulated about Peter's behaviour; for example, it was said that he 'goes to the Kukui [Foreign Quarter] and drinks there; he beats the poteshnyi cavalry with his own royal hands and nothing can pacify him for he gets blind drunk'.[45] Just as in 1682, there were allegations that Peter's party failed to show due respect for their ancestors. It may have been well known, for example, that Peter had failed to arrive in time for a requiem mass for Tsar Fedor scheduled for the latter's saint's day on 8 June, with the result that the service had to be delayed for three days.[46]

The behaviour of Lev Naryshkin and Boris Golitsyn came under scrutiny and they were suspected of various abuses of power, such as robbing the Treasury, holding up petitions to the tsars and insulting Tsarevna Sophia and Tsar Ivan. There was even a farcical incident in which one M. Shoshin, acting as agent provocateur, impersonated Lev Naryshkin by riding round the strel'tsy settlements dressed in a white damask caftan and giving orders for the strel'tsy to be flogged.[47] On 4 August Peter had fanned suspicions when, during a reception at Izmailovo for his wife's nameday, he ordered the arrest of Fedor Shaklovity over a dispute involving a strelets. It was far from implausible that Peter and his supporters would come to Moscow with the play regiments and have it out once and for all with Sophia and her party, and Sophia had nothing to lose by endorsing rumours that Peter and his faction were unfit to rule.

The final break came on Wednesday, 7 August. Shaklovity, in his deposition to his interrogators, claimed that on that date he was summoned by Sophia, who announced her intention of going to pray in the Donskoi Monastery and asked him to prepare a detachment of 100 armed strel'tsy as she feared a recurrence of an incident some weeks back when a murder was committed in the vicinity whilst she was on a visit to the Novodevichy Convent. Just an hour later he was summoned again and informed of a letter announcing that the play regiments intended to come to Moscow on the night of 7 August and 'kill all the sovereigns'. Several units of strel'tsy were mustered and the gates of the Kremlin were locked. Then, in the early hours of the morning, Sophia decided to go to the Kazan Cathedral on Red Square, accompanied by Shaklovity himself and a unit of strel'tsy.[48] This outing, which does not appear in the palace records, is noted in many of the statements made at Shaklovity's subsequent 'trial', including that of a lord-in-waiting, V. Narbekov, who helped to distribute a rouble apiece to the guards who had accompanied the Tsarevna.[49]

Meanwhile, just before midnight on the 7th a message reached Peter at Preobrazhenskoe that (in Gordon's words) 'many streltsees or soldiers of the guards were conveened by order in the Krimlina' and were to come armed to Preobrazhenskoe to kill 'diverse persons, especially the Naryskins'. In Matveev's version, four representatives of the royal body-guard of strel'tsy arrived at Preobrazhenskoe to report that the regular strel'tsy were mustering to carry out Shaklovity's plot – to murder Peter, his mother, his wife, his sister and all his courtiers.[50] This news caused Peter to leap on his horse and flee in panic to a wood, where his clothes and boots were brought to him. He rode the forty or so miles to the

Trinity–St Sergius Monastery, where 'he immediately threw himself upon a bed and fell a weeping bitterly relating the case to the abbot and deseiring the protection and assistance of them'. That night he was joined by his wife and mother and the play regiments, and later the next day the loyal Sukharev regiment of strel'tsy arrived.

Even now the palace records gave no hint of a crisis. Peter, we learn, 'deigned to go to the Trinity Monastery for prayers' (*izvolil ittit' dlia moleniia*), accompanied by the gentlemen of his entourage.[51] Sources hostile to Sophia claim that the Tsar was indeed in fear of his life. In the words of Andrei Matveev: 'The ardour of fury and indomitable anger, robbing reason of all power, prompted people to wicked schemes.' He reports a highly secret meeting at the beginning of August when Fedor Shaklovity is said to have met with representatives of the strel'tsy regiments with the 'most evil intent'.[52] Shaklovity was indeed to be sentenced to death because 'forgetful of the fear of God and of his oath of allegiance to the sovereigns, he plotted to kill Tsar Peter Alekseevich [titles] and his mother Tsaritsa Natalia [titles], spoke many indecent words against the sovereign and his mother and ordered his comrades to set fire to the village of Preobrazhenskoe'.[53] It seems equally likely, however, that Peter's own advisers took advantage of the tension between Peter and Sophia to force a confrontation. Peter's memories of 1682 were still fresh enough for him to respond violently to rumours of a strel'tsy revolt, and the incumbents of the Kremlin were also living on the edge of their nerves. Just a small push was needed.[54]

Back in Moscow Sophia carried out her usual round of engagements as though she were unaware of any crisis. Official records, at least, give no hint that she was, in Matveev's words, 'most sorely troubled by her conscience and in a state of great agitation'.[55] On 9 August there was a procession of icons from the Miracles Monastery, and after the evensong Sophia and Ivan attended memorial services for their parents, first in the Archangel Cathedral then in the Ascension Convent, the respective resting places of Tsar Aleksei and Tsaritsa Maria.[56]

That same day a messenger arrived from Peter to ask the reason for the gathering of so many strel'tsy in the Kremlin and received the reply that it was (as Gordon puts it) 'to guard the Princess to a Monastery whither she was to go for devotions sake'. On 11 August she did indeed set off to accompany an icon of Our Lady of the Don used in the Crimean campaign from the Kremlin to the Donskoi Monastery. She was accompanied by boyars and commanders, and returned to the Kremlin on 12 August.[57] One senses an air of defiance in the face of Peter's challenge, a determination to maintain both her own public presence and official propaganda of the 'great victory'. Peter, meanwhile, 'deigned to continue his sojourn at the Trinity Monastery'.

Sophia did not allow anxieties to disrupt observation of the Church calendar. On 15 August fell the feast of the Dormition of the Virgin, one of the major Orthodox festivals. On the 14th she attended a whole series of services in the Dormition Cathedral and on the 15th was present at a lengthy mass.[58] The next day brought a fresh challenge in the form of a written summons from Peter ordering the strel'tsy and infantry regiments to attend him at the Trinity Monastery by 18 August.[59] Sophia's response was to summon the strel'tsy and delivery (in Gordon's words) an 'eloquent oration', explaining why they should disobey and not 'medle themselves in the differences betwixt them and their brother'. After Sophia withdrew, several voted in favour of going but Sophia returned and 'tooke them up very sharply, telling them that if any went thither, she would cause interrupt them, and strike off their heads'.

Palace records note only that on that day Sophia attended mass in the palace Church of the Saviour.[60] Her thoughts must have been fixed on resolving the conflict, if possible by persuading Peter to return to Moscow and abandon the sanctuary and status afforded by the Trinity Monastery. She could hardly fail to recall that she had resorted to its walls when trying to bring the strel'tsy to heel in 1682. She still had a little time to play with for, as Gordon reports, many were still confused by the novel situation of contradictory orders issuing from two different courts and there were even rumours that the summons from the Trinity Monastery had not been approved by Peter. Gordon and his fellow foreign officers therefore obeyed Vasily Golitsyn's 'express orders not to stirr from Mosko'.

On 17 August Sophia went to the Novodevichy Convent and on the 18th and 19th she was in the Donskoi Monastery, attending a major service conducted by the patriarch.[61] This was the last occasion on which Sophia received Joachim's backing. Shortly afterwards he left Moscow to have talks with Peter and threw in his lot with the younger Tsar's camp. On the 27th yet more letters arrived from Peter ordering officers and ten men from each regiment to join him,[62] but this time it was Sophia herself who responded.

On 29 August after visiting several Kremlin churches for prayers she set off for the Trinity Monastery, accompanied by Vasily Golitsyn and a number of other supporters. Palace records state blandly that 'she, the great sovereign lady, deigned to return to Moscow from that journey on the 31st of August at the seventh hour of the night',[63] but in fact she was forced to return. Matveev records that she set off with several of her sisters and an icon of the Saviour. The party stopped at the village of Vozdvizhenskoe about eight miles to the south of the monastery, where they were met by I.I. Buturlin bearing a message from Peter ordering her to go no further. When Sophia declared her intention of proceeding another messenger arrived to inform her that she would be dealt with 'dishonourably' if she had the audacity to disobey.[64] In Kurakin's version she was threatened with cannon fire if she approached the monastery.[65]

If this challenge failed to convince her that Peter was in earnest, she must have been shaken by what happened the following day. On 1 September as preparations were being made to celebrate the Russian New Year a less than seasonal message came from Peter demanding that Shaklovity and his 'complices' be sent at once to the Trinity Monastery. The order, dated 31 August, stated that 'the blatant criminal Fedor Shaklovity was the initiator of that gathering [of troops], together with other criminals. And they intended to march to the village of Preobra-zhenskoe and murder us, our mother, our sister and our courtiers'.[66]

Sophia's 'vehemently incensed' response was to order that the messenger, Colonel Ivan Nechaev, be beheaded, but there was no executioner available to carry out her orders. The strel'tsy were then summoned and, in Gordon's account:

> the Princess coming downe to the lower part of the stairs [of the Krasnoe porch] had a long speech to them, telling them how some bad instruments betwixt her brothers and them had used all meanes to divide them and had raised great trouble jealousies and dissension, that they had suborned some persons to tell of a conspiracy against the life of the youngest Tzaar and others, and that envying the good services of Fiodor Shaklovite and his continuall paines day and night for the safety and welfare of the Empire they had named him as the contriver of the conspiracy (if there be any such thing) that she to compose these businesses and to search and try out the ground of the business had offered herself to assist, and had taken a jorney thither, but was by the instigation of bad Counsellours about her brother stopped and not suffered to go further, and so to her great ignominy must be forced to returne, that they knew very well, how she had governed the Empire these seven yeares by past that she had taken the Government . . . upon her in a very troublesome tyme that during her direction in the Government she had made a glorious perpetuall peace with the Crian [Christian] Princes their neighbours, that the enemyes of the Crian religion had been forced by their armes in two expeditions to stand in awe of them that of they had received large rewards for their services, that she had been at all tymes very gracious to them that she could not imagine but that they would prove true to her and not believe the contrivances of the enemyes of the welfare and quiet of the empire that it was not the life of Fiodor Shaklovite which they sought but the lyfe of her and her brother and so dismissed them with promise of great favour to those who should prove faithfull and not medle in this business and punishment to those who should disobey and make any stirrs.

This speech was repeated to a gathering of the 'burgers and commons', then followed by yet another 'large eloquent speech'. Those assembled, including Colonel Nechaev, were treated to brandy, in liberal measures because 1 September also happened to be the nameday of Tsarevna Marfa.[67] In Nechaev's own account, Sophia 'was pleased to come out and to say that she understood that her brother, the Great Sovereign Tsar Peter Alekseevich, has commanded you to arrest Fedor Shaklovity and Obroska Petrov and others, but they are good men, and you would be arresting them wrongfully'.[68]

The speech reported by Gordon is a vital piece of evidence. The whole episode presents Sophia as vigorous and determined, quite fearless about speaking in public. Here was a woman fighting for her political life and using all means at her disposal, both threats and blandishments, to retain support. What credence should be given to her assurance that there was no conspiracy? If a plot against Peter did exist and Sophia knew of it, in denying its existence she was merely doing what politicians have done throughout the ages. In Gordon's brief cameo she stands out more clearly than ever as a thoroughly political animal.

The decisive thing was, in the end, that Peter himself believed in the existence of a plot, whilst for his supporters it was more than convenient that their protégé's assumption of power should be accompanied by a complete discrediting of Sophia and her party. As Gordon points out, 'the direction of all effaires at Troitsa' was carried out by Prince B.A. Golitsyn, who on 1 September had written to his cousin Prince Vasily urging him to come to the monastery and swear his allegiance to Peter. The defection of Golitsyn would have been a major blow to Sophia, but for the time being the Prince hesitated, asking Prince Boris to 'be a good instrument and agree the parties'. The 'mild' Golitsyn still hoped for an amicable solution, but it became ever clearer that Peter's party meant to exert their ascendancy by force if necessary.

On 4 September Patrick Gordon reported the arrival in the Foreign Quarter of a letter from Peter ordering foreign officers to attend him immediately and setting out details of the 'conspiracy' devised by Fedor Shaklovity, Silvester Medvedev and about ten strel'tsy against the Tsar, his mother, the Patriarch and other persons. Gordon took this letter to Prince Vasily, but, aware that the Prince was wavering, decided to join Peter regardless of the orders he received. The officers left on 5 September and Gordon records that 'our going to Troitsa was the crisis of this business for all began to speack openly on behalfe of the younger Tzaar'.

As more and more people began to set off for the Trinity Monastery the only thing that remained to make Peter's triumph complete was the arrest of the 'conspirators'. On the evening of 6 September large numbers of strel'tsy came to the Kremlin to arrest Shaklovity. Sophia at first:

spoke very resolutely, denying to deliver him, and persuading them not to medle themselves in the business betwixt her and her brother, but to be quiet, where with they not being satisfyed, they told her that if they could not have him, they would be forced to beat on the Nabat, which is the greatest alarum bell, whereat the Princess seemed to be moved, then these, who were near to her, fearing violence and an uproare told her that it was needless for her to contest in such a matter that if a tumult were raised, many would lose their lives, so it were better to deliver him so she suffered herself to be persuaded and caused deliver him.

There was to be no repetition of May 1682.

Events were nearing their conclusion. On 7 September Shaklovity was taken to the monastery, where he confessed that he had intended to burn the palace at Preobrazhenskoe and put Peter and his mother 'out of the way', then present a petition for Sophia to be crowned. The next day, under torture, he made a written statement in which others were implicated. On 12 September Shaklovity was executed, together with his strel'tsy 'complices' Abrosim Petrov and Kuz'ma Chermny.[69] It seems certain that one of those implicated by Shaklovity's testimonial was Prince Vasily Golitsyn, who probably has his cousin Prince Boris to thank for the fact that no charges of attempted regicide or designs on the crown were brought against him. Writes Gordon:

> It is worthy of observation that notwithstanding Kniaz [Prince] Vas. Vas. was the great prop and columne of the Princess her syde, and was very well knowne to be conscious of all intended against the lyfe of the youngest Tzaar if not a contriver, yet he was not sentenced as a traitor or declared guilty of treason which even by consealing of it he had committed in the highest degree which was done by the power and influence which Cousin German Kniaz Boris Alexeyovits Golitsyn had upon the Tzaar and his counsell of that time.

In the event Golitsyn was accused of condoning Sophia's assumption of autocratic power ('showing preference and favour to their royal sister, he did report all manner of affairs to their sister bypassing them, the great sovereigns') and of negligence in his conduct of the Crimean campaign.[70] For this Golitsyn was deprived of rank and property and exiled to the north of Russia.

Sophia was not present as death and humiliation were heaped upon her erstwhile supporters and her own name, by association, was disgraced. No credence can be given to the tale, reproduced in several later accounts, that she had plans for fleeing to Poland.[71] She attempted to draw the strel'tsy remaining to her, consulted the gentlemen of the duma and even threatened to visit the Trinity Monastery with Tsar Ivan, but all to no avail. In the end she had simply to sit in the Kremlin and await judgement, as all her former authority melted away.

On 7 September the practice of including her name in the royal decrees was discontinued, not by any direct reference to her but simply by stating that 'the great sovereign tsars and great princes Ivan Alekseevich, Peter Alekseevich, autocrats of all the Great and Little and White Russias, decree: that in their great sovereigns' rescripts, and in the chancelleries for all matters, and in petitions, their royal name and title should be written as above'.[72] This order was circulated to the heads of all chancelleries.

The only complaints made directly against Sophia appear in a letter from Peter to Ivan, dated between 8 and 12 September 1689, in which the younger Tsar writes:

> by the grace of God the sceptre of the rule of the forefathers' Russian realm was entrusted to us persons, as is attested by our mother Orthodox Church's solemn act of 1682 and is likewise known to our neighbouring fellow sovereigns, but there was no mention that any third person should rule equally with us. And you know very well how our sister the Tsarevna Sophia Alekseevna chose to rule our state by her own will and how in that rule there was much that was disagreeable to us and burdensome to the people. . . . And now those miscreants Fedka Shaklovity and his accomplices, unheedful of our favour and in violation of their oath, contemplated with other rogues the murder of us and our mother, as they admitted under interrogation and torture. And now, sovereign brother, the time has come for us to rule the realm entrusted to us by God, since we are of age and we must not allow that third shameful personage, our sister the Tsarevna S.A., to share the titles and the government with us two male persons . . . for she chose to interfere in affairs and to include herself in the titles without our leave, and also, as a final insult, she wished to be crowned with the royal crown. It is disgraceful that in our majority this shameful person should rule the state in our stead. I inform and beg you, brother, to give me your paternal permission for our own good and for the pacification of the nation to appoint trustworthy judges in the chancelleries and to dismiss those who are unworthy, to bring tranquillity and joy to our state. . . .[73]

Although the sentiments expressed in this letter are probably Peter's own, one again detects the hand of his supporters in initiating the writing of it. Allusions to the tsars' being 'of age' and 'our majority', for example, appear to have been included for effect, since they glossed over the fact that on traditional reckoning (there was no formal age of majority) Ivan had already been 'of age' when Sophia became regent in 1682 and Peter had reached the age at which Fedor had become Tsar in 1686. 1689 had, of course, no special significance in the matter of formal majorities. This letter quashes any fears on the part of Ivan's supporters that Peter intended to violate the dual tsardom by taking sole power, a move which would undoubtedly have aroused opposition, and secures Tsar Ivan's blessing for a radical reorganisation of government personnel, whilst at the same time putting Sophia firmly in her place. The message is that her rule was illegal and that certain 'miscreants' attempted to extend it, although Sophia herself is not directly implicated in the 'plot' against Peter and his family.

There were certainly attempts to prove Sophia's guilt during interrogations of her supporters in September and later. For example, Prince Andrei Vasil'evich Golitsyn was asked to ratify a statement by Abrosim Petrov to the effect that during a visit to the Novodevichy Convent on 27 July Sophia had complained aloud about Tsaritsa Natalia: 'There was trouble then, but God preserved us, but now they are beginning it all over again. . . . Do you need us? If so, stand up for us; if not, we shall quit the state.' (Prince Andrei claimed that he had been sent to fetch a chair for the Princess and therefore heard nothing.)[74] These somewhat oblique words, even if they were uttered, hardly amount to a statement of homicidal intent. Indeed, in the four weighty volumes of published material from the 'Shaklovity affair' there is no direct evidence that Sophia had ordered the murder of Peter or any member of his family.[75] For such allegation we must turn to later writers. La Neuville, who was in Russia in August 1689 but not in print until 1698, claimed that Sophia decided to kill *both* tsars, to which end she employed Shaklovity to do the dirty work. She had, writes La Neuville, 'foreseen all along that the Tsar Peter's life would one day be the ruin of her authority, and a dangerous obstacle to her ambition, in case she did not remove it in time, and now she repented that she had followed the wise and moderate counsels of Golitsyn'.[76] He believed that Peter 'though fully satisfied of his sister's barbarity, would not publicly expose a princess of the blood'.[77] These allegations remain unproven, for Sophia herself was never subjected to a trial and no records have survived of the discussion of her fate.

Peter, meanwhile, showed no particular haste to take up the reins of power. Whilst the leading posts in the administration were being occupied by men such as B.A. Golitsyn, L.K. Naryshkin, T.N. Streshnev and I.B. Troekurov, Peter himself went off to the Aleksandrova Sloboda and indulged in some of his favourite pastimes: shooting, drilling troops and horse-riding, under the supervision of General Gordon. In the words of M.M., Bogoslovsky, 'In the struggle he had been a symbol rather than an active participant with independent initiative.'[78]

On about 9 September Prince I.B. Troekurov was sent to Tsar Ivan in Moscow with the message that in view of her 'intrigues' Sophia should be confined to the Novodevichy Convent. 'Although she tried to defend herself', writes Matveev, 'she was obliged to part with her sisters with great weeping and, abandoning her former love of power, to go to that monastery where it was decreed that she should live.'[79] To make sure that she stayed there a unit of play soldiers from Preobrazhenskoe under the command of F. Iu. Romodanovsky was dispatched to Moscow. We do not know exactly when this order was carried out, but supervision could not have been very strict for in early October, as Vasily Golitsyn and his family made their way northwards towards their place of exile, a letter and a sum of money from Sophia are said to have reached the Prince in the town of Vologda. Golitsyn himself denied the receipt of a letter, but admitted to receiving a gift of 100 gold roubles. His response was to send a petition asking Sophia to intercede on his behalf and secure his return to Moscow, an odd miscalculation of Sophia's status after the August–September events.[80]

This is not the only indication that Sopia's disgrace and incarceration were less than complete. It comes as almost a shock, in view of the events of the past few months, to read the bland entry in the palace records for 17 September 1689 to the effect that 'for the nameday of his sister the Sovereign Lady and Pious Tsarevna and Great Princess Sophia Alekseevna Tsar Ivan Alekseevich treated the boyars [etc., etc.] to vodka in the palace forecourt. And the boyars and lords-in-waiting and gentlemen of the duma and courtiers were dressed in damask robes.'[81] Did Ivan, perhaps, insist, aware that for all her failings Sophia had always done her best to protect his interests? The same entry tells us that Tsar Peter 'deigned to continue his sojourn at Aleksandrovo Sloboda', where, we can conjecture, he did not raise a glass in honour of his fallen sister.

# CHAPTER 10

# Back to Seclusion 1689–1704

*By internecine strife,*
*I rose to power; by internecine strife*
*I fell again. Young Peter, my half-brother,*
*To manhood grown, began to threaten me*
*And here am I, in this mute convent cell*
*Interred . . . a passionate woman of the world*
*Against her will condemned to take the veil*
*And dedicated forcibly to God.*

(from E. Rostopchina, 'The Nun', 1843)[1]

Foreign commentators on the early years of Peter's reign often assumed that Sophia had left a convent in order to pursue her political ambitions. This, as we know, was untrue. But now Sophia was to share the fate of those many women whom men, for reasons both political and private, have seen fit to put out of the way. In September 1689 the gates of the Novodevichy Convent closed on her for the last time. It was to be both her resting place and her memorial.

Very little documentary evidence survives about the last fourteen years of Sophia's life, but it is fairly easy to reconstruct their setting, for the location has altered much less than the Kremlin, where the maze of churches and chambers of the seventeenth century has been greatly reduced by demolition and reconstruction, and where there is restricted access to the buildings which remain.

The Novodevichy Convent had been one of Sophia's favourite haunts. It was here that she had concentrated her most lavish endowments, embellishing the monastery, which had been founded in 1514 to cel-ebrate the capture of Smolensk from the Poles, with a remarkable complex of buildings in the Moscow Baroque style, constructed by the leading craftsmen of the period.[2] As she entered the convent in September 1689 she would have seen all around her the products of her munificence, much as we see them today; the elegant gate churches of the Transfiguration and the Intercession to the north and south, the Church of the Dormition with its adjoining refectory chamber, and the tall bell tower, the decorative work on its columns interrupted by its founder's downfall. All are of red brick with carved limestone columns, portals and window surrounds, the forms of which bear eloquent witness to the new Westernised directions which pervaded the art of the court and nobility. The sturdy fortress walls were also capped with crenellations in the Moscow Baroque style, and brick and stone living quarters had been built for Sophia and her sisters and decorated inside and out in the latest fashion.

The Cathedral Church of Our Lady of Smolensk was built in the 1520s in imitation of the Kremlin Dormition Cathedral, but even today its interior takes us back to the 1680s rather than to the period of its foundation. Sophia must have looked almost daily upon the magnificent gilded iconostasis, erected on her orders in 1683–5 by master craftsmen from Byelorussia, and at icons painted by leading Armoury artists such as Simon Ushakov and Fedor Zubov, in the same period. The font, metal screens, icon lamps and vestments had almost all been provided by Sophia's generosity. She must have recalled her girlhood when she saw the icon of the family saints of Tsar Aleksei (c.1665) portraying Metropolitan Aleksei, Alexis Man of God, Simeon of Persia, Theodore Stratalites, saints Evdokia, Anna, Marfa, Maria and, of course, Sophia. In the side chapel dedicated to St Sophia the usual icons of supplicants in the Deisis row had been replaced with images of holy women such as Efrosinia of Suzdal'.

One of the most eloquent testimonials to Sophia's patronage is found outside in the bell tower, where bells cast in 1684 and 1688 bear inscriptions announcing that they were commissioned by Tsars Ivan and Peter, and,

> jointly with the great sovereigns, by the will and consent of their sister the Great Sovereign Lady, Great Princess and Tsarevna Sophia of all the Great and Little and White Russias, since she the sovereign lady has been the builder [stroitel'nitsa] of this holy house for many years, and now with even greater zeal sees to its embellishment, as is clear to all.[3]

An oil painting of Sophia with crown and sceptre set into a double-headed eagle survives in the convent to this day.[4] Despite the punitive motives behind Sophia's banishment to the Novodevichy Convent, it seems likely that her many benefactions to the establishment influenced the authority's choice. It was fairly common practice for both men and women to retire in later life to a religious house which they had endowed during their secular lifetime. Conversely, no one could enter a monastery *without* making a special payment. As an unmarried woman of devotional bent, Sophia would have seemed an ideal candidate for the monastic life if we did not know that she went there against her will.

15   Novodevichy convent, iconostasis of the cathedral of Our Lady of Smolensk, (1683 – 5).
(Screen dividing altar from the nave: work of craftsmen from Belorussia)

Although Sophia was living under house arrest, her circumstances
were far from straitened. She took with her a former nurse, Marfa
Viazemskaia, nine chambermaids and two wardrobe mistresses. Each
day supplies of bread, fish, honey, beer, vodka and other victuals were
delivered from the palace. Her name continued to appear in the palace
'needlework book' for the years 1695–9, recording garments sewn for
members of the royal family.[5] Like those who entered the convent of
their own free will, she was able to take her own personal possessions
with her. The monastery treasury still contains many such items: a

244

16   Cups, plates, etc. belonging to Sophia in the Novodevichy Convent Museum

wine bowl engraved with the words 'made by the order of . . . Sophia, Autocrat of all the Great and Little and White Russias, for the sovereign lady in her chambers in 7195 [1686]', a cup of German make (the gift of a foreign embassy), cups and plates engraved with her name, and, most intriguing of all, the 'measuring icon' (*mernaia ikona*) to Sophia's patron saint, made at the time of her birth.[6] Other items – a wooden table, chair, screen of glass and mica – can be seen in the exhibits of the Historical Museum in Moscow. It appears that she also possessed many books, of which a catalogue is being compiled.

After 1689 resources still allowed her to present gifts to the convent, for example an icon lamp set up before the house icon of Our Lady of Smolensk in memory of her mother and father in February 1695.[7] She was even able to make endowments outside the convent. On 10 December 1693 the refectory Church of the Transfiguration in the St Sabbas-Storozhevsky Monastery at Zvenigorod was consecrated. It had been commissioned by Sophia in the Moscow Baroque style to commemorate the 'salvation from the Khovanskys' in 1682. Sophia had made several visits to the monastery during her regency and in the nineteenth century a portrait of Sophia in nun's habit was still recorded amongst its possessions.[8]

In many ways Sophia's life in the convent would have differed little from her life in the Kremlin where, as we know, she was a strict observer of the Church calendar. It should not be supposed, either, that Russian monasteries, either male or female, observed strict rules of seclusion, silence or poverty. Although religious devotions were the focal point of convent life, a recent study has suggested that Muscovite ideology did not expect ascetic saintliness from its women and that pious domesticity remained the ideal inside the convent walls as without.[9] The nuns had no Orders and did not follow a communal rule. They were at liberty to retain external sources of income, to provide their own food and clothing and build their own cells if resources allowed. Convents reflected the structure of lay society, with abbesses and officials chosen from the princely or boyar class, and routine tasks performed by sisters from the lower orders. The Novodevichy Convent had extensive property, some thirty-six villages in twenty-seven regions at the end of the seventeenth century. It owned serfs and was served by its own communities of artisans and craftsmen. This and other religious houses differed from the outside world only in respect of the intensity of the religious observance and the limitations on the mobility of their incumbents. If we recall that Sophia was not forced to take the veil in 1689, then it must be supposed that this last restriction was the one that she found most irksome.

Life in a Russian Orthodox convent, then, was by no means synonymous with isolation from the outside world and its comforts, especially when the establishment in question was located only three miles from the Kremlin. (Today it lies just five Metro stops from the centre of town.) Sophia's main contacts were her five sisters, who resided permanently in the Kremlin palace but made frequent visits to the convent, or kept in touch through letters and parcels. After the death of Tsarevna Anna Mikhailovna in October 1692, shortly after she had taken the veil, the senior member of the *terem* was fifty-six-year-old Tsarevna Tat'iana, the last surviving daughter of Tsar Mikhail, but by all accounts Sophia's place as chief spokeswoman for the tsarevny was taken by her elder sister Marfa.

Sophia must have maintained a close interest in the family fortunes of her brother Ivan, who visited the convent several times a year, just as he had done before Sophia's overthrow.[10] Perhaps she noted wryly that Ivan's wife Praskovia, having given birth to her first child in 1689, produced four more daughters in as many years. For Sophia their sex was no longer crucial and she was not to know that two of them would continue the Miloslavsky line on the throne of Russia – Anna, born in

January 1693, who ruled as Empress from 1730 to 1740, and Ekaterina, born in 1691, whose grandson, the ill-fated Ivan VI, occupied the throne for just twelve months in 1740–1. Their mother Praskovia is said to have avoided meeting Sophia, probably out of political caution.[11]

Tsar Ivan died on 29 January 1696, having carried out his ceremonial duties to the last. Despite his physical and mental handicaps he had lived till his thirtieth year. He had been the lynchpin of Sophia's political ambitions, but there is every reason to believe that she was genuinely attached to him and was present in thought if not in person when he was buried in the Archangel Cathedral on 30 January, the last Russian tsar (with the exception of Peter II) to be laid to rest in Moscow.

Sophia must have experienced mixed feelings at news of the death of her old adversary Tsaritsa Natalia on 25 January, 1694. It is unlikely that she could have derived any real satisfaction from having outlived her rival, however, for Natalia herself had enjoyed little power since 1689. As for Peter, it is unlikely that he set eyes on Sophia between their clash in Kremlin on 8 July 1689 and his interrogation of her in September 1698, to be described below. One nineteenth-century writer believed that he visited her shortly before he set off for Europe in 1697, 'but found her so haughty, cold and intractable that he left in great agitation'.[12] But there are no records of the tsar going to the convent, nor is it likely that he would have wished to pay a courtesy call on someone who held such unpleasant associations.

In any case, he had much to occupy him. Sophia must have known of his campaigns against the Turks in 1695–6, perhaps remembering her own ventures into foreign affairs and the inconclusive southern campaigns of her favourite Golitsyn. Perhaps she experienced a twinge of regret when the war swung in Peter's favour and Azov was taken. And what could have been her reaction to news of Peter's 'Grand Embassy' to Europe? One should not, of course, make the mistake that Sophia herself never had the opportunity to make – that of confusing the Peter of the 1690s with the 'Great' Tsar of Poltava and the reforms. At this stage the reforms were but dimly conceived, and Sophia had no reason to regard herself as the 'relic' of a bygone era, as she was to be regarded by certain future historians. Peter's passion for foreigners, ships and war was already developed by the 1680s and his activities of the 1690s appeared as a natural continuation of boyhood pursuits rather than as harbingers of future greatness.

On the contrary, Sophia must have heard rumours about dissatisfaction with Peter's behaviour, horror at his neglect of the old traditions and Orthodoxy in favour of 'wicked foreign ways'. Did she, like many others, view the visit to Europe not as the epoch-making opening of Russia's 'window on the West' as it was seen in retrospect, but as a sign that Peter had finally abandoned Orthodoxy and was himself to become a 'German' and lose all moral right to his throne? Did she see in Peter's unpopularity a chance of regaining her lost political power? We have no direct insight into her thoughts, but we do know that in some minds Sophia continued to exert considerable attraction as an alternative to Peter. Several incidents in the years following her incarceration could have alerted Peter to this fact.

It was reported, for example, that when Peter was seriously ill in December 1692 his supporters B.A. Golitsyn, F.M. Apraksin and Franz Lefort had horses at the ready to quit Moscow in the event of the Tsar's death and Sophia's return to power.[13] (Tsar Ivan was, of course, still alive, with precedence over the infant Tsarevich Aleksei). There were rumours that a group of strel'tsy had staged a rescue attempt by digging a tunnel under the convent walls and up to the floor of the Tsarevna's rooms, but had been foiled at the last minute by the guards.[14] As ever, it was the strel'tsy who seemed to cherish the most vivid memories of the 'good old days' of Sophia's regency. Just before Peter's departure for the West in 1697 a plot was uncovered, allegedly masterminded by the strel'tsy Colonel Ivan Tsykler, with the aim of murdering the Tsar and restoring Sophia and Golitsyn to power, since there was said to be 'much disorder' (*mnogo nestroeniia*) in the state.[15]

Tsykler, who had supported Sophia in 1682 but hastened to join Peter in August 1689, related under interrogation by torture that:

> in 1682, after the massacre of the boyars and courtiers by the strel'tsy, the Tsarevna summoned him and told him to tell the strel'tsy to cease their disturbances, and he did as she asked. And before the first Crimean campaign, the Tsarevna summoned him and kept telling him to carry out the assassination of the sovereign with Fedka Shaklovity. And the Tsarevna summoned him to her chambers at Khoroshovo and told him through a window again to carry out the assassination of the sovereign with Shaklovity, but he refused to do it.

He claimed that when he advised Sophia that she would do better to be on good terms with Peter, she had accused him of going over to the 'other side' and sent him on the first Crimean campaign as a punishment. After his return she promised him an estate if he would carry out the deed, but he refused and was sent on the second campaign. He also happened to mention that he had been on good terms with Ivan Miloslavsky.

Tsykler's attempts to shift attention away from the present and the blame on to Sophia did nothing to establish his innocence of participation in an ill-devised plot which appeared to reflect anxiety about the aims of the Tsar's trip abroad and about foreign 'guile' in general. He and his 'accomplices' were beheaded in a gruesome spectacle in which the coffin of Ivan Miloslavsky, dead since 1685, was exhumed and placed beneath the block so that the blood of the 'traitors' flowed into it. There was evidently no time to take matters further, for five days later Peter left for Europe.

Sophia was not convicted for the 'Tsykler plot', but Peter may have had the Colonel's allegations at the back of his mind when more serious disturbances broke out amongst the strel'tsy in the following year.[16] These were heralded by the arrival in Moscow in March 1698 of deserters from the Cherny, Chubanov, Gundertmark and Kolzakov regiments. Their complaints centered upon the long period of service away from their homes and families in Moscow. Having fought at Azov in 1695–6 they had been detained there to build fortifications and carry out garrison duty, then, instead of the eagerly anticipated posting home, were deliberately redeployed to the Lithuanian border. They also complained of poverty, non-payment of allowances and ill-treatment by officers, especially by bitterly resented foreigners. They may also have been dimly aware that their 'exile' from the capital reflected Peter's intense suspicion of them as a potential political force. It was obvious that their status had been irrevocably diminished by the expansion of Peter's guards regiments and new-formation infantry units commanded by foreigners.

In addition to personal grievances, the strel'tsy were as ever susceptible to rumour and speculation; it was said that Peter had died abroad, that a 'German' would replace him, that the 'true faith' was in danger and that they themselves were to be at the mercy of the 'boyars' and foreigners like Franz Lefort, who allegedly ill-treated them at Azov. This all led to a revival of some of these naive notions about 'good' and 'bad' rulers that were so much a feature of 1682. In the next few months rule by Tsarevich Aleksei Petrovich under a regency, or a government headed by Vasily Golitsyn or by all or one of the tsarevny, Sophia in particular, were all mooted.

The strel'tsy who went to Moscow in March were fobbed off with promises of back pay, but their basic grievance – 'exile' from Moscow – was still unresolved when it was learned that their regiments were again to be posted away from the capital and those strel'tsy who had complained to Moscow were to be exiled to the Ukraine. Rebellion broke out at Toropets, where the four regiments were stationed. The regiments dismissed their officers and marched on Moscow bearing petitions which detailed their service to the crown and their complaints. One of them ended: 'and we have heard that the Germans are going to Moscow and, following their customs of beard-shaving and smoking tobacco, will bring about the total overthrow of the faith'.[17] On 17 June near the Monastery of New Jerusalem at Istra, twenty miles to the west of Moscow, they found their way blocked by the Preobrazhensky and

Semenovsky guards and other units under the command of Generals Gordon and Shein. The strel'tsy were beaten in a short encounter and immediately afterwards Shein carried out an investigation as a result of which 130 were executed.

In the meantime Peter had been alerted to the troubles. Instead of going to Venice as he had intended, he cut short his journey at Cracow and set off for Moscow, where he arrived on 25 August. In a letter to Romodanovsky Peter had warned that the 'seed of Ivan Miloslávsky is growing',[18] a sure sign that he suspected a conspiracy beneath what appeared to be a straightforward outburst of resentment and frustration. The culprits had to be found, and Peter made it clear that he was dissatisfied with Shein's measures. After a brief pause to cut off his nobles' beards, in order to bring them into line with Western fashion, and to make arrangements for the banishment to a nunnery of his wife Evdokia, whose old-fashioned Muscovite attitudes and ways made her a potential obstacle to his plans to Westernise Russia, Peter ordered a fresh enquiry. Torture chambers were set up at Preobrazhenskoe, trusted helpers such as F.Iu. Romodanovsky, M.A. Cherkassky, I.B. Troekurov and B.A. Golitsyn were summoned to man them, and the remaining strel'tsy were brought in for questioning, using the traditional methods of face-to-face confrontations with hostile witnesses and interrogation by torture, of suspects and witnesses alike.

On the very first day of the investigation, 17 September (Sophia's nameday), fresh evidence came to light. One of the ringleaders, Vasily Zorin, revealed that they had 'intended to go to the Novodevichy Convent and appeal to Tsarevna Sophia Alekseevna to grant their petition and enter into the government as before'. At the end he added that they had gone to Moscow 'with their hopes pinned upon Tsarevna Sophia Alekseevna, for she had ruled the government previously and so now they hoped that she would accept it from them'.[19] Anikita Sidorov's statement, taken on the same day, phrased it thus:

> they were going to the Novodevichy Convent to ask Tsarevna Sophia Alekseevna to rule and were going to take their petition to their homes and write out many such petitions and distribute them around all the districts [slobody] and raise rebellion and go to the New German Quarter and destroy it, and kill all the Germans and the above mentioned boyars; and, having killed them, if the Tsarevna refused to enter into government then the sovereign Tsarevich should rule, seeing that the great sovereign was dead.[20]

This was just what Peter had been waiting for – a clear indication of Sophia's involvement. On the basis of this new evidence lists of five questions were compiled, the first of which went: 'When they, the strel'tsy, went to Moscow, did they intend to make Tsarevna Sophia Alekseevna ruler and by what authority – by a message from her or a letter?'[21] This was crucial, for so far there was evidence only of the reputation that Sophia still enjoyed amongst the strel'tsy but no proof that she had instigated anything. The crucial break came on 20 September, when Vasily Alekseev revealed, after the third bout of torture by fire, that 'there was a letter to them from the Tsarevna in Moscow, and this letter was brought from Moscow to Velikie Luki by Vaska Tuma, and the letter was brought to them in Toropets by Mishka Obrosimov, a sergeant of the Chubarov regiment'.[22] This was what Peter had been hoping for. Alekseev was taken off for further questioning and the affair of the letter was put in the hands of Romodanovsky. Soon more details were added, for example that the letter had been passed to yet a third strelets, Artemy Maslov, who had read it out to the regiments. 'And in that letter it was written that they should march on Moscow and go to the Novodevichy Convent and appeal to Tsarevna Sophia Alekseevna to enter into the government. And in Moscow they were to kill the boyars and destroy the German Quarter and kill the Germans.'[23] The non-extant letter still had to be traced back to Sophia. How had the strel'tsy received it? Here there was much conflicting evidence. One story was that a beggar woman by the name of Mashka Stepanova had passed it on, others said that is was an unknown woman or women, or a sister of the alleged recipient, one Mavruta, who, it turned out, had been dead five years.[24] On 21 September a sixth question concerning the provenance of the letter was added to the interrogators' list.

The focus of the investigation shifted for a while away from Preobrazhenskoe and on to Sophia and her entourage in the convent. Sophia's former nurse Marfa Viazemskaia, attendants Vera Vasiutinskaia and Princess Avdotia Kasatkina and two serving girls were rounded up and asked what they knew. They denied any knowledge of communication between the Tsarevna and the strel'tsy, although the maid Ul'iana admitted that 'when her sisters the tsarevny came to see her and talked amongst themselves she, Ul'iana, was sent outside'.[25] The only substantial evidence came from Vasiutinskaia, who said that in '7206 [1698] at Lent the Moscow strel'tsy came to Moscow and they heard about their coming from the church deacons of the convent. . . . Then after Holy Week Tsarevna Marfa Alekseevna came to the convent and in Tsarevna Sophia's apartments she said, 'The strel'tsy have come to Moscow and they want you to rule.'[26]

On 24 September Peter personally interviewed Tsarevna Marfa, who admitted to telling Sophia that the strel'tsy were 'awaiting her rule', but who denied acting as intermediary.[27] Vasiutinskaia revealed further suspicious behaviour, for example that during Lent a dwarf named Avdotia came to the convent with gifts of food for Sophia from her sisters Ekaterina, Marfa and Feodosia, and when she, Vasiutinskaia, took the food she found a letter in it saying, 'The strel'tsy have come to

Moscow.'[28] In an exchange of letters with her sisters by the same route Sophia asked for more information and is supposed to have said: 'I feel sorry for them, the poor things' ('Zhal' de ikh, bednykh').

On 27 September Peter went to the convent to question Sophia, the first recorded meeting between the two for nine years. Johann Korb, whose account of the execution of the strel'tsy was soon to shock Europe, writes that 'it is said that on first sight of one another both burst into floods of tears'.[29] but although the occasion must have been an emotional one it is hard to imagine that tears would have been the likely response. The short transcript of the interrogation contains no hint of drama whatsoever. Peter, we learn, 'was pleased to speak with his sister Tsarevna Sophia Alekseevna concerning the letter that has come to light in the investigation from her to the four regiments on the Dvina'. She was confronted with Artemy Maslov and another strelets, Vasily Ignat'ev, and their statements. Sophia replied that:

> no such letter, which had come to light in investigation, had ever been sent by her, the Tsarevna, to these strel'tsy regiments; and, as for these same strel'tsy saying that they intended to come to Moscow and invite her, the Tsarevna, to rule as before – this had nothing to do with a letter from her, but was most likely because she had ruled from 7190 [1682].

Maslov and Ignat'ev argued that Vasily Tuma *had* passed on a letter to him via Mikhail Obrosimov and that that letter had been given to Tuma at that very convent by the Tsarevna via a beggar woman. Sophia replied that 'she had never given any such letter to him, Vaska, via a beggar woman – she did not know Vaska, or Artiushka or Vaska Ignat'ev'.[30]

Sophia had admitted nothing and they seemed no nearer the truth about the letter. Korb had evidently heard a version of the 'beggar woman' tale for he reports that, although Sophia was closely guarded, 'yet all these Argus eyes were not able to hinder her from contriving to raise a truly great and most perilous flame of civil war by means of an abject wretched little mendicant that used to frequent the very guard'.[31] Sophia was said to have bribed the beggar to deliver letters hidden in loaves of bread.

In October a new version of events emerged.[32] A strelets claimed to have seen a woman passing a letter to Vasily Tuma in a village outside Moscow. She was identified as one Aniutka Nikitina, but she herself named someone else. Eventually under torture she admitted to having acted as go-between, but then revealed the existence of a second letter passed to the strel'tsy from the tsarevny in the palace. In an identification parade Nikitina picked out Tsarevna Marfa's maid Anna Klushina as the one who had given her this letter.

So the trail led back again to Marfa. She was questioned again by

Peter on 8 October, but admitted nothing.[33] Meanwhile a new trail was discovered when Tuma's sister Ul'ka Dorofeeva was accused of being the go-between. She was interrogated under torture on 15 October but she only admitted to having *seen* some sort of letter in her brother's possession, wrapped in a white shirt.[34]

Simultaneously, the strelets G.L. Gagara 'told the whole truth', namely that Tuma had been given the letter at the back gates of the convent by a nun named Lisafia (or Lisania).[35] Princess Lobanova, one of Tsarevna Sophia's companions, is said to have sent to tell him that the letter was from the Tsarevna herself. Apparently Tuma often received messages when the nuns came out to wash clothes and he asked a nun to convey to the Tsarevna the news that people were saying that Tsar Peter had died abroad and that they wished Sophia to rule. In reply he received orders that the strel'tsy should raise rebellion, kill the boyars and foreigners and soldiers; he was also given assurances that Sophia would rule.

Throughout the enquiry attempts to get at the truth were hampered by the fact that neither Tuma nor the letter appeared to be extant. Artemy Maslov, the closest link that the investigators had with the letter, was not executed until 1707, after Sophia's death, and he continued to amend his story throughout nine years of interrogations. For example, he described the hand that the letter was written in and the seals on it. At one point he claimed that the letter had been ripped up and trampled in the dirt, at another that he had handed it to a relative for safekeeping.[36]

Despite the sheets of testimonial extracted from hapless witnesses and suspects, Peter had failed to prove the link between Sophia and the strel'tsy. There was too much conflicting evidence. Nonetheless, in the words of Korb, she:

> had, the reputation of having intrigued, for the last fourteen years, against her brother's life, and has already been the cause of several seditious movements. She, by her open schemes and factiousness, drove him, who is at once her sovereign and her brother, to consult for his own safety; especially as the later perils bear ample witness that, as long as she was at liberty, there would be nothing stable in Muscovy.[37]

Korb believed that 'she promised to put herself at the head of a new conspiracy of the Strelitz, and communicated her advice to them, suggesting the manner and the frauds by which the Strelitz might bring their dark and malignant designs into effect'.[38] Peter is said to have threatened, 'Mary of Scotland was led forth from prison to the block, by command of her sister Elizabeth, Queen of England – a warning to me to exercise my power over Sophia.'[39]

But in the end Peter, who showed no mercy to the strel'tsy streaming endlessly to the torture chambers and execution blocks and who in

17    Novodevichy convent: the tower in which Sophia is thought to have been confined during the 1698 rebellion

1718 was to condemn his own son to death, stopped short of inflicting physical punishment upon Sophia. Korb reports that on 11 October an assembly of men at all ranks was summoned to decide Sophia's fate, but there is no evidence for this assembly in any other source.[40]

Did anyone intercede on Sophia's behalf? All we know is that on 21 October she took the veil and adopted the name Susanna.[41] Peter's special punishment was of a psychological nature. Korb reports on 28 October that 'not far from the Monastery of the Nuns there were raised thirty gibbets in the shape of a square, where the halter received 230 head of Strelitz who were deserving of a more cruel fate'. Three of the ringleaders, 'who had presented a petition inviting Sophia to take the helm of state were hanged against the walls of the said monastery, close to the window of Sophia's room'.[42] One of them held a petition in his dead hand, 'perhaps in order that remorse for the past may gnaw Sophia with perpetual grief'.[43] The corpses were left there for five months. Korb and some companions went to the convent to see them at the end of November.[44]

This spectacle, especially intended for Sophia's eyes, was just one small part of the punishment heaped upon the strel'tsy. The appalling cruelty of the investigation process, in which fire and knout were freely applied, was matched by the savagery and scale of the executions. In October almost 800 strel'tsy were put to death and a further 350 in February 1699. Only men under the age of twenty were spared – and they were flogged, branded and exiled, with their ears and noses slit. The details of the brutality have been described on many occasions, not least in Korb's somewhat exaggerated account, and they will not be dwelt upon here.

Security on Sophia was tightened. In a letter to Romodanovsky written in October 1698 Peter ordered that:

> her sisters should not be admitted to the convent except in Holy Week and on the Feast of the Virgin [of Smolensk], in July, and not on other days, except in case of illness. To enquire after her health they may send Stepan Narbekov or his son, or the Matiushkins, but others, women or girls, should not be sent. And a letter of permission must be obtained from Prince Fedor Iurievich [Romodanovsky]. And when they are there for feast days, they must not stay [overnight]. And if they stay, they will not be admitted for another feastday. And no choristers [*pevchie*] should be admitted to the monastery. The nuns sing well enough. Just let them be concerned with matters of faith. They should not sing in church 'Save us from misfortune' at the same time as on the porch they pay money for murders. And request of Tsarevna Tat'iana Mikhailovna that she should not visit the monastery except on Easter Sunday and on the feast of 28 July and in case of illness.[45]

This shows that Peter continued to fear the intrigues of the *terem* and of women in general. The ban on choristers may stem from rumours that some of the tsarevny had selected lovers from amongst the young men of the church.

Peter's suspicion of convents is confirmed by a decree of 26 May 1702, ordering that:

18    Portrait of Tsarevna Sophia after the Strel'tsy Rebellion of 1698: painting by Il'ia Repin (1879)

in Moscow in convents the gates should always by locked and experienced guards should be posted there, not young men. And the male sex should not be admitted, not even during the holy singing; and if anyone has to see a nun on business, an acquaintance or a relative, those nuns may go out to the gates to see their acquaintance or relative accompanied by an elderly and experienced nun appointed by the abbess. At their meeting they should speak aloud and not in secret, in the presence of that nun and the guards.[46]

Antushev, whose history of the convent contains many anecdotes, records an undated incident in which Peter, dining in the vicinity of the convent, was summoned there on the discovery of robbery and desecration in the main cathedral. He went there in fear that Sophia was up to no good, but it turned out to be a fairly routine case of theft.[47] Peter evidently never abandoned the suspicion that monasteries and convents harboured plotters and intriguers, as well as fugitives from service to the state. He may also have been influenced by his observation of convents abroad. Between 1724 and 1738 the number of monks and nuns in Russia was to be almost halved, mainly by restricting the

19   Portrait of Peter the Great by Sir Godfrey Kneller (1698)

entrance of newcomers. Nuns, in particular, were subjected to severe restrictions, including injunctions of 1722–3 that all convents be 'permanently enclosed' and that contact with lay people be kept to a minimum. Funds were diverted away from personal use towards the 'common good'.[48]

In the end we must deduce Peter's attitude towards his half-sister from circumstantial evidence. Weber records a speech of Peter's to the effect that Sophia was 'a princess endowed with all the Accomplishments of Body and Mind to Perfection, had it not been for her boundless Ambition and insatiable desire of governing.'[49] William Coxe, in Russia in the 1780s, was told 'by a Russian nobleman of great distinction' that Peter had once said: 'What a pity that she persecuted me in my minority, and that I cannot repose any confidence in her; otherwise, when I am employed abroad, she might govern at home.'[50] Of the two reported speeches, Weber's rings slightly truer than Coxe's, which formed part of a 'rehabilitation' of Sophia. On at least three occasions Peter had reason to fear for his life and throne from rebellions that he supposed to have been initiated by Sophia's intrigues. Having stopped short of executing her, perhaps he simply chose to forget her.

What was Sophia's reaction to the new restrictions imposed in the wake of the 1698 rebellion? Despite her meticulous observance of religious ceremonies during her regency, it has always been presumed that she took the veil under protest, because this step precluded her once and for all from any participation in politics. In 1879 the painter Ilia Repin tried to capture her state of mind in his first painting on a historical theme, 'Tsarevna Sophia Alekseevna a year after her incarceration in the Novodevichy Monastery at the time of the execution of the strel'tsy and the torture of all her servants in 1698'. The angry expression and defiant stance show enormous resolution, whilst the Tsarevna's bulk seems to derive from La Neuville's famous description. A Soviet commentator writes: 'She is unaffected by feminine weakness. Strength and courage are the main features of her character.'[51] In her narrative poem 'The Nun', an extract from which is quoted above, the poetess Evdokia Rostopchina images Sophia lamenting her past glories and asking a much younger nun to be her witness. In one speech Sophia mentions that she had written a memoir, 'in order to bequeath to posterity and to the fatherland a truthful record' but that this was burned by her 'enemies'.[52] There is no evidence that such a memoir existed, nor have other writings from Sophia's hand survived.

Only the mute evidence of artefacts gives some hint of the last years of her life. Plates and goblets engraved with her new name Susanna survive and she continued even now to add to the convent's treasures, for example a shrine containing relics of John Chrysostom, Metropolitan Philip and others, and inscribed: 'In 1700 on the 8th day of October this shrine was installed in the house of the Holy Virgin in the Novodevichy Convent to laud and honour the only praisworthy God of the Trinity by the true initiative and promise of the nun Tsarevna Susanna (Sophia)'.[53] A silver cross in the chapel of the Holy Martyr Sophia is inscribed:

> This lifegiving cross was installed by the initiative of the Pious Sovereign Lady Tsarevna and Great Princess the nun Susanna Alekseevna and the Pious Sovereign Lady Tsarevna and Great Princess Feodosia Alekseevna, in the cloister of the Immaculate Virgin in the Novodevichy Convent in the time of the Abbess Pamfilia with their sisters in Christ . . . 1703 1 July.[54]

As these inscriptions indicate, taking the veil incurred no loss of title and royal status. That Sophia continued to make endowments shows that she was not forced to live in penury. The bill of her upkeep in 1700 was the considerable sum of 5,144 roubles, 15 altyn and $3\frac{1}{2}$ denga.[55]

It is not certain where Sophia's apartments were located or what access she had to the rest of the monastery grounds, but it has been deduced that if the tale of the strel'tsy hanged outside her window is correct then her cell at that time must have been in the Naprudnaia tower, to the west of the so-called Lopukhin wing near the main, northern gates. This is the only tower with a window giving on to the outside world. Sophia has also been associated with the 'Lopukhin' chambers, so called because Peter I's first wife Evdokia lived there for a time until her death in 1731. For a long time the portrait of Sophia with the double-headed eagle was kept there. She may also have inhabited the 'Maria' chambers adjoining the gate Church of the Inter-cession, which was used by the tsarevny as a private chapel.

After 1698, as we know, the sisters were allowed to visit the convent only on a few feast days. It is likely that Sophia never again saw her sister Marfa, who in September 1698 was banished from Moscow on the charge of having informed Sophia about the arrival of the strel'tsy and their desire to see her rule. She was sent to the Convent of the Dormition in Aleksandrova Sloboda where on 29 May 1699 she took the veil under the name of Margarita. She died there in June 1707.[56] Sophia's other sisters also outlived her, and two of them are buried beside her in the cathedral: to the east Evdokia (died 10 May 1712) and to the east of her, Ekaterina (died 1 May 1718). To the north is the tomb of Tsaritsa Evdokia Lopukhina. Her younger sisters Feodosia and Maria died in 1713 and 1723 respectively.

Sophia's own tombtone, like those of the others, is a simple white stone oblong, decorated only with a carved inscription on the lid:

> In the year of the creation of the world 7212 and of our Lord 1704 on the 3rd day of July, on Monday, in the first hour of the day, on the day of the

Holy Martyr Ioakinf and on the day of the canonisation of our father Philip, Metropolitan of Kiev and all Russia, on that day there departed the servant of God, the daughter of the Noble and Pious Great Sovereign Tsar and Great Prince Aleksei Mikhailovich of blessed memory, Autocrat of all the Great and Little and White Russias and of the Noble and Pious Great Sovereign Lady Tsaritsa and Great Princess Maria Il'inichna of blessed memory, the Great Sovereign Lady Pious Tsarevna and Great Princess Sophia Alekseevna, whose nameday was 17 September, and she was 46 years, 9 months and 16 days old and had been a nun for 5 years, 8 months and 12 days, and her given name was Susanna, but in *skhima* she was named by her former name Sophia and was buried in the Church of the Immaculate Virgin of Smolensk in this place on the 4th day of July.[57]

Less than half a century had passed between Sophia's birth and death, but for the people at the top, if not for the mass of the peasantry, the Russia of 1704 was a very different place from the Russia of 1657. In 1700 even the very manner of numbering the years had changed when Peter replaced by decree the Orthodox Creation-based calendar with the Julian calendar by then in use in much of Europe. Sophia's tombstone bore dates in both styles. Peter's unambiguous orientation towards the West was heralded by his Grand Embassy to Europe in 1697–8, after which he launched the campaign to turn his nobles into 'decent, beardless Europeans' by forcing them to adopt European modes of dress and hairstyle. The lives of upper-class women were changed even more drastically than those of men. The *terem,* or those vestiges of it which remained, was swept away. Women were expected to don the latest fashions and join men in public, rather than lurking modestly behind curtains and veils. Enforced celibacy for royal women was also a thing of the past, as Peter launched his nieces and daughters on to the international marriage market.

The first few years of the new century saw a number of innovations – the first Russian newspaper, textbooks in Russian on mathematics and artillery, attempts to open a public theatre. In 1700 the treaty with Sweden ratified during Sophia's regency was finally broken. After initial setbacks, in May 1703 Peter was able to lay the foundation stone of a new Russian city on the Baltic, which a decade later opened its doors to the court and the government as they were forced to abandon the warren of reception chambers, churches and corridors of the ancient Kremlin for a new, purpose-built city. Four of Sophia's sisters lived to witness the dawning of this new age, but Sophia herself died too soon to have much inkling of it.

She had lived a life which combined respect for tradition with receptiveness towards change in the form of closer political and cultural contacts with Europe. She abandoned seclusion in order to attend council sessions and receptions, whilst preserving a demeanour which was, on the surface at least, sober and pious. Yet the strel'tsy who called upon her to replace the 'German' Peter in 1698 either ignored or failed to see the Western-oriented aspects of the Regent's administration. They were amongst the first of many to misinterpret or distort Sophia's image, as our final chapter will show.

# Postscript

'Rarely is even the finest man adorned with these four virtues – ardent faith, reason, wisdom and chastity – but you possess them all,' wrote Patriarch Dionisius of Constantinople to Sophia in 1686.[1] 'Most wise and pious, devoted to God, gracious and merciful in her virtuousness, prudent, illustrious and Christ-loving,' enthused Archimandrite Ignaty of the Novospassky Monastery in an oration of 1687.[2] As late as August 1689 the same cleric composed an exegesis of the Divine Wisdom icon in which Sophia featured as the central figure in the hierarchy of the Muscovite state.[3] A.P. Bogdanov has pointed out that in the 1680s eulogies written for Sophia actually outnumbered those addressed to the tsars.[4]

Such paeans of praise naturally ceased abruptly in September 1689, and for a time, in Russia at least, panegyric outpourings to the 'Pious Tsarevna' gave way to silence. The revival of interest in Sophia was in fact occasioned vicariously by Peter's visit to the West in 1697–8 and by the strel'tsy rebellion that prematurely ended it. From then on Sophia and her regency were almost invariably viewed in relation to the reign of the Reformer and generally came off badly in comparison. The false identification of Sophia and her party with the xenophobic views of the strel'tsy, for example, opened the way for the misconceived association of Peter's predecessors with ignorance and obscurantism, a misunderstanding that the advocates of reform made no attempt to correct.

It is significant that one of the most approving accounts of the regency was written just after Sophia's downfall but just before the beginning of Peter's independent rule. The Jesuit Georgius David firmly linked Sophia and Golitsyn with the forces of progress and tolerance, and the Patriarch and his party with ignorance and prejudice. The latter were given a free hand to persecute the Jesuits in Moscow 'now that Golitsyn has been banished and silenced and the Tsarevna, our only defence [unico nostro praesideo], removed from power'.[5] Although David listed rumours about Sophia's plans to kill Peter, marry Golitsyn, rule with him and unite with Rome,[6] he dismissed them as 'amazing rumours', such as often occur when 'ignorant people have bottled up various feelings then suddenly have the chance to slander others; but we do not believe them'.[7] David blamed his expulsion from Moscow, just a few weeks after the Naryshkins came to power, on 'the fall from favour of Prince Golitsyn and the removal from power of Tsarevna Sophia, who is said, on hearing of [our expulsion] to have groaned out loud'.[8]

David was not the only visitor to Russia to compare the new Naryshkin regime unfavourably with the government of Sophia and Golitsyn. Foy de la Neuville, who has appeared frequently in these pages, described the Tsar's relatives as 'brutes . . . who have begun to destroy everything which this great man [Golitsyn] has achieved by his intelligence and good judgement for the glory and benefit of the nation'.[9] He described Peter as 'agreeable and well-built. The liveliness of his spirit allows one to expect great things of this government if it is well run'[10] – a favourable assessment which is somewhat undermined by later references to Peter's favourite pastimes of bell-ringing, watching houses burn and forcing courtiers to jump into holes in the ice.[11] La Neuville, who was naturally well disposed towards the Catholic and Jesuit cause, is better known, however, for his contribution towards the vilification of Sophia. He has been quoted in nearly all studies of the early part of Peter's reign, and his work is therefore worth dwelling on in some detail.

La Neuville states in his account that he was in Russia from August to December 1689, that is during the crisis which saw Sophia's overthrow and disgrace and when rumours about the Regent, as also recorded by David, were at their height. Because of the absence of references to his visit in Russian sources, it has sometimes been assumed that La Neuville was never in Russia and that his work was an armchair compilation. He has even mistakenly been identified with the contemporary writer Adrien Baillet. But, as Isabel de Madariaga has shown, La Neuville's activities are better documented in French and Polish sources, and he is known to have carried out a number of missions, including the one to Moscow, as the agent of the King of Poland.[12]

A manuscript account of his journey, dedicated to the King of France and signed 'le très humble, très obéissant et très fidèle sujet et serviteur de la Neufville', survives in the Bibliothèque Nationale in Paris, but the work was published only in 1698 under the title *Relation curieuse et nouvelle de Moscovie*. Thereafter, it appeared in several editions and languages, including English and Dutch. It is by far the most influential of all foreign accounts of Sophia's regency, and La Neuville's descriptions of Sophia's character and appearance have been utilised, often second-hand, by historians and novelists up to the present day.

Yet this undoubtedly fascinating and useful work has often been treated with insufficient caution. For a start, the manuscript and printed versions appeared in two rather different phases of the evolution of Sophia's reputation, the book being published in response to interest in Peter I's visit to the West. A comparison between the two texts reveals that the 1698 edition is augmented and amended, possibly by an editor. (Madariaga believes that La Neuville was probably dead by 1698.) To quote but a couple of discrepancies, the much quoted remark that Sophia was 'of a monstrous size, with a head as big as a bushel, with hair on her face, growths on her legs, and at least forty years old', appears in the manuscript in a marginal note, as do other physical descriptions, for example of Ivan and Peter.[13] In printed versions it was incorporated into the text. La Neuville goes on to qualify Sophia's physical hideousness in an equally famous passage: 'although her stature is broad, short and coarse, her mind is subtle, nimble and shrewd'. In the published text there then follows: 'Without ever having read Machiavelli, she has a natural command of all his maxims, and especially this, that there is nothing that may not be undertaken and no crime which may not be committed when ruling is at stake',[14] a reference missing altogether from the manuscript. Evidently, it was felt necessary to emphasise Sophia's negative aspects between the writing of the account (which mentions no event postdating 1690) and its publication.

Even without the later additions and incorporation of marginal notes, however, La Neuville's original assessment of Sophia is sufficiently negative and clearly differentiated from that of the 'great' Golitsyn (in contrast to David, who mentions the two in one breath) that one suspects that his opinion must have been formed whilst he was in Moscow. In fact, he gives us the names of his informants, one of whom was none other than Andrei Artamonovich (referred to in the manuscript as Harthemonovvich) Matveev, whose own memoir, written twenty or thirty years later, was even more hostile to Sophia than La Neuville's.[15] It seems likely that Matveev supplied the Frenchman with some of the more caustic comments about Sophia, whilst information on Golitsyn and his projects was, as we know, provided by the Prince's Foreign Office colleague Spafarius.[16] In any case, La Neuville met Golitsyn and was able to form his own impressions, whereas he probably never even saw Sophia. All in all, La Neuville's *Relation* in its various redactions is a more complex work than has hitherto been supposed, and requires further study.

La Neuville's was not the only work that underwent revisions in the light of political developments in the 1690s. Georg Adam Schleissing, whose initially mildly positive assessment of Sophia's regime was based on observations in 1684–6, substantially reworked his text in the 1690s with remarks to the effect that 'Sophia became so big with lust for power that for a while she succeeded in hanging on to it by spreading such confusion, that nobody could tell who was the cook and who was the waiter.'[17] The Jesuit Philippe Avril, expelled from Russia in January 1689, promised on his return to 'unravel the divers Intrigues of this Princess' in a supplement to his account of his travels, but unfortunately failed to do so.[18] In fact, the seal on Sophia's reputation abroad was set for some time by the work of the Austrian envoy Johann Georg Korb (1672–1741), who was in Moscow during the bloody executions of the strel'tsy rebels in 1698 and 1699. The fact that Peter himself attributed the rebellion to the influence of 'this dangerously ambitious Princess'[19] led him to gather information on the regency and to conclude that Sophia had been the 'torch and trumpet of the many dangerous outbreaks that have hitherto taken place in Muscovy'.[20]

In the wake of La Neuville and Korb, it became commonplace for foreigners writing on Russia to denigrate Sophia, both those who had been in Russia, such as Charles Whitworth (who blamed Peter I's convulsions 'on the effects of poison from his sister Sophia in his youth')[21] or the mercenary Alexander Gordon (who described her as 'a Princess of masculine spirit, unlimited ambition, and great parts')[22] and those who hadn't, such as J. Banks ('an artful and ambitious woman')[23] or the author of *An Impartial History* of 1723 ('she filled the State with continual Plots and Conspiracies').[24] All were under the spell, to one degree or another, of the Petrine cult. As Alexander Gordon said of Peter: 'I do not believe since the creation of the world, ever monarch was at so great pains or did the like.'[25]

Immoderate adulation of Peter also infected some of those Russian writers who left accounts of his reign. By far the most influential was Andrei Artamonovich Matveev (1666–1728). Internal evidence (for example, a reference to the death of Tsarevna Natalia Alekseevna) indicates that his memoir was written down after 1716, and probably after Peter's death in 1725, but, as we have seen, Matveev had already influenced foreign writers such as La Neuville and perhaps even the author of the anonymous Polish *Diariusz*, long before he recorded his reminiscences.[26] Later authors have often treated Matveev's work, particularly his account of the rebellion of 1682, as an eyewitness account, but the work was filtered through many later experiences, in which Matveev served as Ambassador to Holland, France and England, as President of the Naval Academy and on the Senate, in other words, as one of the devoted supporters of Peter's reform programme.

As one of Peter's 'new men' he imbues his memoir with deep mistrust of the 'old ways', and particularly of the strel'tsy, who killed 'purely out of hateful antipathy to all foreigners'.[27] Peter he compares admiringly to the young Hercules, who 'ripped in half and cast aside a serpent whilst still in his cradle'.[28] If we add to this his deeply felt need to avenge and exonerate his father, Artamon Sergeevich, murdered by the strel'tsy at the beginning of the 1682 rebellion, then the picture of Sophia that emerges seems entirely consistent. She is associated with the old ways, a highly ambitious political intriguer who by reason of her sex and Muscovite conventions was unable to operate openly. Matveev's account underlines the covert nature of her activity: messages sent 'from hidden and deep places', rumours spread 'very secretly and cunningly'.[29] Perhaps he was even anxious to counteract earlier published accounts like Butenant's which put a rather positive interpretation on Sophia's public activity during the May rebellion. In Matveev's view, although Sophia may have *appeared* to try to protect Ivan Naryshkin from the strel'tsy, 'in the midst of all this was the most profound Italian politics, where they say one thing and really mean another'.[30]

Even if Matveev had not had such strong personal motives for disliking Sophia, his attitude is largely what one would expect from one of Peter's most enthusiastic supporters. A less positive attitude towards Peter produced a very different appraisal from another contemporary. Prince Boris Ivanovich Kurakin (1676–1727) wrote his *History of Tsar Peter Alekseevich and his Close Associates* towards the end of his life, at about the same time as Matveev was recording his impressions.[31] Kurakin had also served the Tsar since boyhood, participated in the major campaigns of the Northern War and ended his career as a diplomat, but he remained critical of Peter. The seeds of enmity may have been sown by his marriage to K.F. Lopukhina, the sister of Peter's first wife Evdokia. Kurakin disapproved of the low-born Naryshkins; he was critical of Peter's Drunken Synod of Fools and Jesters, in which the Tsar and his retinue indulged in often obscene ceremonies poking fun at the Church; he felt slighted when he did not receive a medal after the Battle of Poltava in 1709.[32] And so, although, like Matveev's, the focus of his memoir is upon power struggles and intrigue, in Kurakin's version Sophia, a woman 'of great intellect and a great politician', earns his approval. In a famous passage, already quoted, he described the seven years of her regency as a period of 'wise government', when the country reached a 'pinnacle of prosperity'.[33]

Kurakin's account, which in any case remained unpublished until 1890,[34] was an exception among contemporary Russian writings on Peter. More typical was the view of Mikhail Lomonosov, himself a creation of the Petrine era: 'Well then, if a man similar to God, according to our understanding, must indeed be found, I know of no other than Peter the Great.'[35]

One of the clearest expressions of Sophia's demotion in the shadow of the posthumous Peter cult is Ivan Golikov's hagiographic compilation *The Deeds of Peter the Great* (1788–9), the twelve volumes of which grew out of a lifetime's fascination with the Emperor. Golikov's unashamed aim was to illustrate the greatness of Peter with the fullest possible account, much of it based on archival sources, of the Reformer's life and reign. Not surprisingly, the sections on Sophia echo La Neuville and Matveev: 'For all her great intellect unfortunately she was of one mind with those politicians who consider all means legitimate which facilitate the acquisition of supreme power.'[36] Even so, a little qualified praise was also admissible: Golikov reports Peter's own alleged opinion of his half-sister: 'She would have been worthy of a place among the Great Sovereigns if only she had not had one great vice, that of inordinate love of power which stifled all her other virtues.'[37] N.M. Karamzin offered a similar view in his 'Pantheon of Russian Authors', first published in 1802:

> 'Sophia . . . was one of the greatest women Russia ever produced. Suffice to say that in respect of her mind and intellectual qualities she was worthy of the name of sister of *Peter the Great*; but blinded by ambition, she aspired to rule alone and to reign alone, thus placing the historian under the sad obligation of being her accuser.[38]

Karamzin's rather positive, albeit qualified view of Sophia was probably linked to his own reassessment of Peter, whom he criticised for alienating the Westernised nobility from their national roots. His partial rehabilitation of Sophia had been anticipated by others. In a work written in refutation of a foreign 'libel' on Russia and generally attributed to Catherine II, we read: 'Much has been said about this princess, but I believe that she has not been given the credit she deserves. . . . She conducted the affairs of the Empire for a number of years with all the sagacity that one could hope for. When one considers the business that passed through her hands, one cannot but concede that she was capable of ruling.'[39]

Catherine was anxious to tone down the image of that 'formidable rival' Peter, whom she found somewhat lacking as an enlightened legislator. She was also interested in the circumstances of Sophia's regency and rule, as she examined precedents in her search for material to refute those critics who felt that she had usurped the throne of her son Paul. With Russian history offering so few examples of strong and capable female rulers it is not surprising that Catherine turned with interest to the 1680s.[40] She was not the only person in Russia to regard Sophia with favour. The St Petersburg academician G.F. Müller (1705–83), who published and analysed a number of original materials on Russian history, wrote: 'She had a subtle mind, and was very diligent about the business of governing. Her rule was just for the people, useful to the state, and renowned throughout Europe, especially as she had Prince V.V. Golitsyn at her side.' At the same time, he accused her of being ambitious and vain, but concedes that she was much more capable than other members of her family, who were obliged to entrust the government to her.[41]

Both Catherine and Müller were quoted in the first major rehabilitation of Sophia to appear abroad, the French historian M. Levesque's *Histoire de Russie*, first published in 1782. Levesque exonerates Sophia for the rebellion of 1682 ('It has not been proven that she was responsible for the strel'tsy revolt which does not even appear to have been premeditated'), of 1689 ('she felt the same horror over the strel'tsy plot as the rest of the nation'), and 1698 ('She had been overthrown; Peter reigned alone, but she was missed. He would have had to blot out Sophia's memory in order to make himself agreeable to the nation').[42] 'It was', he writes,

> a great good fortune for the country that she took the helm of state, which could otherwise only have been governed either by a prince whose feebleness bordered on the imbecilic, or a child who had no one but a young, inexperienced mother to support him on the throne. Sophia handled affairs with intelligence, and people familiar with the art of government have spoken highly of her administration.[43]

He speaks, incidentally, of Sophia's cultivation of *belles lettres* and of her reputation as a dramatist. Despite such accomplishments, Sophia's disgrace was to be followed by libel, which pursued her 'beyond the grave'.[44]

Levesque and his sources are all quoted in the most remarkable apology for Sophia to come out during Catherine's reign, the work of the Rev. William Coxe, Fellow of King's College Cambridge, who in 1782 accompanied Lord Herbert on a visit to Russia. Volume 1 of his *Travels into Poland, Russia, Sweden and Denmark* appeared in 1784. Coxe was sceptical about the English Petrine cult, regretting that the Tsar's 'sublime and unruly Genius was not controlled and improved by proper *Culture*; nor his savage nature corrected and softened by the refinements of art'.[45] He was thus receptive to the revised view of Sophia recently offered by Levesque, Müller (who had been his informant whilst he was in Russia) and, not least, the *Antidote*, just quoted. He took a critical look at foreign accounts, including Alexander Gordon ('a notorious partiality for Peter'),[46] La Neuville ('the grossest contradictions and the most absurd tales')[47] and Voltaire, whom he suspected of being unduly influenced by Peter's daughter, the Empress Elizabeth, and, needless to say, by La Neuville.[48] In a complete chapter devoted to Sophia, Coxe concluded:

> There is scarcely any portion in the annals of the country more important than the minority of Peter the Great, and no character more grossly misrepresented than that of his sister Sophia Alexiefna, who governed Russia

269

during that period. This illustrious princess united, in a very extraordinary
degree, a variety of personal and mental accomplishments; but as she headed
a party in opposition to Peter, the idolatry, which has been universally paid
to his extensive genius, has greatly contributed towards diminishing the
lustre of her administration.[49]

Coxe's rehabilitation of Sophia must itself be treated circumspectly.
His text contains a number of errors (Sophia's date of birth given as
October 1658; exaggeration of her influence during Fedor's reign; dismissal of La Neuville's description of her ugliness by reference to the
English engineer John Perry, who probably never saw her),[50] but it is
valuable as an attempt at a critical evaluation of sources. Coxe also
produces some new material, for example Peter's alleged pronounce-
ment on Sophia quoted earlier.[51]

Coxe's work remained something of an exception amongst foreign
assessments, for the Enlightenment view of Peter and his predecessors
still had several decades to run, and in Russia was even to experience
an extension into the 1850s as a result of Nicholas I's sponsorship of the
doctrine of 'Official Nationality' and the Emperor's personal admiration
for his predecessor. The most influential of the officially commissioned
works of the era was N. Ustrialov's *History of the Reign of Peter the
Great*, volumes 1 and 2 of which included an account of the regency.
Ustrialov, like his Emperor, was of the view that the modernisation of
Russia had been achieved 'by the thought of one man', thus he took a
fairly dim view of the Tsar's predecessors. He wrote off Sophia's regency,
as we saw earlier, as an unfortunate interval which contributed nothing
of benefit to the nation.[52] The ultra-critical *History of the Joint Tsardom*,
already quoted in this work, also dates from this reign.[53]

A more dispassionate reappraisal of Sophia and her era became more
feasible only as the pre-Petrine era was rediscovered, and the simplistic
'darkness into light' and 'nothingness into being' models of the Enlightenment cult were discarded. A more complete picture of the
seventeenth-century 'transition' had been accessible to scholars since
the publication of archival sources, for example by Nikolai Novikov,[54]
in the eighteenth century, but it took the impetus of Romanticism and
national consciousness to produce a genuine interest in early Russian
history.

For almost one and a half centuries Peter's claim to greatness had
been associated with the spread of Enlightenment engendered by his
reforms. Now, under the influence of German Romantic philosophy,
the Enlightenment came to be regarded by some rather as the product
of excessive rationalism and secularism, imposed from above and imported
from abroad. Peter's reforms had broken with true Russian national
principles, especially religious ones, destroying the organic harmony of

the Russian people and their institutions. In the words of the leading Slavophile historian K.S. Aksakov: 'The Petrine Revolution, notwithstanding its outward glitter, testifies to the deep inner evil which can be caused by the greatest genius as soon as he operates alone, distances himself from the people, and regards them as an architect regards bricks.'[55]

The Slavophiles were not violently opposed to all things Western. Indeed, one of the virtues of Peter's Old Russian predecessors was, in their view, precisely that they had been able to borrow what was useful without slavishly imitating Western thought and ways. Academic research into the nature and scope of pre-Petrine 'Westernisation' was to come not from the Slavophiles, however, but from the historians of what Nicholas Riasanovsky calls 'the Age of Realism and Scholarship', the greatest representative of which was S.M. Solov'ev. According to Solov'ev, the 'insolvency of the old ways' was already evident in the reign of Tsar Aleksei, and it was to fall to his immediate successors to undertake the business of reform. His account of the regency, which appeared in volumes 13 and 14 of his twenty-nine volume *History of Russia from the Earliest Times* (1851–79), is still one of the most detailed available.[56] The people 'sensed the inadequacy of the old ways and realised the need for change, but because they were uneducated they were unable clearly to envisage the way ahead and were incapable of taking the initiative. This could come only from above, from the great sovereign himself.'[57]

For Solov'ev, the lever of change in Russian history had always been the ruler, even though the 'great sovereigns' varied widely in their capacity for introducing change. Peter was thus merely the greatest in a series of 'reformers' including Sophia herself, whom Solov'ev dubbed the 'Amazon' (*bogatyr'*) Tsarevna. Fedor and Sophia were both reformers, but, with the former hampered by ill-health and the latter by her sex, could operate only from within the confines of the palace. For reasons of character and upbringing they favoured the Polish influence, which brought new waves of learning and culture to Muscovy, and set up a bridge to the more alien culture of Western Europe. After the publication of Solov'ev's work it was impossible to return to the notion of a Petrine 'revolution' accomplished without any foundations in earlier reigns.

From the 1850s a number of historians worked on extending knowledge of pre-Petrine Westernisation and modernisation, concepts which had been virtually excluded in the one and a half centuries of the Enlightenment cult. These included P.K. Shchebal'sky, who produced the first monograph on Sophia, stressing the importance of the regency as a corrective to the view that Peter had created the 'new Russia' out of nothing, and adding that 'the greater part of governmental activity

was initiated by the Tsarevna herself'.[58] The first attempt at a rehabilitation of Sophia based on a reappraisal of sources was produced by N.
Aristov in 1871,[59] and was immediately challenged by Mikhail Pogodin,
whose study of the first seventeen years of Peter's reign, written to
commemorate the 200th anniversary of the birth of that 'gigantic
colossus', reaffirmed Sophia's guilt for the 1682 rebellion.[60] In other
words, the Petrine cult remained strong.

Many of the works that appeared in this period, for example D.
Mordovtsev's 1874 study *Russian Historical Women*, were simply rework-
ings of Solov'ev,[61] although there were some original attempts to
reassess and discover new sources for the 1670s and 1680s, which in
some cases Solov'ev himself had used rather uncritically. Ivan Zabelin,
for example, considerably extended the picture of seventeenth-century
court life and culture in his studies and publications of contemporary
documents. He described Sophia's break with the conventions of seclusion as a 'bold and daring feat', although he regarded her style of
rulership 'under the cloak of piety' as more Byzantine than Western.[62]
Another careful student of sources, especially foreign ones, was E.
Shmurlo, who specified the extent to which the Petrine cult had
precluded a dispassionate view of events in 1682 and 1689, 'By the side
of Peter, the new "God" of Russia, the creator of a "new life", Sophia
was bound to represent the forces of darkness which threatened to call a
halt to the action of a lifegiving force.'[63]

It seems ironic that in the wake of the October Revolution of 1917,
after a short-lived period of Orthodox Marxist historical writing in
which the spotlight was withdrawn almost completely from individuals,
the Petrine cult enjoyed a revival under the sponsorship of Stalin, who
drew a number of parallels between himself and the Reformer, especially
during the Second World War. Aleksei Tolstoi's novel *Peter the First*,
volume 1 of which first appeared in 1929, even revived with gusto all
the old stereotypical images of pre-Petrine lust for power, palace passion
and intrigue, depicting Sophia in amorous encounters with Vasily
Golitsyn and masterminding the strel'tsy rebellion, whilst Peter associates with plain folk outside decadent court circles.[64] The excesses
of the Soviet Petrine cult were toned down with the arrival of de-
Stalinisation and the 'Thaw' in the 1950s and 1960s.

Soviet historians now tend towards a bipolar view of Peter, who is
acknowledged to have increased Russia's military might and international
standing at the expense of human life; but they still seem uneasy about
exploring the individual contributions of his immediate predecessors.
Not only has the Soviet period seen no monograph on Sophia, but no
comprehensive work on the reign of her father has appeared either,
although a number of aspects of seventeenth-century history have been
separately studied. For example, V.I. Buganov's works on 'popular rebel-

lions' are overtly devoted to the exploration of the social and economic roots of revolt, challenging the 'palace revolution' view of history. Sophia may have played 'a very cautious and clever political game, which in the end led to victory', but Buganov leaves us in no doubt that the outcome was determined elsewhere.[65] There is no interest in Sophia's personality as such. In fact, female rulers, notably Catherine II, have so far failed to find a place in the pantheon of Soviet historical luminaries, amongst whom Peter I and Ivan IV still loom large. Sophia awaits her Soviet biographer in the queue behind Catherine, although A.P. Bogdanov's studies of literary and polemical sources of the period offer valuable materials for identifying the myth and the reality of the carefully cultivated official contemporary image of the Regent and her achievements.[66] Reassessment of national history and attempts to fill in the 'blanks' in Russia's past have provided some of the liveliest debates in the era of glasnost, but so far the focus has been, perhaps understandably, on more recent events, notably 1917 and Stalinism. One awaits with keen anticipation the first substantial signs of 'new thinking' in Soviet historians' interpretations of their own seventeenth century.

In the West, Sophia and her regency have generally been examined only as a prelude to the life of Peter I. The major exception was C.B. O'Brien's 1952 study *Russia under Two Tsars*, which provided an unusually positive view, describing Sophia's administration as 'a government of unusual distinction and promise'.[67] 'All who surrounded Sophia', he went on to say, 'were people of less energy than herself,' thereby according the Regent a vital role in the events of her era.[68] O'Brien's sober and factual study, however, left many sources unexplored and was little concerned with Sophia's personality or private life. The task of fleshing out the bones has generally fallen to biographers of Peter who, drawing uncritically on secondary sources and memoir literature, have consigned Sophia to the portrait gallery of historical fiction.

One of the most sensational comes from the pen of the French novelist and biographer Henri Troyat. 'Her domain', he writes, 'was the whole palace, the outside world. It was as if the awareness that she was ugly, far from moving her to modesty, exalted her ambition.' There follows the statutory quotation from La Neuville, then: 'This virago was possessed by an unbridled sensuality. Although passionately in love with Basil Golitsyn, who was her official lover, she permitted herself indiscretions with the officers of the *streltsy* corps.'[69] Sophia is elsewhere described as 'massive and terrible', 'this fat shapeless woman with the domineering look in her eye', 'of a gluttonous temperament', and so on.[70] It is tremendously readable, but the image is far removed from the possessor of Patriarch Dionisius' 'four chief virtues'.

W. Bruce Lincoln in his collective biography of the Romanovs writes that she 'ruled the Kremlin in a manner reminiscent of Catherine

Medici in sixteenth-century France and her contemporary, Elizabeth Tudor, in England'.[71] Prurient attention to Sophia's relationship with Golitsyn (flimsily founded, as we have seen, in documented sources) seems *de rigueur* in such studies, as do claims rooted in La Neuville that the relationship was stimulated by power politics rather than physical attraction ('her appearance bordered upon the grotesque').[72] Muscovites, we learn, branded Sophia as a 'whore'.[73]

A rather more complex character analysis is attempted in Robert K. Massie's best-selling *Peter the Great*. Massie rejects La Neuville's grotesque description on the grounds that the Frenchman is unlikely to have seen Sophia, and that his portrait is uncorroborated, but he remains in the thrall of the love affair with Golitsyn: 'With Golitsyn she would share power and love, and together they would rule.'[74] Massie is willing to concede that Sophia was 'competent, and on the whole, ruled well'. She even 'helped prepare the way for Peter.'[75] But 'It was not as a Russian ruler but as a Russian woman that Sophia was remarkable. . . . Unfortunately, Sophia's womanhood was not only her distinction, it was also her undoing.'[76] Ultimately, Massie is interested in Sophia not in her own right but as an opponent and precursor of Peter the Great. 'She was, after all, Peter's sister,' he writes.[77] The implications are clear. Sophia shared certain traits with her half-brother: love of power, determination, ruthlessness, even a penchant for the West, albeit less extreme than his.

This point was taken up and developed in NBC's television mini-series *Peter the Great*, based on Massie's book and filmed in the USSR in 1986.[78] Vanessa Redgrave's portrayal of Sophia expressed above all love of power, of which the affair with Golitsyn (played by the British actor Geoffrey Whitehead, perhaps following up Massie's comment that he resembled 'a dashing earl just arrived from England')[79] is seen as a mere corollary. Sophia seeks to bar Peter and his circle, especially the 'hated stepmother', from power, but we are never allowed to forget the familial relationship between them. The scenario imagines a final meeting between Peter and Sophia before she is whisked away (in 1698? The chronology is very muddled) to the Arctic (*sic!*), in which Peter expresses guarded regrets about the necessity of banishing so capable a woman.

The picture that emerges from my own attempt to reassess Sophia and her era may disappoint those whose taste is for historical fiction. If we base our knowledge on reliable contemporary sources alone, we know rather less about certain aspects of Sophia's life than previous writers would have us believe. The notorious relationship with Vasily Golitsyn, for example, is reduced to a couple of letters in cipher, some circumstantial evidence and a lot of malicious gossip. The grotesque appearance, which allegedly motivated Sophia in her quest for political power, turns out to be based on a marginal note in a French manuscript. The legend of Sophia's rule during Fedor's reign appears to stem from the speculation of a few foreign observers in the wake of the 1682 rebellion, whilst evidence of substantial pre-planning of the rebellion on the part of Sophia and her 'party' is found to be absent from most contemporary sources. We are unlikely ever to know more than the small amount we know already about Sophia's inner life, her hopes, her fears and loves, given the lack not only of writing from her own pen but also of any intimate portraits from her family and Russian contemporaries in general. When such people did give voice it was in the stereotyped conventions of the new, courtly panegyric verses and declamations, praising a wise woman who happened to have been baptised with the name Sophia, a pious female ruler in an era when by convention and of necessity the true sovereign, however weak, wicked or ungodly, was described as pious. In the face of such tautology, one may despair of finding any substance behind the image at all.

Yet as some aspects fade, others appear to replace them. Whereas private activities, not to mention private utterances, are rarely recorded, public ones were. Thus although we cannot hope to view Sophia in the psychological detail with which we might scrutinise one of her contemporaries elsewhere, we have ample material for assessing her against models of Muscovite rulership imagery. As we have seen, the evidence of titles, portraits and panegyric points to the formulation of female versions of the time-honoured conventions. Although a woman ruler was a new phenomenon, Sophia pre-empted protest by honouring and adapting the rules observed by her father and brother. There seems to have been little public outcry against a female ruler as such (quite the contrary if we consider the appeals of the strel'tsy in 1698); rather, opposition to her rule originated in Peter's camp in order to prevent her from establishing herself on the throne permanently.

Of the fact that she would have liked to continue ruling in some capacity or another there is little doubt, for she had quite simply become accustomed to being in charge. She had developed a taste not only for the trappings of power but also for the actual business of ruling. The images of Sophia which stick in the mind are of a woman putting men in their place: dismissing Butenant as he waited anxiously to learn his fate in May 1682, scolding the Old Believers in July of the same year, ordering the execution of the Khovanskys in September, receiving ambassadors from Sweden and Poland, chiding Patrick Gordon for even thinking of leaving the tsars' service, heading the welcoming party for Golitsyn, speaking up in her own defence in the Kremlin in August 1689, setting off to confront Peter in the Trinity Monastery, calmly denying the charges against her in September 1698. With the exception of Catherine the Great, who was not even Russian, Sophia has claims to being the most determined and capable woman ever to rule Russia. If this book has helped the 'Pious Tsarevna' and her era to emerge from the shadow cast over them by Peter, it will have achieved its purpose.

# Notes

## Abbreviations Used Frequently in Notes

| | |
|---|---|
| AAE | *Akty, sobrannye . . . arkheograficheskoiu ekspeditsieiu* |
| AI | *Akty istoricheskie* |
| BL | British Library, Manuscript Division |
| Butenant | H. Butenant, 'Wahrhaftige Relation' |
| Chteniia | *Chteniia v imp. obshchestve istorii drevnostei rossiiskikh* |
| DAI | *Dopolneniia k aktam istoricheskim* |
| DDR | *Dopolneniia k tomu IIImu Dvortsovykh razriadov* |
| Diariusz | *Diariusz zaboystwa tyranskiego senatorow moskiewskich* |
| DR | *Dvortsovye razriady* |
| DRV | *Drevniaia rossiiskaia vivliofika* |
| IRI (1959) | *Istoriia russkogo iskusstva*, vol 4 (Moscow, 1959) |
| Matveev | A.A. Matveev, 'Zapiski' |
| Medvedev | S. Medvedev, 'Sozertsanie let kratkoe' |
| MERSH | *Modern Encyclopedia of Russian and Soviet History* |
| PDS | *Pamiatniki diplomaticheskikh snoshenii* |
| PRO | Public Record Office, London |
| PSZ | *Polnoe sobranie zakonov* |
| Rozysknye dela | *Rozysknye dela o Fedore Shaklovitom* |
| SEER | *Slavonic and East European Review* |
| SGGD | *Sobranie gosudarstvennykh gramot i dogovorov* |
| Solov'ev | S.M. Solov'ev, *Istoriia Rossii s drevneishikh vremen*. vol. 13–14 |
| TODRL | *Trudy otdela drevnerusskoi literatury* |
| TsGADA | *Tsentral'nyi gosudarstvennyi arkhiv drevnikh aktov* |
| Tumansky | F. Tumansky (ed.), *Sobranie raznykh zapisok i sochinenii* |
| Vosstanie | V.I. Buganov and N.G. Savich (eds.), *Vosstanie v Moskve 1682 g.* |
| Vosstanie . . . 1698 | V.I. Buganov (ed.), *Vosstanie moskovskikh strel'tsov. 1698 god.* |
| Vykhody | P. Stroev (ed.), *Vykhody gosudarei tsarei i velikikh kniazei* |
| ZhMNP | *Zhurnal Ministerstva Narodnogo Prosveshcheniia* |

See Bibliography for full references.

## CHAPTER 1: RUSSIA IN 1657

1. For a bibliography on seventeenth-century Europe, see below, Chapter 8, note 6.
2. J. Reutenfels, 'Skazanie sviatleishemu gertsogu toskanskomu Koz'me Tret'emu o Moskovii', *Chteniia*, 1906, book 3, p. 140. Translation of *De rebus Moschoviticis* (Padua, 1680).
3. For general background on mid-seventeenth-century Russia, see P. Dukes, *The Making of Russian Absolutism 1613–1801* (London, 1982); V.O. Kliuchevsky, *Course in Russian History: The Seventeenth Century*, trans. N. Duddington (New York, 1968); S.M. Solov'ev, *History of Russia from the Earliest Times*, vol. 24: *The Character of Old Russia*, ed. and

trans. A. Muller (Gulf Breeze, 1980); G. Vernadsky, *The Tsardom of Muscovy 1547–1682*, 2 vols (New Haven and London, 1969). In Russian: A.V. Artsikhovsky (ed.), *Ocherki russkoi kul'tury XVII veka*, 2 vols (Moscow, 1979); A.A. Novosel'sky (ed.), *Ocherki istorii SSSR. Period feodalizma. XVII vek* (Moscow, 1955).

4. *The Travels of Olearius in 17th-century Russia*, trans. and ed. S.H. Baron (Stanford, 1967), p. 173 (henceforth, Olearius). Translation of the 1656 Schleswig edition *Vermehrte neue Beschreibung der Muscowitischen und Persischen*. . . .

5. Reutenfels, 'Skazanie', 1905, book 3, p. 100.

6. For a contemporary example of the Tsar's titles, see *Dvortsovye razriadi*, vol. 3 (St Petersburg, 1852), p. 107. In this, the announcement of Sophia's birth, it is reported 'rodisia Gosudariu Tsariu i Velikomu Kniaziu Alekseiu Mikhailovichu, vseia Velikiia i Malyia i Belyia Rossii Samoderzhtsu dshcher' Gosudarynia Tsarevna i Velikaia Kniazhna Sof'ia Alekseevna'. See also M. Szechtel, 'The Title of the Muscovite Monarch up to the End of the Seventeenth Century', *Canadian – American Slavic Studies*, 13 (1979), 59–81.

7. A useful discussion, albeit in an eighteenth-century context, is found in I. de Madariaga, 'Autocracy and Sovereignty', *Canadian – American Slavic Studies*, 16 (1982), 369–97. The contemporary English translation was 'Self-Upholder'.

8. Dukes, *The Making of Russian Absolutism*, p. 4.

9. N.S. Kollmann, *Kinship and Politics: The Making of the Muscovite Political System 1345–1547* (Stanford, 1987).

10. *Dopolneniia k tomu IIIemu Dvortsovykh razriadov* (St Petersburg, 1854), p. 99.

11. R.O. Crummey, *Aristocrats and Servitors: The Boyar Elite in Russia 1613–1689* (Princeton, 1983), pp. 29, 164.

12. P. Longworth, *Alexis, Tsar of All the Russias* (London, 1984), p. 244. This is the most up-to-date and reliable biography of Tsar Aleksei. More anecdotal and less scholarly, but informative on 'historical colour', is J. Fuhrmann, *Tsar Alexis, His Reign and*

His Russia (Gulf Breeze, 1981). For a discussion of royal epithets in seventeenth-century Russia, see M. Cherniavsky, *Tsar and People: Studies in Russian Myths* (New Haven and London, 1961), pp. 61–71.

13. Longworth, *Alexis*, p. 134.

14. Ibid., p. 117.

15. See *Sobornoe ulozhenie 1649 goda. Tekst. Kommentarii*, comp. A.C. Man'kov *et al.* (Leningrad, 1987); *The Muscovite Law Code (Ulozhenie) of 1649. Part 1: Text and Translation*, trans. and ed. R. Hellie (Irvine, 1988).

16. L. Kochan and R. Abraham, *The Making of Modern Russia* (London, 1983), p. 84.

17. J. Stoye, *Europe Unfolding 1648–1688* (London, 1969), p. 47.

18. For a popular survey, see P. Longworth, 'Tsar Alexis Goes to War', *History Today*, January 1981, 14–18.

19. Ibid., p. 18.

20. S. Collins, *The Present State of Russia* (London, 1671), pp. 64–5.

21. See Longworth, *Alexis*, pp. 120–1.

22. B.H. Sumner, *Survey of Russian History* (London, 1947), p. 294.

23. On the Foreign Quarter, see S.H. Baron, 'The Origins of 17th-Century Moscow's Nemeckaja Sloboda', *California Slavic Studies*, 5 (1970), 1–18; L.A.J. Hughes, 'Foreign Settlement', *MERSH*, 11 (1979), 216–18.

24. See J. Keep, *Soldiers of the Tsar: Army and Society in Russia 1462–1874* (Oxford, 1985), ch. 4. R. Hellie, *Enserfment and Military Change in Muscovy* (Chicago, 1971).

25. S.M. Solov'ev, *Istoriia Rossii s drevneishikh vremen*, vols 13–14 (Moscow, 1962), pp. 135–6.

26. See L.A.J. Hughes, 'The Moscow Armoury and Innovations in 17th-Century Muscovite Art', *Canadian – American Slavic Studies*, 13 (1979), 204–23, and 'The 17th-century "Renaissance" in Russia: Western Influences in Art and Architecture', *History Today*, February 1980, 41–5.

27. Portraits of the False Dmitry (reigned 1605–6) and his bride Marina Mniszech were painted in Poland. On Aleksei's appearance, see p. 28 below.

28. N. Andreyev, 'Nikon and Avvakum on Icon Painting', *Revue des Etudes Slaves*, 38 (1961), 40.

29. Paul of Aleppo, *The Travels of Maca-*

rius Patriarch of Antioch. *Written by his attendant Archdeacon Paul of Aleppo*, vol. 2 (London, 1836), p. 49.

30. Andreyev, 'Nikon and Avvakum', p. 49.
31. Olearius, p. 234.
32. R. Wittram, *Peter I: Czar und Kaiser*, vol. 1 (Göttingen, 1964), p. 58.
33. On the schism, see W. Palmer, *The Patriarch and the Tsar*, 6 vols (London, 1871–6); P. Pascal, *Avvakum et les débuts du raskol* (Paris, 1938); M. Cherniavsky, 'The Old Believers and the New Religion', *Slavic Review*, 25 (1966), 1–39; and pp. 121–4, below.
34. A. Vucinich, *Science in Russian Culture: A History to 1860* (London, 1965), p. 36.
35. N.P. Kisilev, 'O moskovskom knigopechatanii XVII veka', *Kniga. Issledovaniia i materialy*, 2 (1960), 129. See also S.P. Luppov, *Kniga v Rossii v XVII veke* (Leningrad, 1970).
36. For a listing of books published in Moscow in the seventeenth century, see A.S. Zernova, *Knigi kirillovskoi pechati izdannye v Moskve v XVI–XVII vekakh: svodnyi katalog* (Moscow, 1958), and pp. 165–6 below.
37. Olearius, pp. 130–1.
38. Ibid., p. 238.
39. V.S. Rumiantseva, 'Russkaia shkola XVII veka', *Voprosy istorii*, 1978, no. 6, 214–9. See also A.I. Rogov, 'Shkola i prosveshchenie', in Artsikhovsky, pp. 142–54.
40. Collins, *The Present State of Russia*, pp. 92–3.
41. A von Mayerberg, *Voyage en Moscovie d'un Ambassadeur, Conseiller de la Chambre Impériale, Envoyé par l'Empereur Léopold au Czar Alexis Mihalowics, Grand Duc de Moscovie* (Leiden, 1688), p. 52. Translation of *Iter in Moschoviam Augustini Liberi Baronis de Mayerberg . . . ad Tsarem et Magnum Ducem Alexium Mihalowicz. Anno M.DC.LXI.*
42. For texts of some of the tales in English, see S.A. Zenkovsky (ed.), *Medieval Russia's Epics, Chronicles and Tales* (New York, 1963). On the history of seventeenth-century Russian literature, see W.E. Brown, *The History of Seventeenth-Century Russian Literature* (Ann Arbor, 1980). For Russian bibliography, see Chapter 7,

note 178, below.
43. G. Kotoshikhin, *O Rossii v carstvovanie Alekseja Mixajlovica: Text and Commentary*, ed. A.E. Pennington (Oxford, 1980), pp. 29–30.
44. Mayerberg, *Voyage en Moscovie*, pp. 144–6.
45. I. Zabelin, *Domashnii byt russkogo naroda*, vol. 2 (Moscow, 1901), p. 144.
46. G. Vernadsky, *Kievan Russia* (New Haven and London, 1948), p. 154.
47. M.P. Fabritsius, *Kreml' v Moskve. Ocherki i kartiny proshlogo* (Moscow, 1883), pp. 108–9.
48. Kollmann, *Kinship and Politics*, p. 124. She regards Kotoshikhin's theories as 'an explanatory façade'.
49. S.J. McNally, 'From Public Person to Private Prisoner: The Changing Place of Women in Medieval Russia' (unpublished PhD thesis, State University of New York, Binghampton, 1976), p. 69. See also N.S. Kollmann, 'The Seclusion of Elite Muscovite Women', *Russian History*, 10 (1983), 170–87.
50. Olearius, p. 164.
51. Mayerberg, *Voyage en Moscovie*, pp. 148–9.
52. Olearius, p. 73.
53. Reutenfels, 'Skazanie', 1905, book 3, p. 83.
54. Fabritsius, *Kreml' v Moskve*, p. 108. The royal *terem* should not be confused with the Terem Palace (*Teremny dvorets*, built in the Kremlin in 1635–6 and still extant. This was part of the extended Kremlin palace and was not exclusively for women; in fact, it contained some of the Tsar's reception chambers. Records indicate that the tsarevny's quarters were separate from this building and constructed of wood, until they were replaced by a stone building in the 1680s.
55. On the birth of Tsar Aleksei's sixteen children (thirteen by his first wife, three by his second), see Chapter 2, below.
56. Reutenfels, 'Skazanie', 1905, book 3, p. 84.
57. Kotoshikhin, *O Rossii v carstvovanie Alekseja Mixajlovica*, p. 19.
58. For an annotated text of the *Domostroi*, see *Pamiatniki literatury drevnei Rusi. Seredina XVI veka*, ed. L.A. Dmitrieva and D.S. Likhachev

(Moscow, 1985), pp. 70–173.
59. See T.A. Greenan, 'Iulianiya Laza-revskaya', *Oxford Slavonic Papers*, 15 (1982), 28–45.
60. For a recent view, see E. Levin, *Sex and Society in the World of the Orthodox Slavs, 900–1700* (Ithaca, 1989).
61. Olearius, p. 145.
62. Collins, *The Present State of Russia*, p. 19.
63. B. Tanner, 'Opisanie puteshestviia pol'skogo posol'stva v Moskvu v 1678g', *Chteniia* 1891, book 3, p. 47. Translation of *Legatio Polono-Lith-uanica* (1689).
64. Ibid., p. 106.
65. D. Mordovtsev, *Russkie istoricheskie zhenshchiny. Populiarnye rasskazy iz russkoi zhizni* (St Peterburg, 1874), pp. 306–7.

## CHAPTER 2: CHILDHOOD AND YOUTH 1657–1682

1. *Dopolneniia k tomu IIIemu Dvortsovykh razriadov* (St Petersburg, 1854), p. 107 (henceforth, *DDR*). There are no entries for 1657 in vol. 3 itself. (See note 45, below.)
2. *Russkii biograficheskii slovar'*, vol. 13 (St Petersburg, 1909), p. 126.
3. G Kotoshikhin, *O Rossii v carstvovanie Alekseja Mixajlovica. Text and Commentary*, ed. A.E. Pennington (Oxford, 1980), p. 30.
4. *DDR*, pp. 107–9. The princes (*tsarevichi*) of Kasimov, Siberia and so on were descendants of Tatar khans who had served the Muscovite rulers since the sixteenth century. By the mid-seventeenth century most had been converted to Christianity and were still afforded places of honour on formal occasions.
5. This icon is sometimes displayed in the exhibition at the Novodevichy Convent, now a branch of the State Historical Museum.
6. *DDR*, p. 109.
7. Kotoshikhin, *O Rossii v carstvovanie Alekseja Mixajlovica*, p. 31.
8. I.E. Zabelin, *Domashnii byt russkikh tsarei v XVI i XVII st.*, vol. 1, part 2 (Moscow, 1915), pp. 29–30.
9. Kotoshikhin, *O Rossii v carstvovanie Alekseja Mixajlovica*, p. 33.
10. *DDR*, pp. 146–7.
11. *Vykhody gosudarei tsarei i velikikh kniazei Mikhaila Fedorovicha, Alekseia Mikhailovicha, Fedora Alekseevicha, vseia Rusii Samoderzhtsev (s 1632 po 1682)*, ed. P. Stroiev (Moscow, 1844), p. 314 (henceforth, *vykhody*). Unfortunately no such records have survived for the reign of Peter and Ivan.
12. Ibid., p. 339.
13. Nameday celebrations on 17 September are recorded in 1661, 1662, 1664, 1666, 1668, 1669, 1670, 1671, 1674 and 1675. Many were held in the Church of St Evdokia in the Kremlin. In 1669 and 1671 the celebrations took place at the village of Preobrazhenskoe. See ibid., pp. 363, 386, 426, 468, etc.
14. Kotoshikhin, *O Rossii v carstvovanie Alekseja Mixajlovica*, p. 31.
15. I. Zabelin, *Domashnii byt russkogo naroda*, vol. 2 (Moscow, 1901), p. 351.
16. Ibid., p. 552.
17. Ibid., p. 553.
18. A. von Mayerburg, *Voyage en Moscovie d'un Ambassadeur, Conseiller de la Chambre Impériale, Envoyé par l'Empereur Léopold au Czar Alexis Mihalowicz, Grand Duc de Moscovie* (Leiden, 1688), pp. 204–5.
19. S. Collins, *The Present State of Russia* (London, 1671), p. 11. Collins gets the date of birth wrong, perhaps confusing it with the nameday on 8 June.
20. Mayerburg, *Voyage en Moscovie*, p. 250.
21. Collins, *The Present State of Russia*, p. 44.
22. See A.A. Kizevetter, *Den' tsaria Alekseia Mikhailovicha* (Moscow, 1897).
23. *Sobranie gosudarstvennykh gramot i dogovorov, khraniashchikhsia v gos. kollegii inostrannykh del*, vol. 4 (Moscow, 1828), no. 63, pp. 219–23 (hereafter *SGDD*).
24. *Opisanie starinnykh tsarskikh utvarei, odezhd, oruzhiia, ratnykh dospekhov i konskogo pribora*, comp. P. Savvaitov (St Petersburg, 1865), pp. 127–32.
25. Zabelin, *Domashnii byt russkikh tsarei*, p. 116.
26. G.V. Esipov (comp.), *Sbornik vypisok iz arkhivnykh bumag o Petre Veli-*

*kom*, vol. 1 (Moscow, 1872), p. 20.

27. J. Reutenfels, 'Skazanie Sviatleishemu gertsogu toskanskomu Koz'me Tret'emu o Moskouii', *Chteniia*, 1905, book 3, p. 85.

28. I.K. Kondrat'ev, *Sedaia starina Moskvy* (Moscow, 1893), p. 120; N.A. Skvortsov, *Arkheologiia i topografiia Moskvy. Kurs lektsii* (Moscow, 1913), pp. 459–62.

29. Skvortsov, *Arkheologiia i topografiia Moskvy*, pp. 467–8.

30. Kondrat'ev, *Sedaia starina Moskvy*, p. 124; M.P. Fabritsius, *Kreml' v Moskve. Ocherki i kartiny proshlogo* (Moscow, 1883), p. 269.

31. Reutenfels, 'Skazanie', 1905, book 3, pp. 82–3.

32. S.J. McNally, 'From Public Person to Private Prisoner: The Changing Place of Women in Medieval Russia' (unpublished PhD thesis, State University of New York, (Binghampton, 1976), p. 150.

33. Kotoshikhin, *O Rossii v carstvovanie Alekseja Mixajlovica*, p. 32.

34. Reutenfels, 'Skazanie', 1905, book 3, p. 84.

35. Ibid., pp. 84–5.

36. For a biographical sketch of Polotsky, see my entry in *MERSH*, 29 (1982), 8–11. A short study of his literary work is A. Hippisley, *The Poetic Style of Simeon Polotsky* (Birmingham, 1983).

37. See, for example, entries in *Entsiklopedicheskii slovar'*, vol. 30 (St Petersburg, 1900), p. 598; *Sovetskaia istoricheskaia entsiklopediia*, vol. 13 (Moscow, 1971), 362.

38. A.N. Robinson (ed.), *Simeon Polotskii i ego knigoizdatel'skaia deiatel'nost'* (Moscow, 1982), p. 93.

39. *Letopisi russkoi literatury i drevnosti*, vol. 3, book 6 (Moscow, 1861), part 3, pp. 86–7. For a description of the contents of the *Rifmologion*, see Robinson, *Simeon Polotskii*, pp. 259–308.

40. Robinson, *Simeon Polotskii*, p. 132. On Sophia's library, see below, pp. 171–2.

41. On Sophia as author, see below, pp. 172–6.

42. On Nikon, see *MERSH*, 25 (1981), 4–10. The 'Copper Coin' riots of 1662 centred on the devaluation of the currency through the unrestricted minting of copper coinage. See V.I. Buganov, *Moskovskoe vosstanie 1662 g.* (Moscow, 1964).

43. On the Treaty of Andrusovo and its implications, see below, pp. 182 ff.

44. On Razin, see P. Avrich, *Russian Rebels* (New York, 1972).

45. *Dvortsovye razriady*, vol. 3 (St Petersburg, 1852), p. 849 (hereafter, *DR*).

46. On Ivan and his ailments, see below, pp. 91–6.

47. On Matveev, see *MERSH*, 21 (1981), 142–4.

48. *DR*, vol. 3, pp. 872–3.

49. S.M. Solov'ev *Istoriia Rossii s drevneishikh vremen*, vols 13–14 (Moscow, 1962), p. 105 (henceforth, Solov'ev).

50. D. Mordovtsev, *Russkie istoricheskie zhenshchiny. Populiarnye rasskazy iz russkoi zhizni* (St Petersburg, 1874), p. 310

51. Reutenfels, 'Skazanie', 1905, book 3, p. 83.

52. L. Rinhuber, *Relation du voyage en Russie fait en 1684 par Laurent Rinhuber* (Berlin, 1883), p. 29. (On Rinhuber, see below, pp. 190–1.) On the history of the early Russian theatre, see S. Karlinsky, *Russian Drama from Its Beginnings to the Age of Pushkin* (Berkeley, 1985); E. Kholodov, 'Pervye zriteli russkogo teatra', *Teatr*, 1978, no. 8, 97–111.

53. Reutenfels, 'Skazanie', 1905, book 3, p. 88.

54. Kholodov, 'Pervye zriteli russkogo teatra', p. 102; *DR*, vol. 3, pp. 1131–2.

55. On Sophia as dramatist, see below, pp. 172–5.

56. *Russkaia sillabicheskaia poeziia XVII–XVIII v.v.*, ed. A.M. Panchenko (Leningrad, 1970), pp. 108–10.

57. Reutenfels, 'Skazanie', 1905, book 3, p. 93.

58. See *DR*, vol. 3, pp. 973–1632.

59. See N. Moleva, 'Izmailovo', *Znaniesila*, 1971, no. 5, 32–6.

60. *DR*, vol. 3, pp. 1130–2. For texts and background on the first plays, see A.N. Robinson (ed.). *Pervye p'esy russkogo teatra* (Moscow, 1972).

61. *DR*, vol. 3, p. 1153.

62. Ibid., p. 1224. Robinson, *Pervye p'esy*, p. 12.

63. *DR*, vol. 3, p. 1236.

64. Ibid., pp. 1403–4.
65. Ibid., pp. 1487–93.
66. See P. Longworth, *Alexis, Tsar of All the Russias* (London, 1984), pp. 219–25.
67. Robinson, *Pervye p'esy*, p. 12. S.K. Bogoiavlensky, *Moskovskii teatr pri tsariakh Aleksee i Petre* (Moscow, 1914), p. 71 ff.
68. *DR*, vol. 3, pp. 1641–3.
69. Kotoshikhin (*O Rossii v carstvovanie Alekseja Mixajlovica*, p. 35) did list the tsarevny amongst those in attendance at state funerals, but the only one in living memory had been Mikhail's in 1645.
70. Reutenfels, 'Skazanie', 1905, book 3, p. 91
71. See Robinson, *Simeon Polotskii*, p. 294.
72. *Diariusz zaboystwa tyranskiego senatorow moskiewskich w stolicy roku 1682 y o obraniu dwoch carow Ioanna y Piotra* (St Petersburg, 1901), p. 4 (henceforth, *Diariusz*). On the provenance of this work, see below, pp. 57–8. Also L.A.J. Hughes, '"Ambitious and Daring above Her Sex": Tsarevna Sophia Alekseevna (1657–1704) in Foreigners' Accounts', *Oxford Slavonic Papers*, 21 (1988), 65–89.
73. *Diariusz*, p. 5.
74. 'Narratio rerum quae post obitum Alexii Mickalowicz Russorum Imperatoris etc. gestae sunt Moschuae XI Kal. octobris an 1682', in S. Ciampi, *Bibliografia critica*, vol. 1 (Florence, 1834), p. 76. For a discussion of provenance, see Hughes, 'Ambitious and Daring', p. 67.
75. Some eighteenth-century chronicles contain variations of rumours, e.g. I.I. Golikov, *Deianiia Petra Velikogo*, vol. 1 (Moscow, 1788), p. 8, recounts that when Fedor was advised to marry again after the death of his first wife, he replied that 'his father had intended to name Peter as his heir, but did not because of his youth'. Fedor had thus decided to name Peter because of his own ill-health. Fedor's 'wishes', however, were never mentioned in 1682.
76. *SGDD*, vol. 4, no. 103, pp. 333–5.
77. H.E. Ellersieck, 'Russia under Aleksei Mikhailovich and Fedor Alekseevich, 1654–1682: The

Scandinavian Sources' (unpublished PhD, thesis, University of California at Los Angeles, 1955), p. 275.
78. *DR*, vol. 4, pp. 1–24.
79. Ibid., p. 31.
80. Ibid., pp. 35–8.
81. Ibid., pp. 74–6.
82. Ibid., pp. 134–8.
83. See Skvortsov, *Arkheologiia i topografii Moskvy*, p. 437; Kondrat'ev, *Sedaia starina Moskvy*, p. 654.
84. *DR*, vol. 4, pp. 162–3.
85. J. Crull, *The Antient and Present State of Muscovy*, vol. 2 (London, 1698), pp. 199–201.
86. F. de la Neuville, *Relation curieuse et nouvelle de Moscovie* (Paris, 1698.) Quotations translated from The Hague edition, 1699, unless otherwise stated. There is an English translation, *An Account of Muscovy, as it was in the year 1689* (London, 1699). A manuscript of the work survives, entitled 'Récit de mon voyage' (Paris, Bibliothèque Nationale, Département des Manuscrits, NAF 5114), but it differs in many respects from the published versions. Discrepancies will be noted. On La Neuville, see below, pp. 264–5, and Hughes, 'Ambitious and Daring', pp. 83–6.
87. La Neuville, *Relation curieuse et nouvelle de Moscovie*, p. 155. 'Récit de mon voyage', f. 40.
88. On promotions and power networks, see R.O. Crummey, *Aristocrats and Servitors: The Boyar Elite in Russia 1613–1689* (Princeton, 1984), pp. 92–3, and passim. Also Solov'ev, pp. 196–7.
89. Solov'ev, p. 197.
90. 'Mazurinskii letopisets', *Polnoe sobranie russkikh letopisei*, vol. 31 (Moscow, 1968), p. 173. On the provenance of this work, see M.N. Tikhomirov, 'Zapiski prikaznykh liudei kontsa XVII veka', *TODRL*, 12 (1956), 442.
91. On Golitsyn, see L.A.J. Hughes, *Russia and the West: The Life of a Seventeenth-Century Westernizer Prince Vasily Vasil'evich Golitsyn (1643–1714)* (Newtonville, Mass., 1984). Since the completion of the present book, my attention has been drawn to the existence of A.F. Smith, 'Prince V.V. Golitsyn: The Life of an Aristocrat in Muscovite

Russia', (unpublished PhD thesis, Harvard University, 1987.)

92. P. Avril, *Travels into divers Parts of Europe and Asia* (*Undertaken by the French King's Order to discover a new Way by Land into China*), book 4 (London, 1693), pp. 55-6. Translated from *Voyage en divers états d'Europe et d'Asie entrepris pour découvrir un nouveau chemin à la Chine* (Paris, 1692). On Avril, see below, pp. 208-9.

93. La Neuville, *Relation curieuse et nouvelle de Moscovie*, p. 77. (This remark appears in a marginal note in 'Récit de mon voyage', f. 17.

94. La Neuville, 'Récit de mon voyage', f. 40; *Relation curieuse et nouvelle de Moscovie*, p. 156.

95. W. Bruce Lincoln, *The Romanovs* (London, 1981), p. 67.

96. A.K. Tolstoi, *Petr Pervyi. Roman* (book 1, written 1929-30, book 2, 1933-4). The work underwent many revisions. See the version in *Rossiiu podnial na dyby*, vol. 1 (Moscow, 1987), pp. 33-350.

97. La Neuville, *Relation curieuse et nouvelle de Moscovie*, p. 151; 'Récit de mon voyage', f. 40.

98. Ibid.

99. Bruce Lincoln, *The Romanovs*, p. 67.

100. See *DR*, vol. 3.

101. *Vykhody*, pp. 700-1, 780-1.

102. *DR*, vol. 4, pp. 189-90.

103. *SGGD*, vol. 4, no. 130, pp. 396-410.

104. *Akty istoricheskie, sobrannye i izdannye arkheograficheskoiu kommissieiu*, vol. 5 (St Petersburg, 1842), pp. 108-18. See my 'Church Council of 1681-2', *Modern Encyclopedia of Religions in Russia and the Soviet Union* (forthcoming).

## CHAPTER 3: THE REBELLION OF 1682

1. M.I. Belov, 'Pis'ma Ioganna fan Kellera v sobranii niderlandskikh diplomaticheskikh dokumentov', *Issledovaniia po otechestvennomu istochnikovedeniiu* (Leningrad, 1964), p. 24. French copies of Keller's dispatches are located in the archive of the Leningrad division of the Institute of History of the Academy of Sciences (LOII), fond 40 (55-8)

2. See above, pp. 43 ff.

3. Silvester Medvedev, 'Sozertsanie let kratkoe 7190, 91 i 92, v nikh zhe chto sodeiasia vo grazhdanstve', *Chteniia*, 1894, book 4, section II, 43-5 (henceforth Medvedev). For more on this writer and his work, see below, note 10. Another account of Peter's election is 'Zapiski razriadnogo prikaza za 27 aprelia – 25 oktiabria 1682', in *Vosstanie v Moskve 1682 g. Sbornik dokumentov*, ed. V.I. Buganov and N.G. Savich (Moscow, 1976), pp. 254-6 (henceforth, *Vosstanie*). This account, compiled in the Crown Appointments Department (Razriad), was probably written no earlier than September 1683.

4. On the *zemskii sobor*, see above, p. 6.

5. *Polnoe sobranie zakonov Rossiiskoi imperii*, vol. 2 (St Petersburg, 1830), no. 920, p. 399 (henceforth, *PSZ*).

6. *Diariusz zaboystwa tyranskiego senatorow moskiewskich w stolicy roku 1682 y o obraniu dwoch carow Ioanna y Piotra* (St Petersburg, 1901), p. 7 (henceforth, *Diariusz*).

7. *Istoriia sotsarstviia v Rossii* (1682-89 gg.), *sostavlennaia po vernym istochnikam* (St Petersburg, 1837), p. 13.

8. V.I. Buganov, *Moskovskie vosstaniia kontsa XVII veka* (Moscow 1969), p. 86.

9. H. Butenant (later von Rosenbusch), 'Warhaftige Relation der traurigen undt schrecklichen Tragedy hier in der Stadt Moskau furgefallen auff Montag, Dienstag undt Mitwochen, den 15, 16 undt 17 May jetzigen 1682-ten Jahres', in N.G. Ustrialov, *Istoriia tsarstvovaniia Petra Velikogo*, vol. 1 (Moscow, 1858), p. 330 (henceforth, Butenant). Published as *Eigentlicher Bericht wegen des in der Stadt Moskau am 15/16 und 17 May Anno 1682 enstanden greulichen Tumults und grausahmen Massacre* (Hamburg, 1682), and in a slightly revised version as 'Relation der traurigen Tragödie in der Stadt Moscau', *Theatrum Europaeum*, 12 (1691), 441-50. An English translation from Ustrialov, checked against a copy of the MS (Rigsarkivet, Copenhagen, Tyske Kancelli, Udenrigske Afdelung, Russland 40),

is J. Keep, 'Mutiny in Moscow 1682: A Contemporary Account', *Canadian Slavonic Papers*, 23 (1981), 410–42.

10. Medvedev, pp. 40–1. Medvedev, a pupil and later associate of Simeon Polotsky, was one of the most educated Russians of his era. Unfortunately he clashed with the Patriarch (see Chapter 6, below) and was executed in 1691 after Sophia's downfall. For a short summary of his life and work, see my entry in *MERSH*, 21 (1981), pp. 180–2. A recent Soviet account is A.P. Bogdanov, 'Sil'vestr Medvedev', *Voprosy istorii*, 1988, no. 2, 84–98.

11. Butenant, p. 330.

12. See the indictment issued on 30 April 1682, in *Vosstanie*, pp. 20–1.

13. Butenant, p. 331.

14. See J. Keep, *Soldiers of the Tsar: Army and Society in Russia 1462–1874* (Oxford, 1985), ch. 3; L. Hughes, 'Strel'tsy', *MERSH*, 37 (1984), 205–10.

15. On the 'new model army', see p. 10, 110.

16. V.I. Buganov, *Moskovskie vosstaniia vtoroi poloviny XVII v.* (*Avtoreferat st. doktora istoricheskikh nauk*) (Moscow, 1968), p. 24.

17. G.A. Schleissing, *Derer beyden Czaaren in Reussland* (n.p., 1694), pp. 15–16. For more on this writer, see below, pp. 265–6.

18. F. de la Neuville, *Relation curieuse et nouvelle de Moscovie* (The Hague, 1699), p. 152. This comment is missing from 'Récit de mon voyage' (Paris, Bibliothèque Nationale, Département des Manuscrits, NAF 5114).

19. J. Korb, *Diary of an Austrian Secretary of Legation at the Court of Czar Peter the Great*, ed. and trans. Count MacDonnell, vol. 2 (London, 1963), pp. 114–15. For more on Korb, see below, pp. 252–5.

20. *The Present State of Russia* (1729), in *For God and Peter the Great. The Works of Thomas Consett 1723–1729*, ed. J. Cracraft (Boulder, Col., 1982), p. xxvi.

21. S.M. Solov'ev, *Istoriia Rossii s drevneishikh vremen*, vols 13–114 (Moscow, 1962), p. 264 (henceforth, Solov'ev).

22. H. Troyat, *Peter the Great* (London,

1987), p. 13. (Translated from *Pierre le Grand* (Paris, 1979))

23. A.A. Matveev, 'Zapiski Andreia Artamonovicha grafa Matveeva', in N. Sakharov (ed.), *Zapiski russkikh liudei. Sobytiia vremen Petra Velikogo* (St Petersburg, 1841), p. 6 (henceforth, Matveev). Matveev (1666–1728) was the son of Artamon Sergeevich, the favourite of Tsar Aleksei and guardian of his second wife. See A.D. Liublinskaia, *Russkii diplomat vo Frantsii. (Zapiski Andreia Matveeva)* (Leningrad, 1972), and below, pp. 266–7.

24. *Diariusz*, p. 6.

25. This is one of many errors in this account. Artamon Matveev did not arrive back in Moscow for another fortnight.

26. *Diariusz*, p. 7.

27. See E. Shmurlo, 'Pol'skii istochnik o votsarenii Petra Velikogo', *ZhMNP*, 1902, no. 2, 424–48.

28. 'Kniga zapisnaia tsaria i velikovo kniazia Petra Alekseevicha v 190 godu', *Vosstanie*, p. 11. This account, dated 27 April to 25 May, was compiled in the Crown Appointments Department (Razriad). (Henceforth, 'Kniga zapisnaia'.)

29. Buganov, *Moskovskie vosstaniia*, p. 139.

30. 'Narratio rerum', in S. Ciampi, *Bibliografia critica*, vol. 1 (Florence, 1834), p. 77.

31. Korb, *Diary*, vol. 2, pp. 115–16.

32. *Podrobnaia letopis' ot nachala Rossii do Poltavskoi batalii*, part 4 (St Petersburg, 1799), p. 81. According to Buganov, *Moskovskie vosstaniia*, p. 13, this account was compiled at the end of Peter I's reign.

33. I. Zabelin, *Domashnii byt russkogo naroda*, vol. 2 (Moscow, 1901), p. 155.

34. Butenant, p. 331.

35. Ibid., p. 332.

36. 'Kniga zapisnaia', p. 14.

37. Butenant, p. 331.

38. On popular images of rulership, see M. Cherniavsky, *Tsar and People: Studies in Russian Myths* (New Haven and London, 1961).

39. Butenant, p. 332.

40. Ibid., p. 333.

41. 'Letopisets 1619–1691', *Polnoe sobranie russkikh letopisei*, vol. 31

(Moscow, 1968), p. 189. V.I.
Buganov believes that this account
was written by an eyewitness from
one of the Kremlin cathedrals or
churches. See his 'Novye materialy
o moskovskikh vosstaniiakh', *Istoricheskii arkhiv*, 1961, no. 1, 151–3.
42. 'Kniga zapisnaia', p. 15.
43. For rumours about Ivan Naryshkin,
see *Diariusz*, p. 8; 'Narratio rerum',
p. 78.
44. Butenant, p. 334.
45. *Diariusz*, p. 11.
46. 'Letopisets', p. 189.
47. B. Tanner, 'Opisanie puteshestviia
pol'skogo posol'stva v Moskvu v 1678
g.', *Chteniia*, 1891, book 3, section
III, p. 127. Tanner accompanied a
Polish delegation that came to Russia
for peace negotiations in 1678. The
appended letter was dated 30 May,
1682.
48. *Diariusz*, pp. 7–8.
49. Belov, 'Keller', p. 382.
50. Matveev, pp. 10–11.
51. *Vosstanie*, p. 22.
52. Butenant, p. 333.
53. Matveev, p. 16.
54. Butenant, p. 334.
55. Matveev, pp. 12–14. (Buganov,
*Moskovskie vosstanie*, p. 137, points
out that Rodimitsa was not Sophia's
maid but Tsarita Marfa Matveevna's.)
56. See note 23, above.
57. See R.G. Skrynnikov, 'Boris
Godunov's Struggle for the Throne',
*Canadian – American Slavic Studies*,
11 (1977), 325–53.
58. Medvedev, p. 52.
59. 'Letopisets', p. 197.
60. *Diariusz*, p. 8.
61. Matveev, p. 19.
62. Butenant, p. 334.
63. Medvedev, p. 52.
64. Contemporary accounts not already
referred to above are as follows: V.I.
Buganov, 'Novyi istochnik o moskovskom vosstanii 1682 g.', *Issledovaniia
po otechestvennomu istochnikovedeniiu*
(Leningrad, 1964), pp. 318–23
(anonymous author, probably a
commercial scribe); 'Zapisnaia kniga
razriadnogo prikaza za 15 maia –
konets dek. 1682', in *Vosstanie*,
pp. 276–82 (compiled in the Crown
Appointments Department; entitled
'smutnoe vremia'); 'Mazurinskii

letopisets', *Polnoe sobranie russkikh
letopsei*, vol. 31 (Moscow, 1968),
pp. 11–179 (see M.N. Tikhomirov,
'Zapiski prikaznykh liudei kontsa
XVII veka', *TORDL*, 12 (1956),
442–57); 'Podennye zapisi ochevidtsa moskovskogo vosstaniia 1682
goda', pub. A. Bogdanov, *Sovetskie
arkhivy*, 1979, no. 2, 34–7 (the
author probably served in one of the
patriarchal offices).
65. Matveev, p. 20.
66. Butenant, p. 334.
67. Matveev, p. 19.
68. Ibid., pp. 21–2.
69. Butenant, p. 334.
70. *Diariusz*, p. 9.
71. 'Smutnoe vremia', p. 277.
72. In the strel'tsy petition to the government of c. 6 June, sixteen persons
are specifically named. See below,
pp. 71–2.
73. Matveev, p. 22.
74. *Diariusz*, p. 9.
75. Butenant, p. 336.
76. *Diariusz*, p. 9.
77. There are several versions of how
Dolgoruky was killed. See *Diariusz*,
pp. 9–10; Matveev, pp. 26–7; Butenant, p. 336.
78. Keep, 'Mutiny', p. 430, note 26;
Matveev, p. 24.
79. *Vosstanie*, p. 41.
80. See O.F. Kozlov, 'Khovanshchina',
*Voprosy istorii*, 1971, no. 8, 203;
S.K. Bogoiavlenskyi, 'Khovanshchina', *Istoricheskie zapiski*, 10 (1941),
180–221.
81. Butenant, pp. 340, 342.
82. Ibid., p. 336.
83. Ibid., p. 337.
84. Matveev, p. 31.
85. Butenant, p. 339.
86. *Diariusz*, p. 11.
87. Medvedev, p. 58.
88. Matveev, p. 30.
89. La Neuville, *Relation curieuse et nouvelle de Moscovie* p. 152. This remark is absent from 'Récit de mon
voyage'.
90. Butenant, p. 339.
91. 'Letopisets', p. 196.
92. Butenant, p. 344.
93. Ibid.
94. See 'Kniga zapisnaia', p. 18.
95. For an analysis of factions and affiliations in 1682, see R.O. Crummey,
*Aristocrats and Servitors: The Boyar*

Elite in Russia 1613–1689 (Princeton, 1983), pp. 88–97; Bogoiavlensky, 'Khovanshchina', passim.

96. Diariusz, p. 13.
97. 'Mazurinskii letopisets', p. 451.
98. Medvedev, pp. 59–60.
99. Butenant, p. 341.
100. Keep, 'Mutiny', p. 435.
101. Medvedev, p. 60.
102. Ibid., pp. 61–2.
103. Ibid., p. 65.
104. Ibid., p. 66.
105. Ibid., p. 67.
106. A.P. Bogdanov, Pamiatniki obshchestvenno-politicheskoi mysli v Rossii XVII veka. Literaturnye panegiriki (Moscow, 1983), p. 262; 'Sil'vestr Medvedev', 89–90. See also, L. Hughes, 'Sophia, "Autocrat of All the Russias"', Canadian Slavonic Papers, 28 (1986), 267–70.
107. See A.P. Bogdanov, 'K istorii teksta "Sozertsaniia kratkogo"', Issledovaniia po istochnikovedeniiu istorii dooktiabr'skogo perioda (Moscow, 1983); 'K voprosu ob avtorstve "Sozertsaniia kratkogo"', ibid. (Moscow, 1987). On other aspects of the proposed coronation, see below, pp. 140–4.
108. 'Mazurinskii letopisets', p. 176; 'Letopisets', p. 199. See note 41, above.
109. 'Smutnoe vremia', p. 279; 'Zapiski razriadnogo prikaza', p. 257.
110. Sobranie gosudarstvennykh gramot i dogovorov, khraniashchikhsia v. gos. kollegii inostrannykh del, vol. 4 (Moscow, 1828), no. 147, pp. 443–5; PSZ, vol. 2, no. 920, pp. 398–401.
111. Matveev, p. 34.
112. See, for example, PSZ, vol. 2, no. 998, p. 503.
113. PSZ, vol. 2, no. 928, p. 410–11.
114. See Hughes, 'Sophia, "Autocrat of All the Russias"'.
115. Buganov, Moskovskie vosstaniia, p. 143.
116. Vosstanie, no. 207, p. 279.
117. 'Mazurinskii letopisets', p. 176.
118. Vosstanie, no. 207, p. 280.
119. Ibid. Here the petition is dated 14 June; 'Mazurinskii letopisets', p. 176, has two entries for the event, 5 June and a date after 14 June.
120. Vosstanie, no. 27, p. 50 (28 June), and no. 28, pp. 50–1 (30 June). The name was changed back to

Strel'tsy Department on 17 December 1682. See ibid., no. 185, p. 238.

121. Ibid., no. 20, p. 36.
122. Ibid., p. 37.
123. Ibid.
124. Ibid.
125. Ibid., p. 39.
126. Ibid., no. 21, pp. 40–6. This document forms the basis for the reconstruction of no. 20, note 121, above, which exists only in a defective mid-eighteenth-century copy.
127. Ibid., p. 45.
128. Bogoiavlensky, 'Khovanshchina', p. 199.
129. Vosstanie, no. 36, p. 57.
130. Bogoiavlensky, 'Khovanshchina', p. 197.
131. Account of these meetings by the cellarer Savva Romanov, a supporter of Nikita, 'Istoriia o vere i chelobitnaia o strel'tsakh Savvy Romanova', Letopisi russkoi literatury i drevnosti, ed N. Tikhonravov, 5 (1863), part II, 111–48. Quoted here from Solov'ev, p. 278.
132. Zhitie protopopa Avvakuma im samim napisannoe i drugie ego sochineniia, ed. N.K. Gudzi (Moscow, 1960), p. 371. But a note on p. 371 identifies the victim as Ivan Ivanovich Khovansky. More recently, V.S. Rumiantseva, Narodnoe antitserkovnoe dvizhenie v Rossii v XVII veke (Moscow, 1986), pp. 191–2, 234, claims that Khovansky had dealings with and protected dissidents, including Nikita Dobrynin, whilst Governor of Novgorod. The evidence, however, appears in the report of an interrogation conducted in August 1683. See also E. Belov, 'Moskovskie smuty v kontse XVII veka', ZhMNP, 1887, no. 1, 135–6.
133. Solov'ev, p. 279.
134. E.V. Barsov, 'Drevnerusskie pamiatniki sviashchennogo venchaniia', Chteniia, 1883, book 1, p. xxxi.
135. See, for example, G. Edward Orchard (ed.), Massa's Short History of the Muscovite Wars (Toronto, 1982), pp. 131–3.
136. Solov'ev, p. 340.
137. Akty, sobrannye v bibliotekakh i arkhivakh Rossiiskoi imperii arkheograficheskoiu ekspeditsieu imp. Akademii nauk, vol. 4 (St Petersburg, 1836), no. 257, p. 368 (henceforth, AAE).

138. Account of the coronation in Solov'ev, pp. 343–7. See also *Drevniaia rossiiskaia vivliofika,* vol. 6 (St Petersburg, 1788), pp. 403–77.
139. Solov'ev, p. 345.
140. *Vosstanie,* no. 204, p. 261; Solov'ev, pp. 344–7. See below pp. 101–2, for more on the politics of promotions.
141. Bogoiavlensky, 'Khovanshchina', p. 209.
142. Ibid.
143. Romanov, 'Istoriia', p. 136.
144. Ibid.
145. [Archbishop Afanasy of Kholmogory], *Uvet dukhovnyi* (Moscow, 1682).
146. Medvedev, p. 84.
147. Solov'ev, p. 287.
148. Romanov, 'Istoriia', p. 139.
149. Medvedev, p. 34.
150. Bogoiavlensky, 'Khovanshchina', p. 208.
151. Matveev, p. 42.
152. *Diariusz,* p. 25.
153. Alexander Gordon, *The History of Peter the Great, Emperor of Russia,* vol. 2 (Aberdeen, 1755), p. 88.
154. Bogoiavlensky, 'Khovanshchina', pp. 214–15.
155. Matveev, p. 40.
156. Ibid., p. 38.
157. Bogoiavlensky, 'Khovanshchina', p. 211.
158. Ibid., p. 212.
159. *Vosstanie,* p. 295.
160. Bogoiavlensky, 'Khovanshchina', p. 213.
161. *Vosstanie,* no. 46, p. 66.
162. Ibid., no. 48, pp. 68–9.
163. *Dvortsovye razriady,* vol. 4 (St Petersburg, 1855), pp. 192–4.
164. There are discrepancies over the date of departure. The records of the Razriad, *Vosstanie,* no. 63, p. 79, give 20 August; 30 August, given in ibid., no. 204, p. 262, is clearly an error.
165. Ibid., no. 63, p. 79.
166. Ibid., p. 80.
167. Ibid., no. 86, p. 132.
168. Medvedev, p. 94.
169. *Vosstanie,* no. 86, pp. 132–3.
170. Ibid., no. 207, p. 280.
171. Ibid., no. 68, p. 112.
172. Ibid., no. 74, pp. 120–1 (dated 9 September).
173. Ibid., no. 69, pp. 113–17 (dated between 6 and 10 September).
174. Ibid., no. 77, pp. 123–4.
175. 'Mazurinskii letopisets', p. 177.
176. *Vosstanie,* no. 63, p. 82.
177. Ibid., p. 83.
178. Ibid., p. 85.
179. Ibid.
180. Ibid., no. 67, pp. 110–11. Also published in *AAE,* vol. 4, no. 258, pp. 368–9; Medvedev, pp. 98–9. On authenticity, see editors' note, *Vosstanie,* p. 298. Buganov, *Moskovskie vosstaniia kontsa XVII veka,* p. 266, writes: 'The majority of historians deny the authenticity of the letter.' Similarly, Bogoiavlensky, 'Khovanshchina', p. 216. There are discrepancies over dates in documents: 20 August in *Vosstanie,* no. 207, p. 280, is implausible; 8 September, ibid., no. 102, p. 149, probably an error.
181. Matveev, p. 43.
182. BL Sloane 3036 (2). In the catalogue this was wrongly described as 'a copy of a letter from Czars Ivan Alekseevich . . . and Peter Alekseevich . . . to their sister Sophia, complaining that Kneez Chovanki had committed acts by her authority without their order'. The copy of the letter of denunciation is actually appended to a later document. See below, note 197.
183. In the original: 'Vruchit' gosudaryne tsarevne Sofii Alekseevne, ne rospechatav'.
184. 'Mazurinskii letopisets', p. 178.
185. *Vosstanie,* no. 63, p. 86.
186. The death sentence is in *Vosstanie,* no. 86, pp. 130–3.
187. Matveev, p. 45.
188. *Vosstanie,* no. 63, p. 86.
189. Bogoiavlensky, 'Khovanshchina', pp. 212–13.
190. Solov'ev, p. 295.
191. *Vosstanie,* no. 63, p. 86.
192. Ibid., p. 89.
193. Ibid., p. 92.
194. Ibid., no. 93, pp. 138–9; no. 95, p. 144.
195. Bogoiavlensky, 'Khovanshchina', p. 219.
196. *Vosstanie,* no. 63, p. 101.
197. Ibid., no. 102, pp. 149–50: 'The tsars' charter to the Moscow artisans in praise of their "loyalty" to the government during the rebellion'.

The document ends 'and a copy of that letter [of denunciation] is sent to you with this our royal charter for your information'. It was this dual document that found its way into Engelbert Kämpfer's possession. See above, note 67.

198. Ibid., no. 111, p. 157.
199. Ibid., no. 122, pp. 168–70.
200. Ibid., no. 63, p. 98.
201. Ibid., no. 152, pp. 193–6. On the discovery of the relic, reported to Sophia by the Patriarch on 11 September, see *Dopolneniia k aktam istoricheskim*, vol. 10 (St Petersburg, 1872), no. 39.
202. *Vosstanie*, no. 152, p. 195.
203. Ibid., no. 63, pp. 104–6.
204. Ibid., no. 171, pp. 218–9.
205. Ibid., no. 172, p. 225.
206. Ibid., no. 174, p. 226.
207. 'Mazurinskii letopisets', p. 179.
208. *Vosstanie*, no. 178, p. 232.
209. Ibid., no. 171, p. 224.

## CHAPTER 4: THE INNER CIRCLE

1. M.I. Semevsky, *Tsaritsa Praskov'ia 1664–1723* (St Petersburg, 1861), p. 2.
2. F. de la Neuville, *An Account*, p. 103. Ivan was not twenty-eight until 1694, but this account of Muscovy in 1689 was not published until 1698, and the author was generally inaccurate on ages. In 'Récit de mon voyage' (Paris, Bibliothèque Nationale, Département des Manuscrits, NAF 5114), f. 51, the comment on Ivan appears in a marginal note.
3. H. Butenant, 'Warhaftige Relation der traurigen undt schrecklichen Tragedy hier in der Stadt Moskau furgefallen auff Montag, Dienstag undt Mitwochen, den 15, 16 undt 17 May jetzigen 1682–ten Jahres', in N.G. Ustrialov, *Istoriia tsarstvovaniia Petra Velikogo*, vol. 1 (Moscow, 1858), pp. 331, 332 (henceforth, Butenant).
4. 'Narratio rerum', in S. Ciampi, *Bibliografia critica*, vol. 1 (Florence, 1834), p. 76.
5. E. Kämpfer, 'Diarium itineris ad aulam Moscoviticam indeque Astracanum suscepti anno MDCLXXIII',

from the extract published in K. Meier-Lemgo, *Englebert Kämpfer, der erste deutsche Forschungsreisende 1651–1716* (Stuttgart, 1937), p. 13. Another version is printed in F. Adelung, *Augustin Freiherr von Meyerberg und seine Reise nach Russland* (St Petersburg, 1827), pp. 321–71. The texts differ, no doubt because of the poor state of the original MS (BL Sloane 2923), e.g. the remark on ages appears only in Adelung, *Meyerberg*, p. 349. As the latter, who saw the diary in 1814, noted, the MS was 'completely illegible in many places'. The language he described as 'clumsy and barbaric' German with frequent Latin insertions (p. 335). A recent inspection of the MS confirms these remarks.
6. Meier-Lemgo, *Kämpfer*, pp. 14–15.
7. Unless otherwise stated, quotations from Gordon's diary are taken from the transcript of the original, Tsentral'nyi Gosudarstvennyi Voenno-Istoricheskii Arkhiv, f. 846, op. 15, ed. Khr. 1–7. There is a German translation, *Tagebuch des Generals Patrick Gordon, während seiner Kriegsdienste unter den Schweden und Polen vom Jahre 1655 bis 1661, und seines Aufenthaltes in Russland vom Jahre 1661 bis 1699*, ed. M.A. Obolenski and M.C. Posselt, 3 vols (Moscow and Leipzig, 1849), in which this quotation appears in vol. 2, p. 11.
8. Quoted in F. Adelung, *Kritisch-literärische Übersicht der Reisenden in Russland bis 1700*, vol. 2 (St Petersburg and Leipzig, 1846), pp. 370–1. For more on Hövel, see below, p. 187.
9. L. Rinhuber, *Relation du voyage en Russie fait en 1684 par Laurent Rinhuber* (Berlin, 1883), p. 230.
10. G.A. Schleissing, *Derer beyden Czaaren in Reussland* (n.p., 1694), opp. p. 39.
11. Ibid., p. 10.
12. *Vosstanie v Moskve 1682 g. Sbornik dokumentov*, ed. V.I. Buganov and N.G. Savich (Moscow, 1976), no. 204, p. 255 (henceforth *Vosstanie*).
13. Silvester Medvedev, 'Sozertsanie let kratkoe 7190, 91 i 92, v nikh zhe chto sodeiasia vo grazhdantsve', *Chteniia*, 1894, book 4, section II, p. 61.

14. I.A. Zheliabuzhsky, 'Zapisi Ivana Afanas'evicha Zheliabuzhskogo', in N. Sakharov (ed.), *Zapiski russkikh liudei. Sobytiia vremen Petra Velikogo* (St Petersburg, 1841), p. 2. The author (b.1638), who served in government departments and on diplomatic missions, wrote in an annalistic style, apparently in a regularly kept diary.

15. A.A. Matveev, 'Zapiski Andreia Artamonovicha grafa Matveeva', in N. Sakharov (ed.), *Zapiski russkikh liudei. Sobytiia vremen Petra Velikogo* (St Petersburg, 1841), pp. 6–7 (henceforth, Matveev).

16. P.N. Krekshin, 'Kratkoe opisanie blazhennykh del velikogo gosudaria, imperatora Petra Velikogo', in N. Sakharov (ed.), *Zapiski russkikh liudei. Sobytiia vremen Petra Velikogo* (St Petersburg, 1841), p. 26. This author's eulogistic accounts of Peter's reign were written mostly in the 1740s.

17. See M.P. Pogodin, *Semnadtsat' pervykh let v zhizni Imperatora Petra Velikogo. 1672–1689* (Moscow, 1875), p. 101, and R. Wittram, *Peter I, Czar und Kaiser*, vol. 1 (Göttingen, 1964), p. 81.

18. W. Bruce Lincoln, *The Romanovs* (London, 1981), p. 58.

19. See E.S. Ovchinnikova, *Portret v russkom iskusstve XVII veka* (Moscow, 1955).

20. M.M. Bogoslovsky, *Petr I. Materialy dlia biografii*, vol. 1 (Moscow, 1940), p. 54.

21. On these and other allegorical engravings, see below, pp. 140–2.

22. See, for example, R.K. Massie, *Peter the Great: His Life and World* (London, 1981), between pp. 210 and 211.

23. N.N. Voronin and V.V. Kostochkin (eds), *Troitse-Sergieva Lavra. Khudozhestvennye pamiatniki* (Moscow, 1968), p. 110, plate 124.

24. See Semevsky, *Tsaritsa Praskov'ia*; *Drevniaia rossiiskaia vivliofika*, vol. 11 (St Petersburg, 1872), pp. 177–9.

25. La Neuville, *Relation curieuse et nouvelle de Moscovie*, p. 162; 'Récit de mon voyage', f. 41.

26. Krekshin, 'Kratkoe opisanie blazhennykh del velikogo gosudaria', p. 8.

27. La Neuville, *Relation curieuse et nouvelle de Moscovie*, p. 116; 'Récit de mon voyage', f. 34.

28. J. Banks, *A New History of the Life and Reign of the Czar Peter the Great, Emperor of All Russia, and Father of His Country* (London, 1740), p. 48.

29. *Vosstanie*, no. 45, p. 65.

30. *Diariusz zaboystwa tyranskiego senatorow moskiewskich w stolicy roku 1682 y o obraniu dwoch carow Ioanna y Piotra* (St Petersburg, 1901), p. 13 (henceforth, *Diariusz*).

31. Prince B.I. Kurakin, 'Gistoriia o tsare Petre Alekseeviche 1682–1694', in *Rossiiu podnial na dyby ... Istoriia otechestva v romanakh, povestiakh, dokumentakh. Veka XVII–XVIII*, vol. 1 (Moscow, 1987), p. 369.

32. On Golitsyn, see above, pp. 48 ff.

33. See above, ibid.

34. See below, Chapter 5, pp. 109–11, on Golitsyn as reformer.

35. See R.O. Crummey, *Aristocrats and Servitors: The Boyar Elite in Russia 1613–1689* (Princeton, 1783), ch. 4, and lists on pp. 203–5.

36. See above, Chapter 2, note 91.

37. *Polnoe sobranie zakonov Rossiiskoi imperii*, vol. 2 (St Petersburg, 1830), no. 358, p. 471; no. 1134, p. 687 (henceforth, *PSZ*).

38. Matveev, p. 12.

39. S.K. Bogoiavlensky, 'Khovanshchina', *Istoricheskie zapiski*, 10 (1941), p. 192.

40. Ibid., table pp. 190–1; and *Prikaznye sud'i XVII veka* (Moscow, 1946).

41. *Dvortsovye razriady*, vol. 4 (St Petersburg, 1855), pp. 234, 242, 267, 268, etc.

42. The fact that Miloslavsky 'fell', but continued to be honoured, is confirmed by Kurakin, 'Gristoriia o tsare Petre Alekseeviche', p. 363.

43. See *MERSH* 16 (1980), 175–6.

44. S.M. Solov'ev, *Istoriia Rossii s drevneishikh vremen*, vols. 13–14 (Moscow, 1962), p. 262.

45. Crummey, *Aristocrats and Servitors*, pp. 204–5.

46. Matveev, p. 6.

47. Bogoiavlensky, 'Khovanshchina', p. 192.

48. See Crummey, *Aristocrats and Servitors*, pp. 202–5; Solov'ev, pp. 346–8.

49. Crummey, *Aristocrats and Servitors*, pp. 94, 204. P.S. Khitrovo became

50. See my entry in *MERSH*, 34 (1985), 146–8.
51. See A.N. Robinson (ed.), *Simeon Polotskii i ego knigoizdatel'skaia deiatel'nost'* (Moscow, 1982), pp. 48, 58.
52. On Medvedev, see above, p. 54 note 10.
53. See above pp. 69–70.
54. *Diariusz*, p. 13.
55. *PSZ*, vol. 2, no. 998, p. 513.
56. See for example, the royal letter of 9 June 1682 to Charles II in PRO 102/49, no. 47.
57. 'Die Gantze Beschreibung Reusslandts' (1687), trans. L. Lapteva as 'Rasskaz ochevidtsa o zhizni Moskovii kontsa XVII veka', *Voprosy istorii*, 1970, no. 1, 111.

## CHAPTER 5: DOMESTIC POLICY

1. Prince B.I. Kurakin, 'Gistoriia o tsare Petre Alekseeviche 1682–1694', in *Rossiiu podnial na dyby. Istoriia otechestva v romanakh, povestiakh, dokumentakh. Veka XVII–XVIII*, vol. 1, (Moscow, 1987), pp. 364–5.
2. N. Ustrialov, *Istoriia tsarstvovaniia Petra Velikogo*, vol. 1 (St Petersburg, 1858), p. 99.
3. C.B. O'Brien, *Russia under Two Tsars 1682–1689* (Berkeley and Los Angeles, 1952), p. x.
4. *Istoriia sotsarstviia v Rossii (1682–89 gg.), sostavlennaia po vernym istochnikam* (St Petersburg, 1837), p. iv.
5. Z. Schakovskoy, *Precursors of Peter the Great* (London, 1964), p. 224.
6. 'Il vouloit peupler des déserts, enrichir des gueux, de sauvages en faire des hommes, de poltrons des braves, et d'habitations de pastres des palais de pierre' (quoted from F. de la Neuville, 'Récit de mon voyage' (Paris, Bibliothèque Nationale, Département des Manuscrits, NAF 5114), f. 46); *Relation curieuse et nouvelle de Moscovie* (The Hague, 1699), p. 178. For a discussion of this work, see below, pp. 264–5.
7. See *The Muscovite Law Code (Ulozhenie) of 1649, Part 1: Text and Translation*, trans. and ed. R. Hellie (Irvine, 1988).
8. J. Blum, *Lord and Peasant in Russia from the Ninth to the Nineteenth Centuries* (Princeton, 1961), pp. 233–4.
9. *Polnoe sobranie zakonov Rossiiskoi imperii*, vol. 2 (St Petersburg, 1830), no. 1074, pp. 590–616 (April 1684) (henceforth, *PSZ*).
10. Ibid., no. 926, pp. 404–5 (2 July 1682).
11. Ibid., no. 938, pp. 450–1 (7 July 1682).
12. Ibid., no. 1013, pp. 522–34 (20 May 1683).
13. Ibid., no. 1019, pp. 538–9 (8 July 1683).
14. Ibid., no. 1192, pp. 798–800 (9 July 1686).
15. Ibid., no. 1297, p. 930 (25 May 1688).
16. Ibid., no. 1008, pp. 519–21 (25 April 1683); no. 1078, p. 623 (26 May 1684).
17. Ibid., no. 1236, pp. 848–50 (February 1687).
18. Ibid., no. 930, pp. 411–12 (20 June 1682).
19. Ibid., no. 937, p. 450 (7 July 1682); no. 949, pp. 459–60 (7 August 1682); no. 1132, pp. 678–87 (27 August 1685).
20. Ibid., vol. 5, no. 2789.
21. See, for example, ibid., vol. 2, no. 940, p. 451 (11 July 1682: to strel'tsy captains); no. 941, pp. 451–2 (to palace attendants); no. 961, pp. 472–5 (25 October 1682: for the Trinity campaign); no. 1155, pp. 721–2 (to table attendants and crown agents). On rewards for the Crimean campaigns, see below, pp. 203–4, 216–7.
22. *PSZ*, vol. 2, no. 1147, pp. 704–18 (24 December 1685).
23. See Blum, *Lord and Peasant in Russia*, p. 267.
24. *PSZ*, vol. 2, no. 1138, p. 689 (30 October 1683).
25. Ibid., no. 952, pp. 462–3 (29 August 1682).
26. Ibid., no. 1099, pp. 644–5 (16 December 1684).
27. R. Hellie, *Slavery in Russia 1450–1715* (Chicago, 1982), p. 697.
28. For a discussion, see R. Hellie, *Enserfment and Military Change in Muscovy* (Chicago, 1971), p. 257.
29. *PSZ*, vol. 2, no. 992, pp. 499–500

(13 February 1683).

30. Ibid., no. 998, pp. 503–13 (2 March 1683).

31. Ibid., no. 985, pp. 491–2 (3 January 1683); no. 1072, pp. 586–8 (8 April 1683).

32. See A.A. Novosel'sky, (ed.), *Ocherki istorii SSSR, Period feodalizma, XVII vek* (Moscow, 1955), p. 328.

33. 'Comme le dessein de ce prince estoit de mettre cet Estat sur le mesme pied des autres, il avoit fait venir des mémoires de tous les Estats de l'Europe et de leur gouvernement. Il voulut commencer par afranchir les paisans et leur abandonner les terres qu'ils cultivent au profit du Czar moyennant un tribut annuel qui par la suputation qu'il en avoit fait augmentoit par an le revenu de ces Princes de plus de la moitié'. (La Neuville 'Récit de mon voyage', f. 56; *Relation curieuse et nouvelle de Moscovie*, p. 215.)

34. La Neuville, *Relation curieuse et nouvelle de Moscovie*, p. 177. On the mansion, see below pp. 159, 176–7. For discussions of Golitsyn as reformer, see L.A.J. Hughes, *Russia and the West* (Newtonville, Mass., 1984), pp. 91–2; I. de Madariaga, 'Who was Foy de la Neuville?', *Cahiers du monde russe et soviétique*, 28 (1987), 21–30; V.I. Buganov, '"Kantsler" predpetrovskoi pory', *Voprosy istorii*, 1971, no. 10, 154–5; M.Ia. Volkov, 'O stanovlenii absoliutizma v Rossii', *Istoriia SSSR*, 1970, no. 1, 101–2.

35. On Spafarius see D.T. Ursul, *Nikolai Milesku Spafarii* (Kishinev, 1985).

36. A.S. Lavrov, 'Zapiski o Moskovii de la Nevillia', *Vestnik Leningradskogo Universiteta. Seriia 2. Istoriia, iazyk, literatura*, 1986, no. 4, 89–90. On Golitsyn's library, see below, p. 170.

37. 'Son dessein estoit de changer en bons soldats les légions de païsans dont les terres demeurent incultes quand on les menne à la guerre, et au lieu de ce service inutile à l'Estat imposer sur chaque teste une somme raisonnable' (La Neuville, 'Récit de mon voyage', f. 46; *Relation curieuse et nouvelle de Moscovie*, p. 175.)

38. See J. Keep, *Soldiers of the Tsar: Army and Society in Russia 1462–1874* (Oxford, 1985); Hellie, *Enserfment.*, pp. 181 ff.

39. See J. Keep, 'The Muscovite Elite

and the Approach to Pluralism', *SEER*, 48 (1970), 201–31; S.M. Solov'ev, *History of Russia*. Vol. 25. *Rebellion and Reform. Fedor and Sophia, 1682–1689*, trans. and ed. L.A.J. Hughes (Gulf Breeze, 1989), pp. 89–90.

40. O'Brien, *Russia under Two Tsars*, p. 51.

41. PSZ, vol. 2, no. 1002, p. 515 (22 March 1683).

42. Ibid., no. 970, p. 481 (28 November 1682).

43. Ibid., no. 1004, p. 516 (30 March 1683).

44. Ibid., vol. 3, no. 1335, p. 15 (19 February 1689).

45. *Sobornoe ulozhenie 1649 goda. Tekst. Kommentarii*, comp. A.G. Man'kov et al. (Leningrad, 1987), p. 387.

46. See below, pp. 121 ff.

47. *Dopolneniia k aktam istoricheskim*, vol. 11 (St Petersburg, 1872), no. 11, iii (27 April 1684) (henceforth, *DAI*).

48. PSZ, vol. 2, no. 948, p. 459 (7 August 1682).

49. Ibid., no. 1140, pp. 689–99 (11 November 1685).

50. Ibid., no. 1146, pp. 707–8 (23 December 1685).

51. Ibid., no. 1158, pp. 734–5 (22 January 1686); no. 1166, pp. 741–2 (23 February 1686); no. 1172, p. 748 (4 March 1686).

52. Ibid., no. 1257, p. 883 (14 August 1687).

53. See Keep, 'The Muscovite Elite', p. 229.

54. Blum, *Lord and Peasant in Russia*, p. 205.

55. PSZ, vol. 2, no. 1064, pp. 576–8 (26 February 1684).

56. Ibid., no. 1100, pp. 645–7 (19 December 1684). Also *Sobranie gosudarstvennykh gramot i dogovorov, khraniashchikhsia v gos. kollegii inostrannykh del*, vol. 4 (Moscow, 1828), no. 167, pp. 487–8.

57. Ibid., no. 1095, pp. 641–2 (23 October 1684).

58. Ibid., no. 1096, p. 642 (1 December 1684).

59. Ibid., no. 1097, pp. 642–3 (7 December 1684).

60. Ibid., no. 984, pp. 490–1 (3 January 1683).

61. Ibid., no. 1181, p. 765 (19 March 1686).

62. Ibid., no. 977, pp. 485–6 (29 December 1682); no. 989, p. 493 (18 January 1683); no. 1276, pp. 905–8 (8 February 1688), etc.
63. *DAI*, vol. 11, no. 11, iv (30 June 1684).
64. *PSZ*, vol. 2, no. 976, p. 485 (18 December 1682).
65. Ibid., no. 1089, pp. 638–9 (29 August 1684). Also *Akty, sobrannye v bibliotekakh i arkhivakh Rossiiskoi imperii arkheograficheskoiu ekspeditsieiu imp. Akademii nauk*, vol. 4 (St Petersburg, 1836), no. 281, p. 416.
66. *Akty istoricheskie, sobrannye i izdannye arkheograficheskoiu kommissieiu*, vol. 5 (St Petersburg, 1842), no. 75, pp. 108–30 (November 1681).
67. *DAI*, vol. 10, no. 27, p. 77 (19 August 1684).
68. *PSZ*, vol. 2, no. 1101, p. 647 (24 December 1684).
69. Ibid., no. 956, p. 468 (7 October 1682).
70. For Tolstoi's observations and an excellent introduction to late Muscovite sensibility, see *The Travel Diary of Peter Tolstoy. A Muscovite in Early Modern Europe*, ed. and trans. M.J. Okenfuss, (De Kalb, Illinois, 1987).
71. See Hellie, *Slavery in Russia*.
72. G.A. Schleissing, 'Die Gantze Beschreibung Reusslandts' (1687), trans. L.P. Lapteva as 'Rasskaz ochevidtsa o zhizni Moskovii kontsa XVII veka', *Voprosy istorii*, 1970, no. 1, 107.
73. *PSZ*, vol. 2, no. 1133, p. 687 (1 September 1685); no. 1314, pp. 949–50 (3 October 1688).
74. On architecture, see below pp. 150 ff.
75. 'Mazurinskii letopisets', *Polnoe sobranie russkikh letopisei*, vol. 31 (Moscow, 1968) p. 179.
76. *PSZ*, vol. 2, no. 1054, p. 568 (11 December 1683).
77. Ibid., no. 1181, pp. 760–6 (19 March 1686).
78. Ibid., no. 1315, p. 950 (3 October 1688).
79. La Neuville, *Relation curieuse et nouvelle de Moscovie*, pp. 177, 179–80.
80. Ibid., p. 221.
81. 'Il vouloit faire la mesme chose des Cabarets et des autres ventes et denrées croyant par cette conduite rendre ces peuples laborieux et industrieux par l'espérance de s'enrichir'. (La Neuville, 'Récit de mon voyage',

f. 56 (and following directly the quotation in note 33 above)). A. Lavrov believes that Golitsyn's ideas on the reduction of government monopolies may have been influenced by Iury Krizhanich, a copy of whose work *Politika* the prince owned ('Zapiski o Moskovii', p. 89).
82. *PSZ*, vol. 2, no. 1263, p. 300 (13 October 1687).
83. See S.H. Baron, 'Entrepreneurs and Entrepreneurship in 16th–17th-Century Russia', in G. Guroff and F. Carstensen (eds.), *Entrepreneurship in Imperial Russia and the Soviet Union* (Princeton, 1983), pp. 27–58.
84. *PSZ*, vol. 2, no. 1129, pp. 675–7 (14 July 1685). This act also has information on customs duties and the weighing of coin.
85. La Neuville, 'Récit de mon voyage', f. 55.
86. *PSZ*, vol. 2, 1082, p. 626 (3 June 1684).
87. See below, Chapter 8.
88. See copies of royal letters in PRO, SP104/119, ff. 21–2 (24 November 1682), and ff. 48 rev.–50 (4 December 1687): 'We are encouraged not only to desire, but with some confidence to hope, that at Our request Your Imperial Majesties will think fit to restore unto Our subjects trading to, and in Your Imperial Majesties' Dominions all those privileges and rights which were granted unto them by Your Imperial Majesties' ancestors . . .' On the Postnikov mission of 1687, see below, pp. 194–5.
89. See E. Lermontova, 'Shelkovaia fabrika v pravlenie tsarevny Sof'i Alekseevny', *Zapiski otdeleniia russkoi i slavianskoi arkheologii Imp. Russkogo arkheologicheskogo obshchestva*, 10 (1915), 43–74. Documents in *DAI*, vol. 10, no. 51, pp. 173–95.
90. Lermontova, 'Shelkovaia fabrika', p. 56.
91. Ibid., pp. 69–70.
92. La Neuville, 'Récit de mon voyage', f. 45; *Relation curieuse et nouvelle de Moscovie*, p. 174.
93. *DAI*, vol. 10, no. 74, pp. 312–13; vol. 9, no. 31, pp. 109–13.
94. O'Brien, *Russia under Two Tsars*, p. 76.
95. *PSZ*, vol. 2, no. 1121, pp. 669–71 (20 May 1685).

96. See, for example, ibid., nos. 961, 998, 1050, 1051, etc.

## CHAPTER 6: RELIGIOUS AFFAIRS

1. See listings in *Dvortsovye razriady*, vol. 4 (St Petersburg, 1855); L.A.J. Hughes, 'Sophia "Autocrat of All the Russias"', *Canadian Slavonic Papers*, 28 (1986), 265–86. For an eyewitness account of the Epiphany ceremony, see Georgius David, *Status Modernus Magnae Russiae seu Moscoviae* (1690), ed. A.V. Florovskij (The Hague, 1965), pp. 115–17. On ritual, see R.O. Crummey, 'Court Spectacles in Seventeenth-Century Russia', in D.C. Waugh (ed.), *Essays in Honour of A.A. Zimin* (Columbus, 1985), pp. 130–58.
2. *Polnoe sobranie zakonov Rossiiskoi imperii*, vol. 2 (St Petersburg, 1830), no. 1186, pp. 770–86 (26 April/6 May 1686) (henceforth, *PSZ*). On foreign policy, see below, pp. 192 ff.
3. *Russkoe slovo*, 11 (1852), 421–2.
4. *PSZ*, vol. 2, no. 1186, p. 777.
5. On the lengthy negotiations, which involved securing the blessing of the ecumenical patriarchs, including the Patriarch of Constantinople himself, see S.M. Solov'ev, *Istoriia Rossii s drevneishikh vremen*, vols. 13–14 (Moscow, 1962), pp. 382–7 (henceforth, Solov'ev). Documents in *PSZ*, vol. 2, no. 1144, pp. 702–7 (15 December 1685: the new Metropolitan's charter of rights); no. 1191, pp. 795–7 (May 1686: letter to Patriarch Dionisius from the tsars and Sophia); no. 1196, pp. 805–7 (June 1686: from the Greek hierarchs).
6. See below, pp. 192 ff.
7. M. Cherniavsky, 'The Old Believers and the New Religion', *Slavic Review*, 25 (1966), 20. On the beginning of the schism, see above, pp. 11–13.
8. Cherniavsky, 'The Old Believers', p. 13.
9. *Akty istoricheskie, sobrannye i izdannye arkheograficheskoiu kommissieiu*, vol. 5 (St Petersburg, 1842), no. 75, pp. 108–18.
10. Cherniavsky, 'The Old Believers', note 33.
11. V.S. Rumiantseva, *Narodnoe antitser-*

*kovnoe dvizhenie v Rossii v XVII veke* (Moscow, 1986), pp. 235–42 (documents).
12. Ibid., p. 191. The traditional Orthodox cross had eight points, produced by the addition of bars above and below.
13. Ibid., p. 240.
14. G.A. Schleissing, 'Die Gantze Beschreibung Reusslandts' (1687), trans. L.P. Lapteva as 'Rasskaz ochevidtsa o zhizni Moskovii kontsa XVII veka', *Voprosy istorii*, 1970, no. 1, 117–18.
15. *PSZ*, vol. 2, no. 1102, pp. 647–50 (1685). See discussion in J. Cracraft, *The Church Reform of Peter the Great* (London, 1971), pp. 74–5.
16. Solov'ev, pp. 428–9.
17. *Dopolneniia k aktam istoricheskim*, vol. 12 (St Petersburg, 1872), no. 17, p. 122.
18. Ibid., pp. 126–8.
19. Ibid., vol. 11, no. 17, p. 205.
20. Cracraft, *Church Reform*, p. 186.
21. Ibid., p. 65.
22. *PSZ*, vol. 2, no. 1117, pp. 662–3 (5 April 1685).
23. Ibid., no. 1163, pp. 738–9 (7 February 1686).
24. Ibid., no. 1025, pp. 543–8 (June 1683).
25. Ibid., no. 973, p. 483 (1 December 1682).
26. Ibid., no. 1210, pp. 817–20 (20 September 1686).
27. Ibid., no. 1089, pp. 638–9 (29 August 1684).
28. L.R. Lewitter, 'The Russo-Polish Treaty of 1686 and Its Antecedents', *Polish Review*, 9 (1964), no. 3, 18.
29. On the Zierowski mission, see below, pp. 187–8.
30. A.V. Florovskij in introduction to David, *Status Modernus*, p. 9. See below, note 34.
31. P. Gordon, *Tagebuch des Generals Patrick Gordon, während seiner Kriegsdienste unter der Schweden und Polen vom Jahre 1655 bis 1661, und seines Aufenthaltes in Russland vom Jahre 1661 bis 1699*, ed. M.A. Obolenski and M.C. Posselt, vol. 3 (Moscow and Leipzig, 1849), p. 13.
32. Vota did much behind the scenes to secure Russia's alliance with Poland. See A. Theiner (comp.), *Monuments historiques relatifs aux règnes d'Alexis Michaélowitch, Fédor III et Pierre le*

Grand Czars de Russie extraits des archives du Vatican et de Naples (Rome, 1859), pp. 282–3; Lewitter, 'Russo-Polish Treaty', no. 4, p. 137.

33. Theiner, *Monuments historiques*, p. 295.
34. David left two accounts of his time in Moscow: *Status Modernus*, and 'Brevis Relatio revolutionis in regno Moscovitico', in J.S. Gagarin, *Peter Gagarins Neueste Studieen* (Stuttgart, 1857), pp. 154–77, the latter written immediately after his expulsion. 'Sovremennoe sostoianie velikoi Rusi ili Moscovii', *Voprosy istorii*, 1968, no. 1, pp. 123–32; no. 3, pp. 92–7; and no. 4, pp. 138–47, is an annotated translation of *Status Modernus*. On Jesuits in Russia, see A.V. Florovskij, *Češti jesuité na Rusi* (Prague, 1941).
35. David, 'Brevis Relatio', p. 164.
36. A. Olearius, *The Travels of Olearius in 17th-Century Russia*, trans. and ed. S.H. Baron (Stanford, Calif., 1967), pp. 282–3.
37. See A. Pypin, 'Inozemtsy v Moskovskoi Rossii', *Vestnik Evropy*, 1888, no. 1, pp. 275–6.
38. 'Slovo na Latinov i Liuterov: iako v Moskovskem tsarstvii i vo vsei Rossiiskei Zemli ne podobaet im kostela ili kerki ereticheskikh svoikh ver sozidati', *Chteniia*, 1884, book 3, pp. 12–13.
39. David, *Status Modernus*, p. 69.
40. See P. Smirnov, *Ioakhim – patriarkh moskovskii* (Moscow, 1881). On Joachim's publications, see below, p. 166.
41. Quoted from original.
42. *Materialy dlia istorii roda dvorian Savelovykh*, vol. 2 (Ostrogozhsk, 1896), p. 40.
43. Ibid., p. 43.
44. Ibid., p. iii.
45. On Polotsky, see above, pp. 33 ff.
46. Solov'ev, p. 532. Polotsky was actually educated in the Kiev Academy, an Orthodox institution. But see below, p. 129, on allegations of Ukrainian 'heresy'.
47. On Polotsky's works and printing press, see below, pp. 168, 171.
48. A.P. Bogdanov, 'Sil'vestr Medvedev', *Voprosy istorii*, 1988, no. 2, p. 96.
49. David, 'Brevis Relatio', p. 156.
50. *Diariusz zaboystwa tyranskiego senato-row moskiewskich w stolicy roku 1682 y o obraniu dwoch carow Ioanna y Piotra* (St Petersburg, 1901), p. 5 (henceforth *Diariusz*).
51. 'Narratio rerum', in S. Ciampi, *Bibliografia critica*, vol. 1 (Florence, 1834), p. 78.
52. See E. Belov, 'Moskovskie smuty v kontse XVII veka', *ZhMNP*, 1877, no. 1, 106.
53. A. Prozorovsky, *Sil'vestr Medvedev. Ego zhizn' i deiatel'nost'* (Moscow, 1896), pp. 389–93.
54. On Medvedev's library, see below, p. 171.
55. See T. Ware, *The Orthodox Church* (London, 1964), pp. 291 ff.
56. Bogdanov, 'Sil'vestr Medvedev', p. 95.
57. On the debate about schools, see below, pp. 161 ff.
58. Bogdanov, 'Sil'vestr Medvedev', p. 93.
59. 'Khleb zhivotnyi': text in Prozorovsky, 'Sil'vestr Medvedev', pp. 415–30.
60. 'Pokazanie na podverg latinskogo mudrovaniia': ibid., pp. 430–4; Bogdanov, 'Sil'vestr Medvedev', p. 93.
61. 'Oproverzhenie latinskogo ucheniia o presushchestvlenii': Prozorovsky, pp. 434–50; Bogdanov, 'Sil'vestr Medvedev', pp. 93–4.
62. Kniga o manne khleba zhivotnogo': Prozorovsky, 'Sil'vestr Medvedev', pp. 475–538 (this quotation, p. 480).
63. Bogdanov, 'Sil'vestr Medvedev', p. 95.
64. Prozorovsky, 'Sil'vestr Medvedev', pp. 538–77.
65. Bogdanov, 'Sil'vestr Medvedev', p. 95.
66. Ibid., p. 95.
67. A.P. Bogdanov, *Pamiatniki obshchestvenno-politicheskoi mysli v Rossii XVII veka* (Moscow, 1983), p. 30.
68. See *Rozysknye dela o Fedore Shaklovitom i ego soobshchnikakh*, 4 vols (St Petersburg, 1884–93).
69. David, *Status modernus*, p. 67.
70. Ibid., p. 32.
71. F. de la Neuville, *Relation curieuse et nouvelle de Moscovie* (The Hague, 1699), p. 161. 'Et pour rendre leur marriage plus agréable à tout le monde, ils feroient elire pour patriarche le père Sylvestre, moine polonois, et grec de religion, et homme très habile qui aussi tost proposeroit une

ambassade à Rome pour la réunion' ('Récit de mon voyage' (Paris, Bibliothèque Nationale, Département des Manuscrits, NAF 5114), ff. 41–2).

72. David, *Status Modernus*, p. 71. The 'heretics' were primarily Prussians, who made a number of inroads into Russia in 1688–9.

73. *PSZ*, vol. 3, no. 1351, pp. 39–40 (October 1689).

74. David, *Status Modernus*, pp. 67–8.

75. *Sobranie gosudarstvennykh gramot i dogovorov, khraniashchikhsia v. gos. kollegii inostrannykh del*, vol. 4 (Moscow, 1828), no. 207, p. 62.

76. *PSZ*, vol. 3, no. 1358, p. 48.

77. On the Kuhlmann case see, J. Billington, *The Icon and the Axe* (London, 1966), pp. 171–5.

78. See D.V. Tsvetaev, *Istoriia sooruzheniia pervogo kostela v Moskve* (Moscow, 1885).

79. *PSZ*, vol. 2, no. 1186, p. 777.

80. D.V. Tsvetaev, 'Protestantstvo v Rossii v pravlenie Sofii', *Russkii vestnik*, 1883, no. 11, pp. 53–5.

81. See below, pp. 208–9.

82. *PSZ*, vol. 3, no. 1331, pp. 8–9 (21 January 1689). See below, p. 209.

83. *Diariusz*, p. 13.

84. On works by Polotsky in Sophia's collection, see below, p. 171.

85. *Drevniaia rossiiskaia vivliofika*, vol. 10 (St Petersburg, 1791), pp. 424–5.

86. E. Shmurlo, 'Padenie ts. Sof'i', *ZhMNP*, 1896, no. 1, p. 55.

87. P. Longworth, *Alexis, Tsar of All the Russias* (London, 1984), pp. 231, 234.

# CHAPTER 7: CULTURE

1. *Polnoe sobranie zakonov Rossiiskoi imperii*, vol. 1 (St Petersburg, 1830), p. 607 (henceforth, *PSZ*).

2. On Moscow Baroque in general, see bibliography in L. Hughes, 'Moscow Baroque Architecture: A Study of One Aspect of Westernisation in Late-Seventeenth-Century Russia' (unpublished PhD thesis, Cambridge University, 1976), and my essay 'Moscow Baroque: A Controversial Style', *Transactions of the Association of Russian–American Scholars in USA*, 15 (1982), 69–93. In Russian, A.I. Nekrasov (ed.), *Barokko v Rossii*

(Moscow, 1926); M.A. Il'in, 'Problema "moskovskogo barokko" XVII v.', *Ezhegodnik instituta istorii iskusstv. 1956* (Moscow, 1957), pp. 324–9; T.V. Alekseeva (ed.), *Russkoe barokko. Materialy i issledovaniia* (Moscow, 1977). An illustrated survey, and still the authoritative Soviet work on the subject, is I.E. Grabar' (ed.), *Istoriia russkogo iskusstva*, vol. 4 (Moscow, 1959) (henceforth, *IRI* (1959)). There are few reliable general works in English on seventeenth-century Russian art and culture. J. Billington, *The Icon and the Axe* (London, 1966), pp. 116 ff, still offers one of the best surveys. See also G.H. Hamilton, *The Art and Architecture of Russia* (London, 1983), and note 101, below. The term 'Naryshkin Baroque' is sometimes used interchangeably with 'Moscow Baroque' but the former properly dates from the period beginning immediately after Sophia's overthrow when members of the Naryshkin faction erected a number of churches in the new style.

3. The literature on Western Baroque is vast. See, for example, H.A. Millon, *Baroque and Rococo Architecture* (London, 1968); R. Wittkower, *Art and Architecture in Italy 1600–1750* (London, 1958); H. Wölfflin, *Renaissance and Baroque* (London, 1964). The latter, first published in 1888, influenced some of the early commentators on Moscow Baroque.

4. See D.S. Likhachev, *Razvitie russkoi literatury XV–XVII vekov* (Leningrad, 1972), p. 207; 'Barokko i ego russkie varianty XVII veka', *Russkaia literatura*, 1969, no. 2, 41; 'XVII vek v russkoi literature', in Iu. Vipper (ed.), *XVII vek v mirovom literaturnom razvitii* (Moscow, 1969), pp. 299–328. See also L. Hughes, 'The 17th-Century "Renaissance" in Russia: Western Influences in Art and Architecture', *History Today*, February 1980, 41–5.

5. I.D. Davydova, 'Esteticheskie predstavleniia russkikh liudei XVII stoletiia', *Problemy istorii SSSR*, 7 (1978), 31–3.

6. B.V. Mikhailovsky and B.I. Purishev, *Ocherki istorii drevnerusskoi monumental'noi zhivopisi so vtoroi*

*poloviny XIV do nachala XVIII veka* (Moscow and Leningrad, 1941), pp. 92, 95, 113.

7. G.K. Vagner, *Kanon i stil' v drevnerusskom iskusstve* (Moscow, 1987), p. 273.

8. On the Armoury, see L. Hughes, 'The Moscow Armoury and Innovations in 17th-Century Muscovite Art', *Canadian–American Slavic Studies*, 13 (1979), 204–23 (with bibliography). See also above, p. 10.

9. E.S. Ovchinnikova, *Portret v russkom iskusstve XVII veka* (Moscow, 1955), p. 31.

10. A. Viktorov, *Opisanie zapisnikh knig i bumag starinnykh dvortsovykh prikazov. 1613–1725*, vol. 2 (Moscow, 1883), pp. 452–3.

11. Ovchinnikova, *Portret*, p. 31.

12. O.S. Evangulova, *Izobrazitel'noe iskusstvo v Rossii v pervoi chetverti XVIIIv.* (Moscow, 1987), p. 173. See also Hughes, 'The Moscow Armoury', pp. 210–11. The term *perspektivy* seems to have originated in Russian in reference to theatrical scenery.

13. V.G. Briusova, *Fedor Zubov* (Moscow, 1985), p. 199. This document lists materials issued for the work (21 August 1686) to the 'master of perspective' to paint 'Biblical subjects in perspective' (*preospektivnye roznye pritchi*).

14. See Hughes, 'The Moscow Armoury', p. 211.

15. Ibid.

16. On Bezmin, see A.I. Uspensky, 'Ivan Artem'evich Bezmin i ego proizvedeniia', *Starye gody*, April 1908, 198–206.

17. V.G. Briusova, *Russkaia zhivopis' XVII veka* (Moscow, 1984), p. 54; Ovchinnikova, *Portret*, pp. 86–99.

18. 'And in the same month of November on the 26th day in the fourth hour of the day during mass by the will of God the royal apartments of Tsar Peter Alekseevich caught fire, and the apartments of the Tsaritsa and the tsarevny all burned down' ('Mazurinskii letopisets', in *Polnoe sobranie russkikh letopisei*, vol. 31 (Moscow, 1968), p. 179).

19. Viktorov, *Opisanie*, pp. 450–1. No. 964, 'Prikhodnaia i raskhodnaia

knigi', deals with work carried out from 1 December 1684 to 31 August 1685.

20. N.A. Skvortsov, *Arkheologiia i topografiia Moskvy. Kurs lektsii* (Moscow, 1913), p. 446, gives 1809 as the year of demolition. See also descriptions in I. Zabelin, *Materialy dlia istorii, arkeohologii i statistiki g. Moskvy*, vol. 1 (Moscow, 1884), pp. 1283–1337 (a description of the 'decaying' Kremlin palace, made in 1722), and note 23, below.

21. Briusova, *Zubov*, p. 147.

22. Ibid., p. 196.

23. I. Zabelin, *Domashnii byt russkogo naroda*, vol. 1 (Mocow, 1895), pp. 185–7.

24. Ibid., pp. 187–90. See also Viktorov, *Opisanie*, p. 451; Briusova, *Zhivopis'*, p. 53.

25. A. Uspensky, *Tsarskie ikonopistsy i zhivopistsy XVII veka*, vol. 2 (Moscow, 1911), p. 190.

26. Briusova, *Zubov*, p. 196; *Zhivopis'*, p. 53.

27. *IRI* (1959), p. 406.

28. Evangulova, *Izobrazitel'noe iskusstvo*, p. 172.

29. Uspensky, *Tsarskie ikonopistsy*, p. 55.

30. The murals of the princes and tsars of the Royal House of Moscow were painted in the 1650s.

31. On the early Russian portrait, see Ovchinnikova, *Portret*; A.P. Novitsky, 'Parsunnoe pis'mo Moskovskoi Rusi', *Starye gody*, July–September, 1909, 384–403; S.B. Mordvinova, 'Istoriko-khudozhestvennye predposylki vozniknoveniia i razvitiia portreta v XVII veke', in T.V. Alekseeva (ed.), *Ot Srednevekov'ia k Novomu vremeni* (Moscow, 1984), pp. 9–35. The term *parsuna* denotes a 'naive', often icon-like portrait.

32. Quoted in Evangulova, *Izobrazitel'noe iskusstvo*, p. 118.

33. Reproduced in *IRI* (1959), p. 451.

34. See above, p. 10.

35. Evangulova, *Izobrazitel'noe iskusstvo*, p. 71.

36. G.V. Esipov (comp.), *Sbornik vypisok iz arkhivnykh bumag o Petre Velikom*, vol. 1 (Moscow, 1872), p. 57 (16 March 1685). See illustration 36 in Briusova, *Zhivopis'*. See also Briusova, *Zubov*, p. 198.

37. Evangulova, *Izobrazitel'noe iskusstvo*,

p. 123.
38. Ovchinnikova, *Portret*, pp. 86–99. *IRI* (1959), pp. 453–5, dates the painting *c.*1667, and tentatively attributes it to Wuchters.
39. See M.I. Semevsky, 'Sovremennye portrety Sofii Alekseevny i V.V. Golitsyna. 1689', *Russkoe slovo*, 1859, no. 12, 411–58; M.A. Alekseeva, 'Portret tsarevny Sof'i', *Pamiatniki kul'tury. Novye otkrytiia* (Moscow, 1976), pp. 240–9; A.P. Bogdanov, 'Politicheskaia graviura v Rossii perioda regentstva Sof'i Alekseevny', *Istochnikovedenie otechestvennoi istorii. 1981* (Moscow, 1982), pp. 225–46; L. Hughes, 'Portraits of Tsarevna Sof'ia Alekseevna', *Study Group on 18th-Century Russia Newsletter* 14 (1986), 3–4.
40. See Briusova, *Zhivopis'*, ill. 17.
41. See N. Antushev, *Istoricheskoe opisanie Moskovskogo Novodevich'ego monastyria* (Moscow, 1885), p. 52.
42. *Blagodat' i istina*. See Bogdanov, 'Politicheskaia graviura', pp. 231–4; M.A. Alekseeva, 'Zhanr konkliuzii v russkom iskusstve kontsa XVII – nachala XVIII v.', in T.V. Alekseeva (ed.), *Russkoe barokko. Materialy i issledovaniia* (Moscow, 1977), pp. 7–29. For a good reproduction, see D.A. Rovinsky, *Materialy dlia russkoi ikonografii*, vol. 1 (Moscow, 1884), plate 3.
43. Bogdanov, 'Politicheskaia graviura', pp. 231–4. On Shchirsky, see D. Stepovik, *Ivan Shchir'skii* (Kiev, 1988).
44. See below, pp. 168 ff.
45. On the link between poetry and graphic art, see V.A. Grikhin, 'Simeon Polotskii i Simon Ushakov', in A.V. Lipatov (ed.), *Barokko v slavianskikh kul'turakh* (Moscow, 1982), pp. 191–219.
46. See below, pp. 193 ff.
47. *Rozysknye dela o Fedore Shaklovitom i ego soobshchnikakh*, vol. 1 (St Petersburg, 1884), pp. 596–7, 655–62, etc.
48. Ibid.; Bogdanov, 'Politicheskaia graviura', pp. 238–9.
49. On Tarasevich, see D.A. Rovinsky, *Podrobnyi slovar' russkikh gravirovannykh portretov*, vol. 2 (St Petersburg, 1889), pp. 982–8.
50. *Rozysknye dela*, vol. 1, p. 660.
51. See, for example, D.A. Rovinsky, *Podrobnyi slovar russkikh graverov XVII–XIXvv.*, vol. 1 (St Petersburg, 1895), p. 68; vol. 2, (p. 1232; Alekseeva, 'Zhanr konkliuzii', pp. 15–16, ill. 3.
52. Bogdanov, 'Politicheskaia graviura', p. 240 ('Not one example of this engraving has survived').
53. For an illustration, see Alekseeva, 'Portret', p. 244.
55. In Russian: *devstvo, pravosudie, krotost', blagochestie, milost', krepost'*.
55. See Ovchinnikova, *Portret*, plates IV and V. I.M. Kudriavtsev, '"Izdatel'skaia" deiatel'nost' Posol'skogo prikaza', *Kniga. Issledovaniia i materialy*, 8 (1963), 189, 206.
56. Ovchinnikova, *Portret*. plates IV and V.
57. Bogdanov, 'Politicheskaia graviura', p. 225.
58. 'Filled with wisdom from God on high / adorned with the crown of piety and virginity / she dispenses true graciousness and justice / she has marvellous firmness combined with mildness. / By these seven virtues have you won fame / and have fortified the tsardom as with seven pillars / By them are you famed throughout the world / and will be praised for ages to come.' Text in Alekseeva, 'Portret', p. 242.
59. Reproduced in ibid.; Rovinsky, *Materialy*, vol. 1, no. 2.
60. Bogdanov, 'Politicheskaia graviura', p. 243. For Alekseeva's different chronology, see 'Portret', p. 241.
61. The virtues are *magnanimitas, liberalitas, pietas, prudentia, pudicitia, justita, spes divina*. For the verses, see below, p. 169.
62. Reproduced in Alekseeva, 'Portret', p. 243; Rovinsky, *Materialy*, vol. 1, no. 1. The latter describes it as 'taken from Tarasevich's original'. Prints were available at 30 kopeks each. On Catherine and Sophia, see below, pp. 268–9.
63. Ovchinnikova, *Portret*, p. 103.
64. Normally, of course, the reverse procedure was followed. Ovchinnikova (ibid., p. 105) believes that the two may have been commissioned simultaneously. See also Rovinsky, *Podrobnyi slovar'* (1889), vol. 2, p. 988.

65. Reproduced in Alekseeva, 'Portret', p. 247.
66. I.K. Kondrat'ev, *Sedaia starina Moskvy* (Moscow, 1893), p. 681.
67. R.K. Massie, *Peter the Great: His Life and World* (London, 1981), p. 79.
68. Rovinsky, *Materialy*, vol. 1, no. 15. Inscribed: 'A Paris chez Bonnart au coq-rue St. Jaques avec privil'.
69. Ibid., no. 5 (taken from the 1693 Zittau edition of the work). On Schleissing, see pp. 265–6.
70. Rovinsky, *Materialy*, vol. 1, no. 4; Rovinsky, *Podrobnyi slovar'* (1889), p. 968. On other portraits of Golitsyn, see L. Hughes, *Russia and the West: The Life of a Seventeenth-Century Westernizer Prince Vasily Vasil'evich Golitsyn (1643–1714)* (Newtonville, Mass., 1984), pp. 101–2.
71. Bogdanov, 'Politicheskaia graviura', p. 236.
72. See A.A. Novosel'sky (ed.), *Ocherki istorii SSSR. Period feodalizma. XVII vek* (Moscow, 1955), p. 535.
73. *Rozysknye dela*, vol. 4, pp. 3–5, 101, 19, 56. No portrait of Sophia is mentioned, but he did have the nameday saints of the royal family and an icon of the Holy Wisdom.
74. Evangulova, *Izobrazitel'noe iskusstvo*, p. 19. Matveev, who had a Scottish wife, also had Westernised tastes in furnishings, clocks and theatricals, as well as an impressive collection of foreign books.
75. Briusova, *Zhivopis'*, plate 58.
76. Bogdanov, 'Politicheskaia graviura', pp. 242–4; Rovinsky, *Podrobnyi slovar'* (1889), p. 987; *Materialy*, vol. 5, no. 174.
77. Ovchinnikova, *Portret*, pp. 99–100; *IRI* (1959), p. 463.
78. Quoted in Hughes, 'The Moscow Armoury', p. 208. For general surveys of icon-painting during this period, see Briusova, *Zhivopis'*; L. Hughes, 'The Age of Transition: 17th-Century Russian Icon-Painting', *Icons 88* (Dublin, 1988), pp. 63–74; M.V. Alpatov, 'Problema barokko v russkoi ikonopisi', in A.I. Nekrasov (ed.), *Barokko v Rossii* (Moscow, 1926), pp. 81–92.
79. Briusova, *Zubov*, pp. 146–7.
80. Ibid., pp. 149, 156, ills 11–12.
81. Ibid., p. 155.
82. A.P. Bogdanov, *Pamiatniki obshchestvenno-politicheskoi mysli v Rossii XVII veka. Literaturnye panegiriki* (Moscow, 1983), pp. 233–41.
83. On panegyric literature, see below, pp. 167 ff.
84. On Ushakov, see G. Filimonov, *Simon Ushakov i sovremennaia emu epokha russkoi ikonopisi* (Moscow, 1873); Briusova, *Zhivopis'*, pp. 40–2. In English, my entry in *MERSH*, 41 (1985), 119–21.
85. On collaboration with Polotsky, see note 45, above.
86. N.G. Bekeneva, *Simon Ushakov* (Leningrad, 1984), p. 54.
87. Briusova, *Zubov*, p. 198.
88. See ibid.
89. See below, p. 155.
90. Ill. 30 in Briusova, *Zhivopis'*.
91. Ibid., pp. 54–5. On Foreign Office architectural projects, see below, p. 157.
92. The church at Fili has recently been restored and opened to the public as a branch of the State Historical Museum.
93. Briusova, *Zhivopis'*, ills 137–41.
94. Ibid., ill. 158.
95. Ibid., ill. 43.
96. Ibid., p. 29.
97. L. Ouspensky and V. Lossky, *The Meaning of Icons* (New York, 1982), pp. 47–8.
98. Evangulova, *Izobrazitel'noe iskusstvo*, p. 174.
99. See above, p. 11.
100. *Akty, sobrannye v bibliotekakh i arkhivakh Rossiiskoi imperii arkheograficheskoiu ekspeditsieiu imp. Akademii nauk*, vol. 4 (St Petersburg, 1836), p. 200.
101. See references in note 1, above. Also, B. Vipper, *Arkhitektura russkogo barokko* (Moscow, 1978), and J. Cracraft, *The Petrine Revolution in Russian Architecture* (Chicago, 1988).
102. *PSZ*, vol. 2, no. 1133, p. 687, and no. 1314, pp. 249–50.
103. F. de la Neuville, *Relation curieuse et nouvelle de Moscovie* (The Hague, 1699), pp. 177, 178–9; 'Récit de mon voyage' (Paris, Bibliothèque Nationale, Département des Manuscrits, NAF 5114), f. 46.
104. See N.F. Gulianitsky, 'O svoeobrazii i preemstvennykh sviaziakh ordernogo iazyka v russkoi arkhitekture',

*Arkhitekturnoe nasledstvo*, 23 (1975), 14–29.

105. N.Ia. Tikhomirov and V.I. Ivanov, *Moskovskii kreml'* (Moscow, 1967), p. 84. *Dopolneniia k aktam istoricheskim*, vol. 11 (St Petersburg, 1872), no. 90, ii, p. 243 (henceforth, *DAI*).

106. *DAI*, vol. 11, no. 90, ii, p. 243 (3 July, 1686).

107. Zabelin, *Materialy*, vol. 1, p. 186.

108. Quoted in I.M. Snegirev, *Russkaia starina*, 15, 146. On the Novodevichy Convent (now a branch of the State Historical Museum) see Antushev, *Istoricheskoe opisanie*; L.S. Retkovskaia, *Novodevichii monastyr'. Putevoditel' po muzeiu* (Moscow, 1964); Iu. Ovsyannikov, *Novodevichii monastyr'* (Moscow, 1968).

109. For the full text, see below, p. 169.

110. L. Hughes, 'Byelorussian Craftsmen in Late-17th-Century Russia', *Journal of Byelorussian Studies* (1976), 327–41.

111. Ibid., p. 335.

112. For excellent illustrations of this and other buildings, see W. Brumfield, *Gold in Azure. One Thousand Years of Russian Architecture* (Boston, 1983).

113. Zabelin, *Materialy*, vol. 1, p. 805.

114. Ibid., p. 803. On the iconostasis, made by Karp Zolotar'ev, see *DAI*, vol. 11, no. 90, p. 242.

115. E.g. V.P. Vygolov, 'Tvorchestvo zodchego O.D. Startseva' (unpublished dissertation, Moscow University, 1955), p. 16.

116. A.N. Chiniakov, 'Arkhitekturnye pamiatniki Izmailova', *Arkhitekturnoe nasledstvo*, 2 (1952), 193–220.

117. See Z.E. Kalishevich, 'Khudozhestvennaia masterskaia Posol'skogo prikaza v XVII v. i rol' zolotopistsev v ee sozdanii i deiatel'nosti', in N.V. Ustiugov (ed.), *Russkoe gosudarstvo v XVII veke* (Moscow, 1961), pp. 392–411.

118. N. Gorchakov, *Opisanie Donskogo monastyria v Moskve* (Moscow, n.d.), p. 5.

119. The most famous was Ivan Zarudny, who built, amongst other things, the iconostasis for the Peter–Paul Cathedral in St Petersburg. As argued elsewhere, contemporary Ukrainian seventeenth-century architecture, with its preference for stucco work rather than high relief decoration, for pilasters rather than columns (twisted columns hardly occur) and for a vertical articulation, is easily distinguishable from Muscovite. See Hughes, 'Moscow Baroque Architecture', pp. 141, 151–2.

120. See N.N. Voronin (ed.), *Troitse-Sergieva Lavra. Khudozhestvennye pamiatniki* (Moscow, 1968).

121. See Archimandrite Leonid, *Istoricheskoe opisanie Stavropigial'nogo Voskresenskogo Novyi Ierusalim imenuemogo monastyria* (Moscow, 1876).

122. *Dvortsovye razriady*, vol. 4 (St Petersburg, 1855), pp. 321–2 (14–21 January).

123. M.A. Il'in, *Podmoskov'e* (Moscow, 1965), p. 216.

124. Leonid, *Istoricheskoe opisanie*, p. 70.

125. L. Hughes, 'Western European Graphic Material as a Source for Moscow Baroque Architecture', *Slavonic and East European Review*, 55 (1977), 433–43.

126. S. Belokurov, *O biblioteke moskovskikh gosudarei v XVI stoletii* (Moscow, 1898), p. 74.

127. I.E. Grabar', 'Drevnie doma Golitsyna i Troekurova v Okhotnom riadu', *Stroitel'stvo Moskvy*, 10 (1925), 11–15.

128. *Rozysknye dela*, vol. 3, pp. 219–22.

129. G.K. Vagner, 'O proiskhozhdenii tsentricheskikh kompozitsii v russkom zodchestve XVII veka', *Pamiatniki kul'tury*, 3 (1961), 131.

130. *IRI* (1959), p. 247. Data on churches in the Moscow region taken also from V. and G. Kholmogorovy, *Istoricheskie materialy o tserkvakh i selakh XVI–XVIII st.* (Moscow, 1886).

131. Kholmogorovy, *Istoricheskie materialy*, vol. 5, p. 58.

132. *IRI* (1959), p. 249.

133. Ibid., p. 251.

134. S.V. Bezsonov, *Krepostnye arkhitektory* (Moscow, 1938), pp. 77–8.

135. O.I. Braitseva, 'Konstruktivnye osobennosti arkhitekturnykh detalei Vvedenskogo sobora', *Arkhitekturnoe nasledstvo*, 14 (1962), 105–8.

136. M.A. Il'in, *Riazan'* (Moscow, 1954), pp. 87–96.

137. *IRI* (1959), pp. 259, 263; Hughes, 'Moscow Baroque Architecture', pp. 75–88.

138. Cracraft, *The Petrine Revolution in Russian Architecture*, p. 107.
139. S. Collins, *The Present State of Russia* (London, 1671), p. 2.
140. On Polotsky, see above, pp. 22, 33 etc.
141. See A.I. Rogov, 'Shkola i prosveshchenie', in A.V. Artsikhovsky (ed.), *Ocherki russkoi kul'tury XVII veka*, vol. 2 (Moscow, 1979), p. 142.
142. G.A. Schleissing, *Derer beyden Czaaren in Reussland* (n.p., 1694), p. 126.
143. S.M. Solov'ev, *Istoriia Rossii s drevneishikh vremen*, vols. 13–14 (Moscow, 1962), pp. 179–80 (henceforth, Solov'ev).
144. Rogov, 'Shkola', p. 150.
145. A.P. Bogdanov, 'Sil'vestr Medvedev', *Voprosy istorii*, 1988, no. 2, p. 92.
146. Ibid. The text of the 'Akademicheskaia privilegiia' (not to be confused with the 'appeal' of 1685, discussed below (see note 154)) is in *Drevniaia rossiiskaia vivliofika*, vol. 6 (St Petersburg, 1788), pp. 390–420.
147. Solov'ev, p. 257.
148. Bogdanov, *Pamiatniki*, p. 276.
149. Rogov, 'Shkola', p. 152.
150. Ibid., p. 150. Bogdanov believes that Medvedev's school was opened 'at the same time as or a little earlier than Timothy's' ('K polemike kontsa 60x – nachala 80x godov XVII v.', *Issledovaniia po istochnikovedeniiu istorii SSSR XIII–XVIII v.v.* (Moscow, 1986), p. 194).
151. Quoted in F. Adelung, *Augustin Freiherr von Meyerberg und seine Reise nach Russland* (St Petersburg, 1827), p. 363.
152. Bogdanov, 'K polemike', p. 193.
153. Ibid., p. 198.
154. Text in A. Prozorovsky, *Sil'vestr Medvedev. Ego zhizn'i deiatel'nost'* (Moscow, 1896), pp. 383–8; and A.I. Panchenko (ed.), *Russkaia sillabicheskaia poeziia XVII–XVIII v.v.* (Leningrad, 1970), pp. 191–7.
155. Bogdanov, *Pamiatniki*, p. 267.
156. See M. Smentskovsky, *Brat'ia Likhudy* (St Petersburg, 1899), and V.L. Fonkich, 'Novye materialy dlia biografii Likhudov', *Pamiatniki kul'tury: novye otKrytiia*, 1987 (1988), 61–70.
157. S. Smirnov, *Istoriia Slaviano-greko-latinskoi akademii* (Moscow, 1855).
158. Bogdanov, 'Sil'vestr Medvedev', p. 94.
159. G. David, *Status Modernus Magnae Russiae seu Moscoviae (1690)*, ed. A.V. Florovskij (The Hague, 1965), p. 106.
160. G. David, 'Sovremennoe sostoianie velikoi Rusi ili Moskovii', *Voprosy istorii*, 1968, no. 4, p. 147.
161. Bogdanov, 'Sil'vestr Medvedev', p. 95.
162. La Neuville, 'Récit de mon voyage', f. 45.
163. N.P. Kisilev, 'O moskovskom knigopechatanii XVII veka', *Kniga. Issledovaniia i materialy*, 2 (1960), 128.
164. A.S. Zernova, *Knigi kirillovskoi pechati, izdannye v Moskve v XVI–XVII vekakh. Svodnyi katalog* (Moscow, 1958), nos 362, 373–419; Kisilev, 'O moskovskom knigopechatanii', pp. 135–7.
165. Zernova, *Knigi kirillovskoi pechati*, no. 379.
166. Kisilev, 'O moskovskom knigopechatanii', p. 136. A.I. Rogov, 'Knigopechatanie', in A.V. Artsikhovsky, *Ocherki russkoi kul'tury XVII veka*, vol. 2 (Moscow, 1979), p. 156, challenges this total on the grounds that psalters and primers should be included.
167. Kisilev, 'O moskovskom knigopechatanii', p. 160.
168. See A.N. Robinson (ed.), *Simeon Polotskii i ego knigoizdatel'skaia deiatel'nost'* (Moscow, 1982), pp. 46–59.
169. Zernova, *Knigi kirillovskoi pechati*, nos 357–62.
170. Ibid., nos 374–5.
171. Ibid., no. 384.
172. Ibid., no. 377.
173. Ibid., nos 405, 406.
174. As noted earlier, religious books from the Ukraine came under suspicion in the 1680s. Georgius David (*Status Modernus*, p. 107) wrote: 'The Muscovites do not accept one book published in Kiev, out of hatred for the Kievites.'
175. See G. Marker, *Publishing, Printing and the Origins of Intellectual Life in Russia 1700–1800* (Princeton, 1985), on the Russian 'printing revolution'.
176. Kisilev, 'O moskovskom knigopechatanii', p. 214.

177. Ibid., p. 215.
178. For information on this and other seventeenth-century works, see A.M. Panchenko, 'Literatura "perekhodnogo veka"', in Istoriia russkoi literatury. Tom 1. Drevnerusskaia literatura. Literatura XVIII veka (Leningrad, 1980), pp. 291–407; A.S. Demin, Russkaia literatura vtoroi poloviny XVII – nachala XVIII veka (Moscow, 1977); W.E. Brown, The History of Seventeenth-Century Russian Literature (Ann Arbor, 1980).
179. On 'democratic satire', see V.P. Adrianova-Perets, Russkaia demokraticheskaia satira XVII veka (Moscow and Leningrad, 1954).
180. On Medvedev's library, see below, p. 171.
181. On Golitsyn's library, see below, p. 170.
182. For a short study of Polotsky's verse, see A. Hippisley, The Poetic Style of Simeon Polotsky (Birmingham, 1983).
183. For example, his anthology Rifmologion. See Robinson, Simeon Polotskii, pp. 116–33.
184. Bogdanov, Pamiatniki, p. 34.
185. For examples of verses, see ibid.; Panchenko, Russkaia sillabicheskaia poeziia; 'Pridvornye virshi 80x godov XVII stoletiia', TODRL, 21 (1965), 65–73.
186. A.P. Bogdanov, 'Sil'vestra Medvedeva panegirik tsarevne Sof'e 1682', Pamiatniki kul'tury. Novye otkrytiia. 1982 (Leningrad, 1984), pp. 45–54 (in prose).
187. Panchenko, Russkaia sillabicheskaia poeziia, p. 201.
188. See above, note 154.
189. Text in Panchenko, Russkaia sillabicheskaia poeziia, pp. 201–2. The Latin text in ibid., p. 381.
190. Bogdanov, Pamiatniki, pp. 183–4. See also Sofrony's orations on Tsar Ivan's nameday (ibid., pp. 185–6) and to Patriarch Joachim (ibid., pp. 187–8).
191. S.P. Luppov, Kniga v Rossii v XVII veke (Leningrad, 1970), pp. 107–10. This is an analysis of material from Rozysknye dela, vol. 4, 9, 30–3, 55–6, 99, 160, 215. See also Hughes, Russia and the West, pp. 87–8.
192. Presented by Laurent Rinhuber. See below, p. 190.
193. A.S. Lavrov, 'Zapiski o Moskovii de la Nevillia', Vestnik Leningradskogo Universiteta. Seriia 2. Istoriia, iazyk literatura, 1986, no. 4, p. 90.
194. J. Letiche and B. Dmytryshyn (eds), Russian Statecraft: The Politika of Iurii Krizhanich (Oxford, 1985), pp. xlv, lxxv.
195. Entitled Uchenie i khitrost' ratnogo stroeniia (Moscow, 1649).
196. I. Zabelin (ed.), 'Knigi perepisnye knigam', Vremennyk imp. obshchestva istorii i drevnostei rossiiskikh, 16 (1853), 53–67. Analysed in Luppov, Kniga, pp. 118–26. Thanks to Dr A. Hippisley for identification of some of the original titles.
197. C.B. O'Brien, Russia under Two Tsars 1682–1689: The Regency of Sophia Alekseevna (Berkeley and Los Angeles, 1952), p. 50.
198. Luppov, Kniga, p. 116.
199. Robinson, Simeon Polotskii, p. 93.
200. Ibid., p. 283.
201. Ibid., p. 132; E.I. Bobrova (comp.), Biblioteka Petra I. Ukazatel'-spravochnik (Leningrad, 1978), no. 182.
202. Bobrova, Biblioteka, no. 93. For texts, see Bogdanov, Pamiatniki.
203. Bogdanov, Pamiatniki, pp. 132–4. Also in S.N. Brailovsky, 'Odin iz pestrykh XVII stoletiia', Zapiski imp. akademii nauk. Seriia VIII, vol. 5, no. 5 (1902), 475.
204. Bobrova, Biblioteka, no. 94; Bogdanov, Pamiatniki, p. 27.
205. Bogdanov, Pamiatniki, pp. 105–10.
206. Prozorovsky, Sil'vestr Medvedev, p. 466.
207. Bobrova, Biblioteka, no. 228.
208. Only the first two appear in the catalogue of Peter's library; Bobrova, Biblioteka, nos 541 and 328.
209. Diariusz zaboystwa tyranskiego senatorow moskiewskich w stolicy roku 1682 y o obraniu dwoch carow Ioanna y Piotra (St Petersburg, 1901), p. 13.
210. Antushev, Istoricheskoe opisanie, p. 64.
211. W. Coxe, Travels into Poland, Russia, Sweden and Denmark, vol. 1, (London, 1784), p. 418. (For a discussion of this work, see below, pp. 269–70).
212. N.M. Karamzin, 'Panteon rossiiskikh avtorov', in Sochineniia v dvukh tomakh, vol. 2 (Leningrad, 1984), p. 102.

213. O'Brien, *Russia under Two Tsars*, p. 50.
214. N. Moleva, 'Tsar'-devitsa', *Znaniesila*, 1971, no. 1, p. 34.
215. Z. Schakovskoy, *Precursors of Peter the Great* (London, 1964), p. 133.
216. 'Slovar' knizhnikov i knizhnosti drevnei Rusi', *TODRL*, 40 (1985), 162–3.
217. E. Kholodov (ed.), *Istoriia russkogo dramaticheskogo teatra* vol. 1 (Moscow, 1977), pp. 74–5. This work (*Komediia pritchi o bludnem syne*) does not appear in Zernova, and could not have been published by the *Verkhovnaia tipografiia* which, as noted above, ceased operations in 1683.
218. See A.N. Robinson, *Pervye p'esy russkogo teatra* (Moscow, 1972), pp. 16–17; B.N. Aseev, *Russkii dramaticheskii teatr ot ego istokov do kontsa XVIII veka* (Moscow, 1977), pp. 116–17.
219. S.K. Bogoiavlensky, *Moskovskii teatr pri tsariakh Aleksee i Petre* (Moscow, 1914), pp. xiv–xv.
220. Robinson, *Pervye p'esy*, p. 16.
221. G.A. Schleissing, 'Die Gantze Beschreibung Reusslandts' (1687), trans. L.P. Lapteva as 'Rasskaz ochevidtsa o zhizni Moskovii kontsa XVII veka', *Voprosy istorii*, 1970, no. 1, 112.
222. L. Rinhuber, *Relation du voyage en Russie fait en 1684 par Laurent Rinhuber* (Berlin, 1883), p. 229.
223. Bogoiavlensky, 'MoskovSkii teatr', p. xlv.
224. Ibid., p. xvi.
225. *Ocherki russkoi Kul'tury XVII veka*, part 2, p. 280.
226. See above, note 201.
227. S. Karlinsky, *Russian Drama from Its Beginnings to the Age of Pushkin* (Berkeley, 1985), p. 51, note. He refers to J. von Stählin, 'Zur Geschichte des Theaters in Russland', in *J.J. Haigolds Beylagen zum Neuveränderten Russland* (Riga and Mittau, 1769).
228. A.S. Eleonskaia (ed.), *P'esy stolichnykh i provintsial'nykh teatrov pervoi poloviny XVIII v.* (Moscow, 1975), p. 624.
229. Ibid., p. 634.
230. Robinson, *Pervye p'esy*, p. 472.
231. E. Rastopchina, 'Monakhinia', *Moskvitianin*, 5 (1843), no. 9, 8. I am grateful to Mary Zirin for confirmation that this was composed by the eminent poetess E.P. Rastopchina (1811–58).
232. See below, pp. 227–8.
233. S. Moropol'sky, 'Tsarevna S.A. (Zametki)', *Russkaia starina*, 23 (1878), 130–1. On icons, *Entsiklopedicheskii slovar'*, vol. 5 (St Petersburg, 1900), p. 640.
234. Zabelin, *Domashnii byt*, vol. 2 (1901), p. 181.
235. 'Ukaz tsarei Ivana i Petra i tsarevny Sof'i 7196g. Marta 7', *Chteniia*, 1887, book 1, 177–8.
236. Davydova, 'Esteticheskie predstavleniia', p. 24.
237. A.K. Leont'ev, 'Byt i nravy', in A.V. Artsikhovsky (ed.), *Ocherki russkoi kul'tury XVII veka*, vol. 2 (Moscow, 1979), pp. 5–29.
238. Schleissing, 'Die Gantze Beschreibung', p. 115 ('Some still go around in the old Russian style, in big, wide caftans; others dressed almost the same as Poles').
239. See above, p. 170. A full description of the palace can be found in Zabelin, *Domashnii byt*, vol. 1 (1895), pp. 549–66.

## CHAPTER 8: FOREIGN AFFAIRS

1. P. Avril, *Travels into divers Parts of Europe and Asia*, book 4 (London, 1693), p. 78.
2. M. Raeff, 'Muscovy Looks West', *History Today*, August 1986, 17.
3. S.M. Solov'ev, *Istoriia Rossii s drevneishikh vremen*, vols 13–14 (Moscow, 1962), p. 367 (henceforth, Solov'ev).
4. See, for example, *Rossiia i Tridstatiletniaia voina* (Leningrad, 1947); O. Vainshtein, 'Russko-shvedskaia voina 1655–1660 godov. (Istoriograficheskii obzor)', *Voprosy istorii*, 1947, no. 3, 53–72; L.V. Zaborovsky, *Rossiia, Rech' Pospolitaia i Shvetsiia v seredine XVII veka* (Moscow, 1981).
5. Z. Wójcik, 'From the Peace of Oliwa to the Truce of Bakhchisarai: International Relations in Eastern Europe 1660–1681', *Acta Poloniae Historica*, 34 (1976), 256. See his 'Poland and

Russia in the 17th Century: Problems of Internal Development', *Poland at the 14th Congress of Historical Sciences in San Francisco* (Wroclaw, 1975). Also G. Stadtmüller, 'Das Mächtesystema Osteuropas bis zum Ende des 17 Jahrhunderts', *Saeculum Weltgeschichte*, 6 (1971), 423–51.

6. See A. Lossky, 'The General European Crisis of the 1680s', *European Studies Review*, 10 (1980), 177–98; J. Stoye, *Europe Unfolding 1648–1688* (London, 1969), p. 390. Other works on European history consulted in the preparation of this chapter include: D.H. Pennington, *Seventeenth-Century Europe* (London, 1970); D. Ogg, *Europe in the Seventeenth Century* (London, 1961); S.J. Lee, *Aspects of European History 1494–1789* (London, 1982). P. Dukes, *A History of Europe 1648–1948, The Arrival, the Rise, the Fall* (London, 1985); Idem. 'How the 18th Century Began for Russia and the West', in A.G. Cross (ed.), *Russia and the West in the Eighteenth Century* (Newtonville, Mass., 1983), pp. 2–19.

7. See P. Dukes, 'Paul Menzies and His Mission from Muscovy to Rome 1672–1674', *The Innes Review*, Autumn 1984, 93. On ritual, see R.O. Crummey, 'Court Spectacles in Seventeenth-Century Russia: Illusion and Reality', in D.C, Waugh (ed.), *Essays in Honor of A.A. Zimin* (Columbus, 1985), pp. 130–58.

8. See S.A. Belokurov, 'O posol'skom prikaze', *Chteniia*, 1906, book 3, 1–170.

9. Wójcik, 'From the Peace of Oliwa', p. 263.

10. J.K. Babuskhina, 'Mezhdunarodnoe znachenie Krymskikh pokhodov 1687 i 1689 gg.', *Istoricheskie zapiski*, 33 (1950), 159–61.

11. P. Longworth, *Alexis, Tsar of All the Russias* (London, 1984), p. 58.

12. J.M. Letiche and B. Dmytryshyn (eds), *Russian Statecraft: The Politika of Iurii Krizhanich* (Oxford, 1985), p. xv.

13. On Russo-Swedish relations, see G. Forsten, 'Snosheniia Shvetsii i Rossii vo vtoroi polovine XVII veka, 1668–1700', *ZhMNP*, February 1898; *Russko-shvedskie ekonomicheskie otnosheniia v XVII veke. Sbornik dokumentov* (Moscow and Leningrad, 1960); Zaborovsky, *Rossiia*.

14. Wójcik, 'From the Peace of Oliwa', p. 258.

15. H.E. Ellersieck, 'Russia under Aleksei Mikhailovich and Fedor Alekseevich 1645–1682: The Scandinavian Sources' (unpublished PhD, University of California at Los Angeles, 1955), p. 196.

16. Quoted in J. Black, 'Russia's Rise as a European Power 1650–1750', *History Today*, August 1986, 24.

17. *Vosstanie v Moskve 1682 g. Sbornik dokumentov*, ed. V.I. Buganov and N.G. Savich (Moscow, 1976), p. 62.

18. Solov'ev, pp. 365–6.

19. *Sobranie raznykh zapisok i sochinenii, sluzhashchikh k dostavleniiu polnogo svedeniia o zhizni i deianiiakh gosudaria imperatora Petra Velikogo*, ed. F. Tumansky, vol. 5 (St Petersburg, 1787), p. 9 (henceforth, Tumansky).

20. See N. Ustrialov, *Istoriia tsarstvovaniia Petra Velikogo*, vol. 1 (St Petersburg, 1858), p. 117. Envoys went to Warsaw, Stockholm, Vienna, Copenhagen, The Hague, London and Constantinople. On individual missions, see relevant sections in N.N. Bantysh-Kamensky, *Obzor vneshnikh snoshenii Rossii (po 1800 god)*, 4 vols (Moscow, 1894–1902).

21. M. Welke, 'Russland in der deutschen Publizistik des 17. Jahrunderts (1613–1689)', *Forschungen zur Osteuropäischen Geschichte*, 23 (1976), 232.

22. For Russian texts of these letters, see Tumansky, vol. 5, pp. 9–12 (Sweden), 5–6 (Denmark), 17–22 (Netherlands).

23. Copy of the letter in PRO, SP104/19, f. 21 rev.

24. Tumansky, vol. 6, pp. 29–37.

25. A.A. Novosel'sky (ed.), *Ocherki istorii SSSR. Period feodalizma. XVII vek* (Moscow, 1955), p. 531. For an account of the negotiations leading to the 1686 treaty, see L.R. Lewitter, 'The Russo-Polish Treaty of 1686 and Its Antecedents', *Polish Review*, 9 (1964), no. 3, 5–29; no. 4, 21–37.

26. Solov'ev, pp. 379–82.

27. All citations from the Gordon diaries are unless otherwise stated quoted from transcripts of the original (Tsentral'nyi Gosudarstvennyi Voenno-Istoricheskii Arkhiv, fond. 846, op. 15, ed. khr. 1–7).
28. See Lewitter, 'Russo-Polish Treaty', no. 4, pp. 21–4. He points out that the Polish delegates were 'parliamentarians, politicians versed in oratory and the management of diets and dietines rather than diplomats' (p. 21).
29. Tumansky, vol. 4, pp. 103–5. Russo-Austrian relations in the 1680s are lavishly documented in *Pamiatniki diplomaticheskikh snoshenii drevnei Rossii s derzhavami inostrannymi*, vols 6–9 (St Petersburg, 1851–71) (henceforth, *PDS*).
30. For a Russian version of the Emperor's letter, see Tumansky, vol. 4, pp. 124–5; vol. 5, p. 332.
31. Hövel's own account of his trip is in Wiener Staatsarchiv, Russica 1684. Official letters and documents relating to the mission are published in *PDS*, vol. 6. The quotation here taken from N.N. Danilov, 'Vasilij Vasil'evič Golicyn (1682–1714)', *Jahrbücher für Geschichte Osteuropas*, 2 (1937), 551–3.
32. See above, p. 93. Quoted in F. Adelung, *Kritisch-literärische Übersicht der Reisenden in Russland bis 1700* (St Petersburg and Leipzig, 1846), p. 371.
33. *PDS*, vol. 6, p. 294.
34. Solov'ev, pp. 372–3.
35. Tumansky, vol. 4, pp. 148–9. The congratulations are dated 24 March, 1684. A Theiner (comp.), *Monuments historiques relatifs aux règnes d'Alexis Michaélowitch, Fédor III et Pierre le Grand Czars de Russie extraits des archives du Vatican et de Naples* (Rome, 1859), pp. 282–3.
36. Tumansky, vol. 4, p. 166.
37. See *Russko-shvedskie ekonomicheskie otnosheniia*, pp. 443–7.
38. Ustrialov, *Istoriia*, pp. 118–23.
39. For the text of the treaty, see *Polnoe sobranie zakonov Rossiiskoi imperii*, vol. 2 (St Petersburg, 1830), no. 1076, pp. 619–22 (henceforth, *PSZ*). Also, *Russko-shvedskie ekonomicheskie otnosheniia*, p. 447.
40. Ustrialov, *Istoriia*, p. 119.
41. N.N. Molchanov, *Diplomatiia Petra Pervogo* (Moscow, 1984), p. 32.
42. E. Lermontova, *Samoderzhavie Tsarevny Sof'i Alekseevny, po neizdannym dokumentam. (Iz perepiski, vozbuzhdennoi grafom Paninym)* (St Petersburg, 1912), pp. 441–4. See also, L.A.J. Hughes, 'Sophia, "Autocrat of All the Russias"', *Canadian Slavonic Papers*, 28 (1986), 277.
43. Lermontova, *Samoderzhavie*, p. 44.
44. Tumansky, vol. 4, p. 72.
45. See Rinhuber's own account of his journey to Russia: *Relation du voyage en Russie fait en 1684 par Laurent Rinhuber* (Berlin, 1883). (Includes his journal 'Wahrhafter Relation von der Moscowischen Reise . . . 1684'.) The reference to Sophia from ibid., p. 275.
46. Ibid., p. 259.
47. *PSZ*, vol. 2, no. 1085, pp. 636–8.
48. G.A. Schleissing, 'Die Gantze Beschreibung Reusslandts' (1687), trans. L.P. Lapteva as 'Razzkaz ochevidtsa o zhizni Moskovii kontsa XVII veka', *Voprosy istorii*, 1970, no. 1, 123.
49. Tumansky, vol. 4, pp. 200–1.
50. Solov'ev, p. 389.
51. Ustrialov, *Istoriia*, pp. 152–3.
52. Z. Wójcik, *Jan Sobieski 1629–1696* (Warsaw, 1982), p. 375.
53. Text in *PSZ*, vol. 2, no. 1186, pp. 770–86; Ustrialov, *Istoriia*, p. 167.
54. N. Davies, *God's Playground: A History of Poland, vol. 1: The Origins to 1795* (Oxford, 1981), p. 487.
55. Lewitter, 'Russo-Polish Treaty', no. 4, 30.
56. Wójcik, *Sobieski*, p. 379.
57. See E.B. Frantsuzova, 'Iz istorii russko-pol'skikh otnoshenii v poslednei treti XVII v.', *Istoricheskie zapiski*, 105 (1980), 280–93.
58. Lermontova, *Samoderzhavie* pp. 539–40.
59. Ibid., pp. 540–1.
60. Ibid., p. 437.
61. *PDS*, vol. 6, p. 1219.
62. *PSZ*, vol. 2, no. 1197, p. 799; *Sobranie gosudarstvennykh gramot i dogovorov, khraniashchikhsia v gos. kollegii inostrannykh del*, vol. 4 (Moscow, 1828), no. 178, pp. 519–25 (henceforth, *SGGD*).
63. See Hughes, 'Sophia "Autocrat"'.

64. *PSZ*, vol. 2, no. 1197, p. 801.
65. Ibid., p. 803.
66. Lewitter, 'Russo-Polish Treaty', no. 4, p. 30.
67. Bantysh-Kamensky, *Obzor*, vol. 1, p. 235.
68. Treaty in *PSZ*, vol. 2, no. 1250, pp. 860-2 (16/26 June 1687); *Sobranie traktatov i konventsii, zakliuchennykh Rossieiu s inostrannymi derzhavami*, vol. 5 (1880), no. 177, pp. 26-9.
69. PRO, SP104/119, ff. 49-9 rev. For a complete version of this document see my article 'V.T. Postnikov's Mission to London in 1687', *SEER*, forthcoming.
70. Documents of the mission are in British Library, Manuscripts, Add. 41842, Papers of the Earl of Middleton (then State Secretary), ff. 170-93, including Postnikov's credentials; and PRO SP104/119 (State Secretary's Letter book). See L. Hughes, 'V.T. Postnikov's Mission'.
71. This section of Gordon's diary is published in *Passages from the Diary of General Patrick Gordon of Auchleuchries, A.D. 1635-A.D. 1699* (Aberdeen, 1859). See pp. 150-1 for the letter.
72. Ibid., p. 159.
73. Ibid., p. 161. See also S. Konovalov, 'Sixteen Further Letters of General Patrick Gordon', *Oxford Slavonic Papers*, 13 (1967), 75. Originals in BL, Add. 41842.
74. Danilov, 'Golicyn', p. 566.
75. On the mission to France, see F. Grönebaum, *Frankreich in Ost- und Nordeuropa. Die französisch-russischen Beziehungen von 1648-1689* (Wiesbaden, 1968); Solov'ev, pp. 410-13; *Recueil des instructions données aux ambassadeurs et ministres de France*, vol. 1 (Paris, 1890).
76. Lermontova, *Samoderzhavie*, p. 543.
77. For the letter from King Louis, dated 20 December, 1685, see Tumansky, vol. 4, pp. 226-7.
78. *Relation de tout ce qui regarde la Moscovie* (Paris, 1687). See also the set of prints made in Paris to mark the mission, D.A. Rovinsky, *Materialy dlia russkoi ikonografii*, vol. 1 (Moscow, 1884), nos 11-14.
79. Lossky, 'General European Crisis', p. 193.
80. *PSZ*, vol. 2, no. 1205, p. 812.
81. Ibid., no. 1224, pp. 835-42.
82. R.O. Crummey, *Aristocrats and Servitors; The Boyar Elite in Russia 1613-1689* (Princeton, 1984), p. 46.
83. F. de la Neuville, *An Account*, pp. 34-35. The relevant passage in 'Récit de mon voyage' (Paris, Bibliothèque Nationale, Département des Manuscrits, NAF 5114), ff. 18-19, is much shorter.
84. Prince B.I. Kurakin, 'Gistoriia o tsare Petre Alekseeviche 1682-1694', in *Rossiiu podnial na dyby . . . Istoriia otechestva v romanakh, povestiakh, dokumentakh. Veka XVII-XVIII*, vol. 1 (Moscow, 1987), p. 369.
85. Letter to the Earl of Middleton, 7 January, 1687, in Konovalov, 'Sixteen Further Letters', p. 87. Original in BL, Add. 41842, f. 152.
86. BL, Add. 41842, f. 150 (3 December 1686).
87. Tumansky, vol. 2, pp. 311-20; *Drevniaia rossiiskaia vivliofika*, vol. 13 (St Petersburg, 1789), pp. 163-5.
88. The chief sources are P. Gordon, *Tagebuch des Generals Patrick Gordon, während seiner Kriegsdienste unter den Schweden und Polen vom Jahre 1655 bris 1661, und seines Aufenhaltes in Russland vom Jahre 1661 bis 1699*, ed. M.A. Obolenski and M.C. Posselt, 3 vols (Moscow and Leipzig, 1849) (unfortunately the original text for the year 1687 was not available) and letters. See Konovalov, 'Sixteen Further Letters' (but note that he mistakenly places the main events in July, rather than June). These may be compared with Golitsyn's own account (see below, note 93) and official decrees based on it. See also M. Belov, 'K istorii diplomaticheshikh otnoshenii Rossii vo vremia Krymskikh pokhodov (1686-1689)', *Uchenye zapiski Leningradskogo Gosudarstvennogo Universiteta. Seriia istoricheskikh nauk*, 14 (1949), 154-88, which is based on the letters of the Dutch Resident in Moscow, Johann Van Keller.
89. Gordon, *Tagebuch*, vol. 2, p. 175.
90. La Neuville, 'Récit de mon voyage', f. 21.
91. Gordon, *Tagebuch*, vol. 2, p. 176.
92. Letter to his brother, 27 October

1687, in M. Posselt, *Der General und Admiral Franz Lefort. Sein Leben und Seine Zeit*, vol. 1 (Frankfurt, 1866), p. 374.

93. Ustrialov, *Istoriia*, p. 199.
94. Belov, 'K istorii', p. 159.
95. Solov'ev, p. 400.
96. La Neuville, 'Récit de mon voyage', f. 22.
97. *PSZ*, vol. 2, no. 1258, p. 884, 'In the present military campaign in a blatant act of treachery he burned and steppe and colluded with the Crimean Khan' (p. 890).
98. Solov'ev, p. 402.
99. La Neuville, 'Récit de mon voyage', f. 23; Gordon, *Tagebuch*, vol. 2, p. 194; M.M. Bogoslovsky, *Petr I. Materialy dlia biografii*, vol. 1 (Moscow, 1940), p. 80, provides an illustration of the medal. See also Kochen's report, below.
100. *PSZ*, vol. 2, no. 1258, pp. 884–9.
101. Konovalov, 'Sixteen Further Letters', pp. 90–2.
102. Babushkina, 'Mezhdunarodnoe znachenie Krymskikh pokhodov', p. 171.
103. La Neuville, 'Récit de mon voyage', f. 24.
104. C. von Kochen, 'Mosvka v 1687–1688 gg. (Pis'ma Khristofora fon-Kokhen, shvedskogo poslannika pri russkom dvore)', *Russkaia starina*, 1878, no. 9, 122 (henceforth, Kochen). Kochen (originally plain Koch) first came to Moscow in 1683, and again in 1684. He was in Russia without a break from December 1685 to 1690. See Tumansky, vol. 4, pp. 177–83, 197. Georgius David, *Status Modernus Magnae Russiae seu Moscoviae (1690)*, ed. A.V. Florovskij (The Hague, 1965) p. 64, reported 30,000 dead from epidemics alone.
105. Kochen, p. 122. See confirmation in Gordon's letter to the Earl of Middleton, 26 September, 1687: 'Our Government continues still as before and our favourite as great if not greater as ever, albeit in his absence much was done to cast him' (Konovalov, 'Sixteen Further Letters', p. 93).
106. See A.P. Bogdanov, 'Politicheskaia graviura v Rossii perioda regentstva Sof'i Alekseevny', *Istochnikovedenie otechestvennoi istorii. 1981* (Moscow,

1982), pp. 235–6.
107. On portraits, see pp. 140 ff.
108. Theiner, *Monuments historiques*, pp. 328–39.
109. Belov, 'K istorii', p. 170.
110. Ibid., p. 172. The letter is dated 17 April, 1688.
111. Solov'ev, pp. 403–4.
112. *PSZ*, vol. 2, no. 1313, p. 946.
113. *SGGD*, vol. 4, no. 1693, pp. 587–91.
114. La Neuville, 'Récit de mon voyage', f. 25.
115. Quoted from the original in Dukes, 'How the 18th Century Began for Russia and the West', pp. 7–8.
116. Babushkina, 'Mezhdunarodnoe znachenie Krymskikh pokhodov', p. 267.
117. Letter of 8 November, 1688. Belov, 'K istorii', p. 183.
118. Ibid., p. 180.
119. On Vasil'ev's mission, see Danilov, 'Golicyn', p. 568; *PDS*, vol. 7, p. 470.
120. *Sbornik Mukhanova* (St Petersburg, 1866), pp. 230–1.
121. Letter of 11 May. Kochen, p. 128.
122. Gordon, *Passages*, p. 165.
123. Avril, *Travels*, book 4, p. 8. The Polish Ambassador Grzymułtowski confirmed that Golitsyn and his son wore miniatures of Louis XIV on sashes (Lewitter, 'Russo-Polish Treaty', p. 26.)
124. Avril, *Travels*, book 4, p. 71. See also Bantysh-Kamensky, *Obzor*, vol. 4, pp. 19, 85.
125. Avril, *Travels*, book 4, p. 65. See also Gordon, under 9 January, 'the unfortunate Brabander Everand Frontins de Rulley executed in the sloboda for killing Lt. Coll. Shulz in his own defence'.
126. *PSZ*, vol. 3, no. 1331, pp. 8–9.
127. Ibid., no. 1330, pp. 7–8 (20 January, 1689); no. 1332, pp. 9–10 (28 January, 1689).
128. Bantysh-Kamensky, *Obzor*, vol. 4, p. 21 (18 January, 1689).
129. For the most detailed account, see M. Mancall, *Russia and China: Their Diplomatic Relations to 1728* (Harvard, 1971). Also, N.S. Demidova, 'Iz istorii zakliucheniia Nerchinskogo dogovora 1689 g.', in *Rossiia v period reform Petra I* (Moscow, 1973), pp. 289–31.
130. *PSZ*, vol. 3, no. 1346, pp. 31–2 (27

August, 1689).
131. Demidova, 'Iz istorii', p. 290.
132. La Neuville, 'Récit de mon voyage', f. 27.
133. Golitsyn's dispatches, in Ustrialov, *Istoriia*, p. 369.
134. Ibid., p. 370.
135. Ibid., p. 371.
136. Ibid., p. 373.
137. Ibid., p. 374.
138. PSZ, vol. 3, no. 1340, pp. 19–20.
139. Gordon, *Tagebuch*, vol. 2, p. 258.
140. Ustrialov, *Istoriia*, pp. 379–80.
141. *Rozysknye dela o Fedore Shaklovitom i ego soobshchnikakh*, vol. 3 (St Petersburg, 18), pp. 1–2. See also the decree in PSZ, vol. 3, no. 1348, p. 33.
142. Posselt, *Lefort*, pp. 371–5. J.L. Keep, *Soldiers of the Tsar: Army and Society in Russia 1462–1874* (Oxford, 1985), p. 39, also has this figure.
143. David, *Status Modernus*, p. 127.
144. Ibid.
145. La Neuville, 'Récit de mon voyage', f. 30.
146. *Rozysknye dela*, vol. 3, pp. 938–9.
147. I.A. Zheliabuzhsky, 'Zapiski Ivan Afanas'evicha Zheliabuzhskogo', in N. Sakharov (ed.), *Zapiski russkikh liudei. Sobytiia vremen Petra Velikogo.* (St. Petersburg, 1841), p. 10.
148. G.A. Schleissing, *Derer beyden Czaaren in Reussland* (n.p., 1694), pp. 128–9, but note that this reworking of Schleissing's 1687 account (see above, note 48) was published eight years after he left Russia.
149. *Copia-Schreibens des Kniar Gallicryn, Feldherrn der Moscowitischen Armee an den Herrn Jablonowsky, Cron Gross-Feldherrn in Pohlen auss Perekop den 2. Jun. 1689*, Frankfurt (?) (British Library Reference Division, 8010.b.1 (58)).
150. PSZ, vol. 3, no. 1340, p. 20.

## CHAPTER 9: OVERTHROWN 1689

1. Extract from dispatch, quoted in M.I. Belov, 'K. istorii diplomaticheskikh otnoshenii Rossii vo vremia Krymskikh pokhodov (1686–89)', *Uchenye zapiski Leningradskogo Gosudarstvennogo Universiteta. Seriia istoricheskikh*
nauk, 14 (1949), 181.
2. C. von Kochen, 'Moskva v 1687–1688 gg. (Pis'ma Khristofora fon-Kokhen, shvedskogo poslannika pri russkom dvore)', *Russkaia starina*, September 1878, 124 (henceforth, Kochen).
3. Quoted from original. See also P. Gordon, *Tagebuch des Generals Patrick Gordon, während seiner Kriegsdienste unter den Schweden und Polen vom Jahre 1655 bis 1661, und seines Aufenthaltes in Russland vom Jahre 1661 bis 1699*, ed. M.A. Obolenski and M.C. Posselt, vol. 2 (Moscow and Leipzig, 1849), p. 209, and M. Posselt, *Der General und Admiral Franz Lefort. Sein Leben und Seine Zeit*, vol. 1 (Frankfurt, 1866), p. 412.
4. Kochen, p. 126.
5. *Chteniia*, 1911, book 4, pp. 51–2. See also L. Hughes, *Russia and the West: The Life of a Seventeenth-Century Westernizer Prince Vasily Vasil'evich Golitsyn (1643–1714)* (Newtonville, Mass., 1984), p. 58. Kochen, p. 128.
7. R.O. Crummey, *Aristocrats and Servitors: The Boyar Elite in Russia 1613–1689* (Princeton, 1984), pp. 208–10.
8. *Dvortsovye razriady*, vol. 4 (St Petersburg, 1855), pp. 453–4 (henceforth, DR).
9. C.F. Weber, *The Present State of Russia*, vol. 1 (London, 1722–3), p. 38.
10. S.M. Solov'ev, *Istoriia Rossii s drevneishikh vremen*, vols 13–14 (Moscow, 1962), p. 446.
11. Gordon, *Tagebuch*, vol. 2, pp. 227–8. See other references on requisition of troops: pp. 229, 232, 236.
12. *Polnoe sobranie zakonov Rossiiskoi imperii*, vol. 3 (St Petersburg, 1830), no. 1338, pp. 10–11 (henceforth, PSZ). *Drevniaia rossiiskaia vivliofika* vol. 11 (St Petersburg, 1891), p. 194 (henceforth, DRV). Crummey lists only three Lopukhins in the Council in the decade before the marriage, *Aristocrats and Servitors*, pp. 190, 197, 206.
13. Prince B.I. Kurakin, 'Gistoriia o tsare Petre Alekseeviche i blizhnikh k nemy liudiakh, 1682–1694', in *Rossiiu podnial na dyby ... Istoriia otechestra v romanakh, povestiakh, documentakh. Veka XVII–XVIII*, vol. 1 (Moscow, 1987), p. 369.

14. Ibid., p. 370.
15. *Rozysknye dela o Fedore Shaklovitom i ego soobshchnikakh*, vol. 1 (St Petersburg, 1884), pp. 166–7 (henceforth, *Rozysknye dela*).
16. See entries in *DR*, vol. 4, pp. 383–406.
17. Belov, 'K istorii', p. 181.
18. Gordon, *Tagebuch*, vol. 2, p. 230.
19. *DR*, vol. 4, p. 415.
20. P. Avril, *Travels into divers Parts of Europe and Asia*, book 4 (London, 1693), p. 14. On the mission, see above, pp. 208–9.
21. Ibid., pp. 56, 73–4.
22. Ibid., p. 175.
23. Ibid., p. 176.
24. *DR*, vol. 4, p. 433.
25. Ibid., p. 437.
26. Ibid., p. 438. For an announcement of the birth, see *PSZ*, vol. 3, 1339, pp. 18–19.
27. *DR*, vol. 4, pp. 439–40.
28. Ibid., pp. 446–7.
29. Deciphered and published by N. Ustrialov in *Istoriia tsarstvovaniia Petra Velikogo*, vol. 1 (St Petersburg, 1858), pp. 382–4. The originals are in TsGADA, f. 5, no. 2.
30. Information from 15 June to 5 July from *DR*, vol. 4, pp. 449–56.
31. Ibid., pp. 457–8.
32. A.A. Matveev, 'Zapiski Andreia Artamonovicha grafa Matveeva', in N. Sakharov (ed.), *Zapiski russkikh liudei. Sobytiia vremen Petra Velikogo* (St Petersburg, 1841), p. 52 (henceforth, Matveev). See also Kurakin, 'Gistoriia', p. 368. I Zabelin, *Domashnii byt russkogo naroda*, vol. 2 (Moscow, 1901), p. 183, records that Sophia also offended by going bare-headed.
33. *DR*, vol. 4, pp. 459–60.
34. Ibid., p. 462.
35. Ibid., p. 464.
36. Ibid., p. 466.
37. Ibid.
38. *PSZ*, vol. 3, no. 1343, p. 26.
39. Quotations from Gordon in the rest of this chapter, hitherto unpublished in English, are taken from a transcript of the original (unpaginated) MS in Tsentral'nyi Gosudarstvennyi Voenno-Istoricheskii Archiv, f. 846, op. 15, ed. khr. 1–7, kindly supplied by Professor Paul Dukes. See also Gordon, *Tagebuch*, vol. 2, pp. 267–83.
40. G. David, *Status Modernus Magnae Russiae seu Moscoviae* (1690), ed. A.V. Florovskij (The Hague, 1965), p. 65.
41. *DR*, vol. 4, p. 468.
42. Ibid., pp. 469–70.
43. Kurakin, 'Gistoriia', p. 371. He names, in particular, B.A. Golitsyn, L.K. Naryshkin, T.N. Streshnev and G.I. Golovkin on Peter's side; F. Shaklovity, A.I. Rzhevsky and S.F. Tolochanov on Sophia's.
44. E. Shmurlo, 'Padenie tsarevny Sof'i', *ZhMNP*, 1896, no. 1, p. 85.
45. *Rozysknye dela*, vol. 1, p. 31.
46. *DR*, vol. 4, p. 445; *DRV*, vol. 10, p. 310.
47. *Rozysknye dela*, vol. 1, pp. 931–4.
48. Ibid., pp. 167–9.
49. Ibid., pp. 991 ff.
50. Matveev, p. 53.
51. *DR*, vol. 4, p. 471.
52. Matveev, p. 52.
53. *Rozysknye dela*, vol. 1, p. 265.
54. See M. Pogodin, *Semnadtsat' pervykh let v zhizni Imperatora Petra Velikogo. 1672–1689* (Moscow, 1875), pp. 210–22, in which most of the blame is placed on Peter's own supporters.
55. Matveev, p. 53.
56. *DR*, vol. 4, p. 471.
57. Ibid., pp. 471–2.
58. Ibid., pp. 473–4.
59. *Rozysknye dela*, vol. 1, pp. 280–7.
60. *DR*, vol. 4, p. 474.
61. Ibid., p. 475.
62. *Rozysknye dela*, vol. 1, pp. 289–95.
63. *DR*, vol. 4, p. 480.
64. Matveev, p. 54.
65. Kurakin, 'Gistoriia', pp. 374–5.
66. *Rozysknye dela*, vol. 1, p. 297.
67. *DR*, vol. 4, pp. 481–2.
68. *Rozysknye dela*, vol. 1, p. 345.
69. Detailed transcripts of statements, face-to-face confrontations (*ochnye stavki*), torture, charges, etc., of these and others, see ibid., which provides valuable insights into seventeenth-century Russian legal procedures. For another copy of the sentence, see *PSZ*, vol. 3, no. 1349, pp. 33–6 (11 September, 1689).
70. *Rozysknye dela*, vol. 3, pp. 1–2. See also Hughes, *Russia and the West*, pp. 77–8.
71. E.g. F. de la Neuville, 'Récit de mon voyage' (Paris, Bibliothèque Nationale, Département des Manuscrits,

NAF 5114), f. 43; *Istoriia sotsarstviia v Rossii (1682–89 gg.)*, *sostavlennaia po vernym istochnikam* (St Petersburg), pp. 76.

72. *Sobranie gosudarstvennykh gramot i dogovorov, khraniashchikhsia v gos. kollegii inostrannykh del*, vol. 4 (Moscow, 1828), no. 200, p. 611; *DR*, vol. 4, p. 482.

73. *Pis'ma i bumagi Imp. Petra Velikogo*, vol. 1 (St Petersburg, 1887), pp. 13–14.

74. *Rozysknye dela*, vol. 3, p. 1096.

75. See in the index of references to Sophia in *ibid.*, vol. 4, pp. 164–74.

76. F. de la Neuville, *Relation Curieuse et nouvelle de Moscovie* (The Hague, 1699), p. 113–4. The MS version is different: 'La princesse ambitieuse se voyant comme maitresse absolue . . . voulut s'approprier entierement et s'affermir la puissance, la vie de Pierre n'estoit pas un petit obstacle à son dessein, Elle prend la resolution de s'en defaire' ('Recit de mon voyage', f. 33).

77. La Neuville, *Relation curieuse et nouvelle de Moscovie*, p. 140.

78. M.M. Bogoslovsky, *Petr I. Materialy dlia biografii*, vol. 1 (Moscow, 1940), p. 94.

79. Matveev, p. 57.

80. *Rozysknye dela*, vol. 3, pp. 1170, 1207–8, 1468–72.

81. *DR*, vol. 4, p. 486.

## CHAPTER 10: BACK TO SECLUSION 1689–1704

1. E. Rastopchina [Rostopchina], 'Monakhinia', *Moskvitiianin*, 5 (1843), no. 9, 11.

2. On the history and architecture of the Novodevichy Convent, see above, pp. 152–4, and N. Antushev, *Istoricheskoe opisanie Moskovskogo Novodevich'ego monastyria* (Moscow, 1885); I.P. Mashkov, *Arkhitektura Novodevich'ego monastyria* (Moscow, 1949); L.S. Retkovskaia, *Novodevichii monastyr'. Putevoditel' po muzeiu* (Moscow, 1964); Iu. Ovsiannikov, *Novodevichii monastyr'* (Moscow, 1968). Information on the monastery has also been collected on several visits to Moscow, including consultations with staff on a study visit in

September 1983. The nunnery was disbanded in 1922 and the compound is now open to the public as a branch of the State Historical Museum. The refectory Church of the Dormition is a functioning Orthodox church.

3. Antushev, *Istoricheskoe opisanie*, p. 75.

4. Ibid., appendix, pp. xliv–xlviii, and see above, pp. 144–5. In summer 1988 the painting was exhibited in the entrance to the main cathedral.

5. N. Kostomarov, *Russkaia istoriia v zhizneopisaniiakh ee glavneishikh deiatelei*, vol. 2, issue 4 (St Petersburg, 1874), p. 511. A. Viktorov, *Opisanie zapisnikh knig i bumag starinykh dvortsovykh prikazov. 1613–1725*, vol. 2 (Moscow, 1883), p. 361.

6. These objects were inspected in a visit in 1983. Some of the inscriptions are reproduced in Antushev, *Istoricheskoe opisanie*.

7. Ibid., p. 56.

8. S. Smirnov, *Istoricheskoe opisanie Savvina Storozhevskogo monastyria* (Moscow, 1877), p. 52; I.K. Kondrat'ev, *Sedaia starina Moskvy* (Moscow, 1893), pp. 679–81.

9. See M.A. Thomas, 'Muscovite Convents in the 17th Century', *Russian History*, 10 (1983), 230–42.

10. E.g. entry for 1 March 1690, in *Dvortsovye razriady*, vol. 4 (St Petersburg, 1855), pp. 536–7.

11. See M.I. Semevsky, *Tsaritsa Praskov'ia 1664–1723* (St Petersburg, 1861).

12. S. Librovich, *Petr Velikii i zhenshchiny* (St Petersburg, n.d.), p. 23.

13. M.M. Bogoslovsky, *Petr I. Materialy dlia biografii*, vol. 1 (Moscow, 1940), p. 149.

14. S.M. Solov'ev, *Istoriia Rossii s drevneishikh vremen*, vols 13–14 (Moscow, 1962), p. 558 (henceforth, Solov'ev). The incident was reported by I.Ia. Trubetskoi, the captain of the guards. There were tunnels in the convent. See, for example, Antushev, *Istoricheskoe opisanie*, p. 111, and I. Stelletsky, 'Podzemnyi khod pod Novodevichim monastyem v Moskve', *Staraia Moskva*, vol. 1, 1912, pp. 54–64.

15. Solov'ev pp. 548–9.

16. The main published sources of contemporary material on the strel'tsy rebellion of 1698 are as follows: Bo-

goslovsky, *Petr I*, vols 3–4; V.I. Buganov (ed.), *Vosstanie moskovskikh strel'tsov. 1698 god. Sb. dokumentov* (Moscow, 1980) (henceforth, *Vosstanie . . . 1698*). Patrick Gordon was an eyewitness to many of the events. Also, J.L. Keep, *Soldiers of the Tsar: Army and Society in Russia 1462–1874* (Oxford, 1985), pp. 98–102.

17. *Vosstanie . . . 1698*, pp. 40–1.
18. Solov'ev, p. 567.
19. Bogoslovsky, *Petr I*, vol. 3, p. 35; *Vosstanie . . . 1698*, p. 71.
20. *Vosstanie . . . 1698*, p. 73.
21. Ibid., pp. 82–3.
22. Ibid., p. 113; Bogoslovsky, *Petr I*, vol. 3, pp. 47–8.
23. *Vosstanie . . . 1698*, pp. 151–2.
24. Bogoslovsky, *Petr I*, vol. 3, pp. 49–55.
25. Ibid., p. 57.
26. Ibid., p. 58.
27. *Vosstanie . . . 1698*, p. 271.
28. Bogoslovsky, *Petr I*, vol. 3, p. 65.
29. J. Korb, *Diary of an Austrian Secretary of Legation at the Court of Czar Peter the Great*, ed. and trans. Count MacDonnell, vol. 1 (London, 1863), p. 177.
30. *Vosstanie . . . 1698*, p. 128.
31. Korb, *Diary*, vol. 2, pp. 94–5.
32. Bogoslovsky, *Petr I*, vol. 3, pp. 77 ff.
33. Ibid., p. 82.
34. *Vosstanie . . . 1698*, pp. 171–2.
35. Ibid., pp. 172–3; Bogoslovsky, *Petr I*, vol. 3, pp. 103–4.
36. *Vosstanie . . . 1698*, pp. 242–3, 259–60.
37. Korb, *Diary*, vol. 2, p. 91.
38. Ibid., p. 92.
39. Ibid.
40. Ibid., vol. 1, p. 188. See discussion in Bogoslovsky, *Petr I*, vol. 3, pp. 87–8.
41. No formal record survives. The date of Sophia's induction is calculated from the inscription on her tomb, which tells us that on the day of her death she had been a nun for five years, eight months and twelve days.
42. Korb, *Diary*, vol. 1, p. 194.
43. Ibid.
44. ibid., p. 209.
45. *Pis'ma i bumagi Imp. Petra Velikogo*, vol. 1 (St Petersburg, 1887), no. 254, p. 273.
46. I. Zabelin, *Materialy dlia istorii, arkheologii i statistiki g. Moskvy*, vol. 1

(Moscow, 1884), p. 806.
47. Antushev, *Istoricheskoe opisanie*, pp. 114–15.
48. See J. Cracraft, *The Church Reform of Peter the Great* (London, 1971), pp. 251–61.
49. C.F. Weber, *The Present State of Russia*, vol. 1 (London, 1722), p. 138.
50. W. Coxe, *Travels into Poland, Russia, Sweden and Denmark*, vol. 1 (London, 1784), p. 471. Chapter 8 is devoted to Sophia.
51. T.M. Kovalenskaia, *Gos. Tret'iakovskaia Galereia. Putevoditel'. Russkoe iskusstvo vtoroi poloviny XIX veka* (Leningrad, 1980), p. 164.
52. Rastopchina, 'Monakhinia', p. 8.
53. Antushev, *Istoricheskoe opisanie*, p. 55.
54. Ibid., p. 60.
55. *Russkii biograficheskii slovar'* (St Petersburg, 1909), p. 143.
56. See introduction to 'Pis'ma tsarevny Marfy Alekseevny', *Russkii arkhiv*, 10 (1882), no. 5, 27–41.
57. Copied from the plaque on exhibition in the cathedral.

## POSTSCRIPT

1. *Russkoe slovo*, 1852, no. 12, 421–2.
2. A.P. Bogdanov, *Pamiatniki obshchestvenno-politicheskoi mysli v Rossii XVII veka. Literaturnye panegiriki* vol. 1 (Moscow, 1983), pp. 183–4.
3. Ibid., pp. 233–4. See above, p. 146, for a fuller account of this work.
4. A.P. Bogdanov, 'Sil'vestra Medvedeva panegirik tsarevna Sof'e 1682', *Pamiatniki kul'tury. Novye otkrytiia. 1982.* (Leningrad, 1984), p. 46.
5. G. David, *Status Modernus Magnae Russiae seu Moscoviae* (1690), ed. A.V. Florovskij (The Hague, 1965), p. 69. For further biographical and bibliographical details on this and other foreign writers on the regency, see L. Hughes, '"Ambitious and Daring above Her Sex": Tsarevna Sophia Alekseevna (1657–1704) in Foreigners' Accounts', *Oxford Slavonic Papers*, 21 (1988), 65–89.
6. G. David, 'Brevis Relatio revolutionis in regno Moscovitico', in J.S. Gagarin, *Peter Gagarins Neueste Studieen* (Stuttgart, 1857), p. 163.
7. David, *Status Modernus*, pp. 66–7.
8. Ibid., p. 71.

9. F. de la Neuville, 'Récit de mon voyage' (Paris, Bibliothèque Nationale, Département des Manuscrits, NAF 5114), f. 44; *Relation curieuse et nouvelle de Moscovie* (The Hague, 1699), p. 174 (with minor variations).
10. La Neuville, 'Récit de mon voyage', f. 14.
11. Ibid., ff. 48–9.
12. I. de Madriaga, 'Who Was Foy de la Neuville?', *Cahiers du monde russe et soviétique*, 28 (1987), 21–30. See also A.S. Lavrov, 'Zapiski o Moskovii de la Nevillia', *Vestnik Leningradskogo Universiteta. Seriia 2. Istoriia, iazyk, literatura*, 1986, no. 4, 88–91.
13. La Neuville, *Relation curieuse et nouvelle de Moscovie*, p. 152; 'Récit de mon voyage', marginal note to f. 40; Ón Peter and Ivan, marginal notes to ff. 48 and 51.
14. La Neuville, *Relation curieuse et nouvelle de Moscovie*, p. 152.
15. 'Récit de mon voyage', f. 12. 'This young gentleman is highly intelligent, speaks Latin well, enjoys reading, is eager to learn the latest news of Europe, and is particularly well disposed towards foreigners.'
16. On Spafarius, see above, pp. 110, 116.
17. G.A. Schleissing, *Derer beyden Czaaren in Reussland* (n.p., 1694), Introd. (without pagination).
18. P. Avril, *Travels into divers Parts of Europe and Asia* (London, 1693), p. 74.
19. J. Korb, *Diary of an Austrian Secretary of Legation at the Court of Czar Peter the Great* ed. and trans. Count MacDonnell, vol. 1 (London, 1863), pp. 94–5.
20. Ibid., vol. 2, p. 124.
21. C. Whitworth, *An Account of Russia as it was in the year 1710* (Strawberry Hill, 1758), p. 57.
22. A. Gordon, *A History of Peter the Great, Emperor of Russia*, vol. 2 (Aberdeen, 1755), p. 87.
23. J. Banks, *A New History of the Life and Reign of the Czar Peter the Great* (London, 1740), p. 45.
24. *An Impartial History of the Life and Actions of Peter Alexowitz* (London, 1728), pp. 2–3.
25. Gordon, *History of Peter the Great*, p. 262.
26. On Matveev, see above, p. 57–8. The reference to him in *Diariusz zaboystwa tyranskiego senatorow moskiewskich w stolicy roku 1682 y o obraniu dwoch carow Ioanna y Piotra* (St Petersburg, 1901) occurs on p. 14: 'The son of Artamon, when he was in exile with his father, learned Polish, Latin and German, which he will teach to Peter as soon as the present troubles calm down. He doesn't frequent the city, only appearing *incognito* to visit Peter in the palace. . . .' With that the manuscript breaks off.
27. A.A. Matveev, 'Zapiski Andreia Artamonovicha grafa Matveeva', in N. Sakharov (ed.), *Zapiski russkikh liudei. Sobytiia vremen Petra Velikogo* (St Petersburg, 1841), p. 31.
28. Ibid., p. 5.
29. Ibid., p. 7.
30. Ibid., p. 30.
31. On Kurakin, see above, pp. 105, 223.
32. See Prince B.I. Kurakin, 'Gistoriia o tsare Petre Alekseeviche i blizhnikh k nemy liudiakh, 1682–1694', in *Rossiiu podnial na dyby . . . Istoriia otechestva v romanakh, povestiakh, dokumentakh. Veka XVII–XVIII*, vol. 1 (Moscow, 1987), pp. 353–6.
33. Ibid., pp. 364–5.
34. *Arkhiv kn. F.A. Kurakina*, vol. 1 (St Petersburg, 1890).
35. M.V. Lomonosov, 'Slovo pokhval'naia . . . Petru Velikomu' (1755). Quoted in N.V. Riasanovsky, *The Image of Peter the Great in Russian History and Thought* (Oxford, 1985), p. 33.
36. I.I. Golikov, *Deianiia Petra Velikogo*, vol. 1 (Moscow, 1788), p. 12.
37. Ibid., pp. 66–7.
38. N.M. Karamzin, 'Panteon rossiiskikh avtorov', in *Sochineniia v dvukh tomakh*, vol. 2 (Leningrad, 1984), p. 102. On his view of Sophia as author and playwright, see above, pp. 172–3.
39. [Catherine II], *The Antidote, or an Enquiry into the merits of a book, entitled A Journey into Siberia . . . by a Lover of Truth* (London, 1772).
40. On Catherine and Sophia, see E. Lermontova, *Samoderzhavie Tsarevny Sof'i Alekseevny po neizdannym dokumentam. (Iz perepiski, vozbuzhdennoi grafom Paninym)* (St Petersburg, 1912), and N. Moleva, 'Tsar'-devitsa', *Znanie-sila*, 1971, no. 1, 34: 'The

point at issue was not really Sophia at all. Sophia was merely a convenient cover for the debate that had sprung up. The point at issue was Catherine herself.'

41. G.F. Müller (Miller), *Sammlung russischer Geschichte*, in F. Tumansky (ed.), *Sobranie raznykh zapisok i sochinenii, sluzhashchikh k dostavleniiu polnogo svedeniia o zhizni i deianiiakh gosudaria imperatora Petra Velikogo*, vol. 5 (St Petersburg, 1787), p. 221.

42. M. Levesque, *Histoire de Russie*, vol. 4 (Paris, 1782), pp. 78, 102, 152.

43. Ibid., pp. 104–5. Levesque was evidently under the impression that Tsaritsa Natalia was younger than Sophia. The authority referred to is Catherine, whose *Antidote* he quotes at length.

44. Ibid., p. 103.

45. Coxe, *Travels*, pp. 510–11.

46. Ibid., p. 394.

47. Ibid., p. 395.

48. Ibid. See Voltaire's *Histoire de l'empire de Russie sous Pierre-le-Grand*, first published 1759–63.

49. Coxe, *Travels*, p. 394.

50. See J. Perry, *The State of Russia under the Present Czar* (London, 1716).

51. Coxe, *Travels*, p. 417. See above, p. 258.

52. On Ustrialov and the 'Official Nationality' school of history, see Riasanovsky, *Image of Peter the Great*, pp. 115–16.

53. *Istoriia sotsarstviia v Rossii (1682–89 gg.), sostavlennaia po vernym istochnikam* (St Petersburg, 1837). See above, p. 105.

54. For example, *Drevniaia rossiiskaia vivliofika*, 20 vols (Moscow, 1788–91).

55. K.S. Aksakov, 'Zapiska o vnutrennem sostoianii Rossii' (1855). Quoted in Riasanovsky, *Image of Peter the Great*, pp. 145–6.

56. On Solov'ev and late-seventeenth-century Russian history, see my introduction to S.M. Solov'ev, *History of Russia*, vol. 25, *Rebellion and Reform. Fedor and Sophia, 1682–1689* (Gulf Breeze, 1989), pp. xvi–xxiv.

57. S.M. Solov'ev, *Istoriia Rossii s drevneishikh vremen*, vols 13–14 (Moscow, 1962), p. 180.

58. P.K. Shchebal'sky, *Pravlenie tsarevny Sofii* (Moscow, 1856), pp. 1, 99.

59. N. Aristov, *Moskovskie smuty v pravlenie tsarevny Sofii Alekseevny* (Warsaw, 1871).

60. M.P. Pogodin, *Semnadtsat' pervykh let v zhizni Imp. Petra Velikogo 1672–1689* (Moscow, 1875).

61. D. Mordovtsev, *Russkie istoricheskie zhenshchiny. Populiarnye rasskazy iz russkoi zhizni* (St Petersburg, 1874).

62. I. Zabelin, *Domashnii byt russkogo naroda.*, vol. 2 (Moscow, 1901), pp. 144, 181–2, etc.

63. E. Shmurlo, 'Padenie ts. Sof'ii', *ZhMNP*, 1896, no. 1, 41.

64. A.N. Tolstoi, *Petr Pervyi. Roman.* The work underwent many revisions as the ideological climate changed. See edition in *Rossiiu podnial na dyby*, vol. 1 (Moscow, 1987), pp. 33–350.

65. V.I. Buganov, *Moskovskie vosstaniia kontsa XVII veka* (Moscow, 1969), p. 143.

66. See entries under A.P. Bogdanov in bibliography.

67. C.B. O'Brien, *Russia under Two Tsars 1682–1689: The Regency of Sophia Alekseevna* (Berkeley and Los Angeles, 1952), p. x.

68. Ibid., p. 50.

69. H. Troyat, *Peter the Great* (London, 1987), p. 11. (Trans. of *Pierre le Grand* (Paris, 1979).)

70. Ibid., pp. 13, 33, 37.

71. W. Bruce Lincoln, *The Romanovs* (London, 1981), p. 66.

72. Ibid., p. 67.

73. Ibid., p. 76.

74. R.K. Massie, *Peter the Great: His Life and World* (London, 1981), p. 81.

75. Ibid., p. 106.

76. Ibid., pp. 106–7.

77. Ibid., p. 107.

78. See my 'Dragging Them Kicking and Screaming into the Modern World': An Examination of NBC's *Peter the Great*', *Study Group on 18th-Century Russia Newsletter*, 16 (1988), 4–6.

79. Massie, *Peter the Great*, p. 81.

# Bibliography

PRIMARY SOURCES: SEVENTEENTH-CENTURY

*(i) Laws, charters, decrees, public records, etc.*

*Akty istoricheskie, sobrannye i izdannye arkheograficheskoiu kommissieiu*, 5 vols (St Petersburg, 1841–2).

*Akty, sobrannye v bibliotekakh i arkhivakh Rossiiskoi imperii arkheograficheskoiu ekspeditsieiu imp. Akademii nauk*, 4 vols (St Petersburg, 1836).

*Dopolneniia k aktam istoricheskim*, 12 vols (St Petersburg, 1846–72).

*Dopolneniia k tomu IIIemu Dvortsovykh razriadov* (St Petersburg, 1854).

*Drevniaia rossiiskaia vivliofika*, 20 vols (St Petersburg, 1788–91).

*Dvortsovye razriady*, 4 vols (St Petersburg, 1852–5).

Esipov, G.V. (comp.) *Sbornik vypisok iz arkhivnykh bumag o Petre Velikom*, vol. 1 (Moscow, 1872).

Golikov, I.I. (comp.) *Deianiia Petra Velikogo*, 12 vols (Moscow, 1788–9).

*Muscovite Law Code (Ulozhenie) of 1649, Part 1: Text and Translation*, trans. and ed. R. Hellie (Irvine, 1988).

*Opisanie starinnykh tsarskikh utvarei, odezhd, oruzhiia, ratynkh dospekhov i konskogo pribora*, comp. P. Savvaitov (St Petersburg, 1865).

*Pamiatniki diplomaticheskikh snoshenii drevnei Rossii s derzhavami inostrannymi*, 10 vols (St Petersburg, 1851–71).

*Pamiatniki russkogo prava*, vol. 7 (Moscow, 1963).

*Polnoe sobranie zakonov Rossiiskoi imperii*, vols 1–3 (St Petersburg, 1830).

*Recueil des instructions données aux ambassadeurs et ministres de France*, vol. 1 (Paris, 1890)

*Rozysknye dela o Fedore Shaklovitom i ego soobshchnikakh*, 4 vols (St Petersburg, 1884–93).

*Russko-shvedskie ekonomicheskie otnosheniia v XVII veke. Sbornik dokumentov* (Moscow and Leningrad, 1960).

*Sobornoe ulozhenie 1649 goda. Tekst. Kommentarii*, comp. A.G. Man'kov *et al.* (Leningrad, 1987).

*Sobranie gosudarstvennykh gramot i dogovorov, khraniashchikhsia v gos. kollegii inostrannykh del*, 4 vols (Moscow, 1828).

Theiner, A. (comp.) *Monuments historiques relatifs aux règnes d'Alexis Michaélowitch, Fédor III et Pierre le Grand Czars de Russie extraits des archives du Vatican et de Naples* (Rome, 1859).

Tumansky, F. (ed.) *Sobranie raznykh zapisok i sochinenii, sluzhashchikh k dostav-*

313

# BIBLIOGRAPHY

*leniiu polnogo svedeniia o zhizni i deianiiakh gosudaria imperatora Petra Velikogo*, 10 vols (St Petersburg, 1787).

'Ukaz tsarei Ivana i Petra i tsarevny Sof'i 7196 g. marta 7', *Chteniia*, 1887, book 1, 177–8.

*Vosstanie moskovskikh strel'tsov 1698 god. Sb. dokumentov* (Moscow, 1980).

*Vosstanie v Moskve 1682 g. Sbornik dokumentov*, ed. V.I. Buganov and N.G. Savich (Moscow, 1976).

*Vykhody gosudarei tsarei i velikikh kniazei Mikhaila Fedorovicha, Alekseia Mikhailovicha, Fedora Alekseevicha, vseia Rusii Samoderzhtsev (s 1632 po 1682)*, ed. P. Stroiev (Moscow, 1844).

## (ii) Contemporary accounts, memoirs, chronicles, literary sources, letters

### (a) Russian

Archbishop Afanasy of Kholmogory, *Uvet Dukhovnyi* (Moscow, 1682).

*Arkhiv kn. F.A. Kurakina*, vol. 1 (St Petersburg, 1890).

Bogdanov, A.P. 'Podennye zapisi ochevidsta moskovskogo vosstaniia 1682 goda', *Sovetskie arkhivy*, 1979, no. 2, 34–7.

*Copia-Schreibens des Kniar Gallicryn, Feldherrn der Moscowitischen Armee an den Herrn Jablonowsky, Cron Gross-Feldherrn in Pohlen auss Perekop den 2. Jun.* 1689.

*Istoricheskie pesni XVII veka*, ed. O.B. Alekseeva (Leningrad, 1971).

Kotoshikhin, G. *O Rossii v carstvovanie Alekseja Mixajlovica. Text and Commentary*, ed. A.E. Pennington (Oxford, 1980).

Kurakin, Prince B.I. 'Gistoriia o tsare Petre Alekseeviche i blizhnikh k nemy liudiakh 1682–1694', in *Rossiiu podnial na dyby . . . Istoriia otechestva v romanakh, povestiakh, dokumentakh. Veka XVII–XVIII*, vol. 1 (Moscow, 1987), pp. 353–96.

'Letopisets 1619–1691', in *Polnoe sobranie russkikh letopisei*, vol. 31 (Moscow, 1968), pp. 180–205.

Matveev, A.A. 'Zapiski Andreia Artamonovicha grafa Matveeva', in N. Sakharov (ed.), *Zapiski russkikh liudei. Sobytiia vremen Petra Velikogo* (St Petersburg, 1841).

'Mazurinskii letopisets', in *Polnoe sobranie russkikh letopisei*, vol. 31 (Moscow, 1968), pp. 11–179.

Medvedev, S. 'Sozertsanie let kratkoe 7190, 91 i 92, v nikh chto sodeiasia vo grazhdanstve', *Chteniia*, 1894, book 4, I–LII, 1–198.

*Pis'ma i bumagi Imp. Petra Velikogo*, vol. 1 (St Petersburg, 1887).

'Pis'ma tsarevny Marfy Alekseevny', *Russkii arkhiv*, 10 (1882), no. 5, 27–41.

*Podrobnaia letopis' ot nachala Rossii do Polavskoi batalii*, part 4 (St Petersburg, 1799).

Romanov, S. 'Istoriia o vere i chelobitnaia o strel'tsakh Savvy Romanova', *Letopisi russkoi literatury i drevnosti*, ed. N. Tikhonravov, 5 (1863), part 2, 111–48.

*Russkaia sillabicheskaia poeziia XVII–XVIII v.v.*, ed. A.M. Panchenko (Leningrad, 1970).

'Slovo na Latinov i liuterov: iako v Moskovskem tsarstvii i vo vsei Rossiskei zemli ne podobaet im kostela ili kerki ereticheskikh svoikh ver sozidati', *Chteniia*, 1884, book 3, 10–32.

Tikhomirov, M. 'Zametki zemskogo d'iachka 2-oi poloviny XVII veka', *Istoricheskii arkhiv*, 2 (1939), 93–100.

Tolstoi, P.A. *The Travel Diary of Peter Tolstoy: A Muscovite in Early Modern Europe*, ed. and trans. M.J. Okenfuss (De Kalb, Illinois, 1987).

Zheliabuzhsky, I.A. 'Zapiski Ivana Afanas'evicha Zheliabuzhskogo', in N. Sakharov (ed.), *Zapiski russkikh liudei. Sobytiia vremen Petra Velikogo* (St Petersburg, 1841).

*Zhitie protopopa Avvakuma im samim napisannoe i drugie ego sochineniia*, ed. N.K. Gudzi (Moscow, 1960).

(b) Foreign

Aleppo, Paul of, *The Travels of Macarius Patriarch of Antioch. Written by his attendant Archdeacon Paul of Aleppo*, 2 vols (London, 1836).

Avril, P. *Voyage en divers états d'Europe et d'Asie entrepris pour découvrir un nouveau chemin à la Chine.* (Paris, 1692).

—— *Travels into divers Parts of Europe and Asia (Undertaken by the French King's Order to discover a new Way by Land into China)* (London, 1693).

Butenant, H. von. 'Wahrhaftige Relation der traurigen undt schrecklichen Tragedy hier in der Stadt Moscau furgefallen auff Montag, Dienstag undt Mitwochen, den 15, 16 undt 17 May jetzigen 1682-ten Jahres', in N.G. Ustrialov, *Istoriia tsarstvovaniia Petra Velikogo*, vol. 1 (Moscow, 1858), pp. 330–46.

—— 'Mutiny in Moscow, 1682: A Contemporary Account', trans. J. Keep, *Canadian Slavonic Papers*, 23 (1981), 410–42.

Collins, S. *The Present State of Russia* (London, 1671).

Crull, J. *The Antient and Present State of Muscovy*, vol. 2 (London, 1698).

David, Georgius, S.J, 'Brevis Relatio revolutionis in regno Moscovitico', in J.S. Gagarin, *Peter Gagarins Neueste Studieen* (Stuttgart, 1857), pp. 154–77.

—— 'Sovremennoe sostoianie velikoi Rusi ili Moskovii', *Voprosy istorii*, 1968, no. 1, 123–32; no. 3, 92–7; no. 4, 138–47.

—— *Status Modernus Magnae Russiae seu Moscoviae* (1690), ed. A.V. Florovskij (The Hague, 1965).

*Diariusz zaboystwa tyranskiego senatorow moskiewskich w stolicy roku 1682 y o obraniu dwoch carow Ioanna y Piotra* (St Petersburg, 1901).

Gordon, P. *Passages from the Diary of General Patrick Gordon of Auchleuchries, A.D. 1635–A.D. 1699* (Aberdeen, 1859).

—— 'Sixteen Further Letters of General Patrick Gordon', ed. S. Konovalov, *Oxford Slavonic Papers*, 13 (1967), 72–95.

—— *Tagebuch des Generals Patrick Gordon, während seiner Kriegsdienste unter den Schweden und Polen vom Jahre 1655 bis 1661, und seines Aufenthaltes in Russland vom Jahre 1661 bis 1699*, ed. M.A. Obolenski and M.C. Posselt, 3 vols. (Moscow and Leipzig, 1849).

—— Diary original in Moscow, Tsentral'nyi Gosudarstvennyi Voenno-Istoricheskii Arkhiv, f. 846, op. 15, ed. khr. 1–7.

—— Letters in British Library, Manuscripts, Add. 41842.

Kämpfer, E. *Engelbert Kämpfer, der erste deutsche Forschungsreisende 1651–1716. Leben, Reisen, Forschungen nach den bisher unveröffentlichen Handschriften Kämpfers im Britischen Museum*, comp. K. Meier-Lemgo (Stuttgart, 1937).

—— 'Tagebuch über die Reise durch Russland 1683/84', British Library, Manuscripts, Sloane 2923; letters and papers, Sloane 3063, 3064.

Kochen, C. von, 'Moskva v 1687–1688 g.g. (Pis'ma Khristofora fon-Kokhen, shvedskogo poslannika pri russkom dvore)', *Russkaia starina*, 1878, no. 9, 121–9.

Korb, J. *Diarium itineris in Moscoviam* (Vienna, 1700 (?)).

—— *Diary of an Austrian Secretary of Legation at the Court of Czar Peter the Great*, 2 vols, ed. and trans. Count MacDonnell (London, 1863).

*Massa's Short History of the Muscovite Wars*, ed. G.E. Orchard (Toronto, 1982).

Mayerberg, A. von (Mayer, A.) *Iter in Moschoviam . . . ad Tsarem et Magnum Ducem Alexium Mihalowicz, Anno M.DC.LXI.* (no place or date)

—— *Voyage en Moscovie d'un Ambassadeur, Conseiller de la Chambre Imperiale, Envoyé par l'Empereur Leopold au Czar Alexis Mihalowics, Grand Duc de Moscovie* (Leiden, 1688).

Neuville, F. de la. *Relation curieuse et nouvelle de Moscovie* (The Hague, 1699).

—— *An account of Muscovy, as it was in the year 1689* (London, 1699).

—— 'Zapiski de-la Nevillia o Moskovii, 1689', *Russkaia starina*, 1891, no. 9, 419–50; no. 11, 242–81.

—— 'Récit de mon voyage' (Paris, Bibliothèque Nationale, Département des Manuscrits, NAF 5114).

—— 'Liubopytnye i novye izvestiia o Moskovii', in *Rossiia XV-XVII vv. glazami inostrantsev*, ed. Iu. A. Limonov (Leningrad, 1986). pp. 471–529.

*A New and Exact Description of Moscovy* (London, 1698).

'Narratio rerum, quae post obitum Alexii Mickalowicz Russorum Imperatoris etc. gestae sunt Moschuae XI. Kal. Octobris an 1682' in S. Ciampi, *Bibliografia critica*, vol. 1 (Florence, 1834), pp. 75–9.

—— Trans. as 'Povestvovanie o moskovskikh proisshestviiakh po konchine tsaria Alekseia Mikhailovicha', *ZhMNP*, 1835, no. 5, 69–82.

Olearius, A. *The Travels of Olearius in 17th-Century Russia*, trans. and ed. S.H. Baron (Stanford, 1967).

*Relation de tout ce qui regarde la Moscovie* (Paris, 1687).

Reutenfels, J. *De rebus Moschoviticis ad serenissimum Magnum Hetruriuae Ducem Cosmum tertium* (Patavium, 1680).

—— 'Skazanie sviatleishemu gertsogu toskanskomu Koz'me Tret'emu o Moskovii', *Chteniia*, 1905, book 3, 1–127; 1906, book 3, 129–228.

Rinhuber, L. *Relation du voyage en Russie fait en 1684 par Laurent Rinhuber* (Berlin, 1883).

Schleissing (Schleussing, Schleissinger), G.A. *Anatomia Russiae Deformatae oder historische Beschreibung derer beyden auf einem Trohn gesetzten Czaaren Iwan und Peter Alexewitz* (Dresden, 1688).

—— *Derer beyden Czaaren in Reussland* (n.p., 1694).

—— 'Die Gantze Beschreibung Reusslandts' (1687), trans. L.P. Lapteva as 'Rasskaz ochevidtsa o zhizni Moskovii kontsa XVII veka', *Voprosy istorii*,

1970, no. 1, 103–26.

Tanner, B. 'Opisanie puteshestviia pol'skogo posol'stva v Moskvu v 1678 g.', *Chteniia*, 1891, book 3, 125–9'.

## GENERAL

Adelung, F. *Augustin Freiherr von Meyerberg und seine Reise nach Russland* (St Petersburg, 1827).

—— *Kritisch-literärische Übersicht der Reisenden in Russland bis 1700*, 2 vols (St Petersburg and Leipzig, 1846).

Adrianova-Perets, V.P. *Russkaia demokraticheskaia satira XVII veka* (Moscow and Leningrad, 1954).

Alekseeva, M.A. 'Portret tsarevny Sof'i', *Pamiatniki kul'tury. Novye otkrytiia* (Moscow, 1976), pp. 240–9.

Alekseeva, T.V. (ed.) *Russkoe barokko. Materialy i issledovaniia* (Moscow, 1977).

—— 'Zhanr konkliuzii v russkom iskusstve kontsa XVII – nachala XVIII v.', in T.V. Alekseeva (ed.) *Russkoe barokko. Materialy i issledovaniia* (Moscow, 1977), pp. 7–29.

Alpatov, M.A. 'Georg Adam Shleissinger o Rossii kontsa XVII v.', in *Istoriia i istoriki. Istoriograficheskii ezhegodnik. 1979* (Moscow, 1982), pp. 195–203.

Alpatov, M.V. (ed.) 'Problema barokko v russkoi ikonopisi', in A.I. Nekrasov, (ed.), *Barokko v Rossii* (Moscow, 1926).

Andreyev, N. 'Nikon and Avvakum on Icon Painting', *Revue des Etudes Slaves*, 38 (1961). 37–44.

Antushev, N. *Istoricheskoe opisanie Moskovskogo Novodevich'ego monastyria* (Moscow, 1885).

Aristov, N. *Moskovskie smuty v pravlenie tsarevny Sofii Alekseevny* (Warsaw, 1871).

Artsikhovsky, A.V. (ed.), *Ocherki russkoi kul'tury XVII veka*, 2 vols (Moscow, 1979).

Aseev, B.N. *Russkii dramaticheskii teatr ot ego istokov do kontsa XVIII veka* (Moscow, 1977).

Avrich, P. *Russian Rebels* (New York, 1972).

Babushkina, G.K. 'Mezhdunarodnoe znachenie Krymskikh pokhodov 1687 i 1689 gg.', *Istoricheskie zapiski*, 33 (1950), 158–72.

Banks, J. *A New History of the Life and Reign of the Czar Peter the Great, Emperor of All Russia, and Father of His Country* (London, 1740).

Bantysh-Kamensky, N.N. *Obzor vneshnikh snoshenii Rossii (po 1800 god)*, 4 vols (Moscow, 1894–1902).

Baron, S.H. 'Entrepreneurs and Entrepreneurship in 16th–17th Century Russia', in G. Guroff and F. Carstensen (eds), *Entrepreneurship in Imperial Russia and the Soviet Union* (Princeton, 1983), 27–58.

—— 'The Origins of 17th-Century Moscow's Nemeckaja Sloboda', *California Slavic Studies*, 5 (1970), 1–18.

Barrow, J. *A Memoir of the Life of Peter the Great* (London, 1832).

Barsov, E.V. 'Drevnerusskie pamiatniki sviashchennogo venchaniia', *Chteniia*, 1883, book 1, 1–XXXV, 1–160.

# BIBLIOGRAPHY

Bartenev, S.P. *Moskovskii kreml' v starinu i teper'*, vol. 1 (Moscow, 1912).

Bekeneva, N.G. *Simon Ushakov* (Leningrad, 1984).

Belokurov, S.A. *O biblioteke moskovskikh gosudarei v XVI stoletii* (Moscow, 1898).

—— 'O posol'skom prikaze', *Chteniia*, 1906, book 3, 1–170.

Belov, E. 'Moskovskie smuty v kontse XVII veka', *ZhMNP*, 1887, no. 1, 99–146; no. 2, 319–66.

Belov, M.I. 'K istorii diplomaticheskikh otnoshenii Rossii vo vremia Krymskikh pokhodov (1686–1689)', *Uchenye zapiski Leningradskogo Gosudarstvennogo Universiteta. Seriia istoricheskikh nauk*, 14 (1949), 154–88.

—— 'Pis'ma Ioganna fan Kellera v sobranii niderlandskikh diplomaticheskikh dokumentov', *Issledovaniia po otechestvennomu istochnikovedeniiu* (Leningrad, 1964), pp. 374–82.

Bezsonov, S.V. *Krepostnye arkhitektory* (Moscow, 1938).

Billington, J.H. *The Icon and the Axe* (London, 1966).

Black, J. 'Russia's Rise as a European Power 1650–1750', *History Today*, August 1986, 21–28.

Blum, J. *Lord and Peasant in Russia from the Ninth to the Nineteenth Centuries* (Princeton, 1961).

Bobrova, E.I. (comp.), *Biblioteka Petra I. Ukazatel'-spravochnik* (Leningrad, 1978).

Bogdanov, A.P. 'Graviura kak istochnik po istorii politicheskoi bor'by v Rossii v period regentstva Sof'i Alekseevny', *Student i nauchnotekhnicheskii progress. Istoriia* (Novosibirsk, 1977), 39–48.

—— 'K istorii teksta "Sozertsaniia kratkogo"', *Issledovaniia po istochnikovedeniiu istorii dooktiabr'skogo perioda* (Moscow, 1983).

—— 'K polemike kontsa 60x–nachala 80x godov XVIIv. Ob organizatsii vysshego uchebnogo zavedeniia', *Issledovaniia po istochnikovedeniiu istorii SSSR XIII–XVIII v.v.* (Moscow, 1986), pp. 177–223.

—— 'K voprosu ob avtorstve "Sozertsaniia kratkogo"', *Issledovaniia po istochnikovedeniiu istorii dooktiabr'skogo perioda* (Moscow, 1987).

—— 'Literaturnye panegiriki kak istochnik izucheniia sootnosheniia sil v pravitel'stve Rossii perioda regentstva Sof'i (1682–89)', *Student i nauchnotechnicheskii progress*, part 2 (Novosibirsk, 1979), pp. 71–79.

—— 'Nachalo moskovskogo vosstaniia 1682 g. v sovremennikh letopisnykh sochineniiakh', *Letopisi i khroniki. Sb. Statei. 1984* (Moscow, 1984), pp. 131–46.

—— *Pamiatniki obshchestvenno-politcheskoi mysli v Rossii XVII veka. Literaturnye panegiriki*, 2 vols (Moscow, 1983).

—— 'Politicheskaia graviura v Rossii perioda regentstva Sof'i Alekseevny', *Istochnikovedenie otechestvennoi istorii. 1981* (Moscow, 1982), pp. 225–46.

—— 'Sil'vestr Medvedev', *Voprosy istorii*, 1988, no. 2, 84–98.

—— 'Sil'vestra Medvedeva panegirik tsarevne Sof'e 1682', *Pamiatniki kul'tury. Novye otkrytiia. 1982* (Leningrad, 1984), pp. 45–52.

Bogoiavlensky, S.K. 'Khovanshchina', *Istoricheskie zapiski*, 10 (1941), 180–221.

—— *Moskovskii teatr pri tsariakh Aleksee i Petre* (Moscow, 1914).

—— *Prikaznye sud'i XVII veka* (Moscow, 1946).

# BIBLIOGRAPHY

Bogoslovsky, M.M. *Petr I. Materialy dlia biografii*, 5 vols (Moscow, 1940–8).

Brailovsky, S.N. 'Odin iz pestrykh XVII stoletiia', *Zapiski imp. akademii nauk. Seriia VIII*, vol. 5, no. 5, 1902.

Braitseva, O.I. 'Konstruktivnye osobennosti arkhitekturnykh detalei Vvedenskogo sobora', *Arkhitekturnoe nasledstvo*, 14 (1962), 105–8.

Briusova, V.G. *Fedor Zubov* (Moscow, 1985).

—— *Russkaia zhivopis' XVII veka* (Moscow, 1984).

Brown, W.E. *The History of Seventeenth-Century Russian Literature* (Ann Arbor, 1980).

Brückner, A. 'Fürst W.W. Golizyn (1643–1714)', *Beiträger zur Kulturgeschichte Russlands im XVII. Jahrhundert* (Leipzig, 1887), pp. 281–354.

—— 'Materialy dlia istochnikovedeniia istorii Petra Velikogo (1682–1698)', *ZhMNP*, 1879, no. 8, 272–317.

Brumfield, W. *Gold in Azure. One Thousand Years of Russian Architecture* (Boston, 1983).

Buganov, V.I. 'Istochnikovedcheskii analiz dokumentov o moskovskom vosstanii 1682 g.', *Voprosy arkhivovedeniia*, 1965. no. 1, 52–5.

—— 'Iz istorii moskovskogo vosstaniia 1682 g.', *Slaviane i Rus'* (Moscow, 1968).

—— '"Kantsler" predpetrovskoi pory', *Voprosy istorii*, 1971, no. 10, 144–56.

—— *Moskovskie vosstaniia kontsa XVII veka* (Moscow, 1969).

—— *Moskovskie vosstaniia vtoroi poloviny XVII v. (Avtoreferat st. doktora istoricheskikh nauk)* (Moscow, 1968).

—— 'Novye materialy o moskovskikh vosstaniiakh', *Istoricheskii arkhiv*, 1961, no. 1, 151–3.

—— 'Novyi istochnik o moskovskom vosstanii 1682 g.', *Issledovaniia po otechestvennomu istochnikovedeniiu* (Leningrad, 1964) pp. 318–24.

—— *Moskovskoe vosstanie 1662 g.* (Moscow, 1964).

[Catherine II] *The Antidote, or an Enquiry into the merits of a book, entitled A Journey into Siberia . . . by a Lover of Truth* (London, 1772).

Cherniavsky, M. 'The Old Believers and the New Religion', *Slavic Review*, 25 (1966), 1–39.

—— *Tsar and People: Studies in Russian Myths* (New Haven and London, 1961).

Chiniakov, A.N. 'Arkhitekturnye pamiatniki Izmailova', *Arkhitekturnoe nasledstvo*, 2 (1952), 193–220.

Consett, T. *For God and Peter the Great: The Works of Thomas Consett 1723–1729*, ed. J. Cracraft (Boulder, Col., 1982).

Coxe, W. *Travels into Poland, Russia, Sweden and Denmark*, vol. 1 (London, 1784).

Cracraft, J. *The Church Reform of Peter the Great* (London, 1971).

—— *The Petrine Revolution in Russian Architecture* (Chicago, 1988).

Crummey, R.O. *Aristocrats and Servitors: The Boyar Elite in Russia 1613–1689* (Princeton, 1983).

—— 'Court Spectacles in Seventeenth-Century Russia: Illusion and Reality', D.C. Waugh (ed.), *Essays in Honor of A.A. Zimin* (Columbus, 1985), pp. 130–58.

—— 'The Origins of the Noble Official: The Boyar Elite 1613–1689', in

*Russian Officialdom: The Bureaucratization of Russian Society from the 17th to the 20th Century* (London, 1980).
—— 'Reflections on Mestnichestvo in the 17th Century', *Forschungen zur Osteuropäische Geschichte*, 27 (1980), 269–81.
Danilov, N.N. 'Vasilij Vasil'evič Golicyn (1682–1714)', *Jahrbücher für Geschichte Osteuropas*, 2 (1937), 539–96.
—— 'V.V. Golicyn bis zum Staatsstreich vom Mai 1682', *Jahrbücher für Geschichte Osteuropas*, 1 (1936), 1–33.
Davies, N. *God's Playground: A History of Poland*, vol. 1: The Origins to 1795 (Oxford, 1981).
Davydova, I.D. 'Esteticheskie predstavleniia russkikh liudei XVII stoletiia', *Problemy istorii SSSR*, 7 (1978), 19–37.
Demidova, N.F. 'Gosudarstvennyi apparat Rossii v XVII v.', *Istoricheskie zapiski*, 108 (1982), 109–54.
—— 'Iz istorii zakliucheniia Nerchinskogo dogovora 1689 g.', *Rossiia v period reform Petra I* (Moscow, 1973), pp. 289–310.
Demin, A.S. *Russkaia literatura vtoroi poloviny XVII–nachala XVIII veka* (Moscow, 1977).
Dolgorukov, P.V. *Rossiiskaia rodoslovnaia kniga*, vol. 1 (St Petersburg, 1854).
Dukes, P. *A History of Europe 1648–1948: The Arrival, the Rise, the Fall* (London, 1985).
—— 'How the 18th Century Began for Russia and the West', in A.G. Cross, (ed.), *Russia and the West in the Eighteenth Century* (Newtonville, Mass., 1983), pp. 2–19.
—— *The Making of Russian Absolutism 1613–1801* (London, 1982).
—— 'Paul Menzies and His Mission from Muscovy to Rome 1672–1674', *The Innes Review*, Autumn 1984, 88–95.
Eleonskaia, A.S. (ed.) *P'esy stolichnykh i provintsial'nykh teatrov pervoi poloviny XVIII v.* (Moscow, 1975).
Ellersieck, H.E. 'Russia under Aleksei Mikhailovich and Fedor Alekseevich 1654–1682: The Scandinavian Sources' (unpublished PhD thesis, University of California at Los Angeles, 1955).
*Entsiklopedicheskii slovar'*, 43 vols in 86 (St Petersburg 1890–1907).
Evangulova, O.S. *Izobrazitel'noe iskusstvo v Rossii v pervoi chetverti XVIII veka* (Moscow, 1987).
Fabritsius, M.P. *Kreml' v Moskve. Ocherki i kartiny proshlogo* (Moscow, 1883).
Feustreutter, K. *Preussen und Russland von der Anfangen des Deutschen Ordens bis zum Peter dem Grossen* (Gottingen, 1955).
Filimonov, G. *Simon Ushakov i sovremennaia emu epokha russkoi ikonopisi* (Moscow, 1873).
Florovskij, A.V. *Češti jesuité na Rusi* (Prague, 1941).
Fontich, V.L. 'Novye materialy dlia biografii Likhudov', *Pamiatniki kul'tury. Novye otkrytiia*, 1987 (1988), 61–70.
Forsten, Z. 'Snosheniia Shvetsii i Rossii vo vtoroi polovine XVII veka 1668–1700', *ZhMNP*, 1898, no. 2.
Frantsuzova, E.B. 'Iz istorii russko-pol'skikh otnoshenii v poslednei treti XVII v.', *Istoricheskie zapiski*, 105 (1980), 280–93.
Fuhrmann, J.T. *Tsar Alexis, His Reign and His Russia* (Gulf Breeze, 1981).

# BIBLIOGRAPHY

Golitsyn, N.N. *Ukazatel' imen lichnykh upomianutykh v dvortsovykh razriadakh* (St Petersburg, 1912).

Gorchakov, N. *Opisanie Donskogo monastyria v Moskve* (Moscow, n.d.).

Gordon, A. *The History of Peter the Great, Emperor of Russia*, 2 vols (Aberdeen, 1755).

Grabar', I.E. 'Drevnie doma Golitsyna i Troekurova v Okhotnom riadu', *Stroitel'stvo Moskvy*, 10 (1925), 11–15.

—— (ed.) *Istoriia russkogo iskusstva*, vol. 4 (Moscow, 1959).

Greenan, T.A. 'Iulianiya Lazarevskaya', *Oxford Slavonic Papers*, 15 (1982), 28–45.

Grikhin, V.A. 'Simeon Polotskii i Simon Ushakov', in A.V. Lipatov (ed.), *Barokko v slavianskikh kul'turakh* (Moscow, 1982).

Grönebaum, F. *Frankreich in Ost- und Nordeuropa. Die französisch-russischen Beziehungen von 1648–1689* (Wiesbaden, 1968).

Gulianitsky, N.F. 'O svoeobrazii i preemstvennykh sviaziakh ordernogo iazyka v russkoi arkhitekture', *Arkhitekturnoe nasledstvo*, 23 (1975), 14–29.

Hamilton, G.H. *The Art and Architecture of Russia* (London, 1983).

Hellie, R. *Enserfment and Military Change in Muscovy* (Chicago, 1971).

—— *Slavery in Russia 1450–1715* (Chicago, 1982).

Hippisley, A. *The Poetic Style of Simeon Polotsky* (Birmingham, 1983).

*The History of the Life of Peter the First, Emperor of Russia containing a description of Russia or Muscovy, Siberia, Crim Tartary, etc.* (London, 1739).

Hughes, L.A.J. 'The Age of Transition: 17th-Century Russian Icon-Painting', in S. Smyth and S. Kingston (eds), *Icons 88* (Dublin, 1988), pp. 63–74.

—— '"Ambitious and Daring above Her Sex": Tsarevna Sophia Alekseevna (1657–1704) in Foreigners' Accounts', *Oxford Slavonic Papers*, 21 (1988), 65–89.

—— 'Byelorussian Craftsmen in Late-17th-century Russia', *Journal of Byelorussian Studies* (1976), 327–41.

—— 'Church Council of 1681–2', *Modern Encyclopedia of Religions in Russia and the Soviet Union* (Gulf Breeze, forthcoming)

—— '"Dragging Them Kicking and Screaming into the Modern World": an Examination of NBC's *Peter the Great*', *Study Group on 18th-Century Russia Newsletter*, 16 (1988), 4–6.

—— 'Foreign Settlement', *MERSH*, 11 (1979), 216–18.

—— 'Medvedev, Sil'vestr', *MERSH*, 21 (1981), 180–2.

—— 'The Moscow Armoury and Innovations in 17th-Century Muscovite Art', *Canadian – American Slavic Studies*, 13 (1979), 204–23.

—— 'Moscow Baroque – A controversial Style', *Transactions of the Association of Russian–American Scholars in USA*, 15 (1982), 69–93.

—— 'Moscow Baroque Architecture: A Study of One Aspect of Westernisation in Late – Seventeenth-Century Russia' (unpublished PhD thesis, Cambridge University, 1975).

—— 'Portraits of Tsarevna Sof'ia Alekseevna', *Study Group on 18th-century Russia Newsletter* 14 (1986), 3–4.

—— *Russia and the West: The Life of a Seventeenth-Century Westernizer Prince Vasily Vasil'evich Golitsyn (1643–1714)* (Newtonville, Mass., 1984).

'The 17th-Century "Renaissance" in Russia: Western Influences in Art and

Architecture', *History Today*, February 1980, 41–5.
—— 'A Seventeenth-Century Westerniser: Prince Vasily Vasil'evich Golitsyn (1643–1714)', *Irish Slavonic Studies*, 3 (1982), 47–58.
—— 'Shaklovityi, Fedor', *MERSH*, 34 (1983), 146–8.
—— 'Sofiya Alekseyevna and the Moscow Rebellion of 1682', *Slavonic and East European Review*, 63 (1985), 518–39.
—— 'Sophia Alekseevna', *MERSH*, 36 (1984), 165–72.
—— 'Sophia, "Autocrat of All the Russias": Titles, Ritual and Eulogy in the Regency of Sophia Alekseevna (1682–89)', *Canadian Slavonic Papers*, 28 (1986), 265–86.
—— 'Sophia, Regent of Russia', *History Today*, July 1982, 10–15.
—— 'Strel'tsy', *MERSH*, 37 (1984), 205–10.
—— 'V.T. Postnikov's 1687 Mission to London', *Slavonic and East European Review*, (forthcoming).
—— 'Western European Graphic Material as a Source for Moscow Baroque Architecture', *Slavonic and East European Review*, 55 (1977), 433–43.
Il'in, M.A. *Podmoskov'e* (Moscow, 1965).
—— 'Problema "Moskovskogo barokko" XVII v.', *Ezhegodnik instituta istorii iskusstv. 1956* (Moscow, 1957), pp. 324–9.
—— *Riazan'* (Moscow, 1954).
*An Impartial History of the Life and Actions of Peter Alexowitz, the present Czar of Muscovy: From his Birth down to the present Time* (London, 1728).
*Istoriia dorevoliutsionnoi Rossii v dnevnikakh i vospominaniiakh, vol. 1: XV–XVIII veka* (Moscow, 1976).
*Istoriia sotsarstviia v Rossii (1682–89 gg.), sostavlennaia po vernym istochnikam* (St Petersburg, 1837).
Kalash, V. (ed.) *Tri veka. Rossiia ot smuty do nashego vremeni*, vol. 2 (Moscow, 1912)
Kalishevich, Z.E. 'Khudozhestvennaia masterskaia Posol'skogo prikaza v XVII v. i rol' zolotopistsev v ee sozdanii i deiatel'nosti', in N.V. Ustiugov (ed.), *Russkoe gosudarstv v XVII veke* (Moscow, 1961).
Karamzin, N.M. 'Panteon rossiiskikh avtorov', in *Sochineniia v dvukh tomakh*, vol. 2 (Leningrad, 1984).
Karlinsky, S. *Russian Drama from Its Beginnings to the Age of Pushkin* (Berkeley, 1985).
Keep, J.L. *Soldiers of the Tsar: Army and Society in Russia 1462–1874* (Oxford, 1985).
—— 'The Muscovite Military Elite and the Approach to Pluralism', *Slavonic and East European Review*, 48 (1970), 201–31.
Kholmogorovy, V. and G. *Istoricheskie materialy o tserkvakh i selakh XVI–XVIII st.* (Moscow, 1886).
Kholodov, E. (ed.) *Istoriia russkogo dramaticheskogo teatra*, vol. 1 (Moscow, 1977).
—— 'Pervye zriteli russkogo teatra', *Teatr*, 1978, no. 8, 97–111.
Kisilev, N.P. 'O moskovskom knigopechatanii XVII veka', *Kniga. Issledovaniia i materialy*, 2 (1960), 123–86.
Kizevetter, A.A. *Den' tsaria Alekseia Mikhailovicha* (Moscow, 1897).
Kliuchevsky, V.O. *Kurs russkoi istorii*, vol. 3 (Moscow, 1908).

# BIBLIOGRAPHY

—— *Course in Russian History: The Seventeenth Century*, trans. N. Duddington (New York, 1968).

Kochan, L. and Abraham, R. *The Making of Modern Russia* (London, 1983).

Kollmann, N. Shields. *Kinship and Politics: The Making of the Muscovite Political System, 1345–1547* (Stanford, 1987).

—— 'The Seclusion of Elite Muscovite Women', *Russian History*, 10 (1983), 170–87.

Kondrat'ev, I.K. *Sedaia starina Moskvy* (Moscow, 1893).

Kostomarov, N. *Russkaia istoriia v zhizneopisaniiakh ee glavneishikh deiatelei*, vol. 5 (St Petersburg, 1874).

Kovalenskaia, T.M. *Gos. Tret'iakovskaia Galereia. Putevoditel'. Russkoe iskusstvo vtoroi poloviny XIX veka* (Leningrad, 1980).

Kozlov, O.F. 'Khovanshchina', *Voprosy istorii*, 1971, no. 8, 200–5.

Krekshin, P.N. 'Kratkoe opisanie blazhennykh del velikogo gosudaria, i imperatora Petra Velikogo', in N. Sakharov (ed.), *Zapiski russkikh liudei. Sobytiia vremen Petra Velikogo* (St Petersburg, 1841).

Kudriavtsev, I.M. '"Izdatel'skaia" deiatel'nost Posol'skogo prikaza (k istorii russkoi rukopisnoi knigi vo vtoroi polovine XVII v.)', *Kniga. Issledovaniia i materialy*, 8 (1963), 179–244.

Lavrov, A.S. 'Zapiski o Moskovii de la Nevillia', *Vestnik Leningradskogo Universiteta. Seriia 2. Istoriia, iazyk, literatura*, 1986, no. 4, 88–91.

Lee, S.J. *Aspects of European History 1494–1789* (London, 1982).

Leitsch, W. *Moskau und die Politik des Kaiserhofs im XVII Jahrhundert* (Graz and Cologne, 1960).

Leonid, Archimandrite, *Istoricheskoe opisanie Stavropigial'nogo Voskresenskogo Novyi Ierusalim imenuemogo monastyria* (Moscow, 1876).

Lermontova, E. *Samoderzhavie Tsarevny Sof'i Alekseevny, po neizdannym dokumentam* (*Iz perepiski, vozbuzhdennoi grafom Paninym*) (St Petersburg, 1912).

—— 'Shelkovaia fabrika v pravlenie tsarevny Sof'i Alekseevny', *Zapiski otdeleniia russkoi i slavianskoi arkheologii imp. Russkogo arkheologicheskogo obshchestva*, 10 (1915), 43–74.

Letiche, J.M. and Dmytryshyn, B. (eds.) *Russian Statecraft: The Politika of Iurii Krizhanich* (Oxford, 1985).

Levesque, M. *Histoire de Russie*, 5 vols (Paris, 1782).

Levin, E. *Sex and Society in the World of the Orthodox Slavs, 900–1700* (Ithaca, 1989).

Lewitter, L.R. 'The Russo-Polish Treaty of 1686 and Its Antecedents', *Polish Review*, 9 (1964), no. 3, 5–29; no. 4, 21–37.

Librovich, S. *Petr Velikii i zhenshchiny* (St Petersburg, n.d.).

Likhachev, D.S, 'Barokko i ego russkie varianty XVII veka', *Russkaia literatura*, 1969, no. 2, 18–45.

—— *Razvitie russkoi literatury X–XVII vekov* (Leningrad, 1973).

—— 'XVII vek v russkoi literature', in Iu. Vipper (ed.), *XVII vek v mirovom literaturnom razvitii* (Moscow, 1969), pp. 299–328.

Lincoln, W. Bruce *The Romanovs* (London, 1981).

Lipatov, A.V. (ed.) *Barokko v slavianskikh kul'turakh* (Moscow, 1982).

Liublinskaia, A.D. *Russkii diplomat vo Frantsii.* (*Zapiski Andreia Matveeva*) (Leningrad, 1972).

Longworth, P. *Alexis, Tsar of All the Russias* (London, 1984).

—— 'Tsar Alexis Goes to War', *History Today*, January 1981, 14–18.

Lossky, A. 'The General European Crisis of the 1680s', *European Studies Review*, 10 (1980), 177–98.

Lupinin, N. *Religious Revolt in the 17th Century: The Schism of the Russian Church* (Princeton, 1984).

Luppov, S.P. *Kniga v Rossii v XVII veke* (Leningrad, 1970).

McNally, S.J. 'From Public Person to Private Prisoner: The Changing Place of Women in Medieval Russia' (unpublished PhD thesis, State University of New York, Binghampton, 1976).

Madariaga, I. de. 'Autocracy and Sovereignty', *Canadian–American Slavic Studies*, 16 (1982), 369–97.

—— 'Who Was Foy de la Neuville?, *Cahiers du monde russe et soviétique*, 28 (1987), 21–30.

Marker, G. *Publishing, Printing and the Origins of Intellectual Life in Russia, 1700–1800* (Princeton, 1985).

Mashkov, I.P. *Arkhitektura Novodevich'ego monastyria* (Moscow, 1949).

Massie, R.K. *Peter the Great: His Life and World* (London, 1981).

*Materialy dlia istorii roda dvorian Savelovykh*, vol. 2 (Ostrogozhsk, 1896).

Mikhailovsky, B.V. and Purishev, B.I. *Ocherki istorii drevnerusskoi monumental'noi zhivopisi so vtoroi poloviny XIV veka do nachala XVIII veka* (Moscow and Leningrad, 1941).

Millon, H.A. *Baroque and Rococo Architecture* (London, 1968).

Mintslof, R. *Petr Velikii v inostrannoi literature* (St Petersburg, 1872)

*Modern Encyclopedia of Russian and Soviet History*, 46 vols (Gulf Breeze, 1976–87) and supplements.

Molchanov, N.N. *Diplomatiia Petra Pervogo* (Moscow, 1984).

Moleva, N. 'Etot neponiatnyi XVII vek', *Znanie-sila*, 1974, no. 2, 21–4.

—— 'Izmailovo', *Znanie-sila*, 1971, no. 5, 54–7.

—— 'Tsar'-devitsa', *Znanie-sila*, 1971, no. 1, 32–6.

Mordovtsev, D. *Russkie istoricheskie zhenshchiny. Populiarnye rasskazy iz russkoi zhizni* (St Petersburg, 1874).

Mordvinova, S.B. "Istoriko-khudozhestvennye predposylki vozniknoveniia i razvitiia portreta v XVII veke', in T.V. Alekseeva (ed.), *Ot Srednevekov'ia k Novomu vremeni. Materialy i issledovaniia po russkomu iskusstvu XVIII–pervoi pol. XIV v.* (Moscow, 1984, pp. 9–35.

Moropol'sky S. 'Tsarevna S.A. (Zametki)', *Russkaia starina*, 23 (1878), 130–1.

Nekrasov, A.I. (ed.), *Barokko v Rossii* (Moscow, 1926).

Novitsky, A.P. 'Parsunnoe pis'mo Moskovskoi Rusi', *Starye gody*, July–September, 1909, 384–403.

Novosel'sky, A.A. (ed.), *Ocherki istorii SSSR. Period feodalizma. XVII vek.* (Moscow, 1955).

O'Brien, C.B. *Russia under Two Tsars, 1682–1689; The Regency of Sophia Alekseevna* (Berkeley and Los Angeles, 1952).

Ogg, D. *Europe in the Seventeenth Century* (London, 1961).

Ouspensky, L. and Lossky, V. *The Meaning of Icons* (New York, 1982).

Ovchinnikova, E.S. *Portret v russkom iskusstve XVII veka* (Moscow, 1955).

Ovsiannikov, Iu. *Novodevichii monastyr'* (Moscow, 1968).

# BIBLIOGRAPHY

Palmer, W. *The Patriarch and the Tsar*, 6 vols (London, 1871–6).

Pamiatniki literatury drevnei Rusi. Seredina XVI veka, ed. L.A. Dmitrieva and D.S. Likhachev (Moscow, 1985).

Panchenko, A.M. 'Literatura "perekhodnogo veka"', *Istoriia russkoi literatury. Tom 1. Drevnerusskaia literatura. Literatura XVIII veka* (Leningrad, 1980), pp. 291–407.

Pascal, P. *Avvakum et les débuts du raskol* (Paris 1938).

—— 'Pridvornye virshi 80x godov XVII stoletiia', *TODRL*, 21 (1965), 65–73.

Pennington, D.H. *Seventeenth-Century Europe* (London, 1970).

Perry, J. *The State of Russia under the Present Czar* (London, 1716).

Phipps, G. 'Britons in Seventeenth-Century Russia: A Study in the Origins of Modernization' (unpublished PhD thesis, University of Pennsylvania, 1971).

Pierling, P. *La Russie et le Saint-Siège*, 5 vols (Paris, 1901–12).

—— *Saxe et Moscou. Un Médecin diplomat. Laurent Rinhuber de Reinufer* (Paris, 1893).

Plechko, A.M. *Moskva. Istoricheskii ocherk* (Moscow, 1883).

Pogodin, M.P. *Semnadtsat' pervykh let v zhizni imp-a Petra Velikogo. 1672–1689* (Moscow, 1875).

Posselt, M. *Der General und Admiral Franz Lefort. Sein Leben und Seine Zeit*, vol. 1 (Frankfurt, 1866).

Prozorovsky, A. *Sil'vestr Medvedev. Ego zhizn'i deiatel'nost'* (Moscow, 1896).

Przezdziecki, R. 'Les ambassades moscovites en Pologne au XVIème et XVIIème siècles', *Revue de l'Histoire Diplomatique*, 43 (1929).

Pypin, A. 'Inozemtsy v Moskovskoi Rossii', *Vestnik Evropy*, 1888, no. 1, 255–96.

Raeff, M. 'Muscovy Looks West', *History Today*, August 1986, 16–21.

Rastopchina, E. 'Monakhinia', *Moskvitianin*, 5 (1843), no. 9, 1–14.

Rauch, G. von, 'Moskau und die europäische Mächte des 17 Jahrhunderts', *Historische Zeitschrift*, 178 (1954).

Retkovskaia, L.S. *Novodevichii monastyr'. Putevoditel' po muzeiu* (Moscow, 1964).

Riasanovsky, N.V. *The Image of Peter the Great in Russian History and Thought* (Oxford, 1985).

Robinson, A.N. *Pervye p'esy russkogo teatra* (Moscow, 1972).

—— (ed.) *Simeon Polotskii i ego knigoizdatel'skaia deiatel'nost'* (Moscow, 1982).

Rogov, A.I. 'Shkola i prosveshchenie', in A.V. Artsikhovsky (ed.), *Ocherki russkoi kul'tury XVII veka*, vol. 2 (Moscow, 1979), pp. 142–54.

—— 'Knigopechatanie', in A.V. Artsikhovsky (ed.), *Ocherki russkoi kul'tury XVII veka*, vol. 2 (Moscow, 1979), pp. 155–69.

Rossiia i Tridtsatiletniaia voina (Leningrad, 1947).

Rovinsky, D.A. *Materialy dlia russkoi ikonografii*, 12 vols (Moscow, 1884–91).

—— *Podrobnyi slovar' russkikh graverov XVII–XIX vv.* (St Petersburg, 1895).

—— *Podrobnyi slovar' russkikh gravirovannykh portretov*, 2 vols (St Petersburg, 1889).

—— *Russkie gravery i ikh proizvedeniia s 1564 do osnovaniia Akademii Khudozhestv* (Moscow, 1870).

—— *Slovar' russkikh gravirovannykh portretov* (Moscow, 1872).

Rumiantseva, V.S. *Narodnoe antitserkovnoe dvizhenie v Rossii v XVII veke*

(Moscow, 1986).
—— 'Russkaia shkola XVII veka' *Voprosy istorii*, 1978, no. 6, 214–19.
*Russkii biograficheskii slovar'*, 25 vols (St Petersburg, 1896–1918).
*Sbornik Mukhanova* (St Petersburg, 1866).
Schakovskoy, Z. *Precursors of Peter the Great: The Reign of Tsar Alexis, Peter the Great's Father, and the Young Peter's Struggle against the Regent Sophia for the Mastery of Russia* (London, 1964).
Schyler, E. *Peter the Great, Emperor of Russia*, vol. 1, (London, 1884).
Semevsky, M.I. 'Sovremennye portrety Sofii Alekseevny i V.V. Golitsyna. 1689', *Russkoe slovo*, 1859, no. 12, 411–58.
—— *Tsaritsa Praskov'ia 1664–1723* (St Petersburg, 1861).
Semevsky, V.I. *Krest'ianskii vopros v Rossii v XVIII i pervoi polovine XIX veka*, vol. 1 (St Petersburg, 1888).
Shchebal'sky, P.K. *Pravlenie tsarevny Sofii* (Moscow, 1856).
Shmurlo, E. 'Kriticheskie zametki po istorii Petra Velikogo', *ZhMNP*, 1900, no. 10, 335–66.
—— 'Padenie ts. Sof'i', *ZhMNP*, 1896, no. 1, 38–95.
—— 'Pol'skii istochnik o votsarenii Petra Velikogo', *ZhMNP*, 1902, no. 2, 428–48.
Skrynnikov, R.G. 'Boris Godunov's Struggle for the Throne', *Canadian-American Slavic Studies*, 11 (1977), 325–53.
Skvortsov, N.A. *Arkheologiia i topografiia Moskvy. Kurs lektsii* (Moscow, 1913).
'Slovar' knizhnikov i knizhnosti drevnei Rusi', *TODRL*, 40 (1985), 31–189.
Smentskovsky, M. *Brat'ia Likhudy* (St Petersburg, 1899).
Smirnov, P. *Ioakhim–patriarkh moskovskii* (Moscow, 1881).
Smirnov, S. *Istoricheskoe opisanie Savvina Storozhevskogo monastyria.* (Moscow, 1877).
—— *Istoriia Slaviano-greko-latinskoi akademii* (Moscow, 1855).
Smith, A.F. 'Prince V.V. Golitsyn: the Life of an Aristocrat in Muscovite Russia' (unpublished PhD thesis, University of Harvard, 1987.)
Snegirev, I.M. *Russkaia starina v pamiatnikakh tserkovnogo i grazhdanskogo zodchestva*, books 1–18 (Moscow, 1846)
Solov'ev S.M. *Istoriia Rossii s drevneishikh vremen*, vols. 13–14, 5th edn (Moscow, 1962).
—— *Publichnye chteniia o Petre Velikom* (Moscow, 1872).
—— *History of Russia*, vol 24: *The Character of Old Russia*, ed. and trans. A. Muller (Gulf Breeze, 1980).
—— *History of Russia*, vol 25: *Rebellion and Reform. Fedor and Sophia, 1682–1689*, ed. and trans. L.A.J. Hughes (Gulf Breeze, 1989).
*Sovetskaia istoricheskaia entsiklopediia*, 16 vols (Moscow, 1961–76).
Spliet, H. *Russland von der Autokratie der Zaren zur imperialen Grossmacht. Psychische Anomalien der Zaren im Wandel ihrer Genetik* (Luneberg, 1979).
Stadtmüller, G. 'Das Mächtesystema Osteuropas bis zum Ende des 17 Jahrhunderts', *Saeculum Weltgeschichte*, 6 (1971), 423–51.
Stelletsky, I.Ia. 'Podzemnyi khod pod Novodevichim monastyrem v Moskve', *Staraia Moskva*, vol. 1 (Moscow, 1912), pp. 54–64.
Stepovik, D. *Ivan Shchir'skii* (Kiev, 1988).
Stoye, J. *Europe Unfolding 1648–1688* (London, 1969).

Strahlenberg, P.J. *Das Nord- und Ostliche Theil von Europa and Asia* (Stockholm, 1730).

Sumarokov, A.P. *Der erste und wichtigste Auffstand der Strelizen in Moskau im Jahre 1682 im May Monate* (Riga, 1772).

Sumner, B.H. *Survey of Russian History* (London, 1947)

Szechtel, M. 'The Title of the Muscovite Monarch up to the End of the Seventeenth Century', *Canadian–American Slavic Studies*, 13 (1979), 59–81.

Thomas, M.A. 'Muscovite Convents in the 17th Century', *Russian History*, 10 (1983), 230–42.

Tikhomirov, M.N. 'Zapiski prikaznykh liudei kontsa XVII veka', *TODRL*, 12 (1956), 442

Tikhomirov, N. Ia. and Ivanov, V.I. *Moskovskii kreml'* (Moscow, 1967).

Torke, H.J. *Die Staatsbedingte Gesellschaft im Moskauer Reich. Zar und Zemlja im der altrussischen Herrschaftsverfassung 1613–1689* (Leiden, 1974).

Troyat, H. *Peter the Great* (London, 1987).

*A True and Authentik, and Impartial History of the Life and Glorious Actions of the Czar of Muscovy: from his Birth to his Death* (London, 1730(?)).

Tsvetaev, D.V. 'Inostrantsy v Rossii v XVI i XVII vekakh', *Russkii vestnik*, 1887, no. 12.

—— *Istoriia sooruzheniia pervogo kostela v Moskve* (Moscow, 1885).

—— 'Pamiatniki k istorii Protestantstva v Rossii', *Chteniia*, 1883, book 3; i–xxi, 1–150. 1884, book 3, 151–242.

—— 'Polozhenie protestantov v Rossii do Petra Velikogo', *ZhMNP*, 1883, nos. 9 and 10.

—— *Protestantstvo i protestanty v Rossii do epokhi preobrazovanii* (Moscow, 1890).

—— 'Protestantstvo v Rossii v pravlenii Sofii', *Russkii vestnik*, 1883, no. 11, 5–93.

Ursul, D.T. 'N.G. Milesku (Spafarii) i obshchestvenno-politicheskaia mysl' Rossii i Ukrainy kontsa XVII–nachala XVIII v.v.', in *Ideinye sviazi progressivnykh myslitelei bratskikh narodov (XVII–XVIII vv.)* (Kiev, 1978), pp. 80–95.

Uspensky, A.I. 'Ivan Artem'evich Bezmin i ego proizvedeniia', *Starye gody*, April, 1908, 198–206.

—— *Tsarskie ikonopistsy XVII veka*, 4 vols (Moscow, 1910–16).

Ustrialov, N. *Istoriia tsarstvovaniia Petra Velikogo*, 5 vols (St Petersburg, 1858–64).

Vagner, G.K. *Kanon i stil'v drevnerusskom iskusstve* (Moscow, 1987).

—— 'O proiskhozhdenii tsentricheskikh kompozitsii v russkom zodchestve XVII veka', *Pamiatniki kul'tury*, 3 (1961).

Vainshtein, O. 'Russko-shvedskaia voina 1655–1660 godov' (Istoricheskii obzor),' *Voprosy istorii*, 1947, no. 3, 53–72.

Vernadsky, G. *Kievan Russia* (New Haven and London, 1948).

—— *The Tsardom of Muscovy 1547–1682*, 2 vols (New Haven and London, 1968).

Viktorov A. *Opisanie zapisnikh knig i bumag starinykh dvortsovykh prikazov. 1613–1725*, vol. 2 (Moscow, 1883).

Vipper, B. *Arkhitektura russkogo barokko* (Moscow, 1978).

Vlasiuk, A.I. *Novodevichii monastyr'* (Moscow, 1958).

Volkov, M.Ia. 'Ob otmene mestnichestva v Rossii', *Istoriia SSSR*, 1977, no. 2, 53–67.

—— 'O stanovlenii absoliutizma v Rossii', *Istoriia SSSR*, 1970, no. 1, 90–104.

Voltaire, *Histoire de l'empire de Russie sous Pierre-le-Grand* (Paris, 1759–63).

Voronin, N.N. (ed.) *Troitse-Sergieva Lavra. Khudozhestvennye pamiatniki* (Moscow, 1968).

Vucinich, A. *Science in Russian Culture: A History to 1860* (London, 1965).

Vygolov, V.P. 'Tvorchestvo zodchego O.D. Startseva' (unpublished dissertation, Moscow University, 1955).

Ware, T. *The Orthodox Church* (London, 1964).

Weber, C.F. *The Present State of Russia*, 2 vols (London, 1722–3).

Welke, M. 'Russland in der deutschen Publizistik des 17. Jahrhunderts (1613–1689)', *Forschungen zur Osteuropäischen Geschichte*, 23 (1976). 105–276.

Whitworth, C. *An account of Russia as it was in the year 1710* (Strawberry Hill, 1758).

Wittkower, R. *Art and Architecture in Italy 1600–1750* (London, 1958).

Wittram, R. *Peter I, Czar und Kaiser*, 2 vols (Göttingen, 1964).

Wójcik, Z. 'From the Peace of Oliwa to the Truce of Bakhchisarai: International Relations in Eastern Europe 1660–1681', *Acta Poloniae Historica*, 34 (1976), 255–80.

—— *Jan Sobieski 1629–1696* (Warsaw, 1982).

—— 'Poland and Russia in the 17th Century: Problems of Internal Development', in *Poland at the 14th Congress of Historical Sciences in San Francisco* (Wroclaw, 1575).

Wölfflin, R. *Renaissance and Baroque* (London, 1964).

Zabelin, I.E. *Domashnii byt russkogo naroda*, 2 vols (Moscow 1895–1901).

—— 'Knigi perepisnye knigam, kotorye po ukazu sviateishego patriarkha v nyneshnem vo 198 godu sentiabria v den' perepisani v Spasskom monastyre, za ikonnym riadom, podle tserkvi v verkhnei kladovoi polatke,' *Vremennyk imp. obshchestva istorii i drevnostei rossiiskikh*, 16 (1853), 53–67.

—— *Materialy dlia istorii, arkheologii i statistiki g. Moskvy*, 2 vols (Moscow, 1884).

*Domashnii byt russkikh tsarei v XVI i XVII st.* (Moscow, 1915).

Zamyslovsky, E.E. *Tsarstvovanie Fedora Alekseevicha* (Moscow, 1871).

Zenkovsky, S.A. (ed.) *Medieval Russia's Epics, Chronicles and Tales* (New York, 1963).

Zernack, K. *Studien zu den schwedisch–russischen Beziehungen in den 2 Hälfte des 17 Jahrhunderts. Teil I, Die diplomatische Beziehungen zwischen Schweden und Moskau von 1675 bis 1689* (Giessen, 1958).

Zernova, A.S. *Knigi kirillovskoi pechati, izdannye v Moskve v XVI–XVII vekakh. Svodnyi katalog* (Moscow, 1958).

# Index

Names of persons contemporary with the events described in this book are, where possible, given in full. Historians and other later commentators cited within the text are referred to by surname and initials.